As explained in the preface, this p best-seller "is based on the assu‌ that instructional supervision is an zational behavior system that ir with the teaching behavior system . purpose of improving the quality of educa- tion for students." The completely revised fourth edition adds historical perspective to the study of educational supervision and considers the future of educational supervision.

Practical ideas for action are suggested throughout the book for you to evaluate in terms of your own situation. You are introduced also to concepts, theories, and research findings from many fields of study relating to behavior in the super- visory process.

Supervision For Better Schools provides ideas regarding a variety of supervisory practices, procedures, methods, and ap- proaches. It gives you conceptual tools with which to examine your particular situation in order to develop approaches that best meet your needs.

Examples and case studies clarify and illustrate the material. Although each chapter stands alone, each is also a part of an interrelated whole. The first chap- ter introduces the theoretical frame of reference from which the practical ideas of action are derived.

for Supervision and Curriculum Develop- ment, The National Education Associa- tion, and American Association of School Administrators. He has published a chap- ter *The High School of the Future* as well as other books and contributed numerous articles to many professional publications. He is a consultant for many school sys- tems in Tennessee, Alabama, Georgia, Florida, and other East Coast states.

SUPERVISION
FOR BETTER SCHOOLS

Fourth Edition

KIMBALL WILES

JOHN T. LOVELL
The University of Tennessee

Prentice-Hall, Inc., Englewood Cliffs, New Jersey

Library of Congress Cataloging in Publication Data

Wiles, Kimball.
    Supervision for better schools.

    Bibliography: p. 307
    1. School supervision.   I. Lovell, John Thomas,
1921-   II. Title.
LB2805.W5 1974   371.2'013   74-16353
ISBN   0-13-876102-7

To Our Wives
Hilda and Em

© 1975 by Prentice-Hall, Inc.
Englewood Cliffs, New Jersey

Printed in the United States of America

10   9   8   7   6   5   4   3   2

Prentice-Hall International, Inc., *London*
Prentice-Hall of Australia, Pty. Ltd., *Sydney*
Prentice-Hall of Canada, Ltd., *Toronto*
Prentice-Hall of India Private Limited, *New Delhi*
Prentice-Hall of Japan, Inc., *Tokyo*

Contents

iii

Preface

The revision of a book is a difficult process. Decisions concerning what to add, delete, rewrite, update, or reorganize are always hard; in this revision the decisions were complicated by the fact that the reviser was not the original author. Fortunately, the third edition of *Supervision for Better Schools* is a basically sound book that was developed from a stated theoretical frame of reference. In this edition, even though some chapters have been added and others extensively revised, every effort has been made to maintain the continuity of ideas and the style of the previous editions.

The book is based on the assumption that instructional supervision is an organizational behavior system that interacts with the teaching behavior system to improve the quality of education for students. As an organizational behavior system, instructional supervision can be studied and generalizations reached concerning the possible consequences of various supervisory practices, procedures, methods, and approaches. Readers are introduced to concepts, theoretical formulations, and research findings from many fields of study that are assumed to have implications for behavior in the supervisory process. Hopefully, practitioners can use the conceptual tools to study the particular behavior system of which they are a part and develop their own behavior to meet the needs of their unique situation.

Practical ideas for action are suggested throughout the book. An attempt is made to maintain consistency with the general conceptual framework. Readers are urged to check this for themselves and to evaluate suggested practices in terms of their own situation.

The first section of the book defines the boundaries and distinctive characteristics of supervisory behavior, presents the theoretical framework, and provides historical perspective.

The second section of the book defines and discusses concepts, theoretical formulations, and research findings from the studies of leadership, communication, and releasing human potential and explains their implications for educational supervision.

Curriculum and instructional improvement are discussed as functions of supervisory action in the third section. The fourth section covers the development, organization, and allocation of resources for supervision at the school district level; and planning, actualization, and evaluation of supervisory operations at the local school level comprise the fifth section.

The special problems of the beginning supervisor are discussed in the sixth section. In the last section an alternative for the future of educational supervision is developed along with some thoughts about a possible approach for moving toward that future.

Help with the revision came from so many sources that no attempt is made to list everyone. Students and colleagues were most helpful in reading and reacting to the manuscript. A special note of thanks is due Amy Pace, who helped in so many ways.

John T. Lovell

THE NATURE OF SUPERVISION

Chapter 1 defines the boundaries and distinctive characteristics of supervisory behavior. The theoretical framework for the development of the book is presented. Chapter 2 provides historical perspective for the development of a concept of supervisory behavior.

1 Instructional Supervision
Organizational Behavior System

Supervision has many different meanings. Each person who reads or hears the word interprets it in terms of his past experiences, his needs, and his purposes. A supervisor may consider it a positive force for program improvement; a teacher may see it as a threat to his individuality; another teacher may think of it as a source of assistance and support.

Teachers' feelings about supervision differ because of the various ways in which supervisors they have known have interpreted their role. During the past half century, supervision has been in a state of rapid evolution. One supervisor may hold to a philosophy and use procedures that are in direct conflict with those of another supervisor. Any teacher with several years of experience has probably encountered several types of supervisors.

At one time, supervision was a directing and judging activity. In the 1910s and 1920s, the writing in the field of supervision recommended directing and telling people what to do and then checking up to see whether people had done as they were directed. It is easy to see one reason for this emphasis. Teachers were not trained then as they are now. Some started teaching as soon as they had left high school, with very little pre-service education.

In the 1930s, the emphasis was on "democratic supervision." But a survey of the literature reveals that this term meant a type of manipulation in which teachers were to be treated kindly and maneuvered into doing what the supervisor wanted to do all along.

In the 1940s, or even as early as 1932, writers described supervision as a cooperative enterprise. They saw all the people in a school system supervising each other. For "supervision," it would be possible to substitute such phrases as helping each other, counseling each other, planning with each other, or talking with each other about how to improve the teaching-learning situation. In this sense, the task of the person who is designated as a supervisor is to make it easier for people to supervise each other.

This emphasis continued until 1957, the year of Sputnik. At this point, the national government became interested in improving the quality of education, especially in mathematics, the sciences, the foreign languages. Large curriculum projects were developed through the National Science Foundation and with funds made available under the National Defense Education Act of 1958. Supervisors in subject matter fields were added and given the function of improving the program in the fields mentioned above. Many conceived their task to be convincing teachers to adopt a national program and to develop the information and skills necessary to implement the program. Success was interpreted to be changing teachers in the desired direction.

During the 1970s, the role of the supervisor has become increasingly confused. The supervisors with a specific mission to perform have seen themselves as directing the process of change, and their primary question has been one of strategy. Other supervisors, those who see themselves as helping professional people solve their instructional and curricular problems, have continued to work for improvement in the process of decision-making, decision-sharing and curricular change. Teachers have become confused about the meaning of supervision, because they encounter many methods in the supervisors they know, and even a Dr. Jekyll-Mr. Hyde pattern of inconsistency in the same supervisor!

A Concept of Instructional Supervisory Behavior*

Instructional supervisory behavior in the institution of public education continues to evolve in response to a wide variety of forces which are both external and internal to the educational system. External forces include the development of knowledge, the expanding population, science and technology, knowledge coming from behavioral sciences and social sciences, organizational theory, specialization, demands for educational change, the federal government's participation in education, and many others. Critical internal forces include professionalization of teachers, rise of teacher specialization, application of technological developments, growth of teacher labor unions and teacher militancy, growth of organizational complexity, curriculum development, performance contracting, emphasis on behavioral objectives, and acceleration of organizational change, to name only a few.

*This section is an extension of an earlier publication by the author. John T. Lovell, "A Perspective for Viewing Instructional Supervisory Behavior," in *Supervision: Perspectives and Propositions,* ed. William H. Lucio, (Washington, D.C.: A.S.C.D., 1967) pp. 12-27.

It is clear that supervisory behavior exists in the educational organization and is in a constant process of change as a result of a complex set of interdependent factors. The question is not whether there will be instructional supervisory behavior; rather the question is whether man can control the nature of this behavior in such a way as to increase the probability that it will facilitate operationally-defined student learning in certain specified directions. In order to achieve such a condition, it will be necessary to develop a "system" of concepts that can serve as a conceptual framework for viewing the phenomenon of "instructional supervisory behavior." Such a framework would necessarily provide not only a precise definition of instructional supervisory behavior, but also a concept of the total setting in which the behavior occurs. This should give direction to a derivation of the nature, purpose, and function of instructional supervisory behavior as well as some clues to possible consequences of this particular behavior system.

Each educational organization must provide for a variety of behavioral systems which have the general functions of facilitating the achievement of organizational goals and maintaining the organization. Examples of behavioral systems in the educational organization would include the management behavior system, teaching behavior system, counseling behavior system, and instructional supervisory behavior system. It might help to clarify the concept by the introduction of Figure 1.

The broken lines indicate that the educational organization matrix is an open system and that the sub-behavior systems are open and in interaction with each other and the system as a whole. Each of the sub-systems has definable functions that are assumed to contribute to organizational maintenance and goal achievement. The implementation of these functions requires the achievement of certain tasks and the "carrying out" of certain activities which in turn is based on a body of theoretical formulations and empirical findings. This is the base from which appropriate technical skills can be developed and applied on a professional basis. In order to develop such a theoretical base for the instructional supervisory behavior system, it is necessary to define the functions of the system.

One way of conceptualizing the instructional supervisory behavior system is as behavior officially designated by the organization which has the purpose of influencing the "teaching behavior sub-system" in such a way as to facilitate the achievement of the goals of the teacher-pupil systems. (Lovell, 1967, pp. 12-29.) This could be achieved either by effect on the teacher on the assumption that he would in turn influence goal achievement in those teacher-pupil systems in which he works or by directly influencing the teacher-pupil system. It is hoped that Figure 2 (Lovell, 1967, p. 14), will help clarify the idea.

It is clear from the conceptual scheme that the educational institution is assumed to be a sub-system of the society. Inputs provided by the society include the specification of learning goals for students, financial support system, laymen

FIGURE 1
Educational Organization Behavior Systems

control structure, standards of "in-school" student and teacher behavior among others. Student learning is what the schools are "about." In order to achieve the goal of certain definable student learning outcomes, educational organizations provide "teaching behavior-student behavior sub-systems." A formally designated individual working with one or more students to achieve certain learning outcomes constitutes a student-teacher behavior system. When a superintendent, principal, supervisor, or teacher is performing this kind of task, he is participating in the teaching behavior system. The function of this system is to plan and actualize engagement opportunities for students which it is hypothesized will produce certain learning outcomes. It is assumed that it is impossible to predict all needed learning and engagement opportunities; therefore, activities are provided for goal development and engagement development in the student-teacher behavior system.

Instructional supervisory behavior is assumed to be an additional behavior system formally provided by the organization for the purpose of interacting with the teaching behavior system in such a way as to maintain, change, and improve the provision and actualization of learning opportunities for students. The instructional supervisor, operating from his own unique conceptual base, works to achieve certain tasks through various operations and activities. From this frame of reference, instructional supervisory behavior can be a dimension of

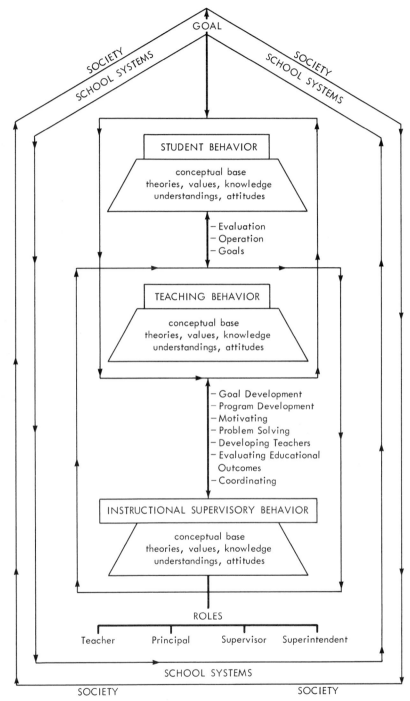

GOAL

SOCIETY
SCHOOL SYSTEMS

SOCIETY
SCHOOL SYSTEMS

STUDENT BEHAVIOR

conceptual base
theories, values, knowledge
understandings, attitudes

– Evaluation
– Operation
– Goals

TEACHING BEHAVIOR

conceptual base
theories, values, knowledge
understandings, attitudes

– Goal Development
– Program Development
– Motivating
– Problem Solving
– Developing Teachers
– Evaluating Educational
   Outcomes
– Coordinating

INSTRUCTIONAL SUPERVISORY BEHAVIOR

conceptual base
theories, values, knowledge
understandings, attitudes

ROLES

Teacher   Principal   Supervisor   Superintendent

SCHOOL SYSTEMS

SOCIETY   SOCIETY

FIGURE 2
Supervisory Behavior: A Conceptual Framework
Source: This figure is based on an earlier work by John T. Lovell (1967).

7

many roles in the educational organization. A superintendent of schools, with special competence in the teaching of reading, working with a group of primary teachers to evaluate a proposed "reading program," would be participating in instructional supervisory behavior. A teacher appointed by the administration to chair a curriculum planning committee would be participating in instructional supervisory behavior to achieve the task. The critical factor is not the title of the role but the nature of the behavior.

It is apparent that the fundamental reason that organizations provide instructional supervisory behavior is to improve the learning situation for children. It is also clear that the thrust or focus of this behavior system is to interact with the teaching behavior system in such a way as to improve the probability of defining, planning, and operationalizing certain learning conditions with which students will interact and achieve appropriate learning outcomes. The definition of instructional supervision in this way gives direction to the formulation of the specific functions of instructional supervisory behavior.

The Functions of Instructional Supervisory Behavior

But why do organizations find it necessary to provide for officially designated behavior which influences teaching behavior? If we are to make any progress in understanding the function of instructional supervisory behavior, then we must set ourselves to the task of answering that question. It was proposed earlier that educational organizations provide instructional supervisory behavior to influence teaching behavior in the following ways (Lovell, 1967):

1. Goal development
2. Program development
3. Control and coordination
4. Motivation
5. Problem solving
6. Professional development
7. Evaluation of educational outcomes

GOAL DEVELOPMENT

The educational system is a sub-system of the society, and therefore the society not only provides human and nonhuman resources but also has certain expectations that the schools will achieve certain goals. Since society is in a constant process of change, the needs of society change and so do the goal specifications. It is necessary for the educational institution to be responsive to these changing expectations, and it is through the instructional supervisory behavior system that teachers and instructional supervisors can continuously examine, evaluate, and change (if appropriate) the goals of the teacher-student behavior systems. The first function of instructional supervisory behavior is defined as the facilitation of the cooperative effort of teachers and supervisors in goal development.

PROGRAM DEVELOPMENT AND ACTUALIZATION

The goals that are developed for the teacher-student systems become the rationale for program planning and actualization. Programs represent the intended engagement opportunities for students. The responsibility for the planning and actualization of programs for a particular group of students rests with a particular teacher or team of teachers. It is proposed that it is a function of instructional supervision to provide technological support to the teaching behavior system in the form of consultations and services.

It is recognized that local schools and school districts have goals and that curriculum planning is done at these levels as well as at the "classroom" level. It is a function of instructional supervision to initiate, coordinate, provide services, and be a part of these activities.

COORDINATION

Organizations come into being as a result of the assumption that there are certain goals that can be achieved more effectively through the patterning of certain specialized parts than could be achieved by the parts separately. The teaching staff is composed of highly specialized and competent individuals, and each teaching unit has its own system of goals and is also a part of a larger system of goals to which it is expected to contribute. Therefore, a particular teaching unit cannot act independently, but rather must act as a coordinated part of a larger system. Educational organizations are concerned with the coordination of teacher behavior in such a way as to assure the achievement of the goals of the teacher-pupil system. Coordination requires a comprehensive system of communication among the various units which assures that each unit will be aware of contributions and expectations of other units. There needs to be a broad base of interpersonal influence. Teachers and supervisors need to participate in the development of goals for the super-system in order to utilize their expertise and to assure their sensitivity to overall system goals. If teachers and supervisors know what is going on, ideas and expertise can be shared. It is proposed that the third function of instructional supervisory behavior is to provide for coordination of the teacher behavior system.

MOTIVATION

Barnard has clarified the idea that the willingness of organizational members to work toward the achievement of organizational goals is an essential characteristic of organizations in general (1938, p. 72). Certainly, this is true in educational organizations. The basic work of the organization is done through teaching behavior systems. It is only through a highly motivated faculty that educational organizations can expect to facilitate student learning in certain directions. Since the instructional supervisory behavior system interacts with the teaching behavior system, it is assumed that one outcome of that interaction would be enhancement of the motivation of both teachers and supervisors to work toward the achievement of the goals of the organization.

PROBLEM SOLVING

It is possible to define instruction as a process through which certain individuals (teachers) are formally designated to provide learning conditions for other individuals (learners) on the assumption that interaction with these conditions will result in certain learning outcomes for the learners. Thus, instruction requires a constant process of examining the relationships among predicted learning outcomes, learning engagements, and actual learning. Failure to achieve the desired engagement opportunities or learning outcomes demands verification, explanation, and "new" attempts with "new" ideas. Thus, human problem solving becomes the central focus for the improvement of teaching and learning in the educational organization. It requires the specification of goals, conditions for achieving goals, and a systematic procedure for getting feedback as to the effectiveness of goal achievement. The facilitation of human problem solving in teacher-student behavior systems is a central function of instructional supervisory behavior.

PROFESSIONAL DEVELOPMENT

Teachers in educational organizations are highly developed and specialized professionals. They have received a level of preparation through which competence in certain conceptual, technical, and human skills has been achieved. But, society's expectations for education continue to change and teachers must change. The growing complexity of education requires more specialization, and teachers must change. Developments in technology, the study of the behavioral sciences, and curriculum developments all have implications for teaching behavior. It is imperative that teachers have an opportunity to continue to learn and develop as professionals, and it is a function of instructional supervisory behavior to provide the necessary initiation, coordination, and support.

EVALUATION OF EDUCATIONAL OUTCOMES

Educational organizations are assumed to be sub-systems of society. The society specifies certain expectations that the educational sub-system will provide to meet certain educational needs of the society. It is essential that the educational institution and society be continuously aware of the extent to which these specified educational needs are being met. It is through the process of evaluation that this is done. Since it is through teacher-student behavior systems that educational goals are achieved and since instructional supervisory behavior interacts directly with these systems, it is logical for the system to provide an external evaluation of the output of the teacher-pupil systems.

Special Characteristics of Instructional Supervisory Behavior

The definition of the functions of instructional supervision gives rise to a whole series of questions which have to do with the special characteristics of this behavior system:

1. Is supervision educational planning, changing, releasing human potential, controlling human behavior, monitoring, overseeing, controlling quality, developing learning goals, providing psychological and logistical support, demanding compliance behavior, controlling the teacher reward system, evaluating student learning outcomes, providing instructional leadership, curriculum planning, and other behaviors that could be mentioned? All have been proposed and discussed by other writers.
2. What should be the nature of the power base from which an instructional supervisor operates? Should the organization provide legitimatized authority for the role or should the supervisor depend on the power of persuasion?
3. What roles should the organization provide and how should they be defined? What titles are appropriate? Do titles such as supervising principal, county supervisor, assistant superintendent in charge of instruction, helping teacher, resource teacher, curriculum director, curriculum coordinator, floating teacher, resource person, and media coordinator have any particular or universal significance? If these roles have universal significance what is it and who defines it? If not, then the question of role definition must be dealt with at the local school district level.
4. What should be the nature of the supervisor's interaction with the teaching behavior system? Are teachers autonomous? Do supervisors intervene only at the request of teachers? Or, should supervisors have conferences with teachers and visit classrooms on a regular basis? What should be the purpose of such visits? Should supervisors work with individual teachers or groups of teachers or both?
5. Do supervisors decide and plan educational changes and experiments and use the teaching behavior system to actualize the plans, or do teachers plan their

own changes and use the supervising behavior system as a support for actualization, or do supervisors involve teachers in a continuous process of evaluation (with emphasis on self-evaluation) for the purpose of planning and actualizing educational changes?

6. The effort to interact with and influence the teaching behavior system indicates the need for effective communication, leadership, human relations, and group work. Is there a knowledge base of theory and research findings that can be used to improve professional practice?

7. Is the effectiveness and appropriateness of the interventions of the supervising system partly a function of the expectations of the teachers, the nature of the situation, the conceptual base from which the supervisor operates and organizational expectations?

It is an assumption of the writers that answers to the above questions (and many others that could be posed) are necessarily partly a function of the context in which the supervisory behavior occurs. Several factors deserve special consideration as important determinants of the appropriateness and effectiveness of instructional supervisory behavior (Lucio, 1967, pp. 12-27). First, teachers do the work of the educational organization. Is it assumed that teachers are primarily technicians who are capable of "carrying out" specifically defined tasks? Or, are teachers thought of as passive instruments of management who will respond to the economic reward system of the organization? Assumptions of this sort about teachers would have important implications for defining the special characteristics of the instructional supervisory behavior system. However, perceiving the teacher as a professionally competent specialist who is capable of creative responses to an emerging situation, and as self-directing problem solver and decision-maker would have quite different implications for the definition of "appropriate" instructional supervisory behavior. The assumptions that are made about teachers are important factors in the determination of the appropriateness of a particular system of instructional supervisory behavior.

It is also apparent from our definition of instructional supervision that it is an organizational system which seeks to influence the teacher-student behavior system. Therefore, the nature of teaching and learning would have important implications for the nature of supervision. Who defines the goals of the teacher-student systems? Who plans the engagement opportunities for students? Who is responsible for the actualization of these engagement opportunities and for the outcomes? Answers to these and other questions are important considerations in the development of appropriate instructional supervisory behavior.

Teaching behavior always occurs within the context of a school system. Since supervision exists to influence teaching behavior, it requires either direct or indirect intervention into the teaching behavior social system. Social systems are characterized by boundaries, internal conflict and tension, defensiveness, openness, equilibration-disequilibration, feedback, problem-solving, and others. The effectiveness or ineffectiveness of the intervention is partly dependent on the nature of the social system in which the teaching behavior occurs.

All teaching behavior and supervising behavior occur within the structure of an organization. Organizations have goals, roles for organizational members, and expectations of these roles. The qualities of supervisory behavior are partly explained by the structure of the particular organization in which the behavior occurs.

The following four factors have been recognized as possible sources of the distinctive features of instructional supervisory behavior in educational organizations:

1. Assumptions made about teachers
2. Assumptions made about the nature of teaching and learning
3. Assumptions made about the nature of "social systems" in the educational organization
4. Assumptions made about the structure of educational organizations

ASSUMPTIONS ABOUT TEACHERS

Educational organizations are characterized by the fact that the teacher normally has achieved a relatively high level of preparation and specialization. The growth of the student population, new knowledge about teaching and learning, technological developments, and the expanding educational needs of members of our society are all factors that have contributed to the improved preparation, specialization, and general competence of teachers. The recognition and acceptance of the teacher as a competent professional makes questionable traditional supervisory behavior such as specifying engagement activities for learners and overseeing or monitoring or even accepting responsibility for the actualization of learning engagements. The complexity of the educational organization demands such a broad base of specialized behavior by many teachers that "supervision" by general administration on the basis of expertise is precluded.

It is also clear that individual teachers utilize many specialities such as subject matter, pupil diagnosis, and teaching methodology. Certainly, it is appropriate for the teacher to have specialized resource people in these areas available for consultation, but the process of weaving the components of the instructional situation into an effective pattern of learning opportunities for a particular group of children requires a creative and emerging response by a freely functioning professional teacher.

The proposition that teachers as human beings have worth and dignity must be considered. What they feel, think, and need is a matter of significance, not just because it is related to the achievement of organizational goals but also because of concern for the teacher as a human being. Acceptance of the worth and dignity of teachers logically leads to supervisory behavior that is characterized by consideration of the psychological and physical well being of "fellow workers" as well as their effectiveness as contributors to the work of the organization.

Recognition of the competence and specialization of teachers provides the basis for instructional supervisory behavior that involves teachers in curriculum development and policy formulation activities, giving and receiving help from each other, and giving and receiving help from other professionals in the organization. The doors of the classroom must be opened so that teachers can interact with each other as well as with the supervisory staff. The potential for interpersonal influence and human growth can be enhanced, and the supervisor is in a strategic position to contribute to the process. Cooperative planning, cooperative teaching, cooperative evaluation, teacher-teacher visitations, teaching demonstrations are examples of activities that can contribute to this process.

It is essential that educational organizations utilize the broad base of expertise of the total staff in the continuous process of problem solving, developmental research, policy formulation, and decision making. One important focus of supervisory behavior is to provide the structure through which it is possible to get the organizational member with the appropriate competence and leadership potential in the appropriate position with the needed time and authority to get the job done.

ASSUMPTIONS ABOUT THE NATURE OF TEACHING AND LEARNING

It is possible to think of teaching as goal identification, development of operations for achieving goals, and evaluation of goal achievement. The goal identification dimension is critical since it provides the rationale for the development of engagement opportunities for students as well as the basis for the evaluation of the effectiveness of the teaching behavior sub-system. The source and formulation of the goals of teaching (including such questions as "Who does it and how?") have always been "nagging" issues in education. No attempt will be made to deal with this issue in a comprehensive way at this point. However, it is assumed that the institution of education is a sub-system of the society and, therefore, the society's expectations of learning outcomes are a significant factor in the formulation of goals. It is also true that the educational institution is organized into school districts and local schools and that these structures also have overall goals. Since teacher-pupil systems are sub-systems of a local school which is a sub-system of school district, a particular teacher-pupil system is interdependent with other teacher-pupil systems in the achievement of the overall goals of a particular school. Each teacher cannot act as an independent agent in the process of goal specification. Rather, the process must be coordinated and controlled in order to assure that each teaching unit will make an appropriate contribution to the ongoing educational experience of each student. The instructional supervisory behavior system must have the required authority, prestige, and resources to work with teachers in a continuous effort to develop, maintain, and evaluate the goals of teacher-pupil systems according to their congruence with the goals of the school system and according to their interdependence with other teacher-pupil systems.

Since teachers are assumed to be professionally competent, they must have the authority and resources to develop and actualize appropriate engagement opportunities for students. They are also responsible for the outcomes. Within the framework of these assumptions it is not appropriate for the instructional supervisory behavior system to prescribe the content or methodology of the teaching behavior system. However, the complexity of teaching is recognized. Teachers cannot be assumed to be specialized in all of the organized bodies of knowledge that have implications for teaching. The content of teaching is normally derived from one or more fields of inquiry that are not only complex but also in a state of rapid expansion of knowledge. Teachers need assistance from specialists who have the special competence and resources to keep abreast of developments in these fields. Teachers also need the help of other teachers who are also specialized. There have also been important developments in educational technology, evaluation and research, curriculum, and behavioral sciences which have important implications for the provision of learner engagement opportunities. The instructional supervisory behavior system should help teachers to take advantage of these developments.

The process of coordination involves the "opening up" of the teacher-student behavior system. Operationally, this means that teachers are participating in cooperative planning, teaching, and evaluation. Such activities require the cooperative development and implementation of educational innovations. It makes it possible for teachers to share engagement opportunities for students, use each other's specialties, and, most important of all, continuously learn from each other. The stimulation, activation, coordination, and evaluation of these activities is an important dimension of instructional supervision.

Just as goal development cannot be left to the individual teacher, neither can evaluation. Rather, it is crucial for the organization to develop a systematic procedure to determine the effectiveness of each teacher-student system according to its contribution to the achievement of the goals of the school. Certainly, this is assumed to be an important feature of the instructional supervisory behavior system. But it also is recognized that teachers must have a continuous source of feedback relative to their effectiveness in achieving desired outcomes. The purpose is not to evaluate the teacher, but rather to provide teachers with data on which engagement opportunities for students can be described, analyzed, evaluated changed, or replaced with more appropriate ones. Historically, this has been a neglected process, but it will receive intensive treatment throughout the book.

THE NATURE OF THE SOCIAL SYSTEMS IN WHICH INSTRUCTIONAL SUPERVISORY BEHAVIOR OCCURS

Instructional supervisory behavior is thought of as an organizational behavior system which interacts with the teaching behavior system. Teaching behavior occurs within the context of a "social system," and so does instructional supervision. It is through the interaction of these two systems that it is possible for the supervisory system to influence the teaching system. In order to understand this process, it is necessary to have some understanding of the nature of social systems.

Social systems can be described in terms of boundary, tension, equilibration-disequilibration, and feedback. (Bennis, Benne, and Chin, 1961, pp. 201-14) The boundary of the social system provides a special identity and is the way the system is differentiated from the outside environment. In the case of a teacher working with a special group of students, the hoped-for behavioral changes in the students represent the goals of the system and the reason for its existence. In open systems the boundary is broken, and therefore, there is the possibility of "input" from the outside into the system and "output" from the inside into the system's external environment. This is the factor that makes it possible for the instructional supervisory behavior system to influence the teaching behavior system. It is possible to do this in at least two ways. First, there can be direct participation in the teacher behavior system such as planning activities, description and analysis of teaching, evaluation, demonstrations and many others.

Second, there can be indirect intervention which focuses on influencing the teacher. It is assumed that the teacher is a significant factor in the teacher-student system and that if the teacher changes, the teacher-pupil system changes. Examples of indirect intervention would be supervisor-teacher conference, special planning committees, workshops, summer school, general conferences and many others. The question of the effectiveness of the intervention has to be asked. What happens in the intervention process?

As a result of input from the outside as well as internal conflict, tension develops in the system and it is thrown out of equilibration. The system must reach out for a new level of equilibration or risk collapse. It is for this reason that systems are often resistant to outside interference. Members of the system are often afraid that they can't meet new demands; often they don't want to make the effort. Therefore, they set up barriers to change. For example, teachers often resist supervisory attempts to become involved by not inviting them into their classrooms, by not doing anything or putting on a show when they come, by not listening to suggestions or not trying new ideas.

At the same time, it is true that teacher-pupil systems are in a constant process of change. The system needs feedback which is a reflection of its output. It is a way of finding out whether goals are being achieved and if they aren't, why not. Such feedback can bring about tension in the system and produce disequilibration which causes the system to seek a new level of equilibration. This is the change process which supervisors hope to set in motion in teacher-pupil systems.

What do we know about the change process in educational social systems? Is this a process that can be controlled, or are men merely the victims of events over which they have no control? Is it possible to study the social system, identify clogged-up parts, weaknesses, and difficulties, and develop changes based on self-determined direction? Can supervisors and teachers work together to improve the learning situation for students? Can supervisors intervene in teacher-pupil systems in such a way as to produce positive benefits for both students and teachers? It is the assumption of the writers of this book that this type of intervention can occur and that it happens as a result of the application of the principles of leadership, communication, cooperative problem solving, and cooperative evaluation. Instructional supervision constitutes an organizational behavior system that can operate in such a way as to throw the teacher-student system into a state of disequilibration. This can occur by sensitizing teachers to new ideas or developments that offer greater promise for achieving goals, and facilitating the process through which teachers get feedback as to their effectiveness or ineffectiveness in achieving goals. Thus, the system must utilize a problem-solving process through which it is possible to achieve a new level of equilibration. Figure 3 helps to show how these ideas fit together.

Teacher A, student B, and student C constitute the teacher-pupil system. The system members are held together by the assumptions that they can achieve certain goals more effectively as a system than as individuals. It is this factor that provides the basis for the continuous striving of the system to achieve certain preferred outcomes. Thus, the system is involved in a continuous process of change, and this change is achieved through some sort of problem solving activity.

There are both external and internal forces which affect the system's process of change. Such factors as "feedback" from the external environment concerning the effect the system is having on external systems, new expectations, allocation of resources, rewards for system members, and threats from the super-system are examples of external factors which can cause tension in the teacher-pupil system and create a state of disequilibration which sets in motion the attempt by the system to achieve a new state of equilibration. Thus, change is achieved through the continuous process of disequilibration and re-equilibration through problem solving activities. Instructional supervisors attempt to facilitate this change process through leadership, communication, cooperative problem solving, and cooperative evaluation. It is through these processes that it is possible to create external forces that will stimulate change in the teacher-pupil system.

Internal forces in the teacher-pupil system can also create tensions that set the change process in motion, i.e., interpersonal conflicts, role conflicts, new system members, new awareness or concern of system members. It is through "indirect" supervision that it is possible to help a teacher develop new insights or awareness that could result in changes in the teacher-pupil system. But it is through direct supervision that it is possible to provide the necessary support system to sustain the change. Leadership, communication, cooperative problem solving, and cooperative evaluation are crucial processes in both direct and

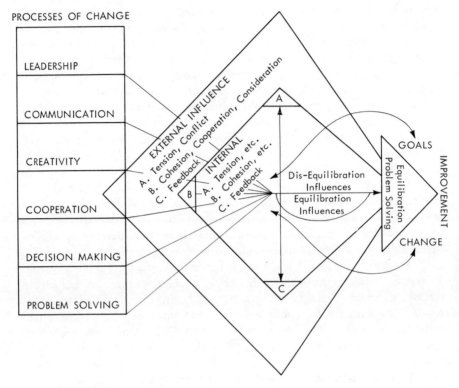

FIGURE 3

Source: This figure is based on an earlier work by John T. Lovell (1967).

indirect supervisory activities. Therefore, special attention is afforded these factors throughout the book.

THE NATURE OF THE ORGANIZATIONAL STRUCTURE IN WHICH INSTRUCTIONAL SUPERVISORY BEHAVIOR OCCURS

Instructional supervisory behavior occurs within the context of an organizational structure. Basically, organizations consist of a group of interdependent parts which exist for the purpose of contributing to the overall goals of the organization. The organization of a particular school or school system is a major factor in the determination of the special characteristics of supervisory behavior. If the emphasis is on control, compliance, hierarchy, and status, then the expectation for instructional supervision would be along these lines. There would be high centrality of decision making and the supervisor would operate from a power base of legitimate authority. The focus would be on the development of general rules and expectations of behavior and the application of general rules through the use of formal authority. Communication would be concerned with getting the "word" to subordinates and getting the "word" back as to how well the work is going. This would require an external system of evaluation.

However, if the emphasis is on functionality, adaptiveness, flexibility, and creative response, then the supervisor would operate from a power base of functional authority emanating from expertise and persuasion. Of course, there would still be general rules but they would be broader and more flexible, leaving more discretionary power to organizational members. Teachers and supervisors would be more accepting of the policies since they would have had a part in their development. Communication would flow freely between and within all levels of the power structure. Teachers and supervisors would be in on the "word," and they would both be significant contributors. There would be a heavy emphasis on evaluation but teachers and supervisors would work together, and there would be greater emphasis on self-evaluation and self-correction. There would be a greater source of feedback for teachers on the output of their own teaching efforts.

It is important to note that organizations are not all one type or the other but rather represent a kind of balance that can be studied and changed. It is crucial for supervisors to understand the organizational structure within which they work, and this factor is given significant attention in later sections.

What Is a Supervisor?

A supervisor is a person formally designated by the organization to interact with members of the teaching behavior system in order to improve the quality of learning of students. No assumption is made that individuals so designated are the sole contributors to the improvement of the teacher behavior system. On the contrary, it is recognized that there is an important informal support system. Teachers help other teachers. Students help each other and teachers. Ideas are shared and skills are developed through the informal behavior system. But, it is also recognized that formally designated leaders have an important role to play. They are the expediters. They help establish communication between persons who have similar problems and resource people who can help. They stimulate staff members to look at the extent to which ideas and resources are being shared, and the degree to which persons are encouraged and supported as they try new ideas. They make it easier to carry out the agreements that emerge from evaluation sessions. They listen to individuals discuss their problems and recommend other resources that may help in the search for solutions. They bring to individual teachers, whose confidence they possess, appropriate suggestions and materials. They sense, as far as they are able, the feelings that teachers have about the system and its policies, and they recommend that the administration examine irritations among staff members.

They provide expertness in group operation, and provide the type of meeting place and structure that facilitate communication. They are, above all, concerned with helping people to accept each other, because they know that when individuals value each other, they will grow through their interaction together and will provide a better emotional climate for pupil growth. The supervisor's role has become supporting, assisting, and sharing, rather than directing. The authority of the supervisor's position has not decreased, but it is used in another way. It is used to promote growth through responsibility and creativity rather than through dependency and conformity.

The Study and Analysis of Instructional Supervisory Behavior

The definition of instructional supervisory behavior in the educational organization sets the stage for the study and analysis of this particular behavior system. What do we now know that would help us predict and thereby control the antecedents and consequences of supervisory behavior? Are there established bodies of knowledge or theoretical formulations that have implications for improving the understanding "of" and practice "in" the instructional supervisory behavior system in educational organizations? A review of the literature did not uncover a "full blown" body of theoretical formulations and empirical findings which could serve as a base for deriving supervisory operations in educational organizations. But the review of the literature did reveal a number of behavior systems for which theories had been developed and which appear to have implications for the study and understanding of Instructional Supervisory Behavior. Those fields which were identified for study included the following:

1. Communication
2. Organization
3. Change process
4. Leadership
5. Mental health
6. Learning
7. Group development
8. Human relations

Figure 4 should help clarify the proposed utilization of these organized bodies of knowledge.

The organizational matrix is composed of a system of interdependent behavior systems which are assumed to be critical to the maintenance and goal achievement of the organization. A number of these behavior systems have been identified. Some have been left open to indicate that no attempt has been made to identify all of the behavior systems.

The instructional supervisory behavior system has been identified as one of these behavior systems, and it is the focus of our study. Eight fields of study

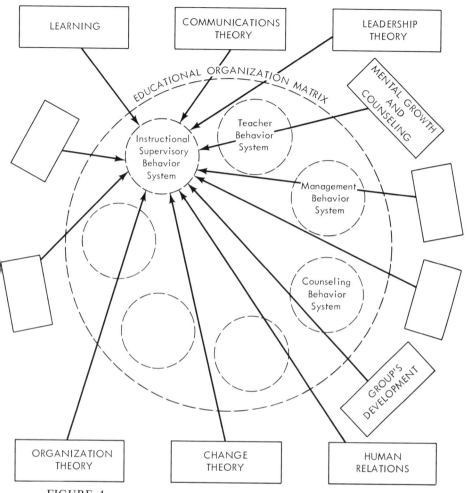

FIGURE 4

Educational Organization Matrix and Fields of Study Assumed to
Have Implications.

have been identified which are assumed to have implications for the study and
understanding of Instructional Supervisory Behavior. Four fields of study have
been left open to indicate that no claim has been made that all fields of study
that might be relevant to our focus have been identified.

A Conceptual Framework

The study of instructional supervision for the purpose of improving
understanding and practice requires a definition of the area of investigation. This

makes it possible to establish boundaries and gives direction for the collection, collation, and development of relevant concepts, assumptions, generalizations, and applications. Naturally, authors who attempt an undertaking of this sort must proceed from their own unique values, assumptions, theories, and general experience. The question is not whether to proceed from a frame of reference but, rather, whether to explicate the general framework or leave it implicit for the reader to interpret. Getzels (1960, p. 38) developed this point in an earlier publication:

> Always, however, we think and work from within some conceptual framework, some theoretical bias, some intellectual stance, which is of course to be held "lightly," but nonetheless held, however, provisionally, until a better one comes along. We are in a more strategic position to move forward both in our own thinking and in communicating with others if we make this bias explicit to ourselves and to others than if we keep it "implicit" under the guise of self-proclaimed neutrality.

It is within this spirit that the conceptual framework for the development of this book on supervision is presented. It is hoped that the use of this book will stimulate discussion, evaluation, and criticism and hopefully the development of a more appropriate frame of reference from which the practice of instructional supervision can continue to evolve.

I. Assumptions
  A. Assumptions about professional workers in educational organizations
    1. Professional workers have worth and dignity.
    2. They possess the capacity to solve their problems and make effective decisions through cooperative action.
    3. They possess potential for growth in ability.
    4. As individuals they are unique.
    5. They have motivation to improve their effectiveness as professionals.
    6. They have specialized competence, and a desire and capacity to be self-directing.
  B. Assumptions about educational organizations
    1. Educational organizations are dynamic.
    2. Organizations exist to serve students, parents, professional workers, and community.
    3. Scientific inquiry is the most effective basis for organizational change.
    4. Man is emotional as well as rational and man's feelings are important and need consideration.
    5. It is possible to enhance our understanding of the educational organization by the utilization of "social system theory."
    6. Instructional supervisory behavior is a sub-system of the educational organization.
    7. The educational organization is a sub-system of the society and,

therefore, the society provides "input" such as specification of educational goals and human material resources.

8. The society is the consumer of the output of the educational organization.

C. Some assumptions about instructional supervisory behavior.

1. Instructional supervisory behavior is behavior which is officially designated by the organization for the purpose of directly influencing the "teaching behavior sub-system" in such a way as to facilitate the achievement of the goals.

2. The functions of this behavior system are
   a. Goal development
   b. Coordination
   c. Program development and actualization
   d. Motivation
   e. Problem solving
   f. Development of professional workers
   g. Evaluation of educational outcomes.

3. The fundamental processes of instructional supervisory behavior are assumed to be
   a. Leadership
   b. Communication
   c. Releasing human potential
   d. Curriculum development.

4. The limits of supervisory authority are defined by the responsibility and requirements of the task.

5. Reliance on scientific knowledge and scientific inquiry in problem solving activities is the most effective approach.

6. The change process is fundamental, but there is recognition of the importance of maintenance operations.

7. It is possible to control to some extent the direction, quality, and amount of change in the "teaching behavior sub-systems of the educational organization."

8. Concepts and theoretical formulations from various fields of inquiry can contribute to the formulation of a theory of supervision.

9. Some of the most valuable sources of concepts for understanding supervisory behavior are the behavioral sciences: psychology (with emphasis on learning, motivation, and mental health), social psychology (with emphasis on leadership, group development, and human relations), sociology (with emphasis on community power structure), and communication.

II. Concepts, theoretical formulations, and empirical findings which have implications for the study and practice of instructional supervision.

A. Mental health, counseling, therapy

1. A person behaves in the manner that he believes best at the moment. (Markey and Herbkersman, 1961)

2. A person changes his behavior as he changes his perception of himself,

his role, or the situation. (Glass, 1964), (Kay and Meyer, 1965), (Kitane, 1962), (Nelson, 1956)

3. The best single predictive indicator of future self-adjustment is the extent to which a person is accurate in his knowledge of himself and his purposes. (McGrath, 1962), (Reader and English, 1947), (Tabachnick, 1962)

4. A person who feels worthy, wanted, and adequate is open to change, finds a wider range of facts and experiences significant, is learning, and is becoming more mature. (Dowis and Diethelam, 1958), (Reader and English, 1947), (Stith and Connor, 1962)

5. A person becomes more open as he lives and works in a situation in which he is accepted, finds it unnecessary to be defensive and closed, and has access to many new experiences. (Ainsworth, 1958), (Feldhusen and Klausmeier, 1962), (Gaier, 1952), (Hallworth, 1961), Mandler and Sarason, 1952), (Palermo, Castaneda and McCandance, 1956)

6. A person is assisted in the process of change by others who convey a feeling of acceptance and a desire to be helpful to him in developing self-direction. (Festinger and Hutte, 1954), Markey and Herbkersman, 1961), (Reader and English, 1947), Stith and Connor, 1962)

B. Learning

1. A human being learns through his interaction with his environment. (Bruner, 1961)

2. The individual selects from the environment the factors with which he will interact. (Bahrick, 1954)

3. A person learns what he perceives that interaction to be, and his perception is a product of his past experiences, his present needs, and his purposes. (Bales, Strodtbeck, Mills, and Roseborough, 1951)

4. The individual's learning is affected by his emotions. Anxiety inhibits performance. (McKeachie, Pollie, and Speisman, 1955), (Montague, 1953), (Watson and Broomberg, 1965)

5. Learning by discovery, the process of rearranging and reinterpreting evidence to enable the individual to gain new insights increases intellectual power, aids in retrieval, and brings satisfaction. (Bruner, 1961), (Gagne and Brown, 1961), (Hale, 1961), (Kersh, 1958), (Kersh, 1962), (Kersh and Wittrock, 1962), (Kittell, 1957)

C. Group Development

1. Group cohesiveness is developed through the interaction of individuals. (Back, 1951), (Harrison and Lubin, 1965), (Polansky, Lippitt, and Redl, 1950)

2. An aggregation of individuals becomes a group when common goals, common values, and norms are developed. (Kiesler, 1963)

3. Cohesive groups are satisfying to members. (Festinger, Torrey, and Willerman, 1954), (Hebb, 1958)

4. Group members are influenced by the norms of the group to which they give allegiance. (Horowitz, Lyons, and Perlmutter, 1950), Nelson, 1956), (Strickland, Jones, and Smith, 1960)

5. The greater the prestige an individual attaches to a group, the stronger the influence of its norms on the individual. (Festinger, Torrey and Willerman, 1954)

6. In highly cohesive groups, members make more effort to reach an agreement, behavior is more influenced by the situation, and inter-action is more effective in producing influence. (Back, 1951), (Gilchrist, Shaw, and Walker, 1954), (Festinger, Torrey, and Willerman, 1954), (Hare, 1952), (Hebb, 1958)

7. Organized groups with past interaction quarrel with frustration, but remain cohesive. (Moos and Speisman, 1962), (Myers, 1962)

8. Groups must develop a structure and organization to make and imple-ment decisions. (Larson and Mill, 1958)

9. High incentive groups tend to learn faster and work more efficiently than low incentive groups. (Bahrick, 1954), (Phillips, 1955, pp. 161-164)

10. The behavior of an individual in a group is affected by the position he has in it. (Bavelas, 1950), (Beal, Rogers, and Bohlen, 1957), (Bovard, 1951), (McClintock, 1963), (Reeves and Goldman, 1957), (Shaw, 1954)

11. Peripheral members of a group are more susceptible to outside influences. (Gilchrist, Shaw, and Walker, 1954), (Thibaut, 1950)

12. Individuals change their perception to accord with the judgment of the group much more in situations in which the group thinks together than in which the leader dominates the group. (Bovard, 1951)

13. High cohesiveness in groups is not necessarily related to high produc-tion. Cohesiveness is related to the susceptibility of group members to be influenced by other group members. (Barnett, 1962)

D. Leadership

1. Leadership is one of the functions in group operation which contribute to the formulation and attainment of group goals. An individual is a leader when he influences group behavior. (Hemphill, 1949), Jennings, 1950), (Markey and Herbkersman, 1961)

2. Leadership function is widespread and diffused throughout the group. A group has more than one leader. Many individuals within the group exert leadership for other group members. (Carter, 1951)

3. The leadership function is fulfilled by different individuals as the situation changes. A group uses the individuals within it who can assist in the solution of the problem confronting it. (Pryer, Flint, and Bass, 1962), (Sterling and Rosenthal, 1950)

4. Leadership is a group role, a product of interaction within the group. (Cornell, 1954), (Hemphill, 1949), (Lewin, 1939), (Markey and Herbkersman, 1961), (Shaw, 1963)

5. Leadership and followership are interchangeable. The characteristics that make an individual a good leader also make him a good follower. (Jennings, 1950), (Sterling and Rosenthal, 1950)

6. The leadership exerted by an individual is determined by the extent to which group members can use an individual's contribution. (Reger, 1962)

7. The extent to which a group is able to use the participation of an individual as a part of the leadership function is determined by their perception of him, his motives, and his competency. (Heinicke and Bales, 1953), (Horton and Wohl, 1956), (James, 1955), (Lippitt,

Polansky, and Rosen, 1952), (Pascoe, 1963), (Reger, 1962), (Strickland, Jones, and Smith, 1960)

8. The leadership that a group uses is partly determined by norms of the group. If an individual violates the critical norms of a group, his participation will not be used as leadership by the group. Group members select for leaders individuals they believe will understand, accept, and maintain the group norms. (Markey and Herbkersman, 1961), (Sterling, and Rosenthal, 1950)

9. Other things being equal, the amount of leadership exerted by an individual is dependent upon the frequency of his interaction with other group members. (Hare, 1952), (Hemphill, 1949), (Shaw, 1963), (Wilkins and Decharms, 1962)

10. Qualities found in individuals who frequently contribute to the leadership function are exhibiting willingness to cooperate, communicating feelings and information, empathizing (Cornell, 1954), (Jennings, 1950), (Wilkins and Decharms, 1962), suggesting new answers to problems, serving others, and emotional stability. (Hicks and Stone, 1962)

11. Leadership is exerted by individuals with and without official status. (Baskin, 1962), (Lewin, 1939), (Shaw, 1963)

12. High-prestige individuals in a group are more spontaneous, make more direct attempts to influence others, and are more open to behavioral contagion than those with low prestige. (Kallegian, Brown, and Weschler, 1953), (Myers, 1962), (Polansky, Lippitt, and Redl, 1950)

E. Human Relations
1. Acceptance of self helps the individual to accept others.
2. Valuing of differences enables each to develop his uniqueness. (Lippitt and White, 1947)
3. Concern for feelings of others is an essential element of effective leadership. (Hemphill, 1949)
4. Membership in cohesive supportive groups decreases the emotional instability of the individuals. (Tabachnick, 1962)

F. Communication
1. Communication is never complete and accurate. Its degree of distortion depends upon the openness of the social situation and the desire of the individuals for complete communication. (Goetzinger and Valentine, 1964)
2. Communication affects efficiency at which groups perform and the ability of the groups to develop adequate organization. (Bavelas, 1950), (Bavelas and Barrett, 1951), (Boag, 1952), (Cohen, 1958), (Cohen, 1962), (Goetzinger and Valentine, 1964), (Guetzkow and Dill, 1957), (Guetzkow, and Simon, 1955), (Gustad, 1962), (Kelley, 1951), (Leavitt, 1951), (Shaw, 1955), (Shaw, 1954)
3. The communication pattern of a group affects its accuracy, emergence of leaders, organization, satisfaction of members, and efficiency. (Back, 1951), (Bavelas, 1950), (Bavelas and Barrett, 1951), (Boag, 1952), (Cohen, 1958), (Goetzinger and Valentine, 1964), (Guetzkow and Dill, 1957), (Kelley, 1951), (Leavitt, 1951), (Read, 1962), (Shaw, 1955)

4. In communication patterns with a high, localized centrality, organization evolves quicker and is more stable, speed and accuracy in solving problems are increased, errors in performance are less, and morale tends to drop. (Bavelas, 1950), (Bavelas and Barrett, 1951), (Gilchrist, Shaw, and Walker, 1954), (Guetzkow and Dill, 1957), (Leavitt, 1951), (Shaw, 1955), (Shaw, 1954)

5. In communication patterns where centrality is evenly distributed, there is high activity, slow organization, and high satisfaction. (Bavelas and Barrett, 1951), (Guetzkow and Dill, 1957), (Leavitt, 1951), (Shaw, 1954)

6. Occurrence and utilization of insight will be found to drop rapidly as centrality becomes highly localized. (Bavelas, 1950), (Guetzkow and Dill, 1957)

7. Increasing the amount of information initially available to an individual in a given position in a communication net has the effect of increasing the individual centrality index of that position or the number of channels available to that position. (Cohen, 1958), (Gilchrist, Shaw, and Walker, 1954), (Goetzinger and Valentine, 1954), (Kelley, 1961), (Shaw, 1954)

8. The position which an individual occupies in a communication pattern affects his behavior while occupying that position. An individual's position in the group affects the chances of his becoming a leader in the group, his satisfaction with his job and with the group, the quantity of his activity, and the extent to which he contributes to the group's functional organization. (Bales, Strodtbeck, Mills, and Roseborough, 1951), (Bavelas, 1950), (Bavelas and Barrett, 1951), (Cohen, 1958), (Cohen, 1962), (Goetzinger and Valentine, 1964), (Guetzkow and Dill, 1957), (Kelley, 1951), (Leavitt, 1951), (Shaw, 1955), (Shaw, 1954), (Shaw, Rothschile, and Strickland, 1957)

9. A recognized leader in a task-oriented group will most probably emerge at the center of the communication pattern. (Bavelas and Barrett, 1951), (Leavitt, 1951), (Shaw, 1954)

10. Communication isolation, a situation in which the individual acts without essential data frequently alienates the individual from the group. (Boag, 1952), (Cohen, 1958), (Goetzinger and Valentine, 1964), (Jenkins and Lippitt, 1951), (Kelley, 1951), (Read, 1962)

11. The completion of the circuit between sender and receiver (feedback) increases the accuracy with which information is transmitted. (Goetzinger, and Valentine, 1964), (Leavitt and Meuller, 1951), (Lysgaard, 1955)

12. The behavior of a group towards a person is affected by the credibility of that person as a source of information. (Aronson and Godlen, 1962), (Bergin, 1962), (Eagle, 1959), (Hoveland and Weiss, 1951), (Runkel, 1956), (Zander, and Cohen, 1955)

13. The message is distorted by feelings of superiority or inferiority of the individuals involved. (Cohen, 1958), (Kelley, 1951)

14. The ability of highly anxious subjects to communicate is less than that of nonanxious subjects. (Cohen, 1958), (Shaw, 1963), (Steiner, 1963)

15. Language that is apparently adequate for superficial communication may not be adequate for understanding deeper meanings. (Bennett and

McKnight, 1956), (Brown and Lenneberg, 1954), (Lionberger and Milton, 1957)

G. Community Power Structure

1. Each community has a power structure in which certain individuals make the decisions of others. In complex (competitive) communities, the power structure may be distributed in several peaks that represent the power figures of different segments of the population. In homogeneous (monopolistic) communities, the power structure may have only one peak and the decision-making is concentrated in a very few individuals. (Kimbrough, 1964)

2. The overt decision-making is not necessarily the real decision-making in community. (Kimbrough, 1964), (Kimbrough and Nunnery, 1971)

3. Decisions made, and actions taken, by legal bodies and community institutions reflect the decisions of the community power structure. (Kimbrough, 1964), (Kimbrough, 1965)

III. Inferred hypotheses

A. Conditional factors such as mutual respect and esteem, trust, and personal satisfaction contribute to the effectiveness of instructional supervisory behavior.

B. Qualities of the organization that affect the supervisory function are rigidity, norms, goals, role perceptions, patterns, communication, use of authority, morale, and cohesiveness.

C. The effectiveness of the supervision is increased when

1. The organizational structure includes a change-inducing agent and is flexible enough to accommodate experimentation and innovation;

2. The norms permit innovation, experimentation, acceptance of diversity and change;

3. The role of perceptions enables each to value the other, to expect to obtain help from the others, to see authority used to hold the group together to make decisions, and to implement those decisions made;

4. Communication channels are opened horizontally as well as vertically, upward as well as downward, and for formulating and evaluating as well as implementing and rating.

D. The persons officially responsible for the function of improvement of instruction — called superintendents, assistant superintendents, directors, consultants, helping teachers, or principals — have the task of creating within the organizational structure an intellectual and emotional environment which provides:

1. Acceptance and support so satisfying that each teacher feels that he belongs and is encouraged to develop his unique potentialities;

2. Many stimuli from which each teacher will choose those that have the greatest meaning and motivation for him;

3. Opportunity for each teacher to grow at his own rate and stage of readiness;

4. Curriculum development programs and in-service education that permit each teacher to work in terms of his purposes and his state of development;

5. A procedure for selecting and distributing materials of instruction that

enables teachers to devote full energy to improving the instruction process;

6. Evaluation conducted in such a manner that evidence involved becomes more self-directing and establishes higher goals for himself;

7. A means of communication where each feels free to reveal his needs, concerns, and values, wants to discover the purposes and perceptions of others, and has access to the data that will enable him to make increasingly intelligent decisions.

8. A system of feedback for each professional person that will help sensitize him to his own effectiveness or ineffectiveness.

9. A technological support system of consultations and services for each member of the staff which includes the development of knowledge and skills in teaching content, methodology, human development, and evaluation.

E. Other staff members — teachers, librarians, secretaries, or custodians — affect improvement of instruction by their attitude, method of operation, interaction pattern, and decisions.

Throughout this book, this theory will provide the basis for advancing hypotheses about the ways in which administrators, directors, supervisors, and resource personnel should work with faculties and individual teachers. Although each practice recommended has proved itself in some school system, it has also been tested against the integrated theory evolved by examination of the inter-relationships of the selected concepts.

Each person who reads the book is encouraged to check the congruence of the recommended practices and the theory, to test the recommended practices against his experience, and, where he finds difference, to explore the degree to which variation in results occurred as a product of divergence in theory.

Theory is the most practical instrument any professional has. It guides his practice and his inquiry. It enables him to engage constantly in a process of self-education.

2 The Evolvement of Instructional Supervision

The current status of the practice and theoretical development of instructional supervision is at least partly a function of its historical evolvement. The assumption on which Chapter 2 was developed is that a look backward provides perspective for analysis and understanding of the present as well as a basis for the development of new ideas, understandings, and practices for the future. There have been major thrusts in the development of instructional supervision, and it is possible in a general way to identify them chronologically. It is apparent that these major movements do not start and stop at some precise time and place. Rather, they tend to start gradually in many places and continue to persist so that threads of past practice can still be found in current practice.

It is hoped that through a study of the historical development of supervision man can learn and profit both from past mistakes and successes. This does not imply the assumption of a cyclical interpretation of history. It does mean that there are present events which have similarities to events of the past. There are suggestions and recommendations for educational change which have been resurrected from the past. Hopefully, a study of the historical origin of these ideas will contribute to sound decisions regarding their current suitability. For example, the current cry for specification of behavioral objectives and educational accountability has roots in the "scientific management movement." This does not mean the ideas are good or bad. It does mean we may already have some relevant evidence.

Major developments in the study and practice of instructional supervision can be organized around the assumptions made about the human being to be supervised. March and Simon (1961, p. 6) have grouped propositions about organizational behavior in three broad classes as follows:

1. Propositions assuming that organization members, and particularly employees, are primarily passive instruments, capable of performing work and
   accepting directions, but not initiating action or exerting influence in any
   significant way.
2. Propositions assuming that members bring to their organizations attitudes,
   values, and goals; that they have to be motivated or induced to participate in
   the system of organization behavior; that there is incomplete parallelism
   between their personal goals and organization goals; and that actual or
   potential goal conflicts make power phenomena, attitudes, and morale
   centrally important in the explanation of organizational behavior.
3. Propositions assuming that organization members are decision makers and
   problem solvers, and that perception and thought processes are central to the
   explanation of behavior in organizations.

The periods of "administrative inspection" and later scientific management were characterized by the assumption of man as a passive instrument or
tool of management that could be manipulated in such a way as to achieve the
goals of the organization. The period of scientific management began in the early
part of the twentieth century and is still an important factor in supervision. In
the later part of the first quarter of the twentieth century, as a result of certain
theoretical formulations and empirical studies, certain questions were raised
about scientific management since it became apparent that it did not explain all
events. This brought on the beginning of the "human relations movement"
which is still a dominating factor in supervisory practice.

Currently, theorists are turning to the assumption of the rationality of
men as well as their emotions and attitudes. This is beginning to influence
supervisory behavior in educational institutions. Accordingly, Chapter 2 is
organized around these major movements as they have affected instructional
supervisory behavior in educational institutions.

Administrative Inspection

Supervision during the early part of the eighteenth century was described
by Burton and Brueckner (1966). Committees of citizens were appointed to
inspect the plant and equipment as well as check on pupil achievement. The
primary focus of these committees was to determine the extent to which
teachers were doing their job based on the "inspection" and to take appropriate
action. Several factors deserve special comment. First, the inspectors were lay
citizens and therefore operating on the assumption that no special professional
competence was required for supervisors. Second, there was no effort to improve
teachers or teaching. There was an effort to determine if children were learning.
If a problem was identified, teachers were expected to improve or else. There
was no assumption of a science of teaching that could be taught or learned.
Third, there is no evidence that these inspectors were particularly concerned

about the emotions, feelings, attitudes, or morale of the teachers. Fourth, the inspectors, lay citizens, held the teachers accountable for the pupil achievement. It is interesting to note the current emphasis on accountability and lay participation.

As schools became larger and it was necessary to have multiple teachers, one teacher would often be singled out as the "principal" teacher and would be assigned certain managerial functions. But these building "principals" did not assume responsibility for improvement of the instructional program at this time (Burton and Brueckner, 1966).

During the early part of the nineteenth century, the schools were growing, population was growing, and people were beginning to crowd into urban centers. This called not only for multiple teachers but also for multiple schools. As a result of the growing complexity of school systems, the functions of lay boards or citizens' committees began to be placed in the hands of superintendents, and the improvement of teaching became an important function of these positions (Ayer and Barr, 1928, pp. 7-28). By the latter part of the nineteenth century, there were twenty-nine superintendents of schools in the United States, and the superintendents were seeking to improve teachers and teaching as well as to reject inadequate teaching (Lucio and McNeil, 1969, p. 4).

As school systems became larger with more and more teachers in more widely scattered facilities, superintendents found it increasingly difficult to meet their responsibilities for supervision of the instructional program. Therefore, they added additional professionals to their staffs, and these personnel became general supervisors and began to develop the role. Since these supervisors were appointed by the superintendent, it was natural that they worked from his office and as his representatives. Thus, there was the development of a highly centralized system of supervision from the central office. This probably helps explain some of the relationship problems that developed between building principals and general supervisors as well as difficulties the schools have experienced in developing the instructional leadership function of the school principal. As schools continued to grow, the highly centralized structure persisted. Today leading educators such as John Goodlad (Goodlad, 1969) and others are suggesting that this is one of the factors that helps explain the difficulty large school systems have experienced in attempts to change.

Another significant development for supervision was the addition to the curriculum of certain new subjects which required special competence that teachers in the schools did not have. "Special teachers" were hired to teach these subjects. In some cases they became "regular" teachers for these subjects. But in other cases they became traveling teachers and taught the special subjects in different schools on different days. This led to these "special teachers" advising and working with the regular teachers, and under some circumstances the regular teachers taught the special courses under the supervision of the special teachers who became special supervisors.

In summary, supervision during the period of "administrative inspection" was conducted on the assumption that the workers (teachers) were passive tools of the organization and they would do, or had better do, what was expected of them. Supervision was telling, inspecting, rating, checking, and monitoring. It wasn't until the latter part of the nineteenth century that improvement of teachers and teaching became a well-established function of instructional supervision.

Scientific Management

At the beginning of the twentieth century the industrial revolution was a dominant factor in American life and the method of science was the major approach used by industry. Scientific management became the dominant theory for organizational improvement largely through the creative and scholarly efforts of a relatively small group of organizational theorists (March, 1961). A spokesman for scientific management was Frederick Taylor whose primary concern was to increase efficiency in industrial organizations. The assumption that the worker was a passive instrument that could be manipulated to achieve the goals of the organization was the same as the assumption for the practice of "administrative inspection," but the methods of science were applied to achieve the greatest possible efficiency. Taylor's principal prescriptions were listed by March and Simon (1961 pp. 19-20) as follows:

1. Use time and methods study to find the "one best way" of performing a job...
2. Provide the worker with an incentive to perform the job in the best way and at a good pace . . .
3. Use specialized experts (functional foremen) to establish the various conditions surrounding the worker's task — methods, machine speeds, task priorities, etc.

These prescriptions clearly establish the use of science to determine the one best method of production. Man was assumed to be motivated by economic gain and foremen "supervisors" established the conditions of work, the best methods for proceeding, and the overseeing of the job. Time and motion studies were used to determine the "one best way" of achieving a special task. Workers were expected to do it that way and supervisors were there to see that they did.
Scientific management had important implications for educational organizations and various educational leaders took up the gauntlet to make public schools more efficient. Cubberley (1916, p. 338) referred to the fact that industry is working to turn out a standard product and to produce it with the most efficient methods. This calls for the scientific study of methods of production and the scientific measurement of the output. He advocated this model for the public schools which were seen as factories with the children as

the raw material to be changed according to the specifications of society and with the greatest efficiency. He called for the use of the methods of science to determine the most efficient methods of teaching and to measure the outcomes of student learning.

Concepts of departmentalization in organizations also had important implications for educational organizations. The general idea was that given a certain set of objectives for an organization it is possible to define the necessary tasks and positions. These positions can be organized into efficient units such as divisions and departments. This contributes to the establishment of a formal hierarchy of authority and responsibility.

Closely related to the work on departmentalization was Max Weber's definition of an "ideal model" for a formal organization which he termed "bureaucracy." Some of the essential characteristics of the bureaucratic model were identified by Blau (1956) as "hierarchy of authority, impersonalization of management, tasks achieved through fixed positions or structures and control maintained through general rules."

Even a cursory examination of Weber's "ideal" type of organization and the structure of educational organizations reveals a close and positive correlation. Careful observers such as Abbott (1965), Miles (1965 pp. 54-72), Moeller (Moeller and Charter, 1966, pp. 444-65), and Anderson (1968) reached similar conclusions. Kliebard (1971, p. 74) explored the influence of bureaucratic ideas in educational organizations.

> The picture that emerges from the apparently frenetic educational activity during the first few decades of this century seems to be one of growing acceptance of a powerful and restrictive bureaucratic model for education which looked toward the management techniques of industry as its ideal of excellence and source of inspiration.

The fact is that there is task specialization in educational organizations. There is an educational hierarchy which determines authority and responsibility in policy development and implementing procedures. There are organizational expectations and general rules which affect behavior in the organization. This does not mean that these factors are apparent to the same extent, if at all, in all organizations. It does mean that bureaucratization and departmentalization were important factors in the evolvement of educational organizations. The superintendent's office was organized into tasks to be accomplished. There were assistant superintendents in charge of business, instruction, personnel, etc., that headed up appropriate departments. Schools were organized by departments according to subject matter areas and grade levels. There was an established hierarchy of line officers (line of authority) and staff officers. Whether or not instructional supervisors should be "line" or staff continues to be a subject of lively debate.

Bobbitt (1912) was one of the important advocates of scientific management for the schools. He was concerned with the elimination of waste, efficiency of workers, and continuous use of facilities. But he was also concerned with finding the most efficient and effective educational methodology and utilizing supervisors to see that teachers carried it out. Kliebard (1971, p. 81) interpreted Bobbitt's writing as follows:

> ... Extrapolating from this and other examples, Bobbitt went on to comment on the functions of specialized supervisors in schools in determining "proper methods" and "the determination of more or less definite qualifications for the various aspects of the teaching personality." The supervisor of instruction occupied that middle-management function roughly comparable to the foreman in industry.

The move toward standardization and particularization of educational objectives and methods had important implications for the evolvement of educational supervision. After objectives had been predetermined and the best way of achieving them had been scientifically established, it was the function of supervision to see to it that the workers (teachers) carried out the specifications. The specifications were complete and there was little or no concern with the teachers as human beings except as instruments for getting the job done. Teachers were paid and were expected to perform with efficiency. If not, they were either taught to do so or relieved of their assignment. Supervision was telling, explaining, showing, enforcing, rating, and rewarding. In a general way this was the status of instructional supervision during the first quarter of the twentieth century. Naturally, there was a variety of patterns. Some systems operated on a laissez-faire pattern in which teachers were expected to produce and were left to their own resources. There were also rigid systems of inspection and rating which had roots in the earlier period of "administrative inspection." But the fundamental assumption was that the teacher was an instrument that could be used and molded by the administration to facilitate the achievement of the goals of the educational organization. Little concern for the feelings, attitudes, and motivations of teachers was expressed. A combination of factors including the development of theoretical formulations and empirical findings as well as certain social developments set in motion a challenge to the "theory" of scientific management and laid the foundation for a growing concern with the psychological well being of organizational members.

Supervision and Human Concern in Educational Organizations

Instructional supervision during the second quarter of the twentieth century was characterized by a growing concern with the nature and needs of human beings in the educational organization. The assumption that human beings in the organization have their own goals, values, feelings, emotions, and needs which affect their need to behave in certain ways and that the organization expects members to behave in ways consistent with organizational needs and goals and that organization needs and human needs are not necessarily congruent was a dominant factor in the theory and practice of supervision.

The famous Hawthorne Studies carried out by Elton Mayo and others (Mayo, 1933); (Roethlisberger and Dickson, 1947) led to serious challenges to the principles of scientific management. The findings that relationships between workers and supervisors could be a more potent factor in production than a variety of environmental conditions shook the scientific thinking about supervision of that day. The conclusion that the informal social system which workers form can be an important stimulant in setting standards for worker production led to a barrage of research and changes in the practice of supervision.

The study of social groups coming from the behavioral sciences also had a profound effect on the growing body of literature on instructional supervision as well as the practice. Lewin (1943, 1944, pp. 195-200), Homans (1950), Lippitt and White (1947), to name only a few, have been significant contributors. The concept of group structure was verified. Sub-concepts such as interaction, activity, and group sentiment were defined to describe the internal structure of groups. Research findings indicated that group members who participate in making group decisions are more likely to accept and act on these decisions. A person's position in the social group can be an important factor in his behavior including his work production. Groups have norms of behavior for their members, and these norms are important factors in the behavior of group members. Those members most attracted to the group are more likely to act according to group norms.

The study of leadership behavior also had an important effect on educational supervision. Of particular significance were the works of Lippitt and White (1947), Stogdill (1948, pp. 35-71), Lewin (1939), Bavelas (1942), and many others. Through these studies, focus was placed on the importance of the behavior of organizational leaders. Questions were being posed and studied concerning the nature of leadership behavior and variables related to leadership effectiveness. The study of the "traits" of leaders and the attempt to correlate certain traits with certain criteria of leadership effectiveness was an early approach. The "styles" of leadership behavior were also studied. Findings indicated that the same groups or similar groups operating under different styles of leadership will develop different group structure and group production. Since the early studies were developed around democratic and authoritarian styles and since the democratic style came out with "favorable" results, "democratic supervision" took on a new significance.

The thirties was a period of depression, economic suffering, and disenchantment with the business community. Angry young men were speaking out against economic oppression and for human rights and democratic principles. Therefore, it is not surprising to find a strong trend to introduce democratic principles in organizational governance. This became an especially important factor in the literature and practice of educational administration and instructional supervision.

The impact of these various strands of thought on the body of professional literature of this period was significant. Even the titles of important textbooks of this period are indicative of the trends of the day:

1. John Bartky, *Supervision as Human Relations*
2. Charles Boardman, *Democratic Supervision in Secondary Schools*
3. William H. Burton and Leo J. Brueckner, *Supervision, A Social Process*

In an earlier edition of *Supervision for Better Schools* Wiles developed a concept of supervision around the sub-concepts of skill in leadership, skill in group process, skill in evaluation, and skill in human relations. Emphasis was placed on building staff morale, releasing the creative energies of group members, shared leadership, cooperative decision making, self evaluation, developing staff leadership. The central focus was on the behavior of the supervisor and how he could influence the behavior of teachers. Significant research was listed which provided the rationale of the book (Wiles, 1950).

Burton and Brueckner (1955) put strong emphasis on social process, social change, principles of democratic supervision, cooperative planning, and leadership but also included the improvement of the educational program through the study of the learner, instruction, curriculum, and the use of materials of instruction.

It is clear that the professors of education had joined the "tide" of the human relations movement. A brief review of the literature and activities of the Department of Supervisors and Directors of Instruction which later became the Association for Supervision and Curriculum Development also revealed a strong and lasting influence of this movement. Democratic principles were defined and applied to the supervisory role. It was assumed that teachers were capable of participating in decisions on teaching and curriculum. The role of the supervisor was to provide a climate where this could happen. Much was written about group process, the importance of morale, cooperative problem solving, worth and dignity of man, leadership, and positive support. Less was written about supervision as maintenance and improvement of quality teaching and learning and the necessity for responsibility and authority.

Even more important was the fact that the Association of Supervision and Curriculum Development emerged as a powerful and influential organization during the forties. Their national meetings were well attended by supervisors, and they were taught group process and democratic leadership not only by the excellent literature and speeches of the organization but by having an opportunity to "live it" during these meetings. Topics were discussed in small groups according to principles of group process. Participants were involved, and the organization grew in strength and national prestige.

Things began to happen in the schools. The title "supervisor" (long associated with overseer or monitor) began to disappear and was replaced by "consultant," "resource person," "helping teacher," "coordinator," and others. The assumption was that it was essential for the needs of teachers to be met and this sometimes became "keeping them happy." The approach was to provide a nonthreatening source of help for teachers. Supervisors worked at developing a comfortable and facilitating climate. Often superintendents would announce that supervisors were "simply" resource people and had no authority in the organization. This was quite a change from the first quarter of the century when there was a highly centralized system and supervisors came from the central office as personal representatives of the superintendent. During the period of "scientific management," courses of study were developed by "curriculum experts" in the central office and the supervisors took the "word" to the local schools where they checked to see that the "word" was being carried out. What a shift! The curriculum was now being defined as what happens to students under the direction of the school (Caswell and Campbell, 1935) and the basic agency for school improvement had shifted from the central office to the local school (Miel, 1946, p. 69). Supervisors were resource people, on call, waiting for requests for services.

Some supervisors became dispensers of happiness using slaps on the back and offerings of coffee and cookies as important techniques. In some cases, supervisors were able to work effectively in this setting and maintain close contact with teachers and the instructional program. But in many situations, supervisors lost significant contact with local schools, teachers, and the instructional program. Problems developed. Teachers did not request services. Many principals of local schools were not trained, experienced, or inclined to assume responsibility for leadership for the instructional program. Roles, responsibility, and authority were unclear in many situations and contributed to poor communication and working relationships between central office supervisors and local school principals. There were also many incidences of poor working relations between supervisors and teachers. Services weren't requested. When they were, supervisors were often more interested in being "democratic" than in helping teachers identify and solve problems. Many teachers did not trust the new approach that supervisors were using and felt that they were still "supervisors." Supervisors failed to live up to expectations of teachers who longed for the "old" supervisors.

The picture was not all rosy. There were serious problems, and it was becoming clear that the "human relations" approach was not the total answer. Practitioners were raising questions and demanding answers.

The Movement Toward Interaction Theories

During the third quarter of the twentieth century, the challenge to formal bureaucracy has continued, the concern for humans in the organization has continued with new focus on organizational members as rational decision makers and problem solvers. The utilization of research and theory coming from the behavioral sciences has continued and intensified, and there has been an effort to develop interaction theories of supervision.

CHALLENGE TO BUREAUCRACY CONTINUES

Many students of bureaucracy became increasingly concerned with the unexpected consequences of bureaucracy: Merton (1940, pp. 560-68), Selznick (1949), Gouldner (1954), Argyris (1961), Kliebard (1971), Arnstine (1971), Miles (1965), Blau and Scott (1962), among others. Merton, for example, found that the demand for control with the intended result of emphasis on reliability also resulted in rigidity of behavior (unintended) and an amount of difficulty with clients (unintended). The difficulty with clients resulted in a greater felt need for defensibility of individual action which leads to greater emphasis on reliability and more difficulty with clients.

Gouldner and Selznick defined additional dysfunctions. Argyris (Petrullo and Bass, 1961, pp. 331-36) identified the following propositions describing the impact of the formal organization on the individual:

Proposition I. *There is a lack of congruency between the needs of healthy individuals and the demands of the formal organization.*

Proposition II. *The resultants of this disturbance are frustration, failure, short-time perspective and conflict.*

Proposition III. *Under certain conditions the degree of frustration, failure, short-time perspective and conflict will tend to increase.*

Proposition IV. *The nature of the formal principles of organization cause the subordinates, at any given level, to experience competition, rivalry, intersubordinate hostility and to develop a focus toward the parts rather than the whole.*

Proposition V. *Employees react to the formal organization by creating informal activities.*

Proposition VI. *Employee adaptive behavior maintains individual self-integration and simultaneously impedes integration with the formal organization.*

Proposition VII. *Adaptive behavior of employees has a cumulative effect, feeds back into the formal organization, and further entrenches itself.*

Proposition VIII. *Certain management reactions tend to increase antagonisms underlying adaptive behavior.*

Kliebard developed the thesis that the assumptions and needs of bureaucratic educational organizations lead to "dehumanization of education, the alienation of means from ends, the stifling of intellectual curiosity," and he describes this as a tragic paradox (Kliebard, 1971, p. 92). Arnstine developed the idea that intellectual freedom is a necessary ingredient in the educational process and that though it is possible to think about intellectual freedom without political freedom, it is never possible to actually have it. Since bureaucracy cannot tolerate political freedom, it is necessary to shake the shackles of bureaucracy in school governance in order to have an effective system of education (Arnstine, 1971, pp. 5-8). Blau and Scott (1962, p. 242) defined the following dilemmas of formal organizations: "1. coordination and communication; 2. bureaucratic discipline and professional expertness; 3. managerial planning and initiative."

Likert (Petrullo and Bass, 1961, pp. 292-93) summarized prevailing standard operating procedures for most organizations and specified the implications. Then he listed typical conclusions and sources of research that seriously challenge the assumptions of the classical conception of organizations. Among his conclusions were that: employers who were concerned with employees rather than just getting out the work were more likely to get better performance; inferior performance was associated with "close" supervision; broad distribution of power and wide participation in decision making was associated with organizational effectiveness; pressure to produce was not associated with greater production.

It became increasingly apparent that the formal bureaucratic model had serious disadvantages for organizations in general, but was especially inadequate for the institution of education because of certain special characteristics:

1. The fact that the "work" of the organization is done by highly trained and specialized professionals
2. The difficulty of measuring and evaluating the "output" and "input" of the educational organization
3. The fact of "person" specialization rather than "task" specialization
4. The relative isolation of the teacher-pupil system and therefore, the lack of a comprehensive system of "supervision"
5. The need for intellectual freedom
6. The nature of human relations in the learning process
7. The need for flexibility and adaptability.

It is true that in the educational organization there is a need for control, general rules, and consistency of response. But, there is also a need for creative response, initiative, adaptiveness, and freedom of movement. The effort to control sometimes leads to teacher dissatisfaction, rigidity, and defensiveness. These conditions tended to stifle creative problem solving, flexibility, and willingness to learn new skills and try new ideas. Communication channels were often blocked, and the opportunities for teachers to share ideas and learn from each other was often stifled. It became increasingly clear that educational organizations needed a structure that not only provided for coordination of personnel but also for psychological support; growth and development, creative response, recognition of achievement, and nonthreatening opportunities to participate in school improvement through experimental and developmental activities.

UTILIZATION OF THEORY AND RESEARCH FROM THE BEHAVIORAL SCIENCES

Evidence is mounting that scholars in the field of instructional supervision are utilizing theory and research from the behavioral sciences. Even a cursory examination of recent textbooks on instructional supervision revealed a strong reliance on research and theory from such fields as communications, leadership, organization, mental health, psychology, business and sociology. The Association for Supervision and Curriculum Development organized a commission on supervision theory which had representatives from various research areas with a specific charge to examine research in these areas for the purpose of developing greater understanding for their implication for the study of instructional supervisory behavior. The work of this group resulted in a publication (Lucio, 1967). Other publications, as well as general meetings and the work of commissions, show similar concerns.

THE LAST TWENTY YEARS

During the last twenty years there has been an important effort to harmonize theoretical and research developments coming from both the doctrines of scientific management and human relations. After careful review of research and theory, Likert (Petrullo and Bass, 1961, pp. 293-95) concluded "that there are important inadequacies in the organizational and managerial theories upon which most American business organizations and government agencies base their present operating procedures." He suggested that there is a need for a modified theory of management which would build on the best of existing practices, such as specification of operational goals, greater efficiency in the utilization of human and material resources of production, and more effective methods of budgeting.

His second major concept was the necessity for a high level of motivation throughout the organization for the achievement of organizational goals. In addition to the classic economic motives, he identified certain motivational factors that emerge from psychological needs of workers such as the need for belonging, esteem, recognition, achievement, and creativity.

The third concept was coordination of human effort. Such coordination requires provision for communication in all directions, broad basis of mutual influence, and wide participation in decision making based on expertise rather than position.

Likert's fourth concept defined the importance of measurement not only in the classical sense but of those human dimensions such as motivation, communication effectiveness, and decision making effectiveness.

To test the modified theory Likert (Petrullo and Bass, 1961, p. 305) identified clusters of organizations which more nearly exemplified the "modified theory" and clusters of stations which least exemplified it. He found the former clusters displayed to the greatest extent the following factors: greater production, more complete and authentic communication, wider distribution of interpersonal influence, decentralized decision making, identification with organizational goals, and increased motivation and less interpersonal conflict.

The modified theory emphasizes the importance of human participants in the enterprise of the organization. The indication is not so much to move from "scientific management" to "human relations" but rather to revise or modify existing organizational theory so as to maintain the best of existing practice as well as to recognize the need for change.

The modified theory clearly recognizes the complexity of motivation and the need for a broad based interpersonal influence system that would use the ability and creativeness of organizational members.

Argyris (Petrullo and Bass, 1961, p. 343) made a careful review of certain difficulties in formal organizations and developed a tentative model for changing the nature of organizations. He identified seven dimensions for understanding the organizational mix. The need for control was emphasized, but for control that is a function of human awareness of the needs of the organization and the way the parts fit together in relationship to individual and organizational goals.

McGregor compared two sets of contrasting assumptions which could serve as a frame of reference for the management of organizations. In theory X and theory Y, management was assumed to have the responsibility for organizing the elements of production to achieve certain economic ends. But in theory X man was assumed to be lazy, irresponsible, unresponsive, incapable and/or unwilling to be self-directing and self-controlling, and resistant to change. Therefore, it was necessary for management to direct, control, motivate, inspect, and modify the behavior of organizational members to fit the needs of management.

But, in theory Y people are not assumed to be naturally lazy, unmotivated, and incapable of self-direction. Rather, they have become that way as a result of management practices. Therefore, it is the function of management to provide the structure in which organizational members can develop their talent, creativeness, and motivation through participation in decision making and problem solving activities. It is assumed that people can achieve their own goals by self-directed work toward the goals of the organization (Bennis and Schein, 1966).

Much of the work on the study and analysis of the organizational environment has been done with focus on industrial organizations. Certainly, we take the position that such work has important implications for educational organizations. But, some work is being done in educational organizations. Halpin and Croft (1963, pp. 55-67) have made an important contribution to this body of literature. They developed the Organizational Climate Description Questionnaire as a way of describing the climate in various schools. The work resulted in the delineation of six distinctive climates in schools which range from open to closed. The six climates were defined by the analysis of the behavior that was described through the administration of the eight subtests: disengagement, hindrance, esprit, intimacy, aloofness, production emphasis, thrust, consideration. Teachers in the organization tested responded according to the group's characteristics with respect to disengagement, hindrance, esprit and intimacy and official leaders' characteristics with respect to aloofness, production emphasis, thrust, and consideration.

In the open climate the groups were extremely high on esprit and low on disengagement and hindrance. They were "with it" and worked well together without the need for great intimacy. The group leader's behavior was perceived as high on thrust and consideration, but low on aloofness and production emphasis. He was perceived as being highly motivated to work hard, but did not have to provide close supervision or emphasize production by subordinates.

The closed climates were characterized by high disengagement, hindrance, intimacy, aloofness, and production emphasis and low esprit, thrust, and consideration. The other climates — autonomous, controlled, familiar and paternal — were also described.

Halpin and Croft (1963, pp. 112-16) were much interested in the fact that they observed that the behavior of organizational members in the more open climates was much more "authentic" than behavior in the more closed climates. In the closed climate it almost appeared that people were playing a part in a play, whereas, in the open climate the action was for real.

The above references are examples which were chosen from a growing body of literature which is concerned with both organizational goals and human goals and the way they relate one to the other. The need is for an organizational structure that recognizes

1. The organizational member's need to use his creative talents and the organization's need for those creative talents
2. The organizational member's need to be involved in decision making and problem solving and the organization's need to have decisions made and problems solved
3. The organizational member's need to be in on communication and contribute to it and the organization's need for communication
4. The organizational member's need to be authentic and the organization's need for authentic behavior
5. The organizational member's need for control and a chance to participate in

the development of the control structure and the organization's need for a control structure

6. The organizational member's need for recognition, creative work, satisfaction of well done work and the organization's need for highly motivated workers.

AN EMERGING POINT OF VIEW

Based on the research, theory development, and practice of instructional supervision duing the past few years, certain key ideas are taking shape which could have important implications for the practice of instructional supervision. Since the shape and form of the chapters which follow are at least partly a function of these various threads of thought, an attempt will be made to identify them and briefly discuss their implications for instructional supervisory behavior.

Instructional supervision will continue to be seen and studied as an organizational sub-system which has the function of directly influencing teaching behavior in such a way as to facilitate student learning. Since educational organizations are under pressure to change for improvement and since they have experienced great difficulty in bringing about significant and lasting change, it appears that instructional supervision will be more and more involved in the change arena.

Many factors indicate that there will be an increased emphasis on the specification (where feasible) of operational goals, definition of learning conditions, and evaluation of outcomes. With the recognition of the need for organizational members to be sensitive to overall organizational goals and the realization that one of the best methods to achieve this is through teacher involvement, it is apparent that instructional supervisors will be increasingly concerned with involving teachers in policy development, problem solving, and decision making activities. These propositions are based on the assumption of teachers as professional educators with specialized expertise.

The motivation of teachers will continue to be a matter of grave concern to instructional supervisors, but relatively less emphasis will be placed on monetary rewards and working conditions and more emphasis will be placed on the teacher's need for recognition, creative experience, satisfaction of a job well done, belonging, and self esteem. Supervisory activities will be provided for these kinds of needs.

Leadership effectiveness is not just a function of formal position, but is a function of complex factors including appropriate specialized competence and level of esteem by colleagues. Since these attributes are broadly distributed among faculty members, it would be appropriate to broaden the allocation of formal supervisory authority to carry out certain kinds of supervisory behavior. Of course, it will also be the function of instructional supervision to identify and organize the personnel for these activities.

The processes of coordination and quality control will become increasingly important, but greater emphasis will be placed on teacher participation in the development of organizational goals. There will also be greater emphasis on self-direction, self-evaluation, and self-correction. This involves the utilization and development of many kinds of instruments that will make it possible for teachers to have more definitive information about the outcomes of their teaching efforts. Interaction analysis, video taping, and micro teaching are examples of such procedures. Instructional supervisors will be expected to provide leadership in these activities.

The rapid expansion of knowledge both in content of subject matter and teaching methodology has important implications for teaching. Even though teachers are assumed to be professionally competent, it is not appropriate to assume that they do not need a highly specialized support system. Changes in technology, behavioral sciences, curriculum, evaluation, and learning resources are important factors. The fact that teachers need to keep abreast of these changes and need help to do so represents an important challenge to instructional supervision.

The growing complexity of educational organizations, the development of specialization, teacher involvement in policy development and decision making, and difficulty of coordination emphasize the need for authentic communication, not only down, but "up" and "sideways." To function as decision makers and problem solvers, teachers must have the total picture, and this requires quality communication. The challenge to instructional supervisors is clear.

In summary, educational organizations will continue to be concerned with the specification of learning outcomes, conditions for achieving the outcomes, and evaluation. This has been and will continue to be a primary function of instructional supervision. But, the growing concern for human beings in the organization will continue and intensify with a growing focus on teachers as problem solvers, decision makers, and change agents. A prime function of instructional supervision will be to involve, lead, and coordinate teachers in these kinds of activities. The salient point is to get the allocation of human resources, effort, authority, and expertise for the appropriate problem.

THE PROCESSES OF
SUPERVISION

Process is a concept often used to refer to any aspect of social interaction. (Longworthy, 1964, p. 538). The term is used in this context to refer to categories of supervisory behavior that are fundamental and persistent in a wide array of supervisory activities. Chapter 3 is developed around the process of releasing human potential. Chapter 4 considers leadership behavior as a process of supervision. Chapters 5 and 6 are built around communication as a crucial process of supervisory behavior.

3   Supervision Is
Releasing Human Potential

Supervision is an organizational behavior system which has the function of interacting with the teaching behavior system for the purpose of improving the learning situation for children. The position has been developed that supervisory behavior is not just a function of supervisors but rather is a function of various roles depending on the needed ability for a particular undertaking. The focus of the "supervisor's" roles is not so much to be competent in all areas and to be the "formal" leader in all situations but, rather, to facilitate the release of the human potential of organizational members that makes available a more competent staff to conduct the human interaction that is called education.

Human Potential Is Not Fully Utilized

To determine how to be most helpful in the release of human potential, the supervisor needs to become well informed about human development, especially motivation and learning. Studies from anthropology, psychology, and human growth and development indicate that each person is born with more potential than he uses, that no matter who he is, no one develops all the potential with which he is born. People are born with different capacities, but no matter how limited or how extensive their potential, no one ever develops all that he has. Since no one ever fully develops all his potential, there is, in effect, no ceiling. Even on the most limited person, there is a ceiling that is higher than he will ever reach.

The experiences a person has determine which of the possible potentials he will develop. The kind of early experience a person has determines the extent to which he will use, or be able to use, a greater portion of his potential. These early experiences can build the kind of structure which is restrictive, which causes him to see himself as less adequate and therefore less able to explore new experiences and develop more potential; or they can build the opposite, an open structure.

The earlier experiences that will develop openness are provided, the greater the possibility of developing additional potential. If the early experience is restrictive, it builds a kind of structure that makes it less possible to expand into other areas. As a person interacts, he forms a structure of knowledge, a concept of self, a concept of other people, and a concept of the world about him. As he builds his structure of knowledge and structure of personality, he is determining by the concepts formed how extensive his future experiences can be and how much he can move in the direction of realizing his potential.

Even though early experiences are very important, the human being continues to develop some of his potential all his life. The amount depends upon his experiences and the environment in which he lives. If he is fortunate enough to live in a heterogeneous, changing society that provides many positive experiences, he will develop more of his potential.

Lionberger (1957), in his study of how farmers change their habits of farming, found that it is much more difficult to bring about change in the farming process in a homogeneous community where people live with others like themselves than in a heterogeneous community where many kinds of people live together. Interaction with people who are different provides challenge and a choice of patterns.

If the environment is a changing one, the individual knows it is possible for him to be an innovator and play a different role. The belief that change is possible affects the individual's freedom to try. If the society is one in which the patterns are fixed and little change is apparent, the individual develops only the potentials that are appropriate to his assigned role. But if he believes he can be more than he is, he will dare to try to develop unused potential.

If, in his interaction with other individuals in the society, he has many positive experiences, he develops the kind of personality and knowledge structure that makes it possible for him to dare to seek new and different experiences that increase his range of understanding and skills. Positive experiences are ones which bring satisfaction to the individual. Support! Expression of faith in his ability! Success in achieving goals! Any experience that increases the individual's belief in his worth and his ability to solve the problems that confront him is a positive experience.

Carl Rogers (1971, pp. 215) posed the rhetorical question, "Can schools grow persons?" and answered with a definite "no." Rather, he indicated that only "persons can grow persons." Thus, it is through our interaction with others that we develop into the kind of person we become. Rogers goes on to define a person as follows:

And what do I mean by persons? I think I have never tried to define that exactly, and what follows is certainly not precise. To me, a person has several qualities. He is an individual whose locus of evaluation is internal. He is not governed by the "shoulds" and "oughts" of conformity, nor necessarily governed by the rules of his institution, if they conflict too deeply with his own values. And he is a person with values, values which are not simply words or beautiful statements, but values which he lives. . . .

A person is openly expressive of where he is, who he is. He does not live a facade or a role, hiding behind the convenient front of being a "teacher," a "principal," a "psychologist." He is real, and the realness shows through. Hence he is unique, and this means that there is enormous diversity in persons — diversity in philosophy, in approach to life, in opinions, in ways of dealing with students. Thus, when there are persons in educational institutions they become controversial, difficult, not easily fitted into categories; consequently life is exciting — and even worthwhile.

A person with sufficient positive experience develops a self concept that enables him to be more open to experience. Because he feels adequate, he does not fear strangeness and welcomes new problems, sensations, opportunities, and challenges. He does not need to seek cover by retreating to the known, the tried, and the tested. He dares to risk failure and rebuff. He is not afraid to reveal himself. He feels that he is a person of worth and that he will be able to cope with whatever the failure brings.

If a person with an adequate self concept exists in a school in which inclusiveness rather than exclusiveness is valued, he does even more to develop his potential. If exclusiveness is valued, the adequate person may never find the situations that produce challenge and growth. If inclusiveness is prized, the individual's contacts in a heterogeneous population with different ideas, values, and procedures will be sufficiently great to test his thinking and his ability to resolve conflicts that arise. An example of openness to experience follows:

A consultant was working for a school in a Georgia town that had taken its first steps in school desegregation. He conducted the first integrated meeting of the professional staff of the school system. The Negro teachers entered first and pursued the strategy of taking seats throughout the room so that there would not be a Negro group and a white group. As the whites came into the room, they took seats among the Negroes. The consultant made a presentation and asked the staff to break up into discussion groups to discuss it. He felt a resistance to his suggestion, so he designated the people who would be in each discussion group — he wanted to be sure each group was mixed. As they started to discuss, he observed the same phenomenon throughout the hall. If the Negroes happened to be sitting in front, not a single Negro turned his chair around to talk to the whites behind, and the whites talked to the back of the Negroes' heads. If the whites were in front, they did not turn around, and the Negroes talked to the back of the whites' heads. After this had gone on for about ten minutes, he noticed a Negro girl who turned her chair halfway. A little bit later, she turned her chair all the way, and another Negro girl turned her chair halfway. He walked over to them and said to the first Negro girl, "How did you get the courage to do it?" She said, "Well, I thought I could profit by it."

As the consultant was getting ready to leave, he asked if they would be interested in his reactions to what went on. When they agreed, he remarked he had noticed that when they moved into the discussion group where they had an opportunity to engage in the kind of professional experience that many of them had not engaged in before, that only one person in the room really took advantage of it. He asked, "Why?" and began to talk about using opportunities for growth. After the session was over, at least 25 people came by and said to him, "I'm very thankful that you said what you did, because what you were doing was helping open the doors so that more of us felt free to be more open."

The Negro girl provided the necessary leadership. Even in this kind of situation with 300 persons involved, one person who was more open to experience could take the initiative that then made it possible for other people to be more open.

Not all teachers were equally open to experience. The ones who needed to have the administration provide increased opportunities to develop openness did not utilize the situation that was presented.

A human being seeks to maintain his existence and enhance himself. The action he takes depends upon his interpretation of the situation and his perception of himself and his role. At any given moment, he behaves in the manner that he believes best. If his behavior is to be changed, then his perception of himself and his skills, his role, or the situation must be altered.

The preceding paragraph describes human motivation and indicates the way a person can be assisted to release his potential. As long as an individual is concerned only with maintenance, the potential released can be limited. Teachers concerned with low salary and morale problems will not be concerned with developing their ability as teachers. But if maintenance is attained, the desire for enhancement offers the key to development. Maslow (1954) has developed a hierarchy of human needs which consists of interdependent levels. The first level was defined as physiological. When man's need for air, water, or food is not satisfied, then this need becomes a highly potent motivator of human behavior and continues to exist as a powerful influence on an individual until the need is met. But, when the first order of need is satisfied, then the next level of need becomes the focus of motivation for the behavior of the individual. Other levels of needs include security or safety, belonging, ego development, and finally, self-actualization. When members of the faculty are relatively well fed, clothed, and sheltered and feel safe and secure there is the possibility of motivation to belong and become an accepted part of the organization, social groups, or professional group. The achievement of these needs contributes to the individual's concern for personal growth, professional growth, recognition, and esteem by fellow workers. These are powerful, pervasive, and continuing needs for organizational members. It is through the teacher's motivation at this level of need fulfillment that it is possible to release faculty energy to improve the quality of education for students.

The highest order of need in the Maslow formulation is the need for self-actualization. This is the "capstone" of man's attempt to become what he can become. The possible fruits are great personal accomplishment, creative problem solving, and exceptional dedication. The facade is removed and the human being is "open" to "become."

Herzberg (1959) made an intensive study of motivation in industrial organizations. Using a technique of content analysis of stories over periods of high and low morale of workers, he found that positive feelings workers have about their work come from the workers' sense of personal worth and self fulfillment and that these positive feelings were related to achievement, work itself, recognition, and responsibility. Job dissatisfiers were found to be factors defining the context in which the work was done such as physical surroundings, supervision, and company policies. The elimination of the dissatisfiers did not lead to high satisfaction since high satisfaction was a function of other factors.

Hahn (1961) did a similar study in the U.S. Air Force and got results that tend to support the Herzberg findings. The "stories" describing the "good day" situations tended to fall in the self-realization category and included such factors as "recognition," productive self-effort, sense of belonging, cooperative effort. Dissatisfying experiences were generally associated with the general job environment category.

The studies of motivation of teachers have produced similar findings. Ralph Savage (1967) made a study of teacher satisfaction and dissatisfaction in the educational organization. His findings supported the findings of the Herzberg study. Sergiovanni (1967) found that achievement, recognition, and responsibility were statistically significant contributors to teacher satisfaction. The absence of these factors was not found to contribute to dissatisfaction. The factors which were found to be significantly related to teacher dissatisfaction include interpersonal relations with subordinates, superiors, peers, and technical supervision, school policy and administration and personal life.

There is considerable evidence that supervisors who seek to release the potential of organization members need to produce opportunities for teachers to feel more adequate as professionals, to see greater significance, possibilities, and responsibility in their role, and to perceive the situation as one in which improvement is not only possible but highly valued. Teachers need to feel that their contribution to the achievement of organizational goals is recognized and valued. A friendly pat on the back is nice, but far from adequate. What is essential is a positive logistical and psychological support system as the teachers "push out" to explore and test new approaches to teaching. When the effort is complete, a sense of personal achievement of a job well done is essential. Words of praise are not enough. Rather, definitive feed-back on the outcomes of their teaching effort is required.

A sense of personal responsibility contributes to high satisfaction and motivation. An opportunity to participate in decision making and policy formulation contributes to a sense of responsibility to carry them through. Further, faculty should be used for official leadership responsibilities on an ad hoc basis and according to expertise and with appropriate authority. Activities such as these contribute to the teacher's sense of worth, self-concept, and a sense of personal well being.

The Need for an Adequate Self-Concept

A supervisor must have confidence in himself. Psychology contains much evidence that scapegoating and the desire to belittle or to hurt others come from feelings of insecurity. When people are sure of themselves, of their ability to meet situations, of the value of their ideas and purposes, of their value as persons, they do not feel a constant need for having other people tell them that they are important, valuable, and worthy. They don't have to build up feelings of superiority in order to eliminate the gnawing feelings of inferiority. They do not have to show themselves that they are better than someone else.

When a supervisor has confidence in himself and in his ability to deal with situations, he doesn't feel the need for being constantly on guard. He can treat others as equals and believe that all are working for the good of the school. He doesn't have to be afraid the other person is after his job or getting the best of him. A person who is not sure of himself must watch the way situations are developing to see whether or not he will be capable of dealing with them when they arise. He will take the necessary action, often harmful to others, to keep situations in which he may fail from arising. To avoid feelings of insecurity, a supervisor must know his role and must have the training that gives the skill to perform it.

An example of insecurity caused by lack of understanding of the function of an offical leader is the false assumption on the part of some principals that they should know more about the subject matter in all fields than the teachers working in each field. That is an impossibility. As a result of the insecurity arising from this assumption, they issue orders about the way subjects should be taught and about the content of courses; they give instructions without any consultation with the members of the staff involved. These principals avoid joint thinking, because they are afraid their lack of knowledge will be revealed. This unnecessary insecurity, with its resulting malpractice, occurs because these offical leaders have not recognized that their function is one of coordination, and that they are not expected to serve as the only technicians and specialists in the field.

If an official leader eradicates his feelings of superiority, his sense of adequacy increases. This apparently contradictory statement is true. If he eliminates the assumption that the official leader is chosen because of superior intelligence and ability, he does away with the necessity always to be better than any member of the group. He makes it possible to admit mistakes, to ask for help, and to recognize and use superior skill in the group. If he accepts the official leader's function as one of helping the group to achieve unity and to release its inherent leadership, he can feel adequate by performing these tasks well. He does not have to feel inadequate because he must cover up his inability to do the impossible.

Insecurity plagues some supervisors, because they establish a stereotype of the way a person in an official leader's position should act. They fail to recognize the need for being themselves, the need for accepting their own personalities as valid for leadership; they try to assume a dignity and a manner of behavior that are alien to them. As a result, they keep other people away from them in order to keep the falseness of their assumed personality from being detected.

But remaining secure involves more than accepting one's present status. In order to maintain self-confidence, it is necessary to continue to study and grow. If the supervisor fails to keep abreast of the new developments in education, he finds himself rejecting new activities and those members of the staff who are participating in them. He begins to belittle others and their achievements in order to maintain his own feeling of adequacy. He clings to things that he knows, rather than encouraging something new, because he is sure of his understanding in the tried method of operation.

It is necessary also to study the results of one's past action and to recognize that mistakes can be learning experiences. If the leader looks upon mistakes as something to hide, then his performance becomes something that decreases his own self-confidence. Everyone makes mistakes. If he looks upon mistakes as a way to grow, his failure in the present situation helps to build his confidence in himself, because he uses failure to increase his adequacy for new situations that will arise.

When a leader is sure of himself in the sense described, he can stop analyzing situations to see whether they will upset him or make him feel successful and can begin to study them to see whether or not they are going to make other people feel more adequate and become stronger persons. His self-confidence increases the self-confidence of the staff. Compare the boss who is in perpetual fret, afraid the task will not be done on time, afraid his superior will not like the way the work is being handled, and afraid that he is not treating everyone right, with the supervisor who is aware of all the difficulties, yet shows by his every action that he knows that he can meet any situation and that the staff will be able to do its part. No one likes to work for a worry-wart or even a supervisor who gives the appearance of being one.

A supervisor needs to ask himself: "Am I always frowning? Do I ever have time to take a few minutes to relax and joke with the faculty? Am I afraid to have visitors observe in the school? Must I always be behind a desk or table during an interview or talk?" These are little things, but if the answers do not satisfy the supervisor, they probably do not satisfy the staff.

An offical leader must believe in the worth of others — all others. He must believe that each principal, teacher, and each child in the school has value and a contribution to make; that the failure of any individual to make a contribution is evidence that the group is not achieving its full potential. Such faith is basic to an environment in which everyone respects the worth of everyone else.

People tend to live up to what others expect them to be. If the supervisor does not believe that others are worthwhile, that they are trustworthy, that they have a real contribution to make, they won't profit from his leadership. If he has faith in them and believes in their potentialities, they will grow and mature through their contact with him. When a supervisor evidences faith in teachers' worth and their willingness to accept each other, he leads them to demonstrate these qualities in their relationships.

But the supervisor dares not make an exception. If he starts denying the value of anyone in the situation — principal, teacher, pupil, or parent — he sets the stage for other persons to begin classifying as unworthy and unimportant individuals with whom they differ.

If some teachers have lost their enthusiasm and their desire to grow and be better teachers, it is possible that it has come about as a result of the supervisor's lack of faith in them or as a result of frustrations in the teaching situations that have led them to feel that the official leader does not believe they are important. An official leader can demonstrate lack of faith in many ways. He may be blunt and undiplomatic:

> In a large city high school the principal was speaking to the student honor society about types of service. To illustrate a negative kind of service, he said, "There are not more than twelve teachers on this staff who will assume new responsibilities or do anything for me unless I pay them overtime or give them a free period." The faculty members present immediately began to speculate on which twelve were the ones who would do the principal's bidding.

Not only did the principal, by a display of lack of faith, decrease the possibility of growth in his faculty by condemning them as unworthy, he also increased the students' doubt of the teachers' worth. Such chance remarks are significant in two ways. They are indices to the kind of relationships that exist in the school group and they intensify the emotions already aroused.

In attempts to help teachers, supervisors can act in such a way that the respect of members of a staff for each other is jeopardized. A substitute teacher cites the following experience:

> While I was taking over an English class for the day at a junior high school, the assistant principal in charge of English decided it was her day for

showing up an underling. I was doing remedial reading work when Miss Brown stepped in, looked at me sourly, and exclaimed, "That's not the way it is done, Mrs. Jones." She then, in very audible and definite tones, corrected me in front of the students at every turn of the lesson. Every time I am observed, I think of the incident and feel like crouching under a seat.

In this action, the supervisor showed no respect for the worth of the substitute teacher. Such supervision has discredited the use of observation as a technique for improving instruction. It has separated supervisors and teachers. All other supervisors this teacher encounters are suspected and feared until they prove themselves. Improvement of teaching must start with a respect for the personality of the teacher and the work he is doing.

Teachers react negatively to an attempt to impose a philosophy and procedure upon them. Attempted imposition makes clear that the supervisor considers himself more intelligent than the teacher and engenders active resistance by the most intelligent, aggressive staff members.

In one school where the principal was trying to institute more progressive practices, the members of the staff who would not accept the newer theories were disregarded and their teaching practices were scorned. An older member of the staff, the head of the English department, suffered in silence and then began an opposition campaign. The faculty split and the principal became ineffective.

A new supervisor entered the scene. He disregarded the philosophic differences altogether. He began working with each staff member on improving the phase of his teaching that seemed most important to that teacher. The results were vastly different. The head of the English department began a special study of ways to improve her teaching of remedial reading. Soon she was telling the faculty about specific programs she was carrying on that were far in advance of any practices in the school. The same reaction was induced in the other teachers in the areas of their special interests.

Teachers are not all alike. They do not have the same concerns or abilities. If a supervisor believes in everyone's worth, he must be willing to accept differences and to value each person for his special contribution. He must recognize that the staff is richer because of the presence of each person, regardless of the limitations of the various staff members. Official leadership must make allowances for differences in the temperament and tempo of various individuals and must encourage the staff to do so too. Attention must be centered on the special contribution that each staff member can make and on creating the situation in which he will want to make it.

This point of view affects the way the supervisor will work with staff members who are problems to him. He realizes that his responsibility is to provide the pupils with the best possible learning situation; he knows that improvement is necessary; but he knows too that he must proceed in such a manner that the worth of teachers is accepted and increased.

There is a tremendous difference in teachers in their openness to experience in terms of looking at education and curriculum. Some are quite sure that there are no answers other than those demonstrated in the pattern of school that they went through, and they hunt ways of working more effectively to fulfill the roles they saw their teachers perform. Some have a very narrow conception of what education should be or what it can be. They see education as being restricted to certain disciplines and see curriculum improvement as consisting of revising the content of a subject. Others think that perhaps education can be better than it has been, and that they can be a part of it. Others are completely open and say, "Let's forget the present pattern of education; let's see what it can be." There is a tremendous amount of difference in what each of these kinds of teachers can do. What a person gets from any situation depends on the size of the basket he takes to it. Some see their function as innovators, and they view education as an innovative process. Others see their function as holding on to what has been, and they hunt for arguments to defend what they're already doing.

People, in terms of their past experiences, are not equally responsive to the kind of supervisory structure that enables them to be more creative. As a result of previous experience, people have different degrees of readiness for change. Supervisors need to give serious consideration to the uniqueness of each member of the faculty.

Supervisory Action
to Release Human Potential

Supervisors must use the power of their position to create an environment conducive to the release of human potential. There are at least two basic sources of power. First, there is the authority that the supervisor has because of the official position he holds in the organization. This source of power normally manifests itself in control of a variety of resources which can be used to influence the behavior of organizational members. It is this source of power that makes it possible for the supervisor to call meetings, provide materials, provide consultants, release teachers from normal duties and support their attendance at professional meetings.

Some persons question any use of authority. This is not our position. Rather, authority is accepted as a legitimate factor in the interpersonal influence system. It is the use of authority according to the values of the supervisor that is good or bad. Since the release of human potential is assumed to be desirable, the use of authority to achieve that condition is also desirable.

In terms of what is known about interaction and the way people grow, the supervisor has a responsibility to use the authority that he has to hold people together until they can explore issues and alternatives and arrive at a decision that is acceptable, not to him, but to the group. He has a responsibility to develop and use the skill of helping people to examine alternatives in terms of values held and to test their values. His job is to see that people live by the existing policies that the faculty has established and to see that any one of these policies can be challenged and modified by the staff's thinking together intelligently about the policy.

A second source of power is the esteem that faculty members have for the supervisor. If they value his competence and trust his motives then they will value his suggestions, ideas, and desires and thereby, increase the supervisor's power in the group. Conversely, if he has not earned their esteem through interactions in the past then there is little chance that the supervisor will be a highly influential person in the informal organization.

The supervisor who wishes to release human potential uses his power to create a working environment with the following elements:

1. All persons have a sense of belonging. Teachers want to feel that they belong to the group with which they work. Studies of work groups in industry have found that this desire is one of the most important in determining how a person produces. Desire to be accepted or to remain a part of the group is more powerful in conditioning the amount of work a person will do than is even his take-home pay. For example, a person working on a piece-rate will slow down and decrease the amount of money earned in order to avoid the charge of rate-breaker by his fellows. These may be the psychological groups in which there is a lot of interaction, as in a departmental or grade-level group; they may also be members of groups that drink coffee or beer together or bowl together. Industry has discovered that these small psychological groups are the basis of morale rather than the things done by the whole organization. Supervisors have to be careful in fostering change and innovations, so that they do not destroy the psychological support of the groups that already exist.

In addition to existing psychological groups, there is need for a place where there can be free interaction in the exploration of a new area without reference to assigned tasks and present duties; a place where people may explore new frontiers in ideas and form cooperative projects to work together.

2. Many stimuli are available. Not all people have a common degree of readiness for an experience. Each person marches to his own music. He sets his own goals and he looks for the elements in his environment that will enable him to move at his speed in the direction he desires. If each staff member is to find a stimulus to excite him and release his potential, the setting must contain many challenges and opportunities. Routine successes or intense failures will not suffice. Sufficient frustration to cause expenditure of effort must be present.

3. Encouragement to explore. It is important for a person who is in an official leadership role to try to make some judgments about readiness for change in the members of the staff. He must not pretend they're all alike. He recognizes there are differences and tries to be as accurate as possible in his assessment of those differences; he does not rate them, but uses them to give himself guidance in planning his strategy to help people grow. His job is placing the major portion of his energies in helping and facilitating the venturing, the innovating, and the exploring of the people who are most ready. Not the ones who are least ready, but the ones who are most ready!

Some people are less willing to change because of firmer commitment to the values they hold. They find that anything that represents much change is threatening to them. The people who hold to the status quo are valuable people on the staff. They are the people that help keep the program stable, making it possible for other people to venture. This stabilizing group helps to determine the norms of the staff, and the innovation group, as it works, helps to shift the norms. Present group norms move in the direction of the venturing if the structure is such that it is possible for some people to venture. But the innovators must be valued and encouraged if the status quo adherents are not to create rigidity with little development of additional potentialities.

A strategy for change must be a strategy for releasing the potential of people; otherwise it becomes a change that decreases the possibility for continuing change. Some people who are most ready to change may, at present, be much less able professional people than some who are less ready to change. But if the release of potential is the strategy, the person who is ready to change will be more powerful and able to produce further change.

4. Opportunity to explore.   All groups develop norms, and these norms determine the extent to which people may change and still remain a part of the group. Even though there is a degree of permissiveness within the norms of groups, there must be an administrative operation in which permissiveness is fostered and implemented.

The supervisor cannot tell people when to move; teachers have to take the step. The supervisor's major role is to make opportunities to participate possible. Almost every staff member should become a member of an innovative group where the norms are (a) how can we learn more about the educative process? and (b) how can we better implement what we know? The major norm must be one of constant improvement rather than one of holding to what exists.

Opportunity to explore is provided (a) by the administration indicating its desire for constant experimentation designed to lead to improvement, (b) by the provision of funds for research and dissemination, and (c) by the organization of study groups with common interests who explore hypotheses concerning ways of reaching desired goals. If the staff believes that change is desired and possible, some members will seize the opportunity to explore.

5. Individual interpretations valued.   Potential is released if the individual is encouraged to develop his own judgments. Teachers are professionally trained and their education has prepared them to make professional judgments, not to be robots following a prescheduled routine. Little, if any, difference in professional education and experience exists between the supervised and the supervisor. Directives and demands that insist upon conformity decrease the competency of the professional by belittling his judgment and, thereby, his confidence or by depriving him of the opportunity to increase his skill by experience. If a supervisor wants to release potential, he values professional judgment, he encourages questioning of existing policy and practices, and he values the diversity of opinion that is the product of differing backgrounds.

6. *Heterogeneous staff sought.* If a heterogeneous community is more conducive to change, and it seems to be, the supervisor should seek teachers with different education, experiences, and ways of looking at the educative process. Staff growth will occur through interaction, and the potential of both supervisor and teachers will be released if the difference is valued and used.

The supervisor does not have to worry about people with ideas that oppose his. Each person's ideas will have to stand the test of the intellectual marketplace. If the supervisor can aid the faculty to reach a norm where all feel responsible for becoming increasingly better students of the educative process, then success will be impossible for any quack or person who advocates a point of view without presenting evidence that it will provide the growth hoped for in people. It is not the supervisor's role to stop any proposal. His role is to make sure that the group gets to examine it and the alternatives.

7. *The organizational structure and process promote communication.* The only way the potential of people is released is through communication – through interaction. An individual's potential is released as he interacts with people in such a way that his vision is increased, his horizon expanded, and his present limitation of thought challenged. An organizational structure has value for releasing human potential only as it increases the possibility for depth communication.

8. *Help with personal problems.* People will grow intellectually and professionally through the interaction involved in solving educational problems if they are not too deeply troubled with personal problems. A person's potential for growth is not released if he is under emotional tension. Actions by supervisors to reduce tension contribute to the release of human potential.

Teachers are under tension. In American society, one out of every twelve persons spends part of his lifetime in an institution for the improvement of mental health. Teachers are no exceptions. Such factors as specialized behavior standards for teachers and lack of acceptance and appreciation by the community serve to aggravate existing mental and emotional disturbances in members of the profession. Teachers need all the help they can get in maintaining their emotional health. Supervisors can help decrease the emotional tension of teachers if they listen to teachers' concerns.

If it is accepted that a function of official leadership is to set the emotional tone of the school, then help with the personal problem of teachers becomes a basic concern of supervision. All other activities at the school are built upon the foundation of the faculty's good mental health. Supervisors must realize that they cannot hope to work with the teacher on the improvement of teaching unless other worries and disturbances are decreased to the point where they are not paramount in the teacher's mind.

Teachers are not supermen; they are hampered by the same worries, fears, and anxieties that handicap other people. They need someone that they feel understands them and their problems and sympathizes with them in their difficulties; someone with whom they can talk out their concerns, confident that the person will not hold their ideas against them; someone they trust. They need a friend. Teachers do not turn to someone they distrust, someone that they cannot respect as an individual, someone they feel is lacking in warmth and sympathy. A supervisor must be the type of person they want for a friend. He must be approachable, genuine, and sensitive to the way others feel.

A supervisor cannot force troubled teachers to come to him. The results would not be good if he could. He can only display concern for how they feel and a willingness to listen. Some of the troubles he hears will not be connected with the school program or the school buildings. They may deal with home problems, social problems, or financial problems. All may be equally important. A problem is as important as the teacher thinks it is.

Supervisors are not trained as counselors. They do not have to be. There are certain things they can do, certain rules they can follow, that will enable them to fill a genuine need. The need is to enable tense persons to talk out their problems and to help them work toward a solution of their problems. He makes no pretense of giving psychiatric aid.

When a teacher has a problem and wants to discuss it, the supervisor may be able to use certain helpful procedures that have been worked out by counselors.

1. The supervisor should not display any kind of authority. He is a listener. He is not there to give advice or to tell the other person what to do.

2. He listens in a patient and friendly but intelligently critical manner. "Critical" should not be misinterpreted. By "critical," it is meant that the listener follows the presentation, raises questions that help to clear up points that the narrator may be overlooking, and singles out items that may be important, but which the teacher has not correctly evaluated.

3. The questions that the supervisor asks should be of a type that alleviates the teacher's fear and anxiety about discussing his problems. Many times when people are troubled, they have difficulty in talking about their trouble. They want to talk, but they hate to tell other people the things that are bothering them. Questions have to come out of sympathy and understanding.

4. An important type of question for a supervisor to ask is one that gets at the implicit assumption that the individual is making in thinking about a situation, an assumption he may not be willing to make explicit. Questions that get at basic reasons are the kind that help people think through their problems

for themselves. However, such questions should not be too direct. Neither should they be asked as though the person who asks the questions has greater understanding than the person telling the story.

5. One of the techniques of the supervisor is to praise people for reporting facts or feelings adequately. Such praise leads the story teller to analyze situations more carefully and to be fair to himself and others involved.

6. Another important technique is never to argue, even though the supervisor feels that the teacher is wrong. In a counseling situation, a supervisor should never discuss a point in an attempt to prove that the teacher is wrong. The supervisor's function is to encourage the other person to get his problem off his chest, not to solve the problem for him. In fact, there is no need for the interview to end with any solution at all, unless a solution develops through the teacher's new insight.

7. Last, the supervisor should never give advice or moral admonition. Whenever the supervisor steps into the role of moral adviser, he loses whatever chance he had of helping the other person. He gives the teacher feelings of guilt, or at least intensifies any feelings of guilt that the teacher has. In such a position, he cannot enable the teacher to work out problems for himself. Instead, the teacher becomes concerned about working out solutions that satisfy the supervisor. Instead of relieving the teacher's tension, which is the purpose of such activity, the counselor increases the tension by having the individual become concerned about satisfying the counselor.

The foregoing statements should not be interpreted to mean that the supervisor can help all teachers. Some teachers are too mentally ill for him to help. His function is to refer such teachers to the type of psychiatric aid they need. If a supervisor is really going to be effective in making referrals, he must first of all have the confidence of his teachers; otherwise, they will reject his suggestion that they secure competent advice. Further, if he has teachers who talk through with him the things that are bothering them, he will be in a much better position to know which teachers are in need of assistance that he is not qualified to provide.

The supervisor should not expect to assist all people in releasing their potential. No one can. The supervisor is only one of many interested in releasing the potential of the people. If the supervisor thinks releasing potential is his exclusive responsibility and sole right, then he is doomed to failure. Although it is important for the supervisor to build a structure and have a strategy for releasing the potential of people, the cornerstone of both goals must be his recognition that the major portion of assistance will come from one teacher to another. The innovators will provide the leadership for others who wish to crack their shell and act.

4 Supervision Is Leadership

Leadership behavior is defined as behavior on the part of one individual which influences the behavior of other individuals. Therefore, leadership behavior is assumed to be one important element of instructional supervisory behavior. As a supervisor begins to work in the organizational behavior system it would be helpful to have a functional concept of leadership, a clear picture of the influence position he wishes to attain, and an explicit view of the way he plans to use this position to influence the behavior of others in the organization. Accordingly, it will be the purpose of Chapter 4 to develop a concept of leadership behavior as one aspect of instructional supervisory behavior. Further, certain theories of leadership behavior and empirical findings have been identified and later applied in the discussion of the leadership behavior of the supervisor.

The Nature of Leadership

Much help is available in determining the nature of leadership. Since 1900, there have been over 300 separate pieces of research into the nature of leadership. The results challenge many accepted stereotypes about leadership.

Some persons see a leader as an eloquent speaker, a person of superior intellect, or a servant of man. Other beliefs held by some people are: a person who is a leader in some situations will be a leader in all situations; some people are born leaders and others are not; leadership is restricted to a few people; a status position gives a person leadership; leadership is a prestige position; a leader is a person who can influence other people to accept his goals.

The research results do not support these hypotheses. One of the earliest approaches to the study of leadership was an attempt to find relationships between traits and leadership. Conclusions were generally negative. No strong positive correlations exist between intelligence and leadership, scholarship and leadership, or height and leadership, unless the trait gives the individual an advantage in the situation in which he exerts leadership.

Another approach to the study of leadership was the "styles of leadership." A great number of studies were conducted to explore the relationship between certain styles of leadership and group achievement, and group climate. These studies established that the same groups or similar groups operating under different styles of leadership will develop different climates and patterns of achievement.

The evidence is clear. The style of leadership defined variously as democratic, indirect, initiating structure and consideration is more likely to be associated with "superior" group achievement and group maintenance. It is especially interesting that Halpin and Winer using the method of factor analysis identified initiating structure and consideration as two critical dimensions of leadership behavior. These findings are consistent with the descriptions of democratic leadership as it was operationally defined in the Lewinian studies. Halpin (1966, pp. 123-24) verifies this notion as follows:

> In fact, it is our impression – and here we are speculating – that what ordinarily is referred to as democratic administration or democratic leadership is precisely what we have defined "operationally" as leadership behavior characterized by high initiation of structure and high consideration.

The fact that these independent investigators who were using distinctive methods came out with quite consistent results strengthens the generalization.

Results from the traits and styles of leadership approaches have led to a different approach to the study of leadership. Marks, Guilford, and Merrifield (1959) concluded, "We are almost forced to agree with the numerous reports . . . which view leadership from a behavioral and situational point of view . . . In essence, this view means that leadership is a function of the situation and its requirements, and of the followers and their expectations as well as of qualities of the leader."

In general the studies of leadership have investigated questions such as who attempts leadership and why? Who is effective in what situation and why? The following conclusions have been reached:

1. Leadership is a group role.   No one is a leader walking down the street by himself. He is able to exert leadership only through effective participation in groups.

2. Leadership, other things being equal, depends upon the frequency of interaction. If a person usually shuts himself behind the office door and does not have time to interact frequently with the staff, he probably will not exert much leadership in it.

During the early 1930s the government tried to find out where farmers secured the ideas that they tried as they changed their farming practices. They did not get them from the slick paper pamphlets put out by the government or even from the county agent, unless he was a real part of the community. They secured the ideas that they tried from the fellows who sat with them at the store and said, "I tried this and it worked."

Apparently, a person can exert leadership in a group only when he has enough values in common with that group for them to accept him as a member. If he is an outsider, or so far ahead that the group feels that he does not have values in common with it, he cannot exert leadership.

3. Status position does not necessarily give leadership. Successful leadership is a function of both formal authority and earned esteem. The fact that a supervisor holds a formal position does not assure his effectiveness as a leader (Bass, 1960).

4. Leadership in any organization is widespread and diffused. The role of a status leader is not just leading a group but also coordinating and focusing as well as helping the group use the leadership that exists within it. If a person hopes to exert leadership for everybody, he is doomed to frustration and failure, because there are many different people within any organization or group who exert leadership for other people.

In his studies of the street-corner gang, Whyte (1943) found that gangs had more than one leader. Each gang had one leader who had two or three lieutenants, and these two or three lieutenants had people who followed them, not the gang leader. If the gang leader couldn't carry the lieutenants with him, he couldn't carry the gang with him.

A study was made of leadership among students in P.K Yonge High School at the University of Florida. Over 240 students were asked these questions: If all the football equipment were destroyed, which person would you choose to head a campaign to raise funds to buy new equipment? If we were going on the radio to explain our school program to the public, which people would you choose to be on the panel? Seven types of activities were sampled. More than 200 out of the 240 were identified by their fellows as the persons they would choose.

5. The norms of a group determine the leader. A group turns for leadership to those people that it sees supporting its norms. Hackman and Moon (1950) asked graduate students who had worked together to select (1) the person they would like to have be chairman of a committee on which they served and (2) the persons they would want as members of a committee that they chaired. The same persons were chosen for both roles. The same people were rejected for both roles. If the individual has the knowledge and competencies needed in the situation, the qualities that enable him to be an effective group member make it possible for him to be a leader or a follower.

This leadership generalization raises one of the major problems for status leaders: If the person who is used by a group as a leader is a person who supports the norms of the group, how does a status leader who has an official responsibility for constantly improving the program work to challenge and raise the norms without losing his leadership?

6. *Leadership qualities and followership qualities are interchangeable.* The person who is an effective leader is also an effective follower.

7. *Persons who try to persuade too much or who give evidence of a desire to control are rejected for leadership roles.* Lippitt and White (1947) studied the effect of three different kinds of adult leadership on groups of fourteen-year-olds. One directed and told and used punishment to make people do what he wanted done. Another attempted to plan with people, encouraged members to work with people they liked to work with, and sought to help the group members evaluate with him the progress that they were making. The third did practically nothing. He just sat back. He helped when he was asked. Lippitt and White found that the third type, the *laissez faire* type, was the least effective. Authoritarian leadership was not as effective as the second type of leadership in getting people to work together. The authoritarian type of leadership produced thirty times as much aggression in persons toward other persons in the group as the democratic type of leadership.

Lewin (1939) during the war, attempted to get people to eat different foods. In one type of situation, a home economist talked to people and told them they should eat certain new foods; only four per cent of the people who listened changed their eating habits. In another situation, the same home economist sat with the members of the group as they talked about what they could do to further the war effort and made the same suggestion; 25 percent of the people made a change in their eating habits.

8. *The feeling that people hold about a person is a factor in whether they will use his behavior as leadership.* A person's behavior within a group must be such that people can accept him as a person of worth if they are going to give his contributions adequate consideration.

Helen Jennings (1950) reports a study of leadership among teenage girls in an institution for delinquents. She found that the leaders were the girls who were sensitive to the feelings of other people and who did not wear their own feelings on their sleeves. If an individual wants to exercise leadership with others, he must be concerned with their feelings and not be disturbed by the statements and actions of others. If supervisors want to be effective in working with teachers, they will work in terms of how teachers feel about action that is occurring.

9. *Leadership shifts from situation to situation.* Sterling and Rosenthal (1950) found that if a group was being attacked by outside groups, the group

turned to its more aggressive members for leadership; if it was going out to have a party and have fun, it turned to its fun-loving members for leadership. The group will use the leadership of people that it feels can contribute to a particular operation, unless the structural organization prevents it.

Cowley (1928) compared leaders in situations ranging from college campuses to prisons. He found that the same type of person is not a leader in different groups; that leadership isn't a common quality that makes it possible for a person to lead in any group, that leadership is a group function and is determined by whether or not the person involved has qualities and values viewed as valuable by the group.

The research leads to the conviction that leadership is an element of group operation that enables a group to agree on goals and achieve those goals; that it is a function to which many people contribute; and that the group selects which person's contribution will be used by that group for leadership.

Chowdhrey and Newcomb (1952) found that the difference between the people who were leaders and those who were not effective leaders was that the leaders in a group could predict what the group wanted to do on critical issues. Nonleaders could sense group sentiments on noncritical issues, but only the leaders were able to sense the group's feelings on critical issues.

Hemphill (1949) summarized all the leadership research until 1947 by saying that the difference between those people who are effective leaders and those who are not is that the effective leaders are concerned with the feeling tones of the group with which they work.

Myers (1954), investigating the research in leadership that had been done from 1900 to 1952 in the armed services, in labor, in industries, and in education, reached the conclusion that the only common elements that can be identified in leadership are social insight (being sensitive to the feelings of other people); initiative (doing things, instead of sitting back and waiting for things to happen); creativeness (the ability to come up with new ideas); and having information, hopes, values, and skills that can be used.

Apparently, if a person hopes that his contributions will be used as leadership by the group, he will:

1. *Exert initiative.* If he goes into a situation and sits back and waits for people to come to him, people won't interact with him as frequently as they do with the person who exerts initiative. It's this willingness to take the steps needed to be taken that increases the possibility of exerting leadership.
2. *Give evidence of a desire to cooperate.* The armed services did a study of supply sergeants and found that the supply sergeant who was willing to cooperate with the men in his group was the most effective supply sergeant.
3. *Communicate his feelings and his thoughts.* Probably no kind of person is more disturbing to most people than "the great stone face" who sits like a sphinx and lets others wonder what he is thinking.
4. *Empathize with those he hopes to lead.* He is able to put himself in the other person's shoes to see how it feels there.

5. *Be creative or original.* He comes up with an answer. The extent to which a person is able to advance ideas that will be helpful to a group in solving a problem determines the extent to which his leadership is used.

6. *Be of service.* Some people think a leader dominates the group to get them to do what he wants. Leadership research indicates that a person will be used more frequently when he has something that is of service to a group.

7. *Be knowledgeable about the area of group concern.* Such knowledge will increase the probability that successful leadership attempts will turn out to be rewarding to group members and thus, contribute to the esteem which group members have for the individual. This increases the probability that the next attempted leadership will be accepted by the group (Bass, 1960).

8. *Attempt to be perceived by followers both as considerate and "initiating of structure."* For the supervisor who wishes to be effective, the expression of concern or even meeting the personal needs of fellow workers is important but not sufficient by itself. It is also necessary to be willing and able to initiate structure into group interaction. This is the "getting out the work" dimension of leadership behavior. It appears that these factors are independent of each other but both are important contributors to leadership effectiveness. (Halpin, 1966, pp. 81-127)

9. *Work to be perceived by teachers as putting great emphasis on both telling and listening or asking for information, raising questions, and reflecting.* This was verified in a study by Blumberg and Amidon (1965). When working with supervisors, teachers are likely to evaluate the interaction in a favorable way if the supervisor is both willing to tell and listen with a positive concern or if the supervisor is just reflective with concern and interest. But, if the supervisor is perceived as just telling and criticizing or as relatively passive, then the teacher is likely to perceive the situation as relatively less productive.

Leadership is any contribution to the establishment and attainment of group purposes. It may be exercised by the supervisor or by any member of the staff. A definition that restricts leadership to persons in official positions is a denial of reality. Any person may make a contribution to the success of the group.

A group and leadership are mutually dependent. Neither exists without the other. A person cannot be a leader apart from a group. Neither can a group develop without leadership. Unity must be established, otherwise the group remains a collection of individuals. Someone must have a basic concern for developing group feeling and coordination. Leadership is a crucial force that someone must exert if a group is to come into being and continue to exist.

Leadership may be official or emerge from the group. Official leadership is appointed by some authority outside the group or elected from within the group by the group. Leadership may come from any member of the group; it is recognized as the group incorporates the contribution into its purposes or procedures.

Supervisors are official leaders who are almost always appointed by an authority outside the group in which the supervisor works. Throughout this book, attention is focused on the official leader and the way he provides the most helpful leadership for the staff of the school in which he works.

The "Power With" Approach to Leadership

Some supervisors attain their position through examination or appointment, without any real understanding of their function. Through observation of supervisors they have known, they have drawn the conclusion that their job is to decide, to direct, and to rate each teacher on how well he contributes. Such supervisors believe that they have been promoted because of superior intelligence and performance, and that their status should be respected. They feel that their word should carry more weight than that of a classroom teacher and that any questioning of their statements is a threat to their status. Closely related to this misconception of function is the understanding of the meaning of authority as "power over." When a supervisor feels that authority means "power over" others, he quickly isolates himself from the group, because he believes that he must be above the group.

In a "power over" situation, the supervisor makes no effort to hide his authority. He stresses it. He uses his position and his authority to get people to do the things he thinks need to be done. No attempt is made here to classify the quality of his purposes. Let us assume that they are good. He feels that he knows what a good learning situation is and that he has insight as to how teachers can provide this type of learning for youngsters. He takes the steps he believes necessary to get these conditions for students in his school.

A leader in a "power over" situation wants people to give unquestioning support to his policy. To question is to challenge, and a challenger must be subdued. The supervisor makes the decisions and tells the staff what to do. Certain members of the staff are delegated certain responsibilities. If they do not do what they are told, they are punished by such means as reprimand, decrease in authority, failure to receive an increase in pay, or, if the offense is serious enough, replacement. "Little black books," rating blanks, and other means of registering deviations from duty become tools of the supervisor.

The leader can control through fear or through respect. People must either be afraid that they will be punished for not carrying out the wishes of the leader or they must respect the leader so much that they will not think of disobeying his wishes. Both are dictatorial types of control.

One result of such power is having group members behave as the leader wishes only when he knows about it. But the leader cannot always be present. Those who fear him least or respect him least begin to loaf on the job. A spy system results. Discipline can be maintained only by having a channel through which information is supplied to the leader.

In a "power over" situation, the leader is forced to see that no one else is gaining too much power. If someone in the group becomes too powerful, the leader's authority will be jeopardized. The leader must guard against too much communication among the members of the staff. Out of situations in which staff members have an opportunity to exchange opinion, new loyalties and new respects develop. Too much respect for another member of the staff is a challenge to the authority of the leader.

One of the difficulties of the "power over" leadership lies in securing new ideas. The leader must rely entirely on his own intelligence. He may try to open channels of communication with the members of his staff, but the ideas that he gets will deal only with ways of implementing his plan. No staff member will dare to challenge the leader's blueprint. To make such a challenge is to risk punishment. To accept such a challenge is to jeopardize authority.

It is obvious that something is wrong with the assumption that leadership and authority consist of maintaining power "over" people. A "power over" approach decreases the possibility of releasing the full power of the group. It limits the potential accomplishment of the group. Some other assumption must be more productive for obtaining the type of relationship a leader wants to have with his fellow human beings and for obtaining better ways of tapping the talents of the group.

Out of the research in group dynamics and democratic ways of working have come helpful suggestions. It has been found that: A group with a harsh, dominating official leader is characterized by intense competition, lack of acceptance of all members, buck-passing, avoidance of responsibility, unwillingness to cooperate, aggression among members and toward persons outside the group, irritability, and a decrease in work when the supervisor is absent. A group with a benevolent autocrat for an official leader loses initiative, shows regression to childlike dependence, becomes increasingly submissive, does not continue individual development, cannot accept added responsibility easily. A group with an official leader who exerts no leadership is disinterested, indifferent, lacks purpose or goals, obtains no sense of achievement, and fails to produce. A group in which the official leader concentrates his efforts on helping the persons for whom he is responsible to operate as a group is characterized by cooperation, enthusiasm, acceptance of greater responsibility, a sense of importance of the work being done, and a recognition among members of the worth of each other. The last of these types of relationship between the official leader and the staff seems to offer the greatest amount of promise for releasing the full power of a staff.

Under the group approach to leadership, a leader is not concerned with getting and maintaining personal authority. His chief purpose is to develop group power that will enable the staff to accomplish its goal. He does not conceive of his power as something apart from the power of the group. He is concerned with developing the type of working relationships that will give him power "with" the group.

If the supervisor makes the "power with" approach, he begins by assisting the group members to plan together. As problems arise in the organization of the group and in the steps taken to reach goals, the supervisor expends his effort in thinking of ways in which the group can attack the problem, instead of ways in which he can influence the group to accept his opinion. The chief questions for the group to answer become: What is the job? How can we do it better? In answering these questions, the members of the group find that they are taking orders from the situation rather than from the supervisor.

If a faculty is governed by the situation, no one has power over anyone else. Decisions are made as to who will exercise which functions on the basis of skill and training. The supervisor participates in the discussion, exercises his full intelligence, and gives the group the benefit of his best thinking. But his thinking is tested just as carefully as is the thinking of any other member of the group. He does not expect his ideas to be accepted as official rulings.

An official ruling under such an approach becomes the statement of the staff's final decision. After a group has given full consideration to the ideas and the proposed solutions of all members, consensus is sought. Wherever possible, decision is delayed until consensus is reached. If time does not permit, as much agreement as possible is attained, and the dissenting members of the staff are asked to go along with the majority decision, with the understanding that the policy will be reconsidered if it appears unsatisfactory in the light of experience.

An executive decision is only a moment in the total process of the solution of the problem. It is the final statement of policy that the official leader is asked to administer. The solution begins with a clear definition of the problem, involves analysis of the factors of the situation, is based on procedure formulated by group decision, is stated as an official decision, and is implemented by the activities agreed upon by the group members as their responsibility in carrying out the decision.

In such a situation, authority and responsibility are derived from function, not from delegation or position. For example, if the faculty is confronted with a problem of mental hygiene, it calls in a specialist or refers the decision to the best-trained member of the staff. The staff accepts his decision, not because he is the person invested with authority by right of his position, but because the group respects his training and background and deems him the member best qualified to render an intelligent decision. Under such a procedure the official leader does not lose power. He is free to utilize all the resources of the staff. He realizes that he is performing his function best when he calls to the fore the best authority in the group. Authority is identified with training and information; it is used for "power with," not "power over." If the staff does not agree upon the best authority to accept, the question is open once more to group problem-solving. Turning to the best-trained person is only a short cut in interpretation of data.

When a faculty operates on the basis of power "with" the supervisor, many persons have the opportunity to lead. Any contribution to the attainment of group goals is accepted as leadership. Each faculty member is called upon to exert leadership in proportion to his special skills and place in the faculty. Under such a method of operation, the supervisor's function is to coordinate the activities of the group. In other words, he is focusing the power of the group. He creates group power through coordination of activities.

Group power is the total capacity of the staff, centered upon the attainment of definite goals and operating through relationships built up under the guidance of the supervisor. A real leader in this type of staff operation is the one who can help the group organize its knowledge, make it available to all members, and use it to exert the full power of the group in the solution of problems. An effective supervisor is one who can relate the different wills and abilities of group members so that they become a driving, unified force. The problem for the supervisor is to learn how to develop power, not where to place it.

A good leader helps the members of his group feel increased responsibility; He enables teachers to attain importance by sharing with them responsibility for the program. He does not allow his position to interfere with the opportunity for others to assume responsibility. Even though final responsibility rests with the supervisor, teachers and committees are given full authority to carry out their own tasks. As a result, all have joint responsibility. It is a shared responsibility, not a division of responsibility, among members of the staff. An official leader can share all his responsibility and authority. He is able to share it as he makes available opportunities to participate in the decisions on how it will be used. The question of delegated authority is less important under this approach. The total program of the school becomes the responsiblity of the total staff, and the official leader looks upon himself as chairman of the group. When the school board or the community asks for an explanation of some phase of the school program, the official leader alone does not give it. He takes with him to explain the portion of the program under question the members of the staff who have primary responsibility for that phase of the program. By such a procedure, the official leader does not lose power or increase the vulnerability of his position. He increases his strength because his actions have the full support of his staff. The full power of the group is back of the position taken by the leader. When the total staff makes decisions that represent the best efforts of group intelligence, the supervisor is in a stronger position than when he makes decisions alone and asks group members to carry them out.

Following the "power with" concept, the leader is able to build group loyalty, a sense of personal responsibility for the accomplishment of group goals, and a unity of effort that are impossible under the "power over" concept. He creates cooperative working relationships with the members of his staff rather than personal control over the actions of individual members. Under the "power with" approach, there is actually greater control of individual staff members. If a group member decides to establish personal goals that oppose group purposes, the total pressure of group opinion is brought to bear to bring him back to group goals. The opinion of fellow workers is a much more effective control than is any action that can be taken by an administrative or supervisory official.

When the official leader decides he is going to work within the group, he is faced with the necessity of working cooperatively with people. In fact, he must become highly skilled in group processes in order that he may fulfill his major function of helping the group members to think, reach decisions, and take action together.

It must be recognized in all work with groups that a group does not start as a mature one. If the members of the staff have not had group work experience, the progress toward group maturity may be slow. Even where staff members are sophisticated in group processes, it will take time to develop group spirit and common concern. The more immature the group, the greater amount of direction it will be necessary for the official leader to exert. As quickly as possible, however, status leadership will want to pull into the background and allow group members to assume more and more responsibility. As more people have an opportunity to develop skill in group processes, the total group achieves more maturity.

A leader can tell whether his staff is attaining group maturity by the extent to which it moves in the direction of developing a clear sense of direction, an ability to improve upon its own procedure, and a high degree of satisfaction from the work process.

How should the supervisor begin?

A framework is necessary. The group members need to know the boundaries within which they can work, the extent of responsibility and authority the group has. The official leader should be very definite with the staff concerning the decisions he can and will share. He should make clear the boundaries of his authority; each staff member should know the areas in which the supervisor can make decisions and the areas in which he cannot go beyond recommendations.

Operating under the "power with" concept, the supervisor shares the authority that is given him in the situation. He cannot, in fairness to the group, share authority that he does not have. If he does, and if the group makes decisions that are reversed by outside controls, the group's confidence in itself and its power will be decreased. A supervisor cannot go beyond the rulings of the board of education or the state department of education. He cannot go beyond the mores of the community. It is possible, however, for the supervisor and the staff to decide what they want to recommend to governing boards or to the community. Recommendations issued as the result of group thinking will be more effective in securing acceptance by outside authority than will be the declarations of a single individual. Cooperative thinking with other groups involved will be even more effective.

There may be areas of his authority that an official leader is unwilling to share with his staff. If he is afraid to risk the results of group thinking on certain problems that he faces, he should make plain to the staff which decisions he is reserving for himself and his reasons for imposing the restrictions. The staff may or may not accept the official leader's thinking, but the results will be less disastrous to group operation and staff growth than if the leader were to pretend he had no reservations about sharing his decision-making authority and then to veto a decision of the group.

Time must be provided for thinking together.   A staff does not become a group because a collection of individuals have been assigned to one building. It becomes a group as the members begin to develop common purposes and common values that tend to control the pattern of behavior of the individuals on the staff. Common concerns, purposes, and values are reached through sharing. There is no alternative. It takes time together. Official leaders must recognize that time spent on thinking together is not wasted; nor is it an indication that democratic processes are inefficient. It is the basis for effective and efficient work. The amount of time spent together can be decreased as the group continues as a unit, because the common concerns, purposes, and values will have been established and will need revision only in terms of new problems and solutions. But time together for solving group problems can never be eliminated completely as long as the staff remains a group.

However, discussion is only a part of a group's development. Experience together is an equally important element. The two must be combined. Without common experience to give common meanings, discussions may produce confusion through semantic difficulties. Action without time for analysis is likewise ineffective in developing a group. Unless there is opportunity to sit down together and interpret what is happening, the experiences may actually separate individuals because of the variety of interpretations. Experience provides common meanings only when there is analysis of it and agreement concerning it.

Let the staff know the method of work that is being used.   This suggestion may sound as though the supervisor is directing rather than allowing cooperative thinking. But it is essential that the staff know the procedures they are following. Teachers need to understand the processes if they are going to become enthusiastic participants in a group. The method of operation must be stated. Vagueness will lead to hesitation and drawing back. One way to achieve this understanding is for the official leader to suggest a way of working. He should propose the best procedure he knows and then open the meeting to other members of the group to propose suggestions for improvement in the plan he has outlined. Quite likely, if this is the first experience the staff has had with that official leader, no supplementary ideas or alternate plans will be suggested. The group, not trusting its official leadership, may sit back and wait to see how he operates.

The opportunity for change of procedure must be maintained.   Although group members may not suggest any variation from the plan of operation suggested by the status leader at the first meeting, these suggestions will come as soon as the members of the staff decide that the official leader can be trusted and that he means what he says. Suggestions for change in procedure indicate that the group is beginning to accept the leader.

During the initial stage of group development, the official leader must be very careful to keep the word "I" out of the picture if he wants the staff to start thinking of itself as a group. The emphasis needs to be placed on cooperative work. The use of "we" instead of "I" leads to integration of interests. The use of "I" produces a division — "My staff and I" — and encourages other people to think in individual terms.

An absolute requirement for the initial staff decision-making is that a group problem be attacked first. A problem gives a collection of people a purpose. Without the purpose there is no need for the members of a group to continue to associate themselves. The problem's solution is the common enterprise that requires thinking together, planning together, and taking action together. The problem cannot be the supervisor's. It must be important to the staff if they are to be willling to spend time in solving it.

The supervisor must start where the staff is. If the staff agrees on the most important problems facing it, the situation is an easy one. If there is lack of agreement on problems, time must be taken to help the staff reach agreement. As a temporary measure, the official leader should encourage the group to select a small problem in which there is general concern as a starting point for work. As the staff works together on the problem, the members will develop a greater number of common concerns. As individuals have experience together, agreement on importance and priority of problems increases.

Although it is well to proceed cautiously until the staff has learned that the official leader's suggestions are not a command, the supervisor, as a member of the group, needs to make his concerns known. His comments may lift to the level of consciousness a problem that is bothering the staff.

The supervisor must stress faculty-planning sessions as a place in which ideas can be advanced without fear of embarrassment. He must recognize that certain members of the staff will be embarrassed by disagreement, because their experience has led them to believe it is a mistake to advance an idea that is not accepted by the group. The leader will want to take steps to assist the group to understand that if people accept each other and want to help each other, ideas can be tested without anyone's being hurt. If the staff has not had such an interchange of ideas, it is well to tone down criticism at first until people begin to feel safe with the official leader and with each other.

The supervisor should keep in mind that agreement on hypotheses is more difficult and less clear-cut in group thinking than in individual thinking. Where forty or fifty people with different sets of values examine the same data, the chance of arriving at an agreement on a single hypothesis are much less than when one individual with one set of values examines the data. Group agreements on hypotheses have a degree of compromise in them.

The Supervisor's Role in the Group

The study of leadership based on interaction theories has emphasized leadership behavior as the performance of needed group functions. Cartwright and Zander (1960, p. 492) have defined this approach as . . . "the performance of those acts which help the group achieve its preferred outcomes. Such acts may be termed 'group functions.' More specifically, leadership consists of such actions by group members as those which aid in setting group goals, moving the group toward its goals, improving the quality of the interactions among the members, building the cohesiveness of the group, or making resources available to the group."

Lippitt (1955 pp. 556-57) has described the functions of leadership as attempting "to discover what actions are required by groups under various conditions if they are to achieve their objectives and how different members take part in these actions."

Leadership behavior will vary among group members according to the demands of the situation, the expectations of followers, and the competence and esteem of group members. The supervisor or official leader would participate along with other group members in carrying out needed group functions; but, according to Lippitt, the official leader has a special responsibility to be sensitive to the group's functional needs and to see that they are carried out. It isn't necessary or desirable for the supervisor to have all of the ideas or to do all of the pushing. However, it is crucial to see that problems are identified, ideas are generated, and action is implemented; and the supervisor has special responsibility in these areas.

As an official leader in the organization, the supervisor has certain prescribed authority, status, and position that others in the group do not have. It is important to use this source of power to provide a work climate that supports leadership attempts, questioning, information giving, and challenging from all members of the staff. It is true that such authority contributes to the leadership power of the supervisor. But, it is also true that if authority is used to threaten, cut people down, inhibit, and belittle staff members it can reduce the effectiveness of the supervisor. This is because leadership success is partly a function of the esteem the group members hold for the supervisor, without which he can never achieve his full potential as a leader.

The supervisor's first step is to win acceptance as a member of the group. As an outsider given charge of the group, he is viewed with suspicion by the members of the group and will be so regarded until he proves himself by the way he works with them. Merei's research (1949) indicates that only as the leader is accepted as a working member can he hope to exert maximum influence on the group's direction and purposes.

If a supervisor begins his work by telling the staff what he has decided they must do, there is a high probability that he and his goals will be rejected. If he has goals that he hopes will emerge, he contributes them as ideas for group consideration after he has been accepted as a working member of the group. But he invites failure if he offers his point of view as statements of official position or direction.

If the supervisor acts in terms of evidence from leadership research, he uses his influence to deepen teachers' insight into the methods of group thinking, and into the importance of building the program on scientific evidence gained through experimentation. His emphasis is on constant improvement, using the concerns of the group as the starting point.

In the process of improvement, he constantly seeks: to increase the unity of the group, to encourage diversity and the experimental approach, to enrich the group thinking, to build the security and self-confidence of the group, to help the group see clearly the boundaries of its authority, to increase interaction and sharing of experience, and to extend the opportunities for leadership.

As official leader, the supervisor wants to spread the leadership in the group, because he recognizes that sharing leadership helps the members grow in ability and thereby increases the strength of the group. He works to keep the organization of the group from concentrating responsibility in a few people.

One of the problems that a supervisor faces as he attempts to spread responsibility is the manner in which certain staff members regard themselves. They glory in their chairmanships and want them. An attempt to give more people an opportunity to serve as leaders is a threat to those who yearn to monopolize the leadership roles. Other teachers feel inadequate and afraid. Out of a desire to shirk responsibility or a sincere belief that their leadership will not be sufficiently skillful, they try to avoid leadership roles by renominating the persons who have served before or by insisting that everything has been going so well that it would be undesirable to institute any change.

The attitudes that staff members have developed toward one another may also hinder the attempt to spread leadership. Any staff will have developed confidence in certain persons. Through the years, the staff will have come to respect their judgment and their ability to guide studies and committee work. Other staff members, through erratic and ill-timed statements, have lost the faith of their fellows. They are considered weak and inept. The probable success of an activity is enhanced or decreased by the person designated to lead it. If a person is selected whom the staff considers able, the other members will want to work with the committee and will give a fair hearing to the proposal that results. If a teacher who is considered unskilled, self-seeking, unintelligent, or shallow is selected as chairman, the others will seek ways to avoid working with him, and the proposal that results will have less chance of acceptance.

After the supervisor has been accepted by the group, he may raise questions that will cause other members of the group to reexamine their position and procedures. Out of these self-analyses by members of the staff, a concern may develop that will lead the group to undertake an improvement in the phase of the program about which the official leader raised a doubt. But he cannot force the group to accept his concern. It must be a concern of the group, not of the supervisor alone.

The place defined for the official leader does not make him a less dynamic person. It increases his potential power. It allows a person with leadership to get into a position where he can use it. Qualities that generate enthusiasm and unity are wasted if preconceived ideas of status and organization prevent an official leader from using these qualities effectively.

A supervisor has the responsibility of helping a staff to establish or improve the organization necessary to study and improve the program. It may not be easy. The existing organization may not have made provision for curriculum study, research experimentation, or in-service education. The plan of organization may have been devised to provide for carrying out directives but not for participation in problem identification, decision-making, or policy planning. The supervisor in many situations will find it necessary to take the initial steps to secure a modification in the organizational structure that makes possible wider participation in the leadership function. In some cases it will be necessary to suggest modification to the administrative leadership and in others to propose to the teaching staff participation in developing a new plan.

An organization cannot be forced on a group. Modification of any existing structure grows out of an attempt to decrease dissatisfactions. The first step of the supervisor is to provide opportunity for dissatisfactions to be stated and then to create the channel through which suggestions can be made concerning an organization that will decrease the dissatisfactions.

An effective organization of a group is a structure through which it can study and solve its problems. The supervisor can perform his official leadership role by creating the committee to propose a new organization and by suggesting a range of alternatives to consider.

Leadership Pitfalls

A pitfall in supervisory leadership comes in not recognizing the necessity for exerting initiative. But initiative should not be designed to control. It should be exerted to help people develop an organization through which they can make decisions that are to be implemented.

A second pitfall is not having an organization sufficiently defined and described, so that people know the functions that are performed by different individuals, know the channels through which to get a problem considered, know the procedures by which problems will be examined and studied, and know that when a decision is made action will be taken to implement it. Moving into effective leadership does not mean moving away from structure. It means providing a kind of structure that implements the values that help people to grow.

A third pitfall is not moving in on a problem when it arises. Pretending that a problem will go away if it is ignored doesn't make it go away. If a vital problem is ignored by official leadership, feelings begin to build, and the acids of anger and fear begin to erode the objectivity of the participants.

The fourth pitfall is not emphasizing what is right instead of who. In any situation, the question should be, "In terms of our values and this situation, what is the right thing to do?" When this approach is made the individuals involved are controlled by their values and the situation rather than being controlled by personal power. Official authority is used to help the group apply the criterion and to implement the decision.

A fifth is not using the authority of the official position to hold the group together until decisions are reached. One of the primary uses of the legal authority of the status leader is to hold the group together until they reach a decision. In a deadline situation, the supervisor may say, "If we cannot reach a decision by December 1, I will have to make it." If it is possible for people who disagree to walk away from the conference table when they do not happen to agree with the way a decision is going, chaos results. The supervisor uses his authority to hold together people who have different values until the decision is made.

The sixth pitfall is not exercising executive authority to carry out policy. At times, the supervisor must say to some people who are not living up to policy, "This you must do." Leadership is not an abdication of the use of executive power, but the use of executive power to implement agreed-upon solutions to problems.

Another pitfall is not distinguishing clearly between policy-forming procedures and executive action. Many people say, "This supervisor took that action." Whether the action was democratic or undemocratic is not determined by whether he said something had to be done, but how the decision that he was implementing was reached.

Another fault is not making clear to the group involved the limitation of its authority to make decisions. No one can share decisions beyond the authority that he has. Anyone creates frustration within groups with which he works if he lets them think they can make a decision that he doesn't have the authority to make. It's very important for a supervisor who is sharing decisions to say, "Here is the limit to the kinds of decisions we have the authority to make.

Still another pitfall is not sharing the information the supervisor has. It works two ways: not keeping the person above him in the line of authority informed and suddenly having him discover an action of which he knows nothing; and, secondly, not keeping the people on his staff informed of all the facts. The decision as to which information to share is hard to make. No one wants to clutter up the desks of the staff or his supervisor with unnecessary information, but he also has the responsibility of keeping them fully informed if he hopes they will assume responsibility, cooperate, or support him.

Another is not working in terms of the expectations of the group. If a supervisor goes into a situation and works in a way that is contrary to what people expect of persons in his role without taking time to talk through with them the process and their expectations, he can get into a situation where people will interpret his actions as weak or inconsistent or manipulative. Misinterpretation is almost certain if he goes against their expectations. It's necessary to talk through to common perceptions the roles being played.

The eleventh is for the supervisor not to be sure of his guiding principles as he makes his day-to-day decisions. In terms of the leadership research, these guiding principles boil down to three:

1. As far as possible, bring people into the making of decisions that will affect them. Make an inclusive approach, rather than an exclusive approach.
2. Respect the personalities of all who are involved. Consult the other person before taking action that will affect him.
3. Base decisions on evidence, using the best problem-solving techniques available.

The twelfth pitfall is not understanding that the supervisory role has many facets; it is not recognizing that in a role as official leader of a school, a person has responsibility for promoting group unity, for developing structure and policy, for contributing ideas, for implementing policy, and for helping groups develop better ways of working.

A major mistake for a supervisor is to want to be the person who is in on all decisions, and who administers all the program. No matter how good a person is, he cannot do everything. If he has worked with people so that they have come to some common commitments about the way of life and the kind of growth they want for children, he doesn't have to be in on all the decisions. Others will be able to make intelligent decisions and implement the values held.

5 Supervision Is Communication

The work of the supervisor is to influence teaching behavior in such a way as to improve the quality of learning for students. This can be achieved by working directly with teachers in the planning for teaching, the description, analysis, and evaluation of teaching, and in the development and implementation of new approaches to teaching based on the evaluation. Supervisors also work with teachers in the development of general goals for school systems and local schools from which teaching objectives can be derived. Teachers and supervisors work together in the development of proposed learning engagement opportunities for students. All of these activities are instructional supervision, and effective communication is an essential ingredient in the process.

Communication has deep significance for human organizations since individuals make specialized contributions to the achievement of the overall goals of the organization. The degree of coordination, ability to use specialized expertise of members, and degree of group unity are at least partly a function of the quality of communication. In the most critical sense, communication is the basis of cooperative effort, interpersonal influence, goal determination, and achievement of human and organizational growth.

Communication in an Organization

A communication system exists in any institution, whether it is a corporation, nation, family, or school system. It is the means of transmitting information, emotions, values, and insights. If it is used to develop cohesiveness and commitment among members of a group, depth as well as accuracy is important.

As far as group development is concerned, communication is necessary if a group is to be formed. Group cohesiveness depends upon common goals, so it is necessary for group members to communicate enough to discover what they hold in common and to identify the areas of difference that should be studied further. If group members are really to value each other through interaction, it is necessary to have the type of communication that will get below the superficial layer of outward appearances. If group interaction is not an attempt to learn purposes, values, insights, understanding, and knowledge held by the others, the group's bonds will be formed only by what people can observe.

Without depth communication, the people remain an organization without loyalty to each other or to a set of purposes. Each person is really alone. Each is controlled by the organizational structure that gives power to the person sitting at the crossing of the channels used for transmitting information. If organizations are to become cohesive groups, the communication must make it possible for group members to form adequate judgments about the worth of each other through having the opportunity to discover the real motivation of fellow members.

The Nature of Communication

Communication is more than talk. It is an attempt by the individuals involved to share their own feelings, purposes, and knowledge, and to understand the feelings, purposes, and knowledge of the others. Gestures, facial expressions, posture, space arrangements, and time enter into the interaction. Between two people, communication is a two-way process. As more individuals are involved, the processes multiply.

Earl Kelly (1952, p. 78) defined communication as: "the process by which one human being can to a degree know what another thinks, feels or believes. It is the means by which an individual's need for others can be satisfied. It is the source of all growth except body building, and the key to human relatedness."

It is obvious from this conceptualization that if the supervisor wishes to influence or be influenced by teachers, he must communicate. Communication is the means of learning and growth and therefore, a fundamental element of the supervisor's effort. The facilitation of supervisor-teacher, teacher-teacher, and teacher-student communication must become a basic focus of the supervisory behavior system.

C. C. Schrag and O. N. Larsen (1954, p. 360) developed a definition of communication: "Communication may be defined as the transmission of meanings through the use of symbols. When men interact by means of symbols, they are engaged in communication. The sender and receiver have communicated only if they identify themselves with each other's situation."

Most concepts of communication include a sender, receiver, message, channels, medium, and effect.

Sender.   The sender is the individual or group that wishes to transmit a message to a receiver. There are many factors which affect the message he sends. The message will be affected by what he wishes to say and his purpose for saying it. The content of the message will be limited by the availability to the sender of symbols which convey the message. Such symbols must necessarily be selected in terms of the past experience of the sender.

The sender may also have certain things which he wishes to conceal. This is a function of his purpose and intent and is conditioned by the way he perceives the receiver. It is also true that the sender may reveal many things without knowing it.

The concept of self which the sender holds and especially the way he sees his relationship with the receiver of the message could be important factors in the way the message is worded, what the sender is willing to reveal, what he feels he must not reveal, and the expectations he holds for the receiver's response. For example, if the receiver is a superordinate of the sender, then an effort might be made to include only information that would tend to enhance the position of the sender. The message might also be worded in such a way as to express deference for the receiver. Such factors may be a function of either conscious or unconscious motivations of the sender.

Message.   The message is the symbol of the idea, event, information, or attitude which the sender is using to stimulate the receiver of the message in some specified way. The problem is that symbols are far from perfect representations of reality. They have to be interpreted and given meaning by humans. As messages become more complex, meanings and interpretation become more complicated and more dependent on a common field of understanding between senders and receivers.

Channels.   Channels are the networks or linkages through which messages travel from sender to receiver. In face to face communication the channel is normally a direct line, but in organizational communication different kinds of channels develop and sometimes messages have to be interpreted and reformulated at different stations before the intended receiver gets it. The "wheel," the "circle," and the "all channel" are patterns of communication that have been defined and studied (Guetzkow and Simon, 1955).

In the chain each person in the network has direct contact with only two individuals. In the wheel, one individual has contact with all others, but they only have contact with the one individual. The individual in the center of the communication normally emerges as the leader. In the "all channel" all members of the network have contact with all other members. It was concluded from the study that the nets influenced group performance only in terms of influence on the group's ability to develop adequate organizations.

In educational organizations, formal messages flow downward and upward through the hierarchy. There are also horizontal linkages between peers. All of these formal channels are important. However, in educational organizations, the normal flow is downward. Superintendents send messages to assistant superintendents, and assistant superintendents send messages to principals and on through the channels to teachers and students. Even downward channels present problems since messages often change during their downward flow. This occurs as a result of misinterpretation, lost meaning, and blockages. Often it is to the advantage of the official leader to withhold information or change meanings to protect his own position in the organization.

Upward channels are even less effective in the educational organization but quite important. It is essential for educational leaders to get feedback from students, teachers, supervisors, and principals. Students and teachers represent an important source of ideas for improvement. It is also necessary to know how policy statements, directives, and other kinds of messages are being received and acted on. This is an important source of information about teacher satisfaction and dissatisfaction and is therefore, an important factor in teacher motivation. But upward flow of communication can be very threatening to formal leaders in the organization. It can also be very threatening to students and teachers. Therefore, it is often distorted and inaccurate. Teachers say what they think the principal wants to hear and principals say what they think the superintendent wants to hear. Sometimes principals block or distort information that they feel may make their performance look bad.

Research in this area is scarce, but some is beginning to appear. A group of researchers from the Manchester College of Science and Technology found that in hospitals with communication flowing mainly downward, there were higher nursing staff turnovers and slower recovery of patients than in hospitals characterized by a better balance of upward and downward communication (Revans, 1964; Sergiovanni and Starratt, 1971, p. 171).

Horizontal patterns of communication have left a great deal to be desired. Teachers in classrooms that are on the same floor or even side by side often have little communication, thus depriving themselves of an opportunity to learn, get psychological support, or share expertise with each other. Team teaching, small group work, and cooperative problem solving can help. There is a grave need to improve the quantity and quality of horizontal communication in schools.

Keith Davis (1966, pp. 185-95) studied informal patterns of communication in organizations and identified the "single strand" and cluster chain. The single strand is a message that is passed along by a series of individuals. The cluster chain involves a network of informal groups that communicate with each other on a regular basis along with interconnecting links. If an individual understands these patterns, then it is possible to pass the word along to certain key individuals with the knowledge that it will make the rounds.

Davis indicates that the informal system of communication can cause trouble. It can start and spread untrue rumors or true rumors that can disrupt the organization. But, nevertheless, this is a normal part of any organization, it is here to stay, and it can provide positive benefits. He contends that the grapevine provides accurate information most of the time and that management can increase communication effectiveness by increasing their understanding and use of informal channels of communication.

In a certain college of education, the faculty became divided on a crucial issue. There were two groups that represented the opposing positions. Certain members of the faculty were clearly in one or the other group. Other members of the faculty tried to identify with both groups. In general, the "fence straddlers" were left out of real communication in both groups because they were not trusted. But they became "messengers" for both groups. When a group had a message that they wanted the other group to receive without knowing that it had been sent, the information would be "leaked" to the "messengers." This is using the informal channels of communication.

Medium.   Messages can be sent either orally or in writing or both. Bulletin Boards, morning reports, news letters, written notes, letter, minutes of meetings, and written group reports would be examples of written communication. Faculty meetings, conferences, classroom visits, intercoms, closed circuit television, and informal contacts at lunch and other social situations would be examples of oral communication. The medium that is used is an important factor in the effectiveness of the message.

McLeary (1968) found that principals relied heavily on classroom visits, conferences, and small group meetings to communicate with individual teachers. General faculty meetings and departmental meetings were used most often to communicate with the staff as a whole. A significant number of principals felt that increases in the size and complexity of schools made it more difficult to communicate effectively.

There is a need for teachers and administrators in an organization to communicate. In the past there has been a heavy reliance on informal face-to-face communication. But with the increase in complexity of the educational organization, the growth in size, and the growing tendency toward a separation of teachers and administrators, communication has become more difficult. It has been advocated and explained in other sections of this book that there is a need to broaden the base of supervisory behavior so that more and more teachers perform in the supervisory behavior system on an ad hoc basis. This procedure should contribute to the effectiveness of both oral and written communication among teachers and between teachers and administrators. Procedures such as cooperative teaching and cooperative evaluation should also help. The idea is to provide a structure in which teachers and supervisors can work together to improve teaching skills, the content of teaching, and the actualization of the instructional process. The utilization of procedures such as micro-teaching, collegial supervision, and "clinical supervision" should help to improve the flow of communication. These procedures are discussed in Chapter 8.

Receiver. The receiver is the person or group that is the target of the message. His interpretation, understanding, feelings, and total reaction to the message is a function of many factors: his understandings of the symbols used, what he wants and needs to hear, his perception of the sender and his intent, what he wants to conceal from himself, and the limitation of the physical structure of the situation. Communication in organizations and among individuals is tremendously complex and difficult. Absolute congruence between communicator and receiver is never possible. It is only possible to constantly work to increase mutual understandings.

Interaction between individuals or within groups is not necessarily communication that results in increased agreement upon goals or understanding of each other. Interaction may at times result in even greater misunderstanding of the situation, the feelings, purposes, and expectations of others, and the way people can help and support each other.

Skill in the area of communication is of utmost importance to the supervisor. Any supervisory action involves working with another person. If the interaction between the supervisor and the others with whom he hopes to relate is not real communication, neither the supervisor nor the other person will be deeply affected.

NONVERBAL COMMUNICATION

Little attention is paid by many supervisors to the nonverbal situation, and this oversight constantly interferes with the effectiveness of supervisory communication. Physical arrangements affect communication. The way furniture is arranged, including positioning, and the symbolism involved make a difference. Most people are aware that to seat participants in a group in such a manner that they can see each other increases the possibility of better communication. Seating group members in such a way that certain individuals can get greater feedback gives those individuals greater control of the communication channels and restricts most of the ideas considered to those suggestions that the favored individual will sanction. Making it possible for each person to have equal feedback by the physical arrangement of the meeting increases the possibility that the group will have freer choice to determine the ideas that are important.

Color has an effect on communication. Harsh, bright colors cause a person to withhold his true feelings and ideas. Soft, light colors contribute to the relaxation of the individual and encourage him to be more self-revealing.

Gestures communicate. Hall (1959), in *The Silent Language* describes in detail how communication among people of different cultures is affected because of lack of mutual interpretation of gestures. Even within a single culture, people interpret gestures differently because of variation in past experiences. One graduate student becomes offended when a professor points a finger at him, while the person sitting in the adjoining seat sees no offense. Some policemen have come to believe, as a result of their experiences, that gestures, particularly unconscious ones, are more revealing of true feelings than actual words. They have become so accustomed to communication situations in which words are used to direct or maneuver, that they distrust verbal communication. They develop a skill in interpreting unplanned gestures.

The posture and the degree of hurriedness of gestures affect communication. If a supervisor wants a conference to be one in which the communication is open, his posture must be relaxed, indicating lack of hurry. He must not move too quickly to respond to an idea. Any indication of tenseness or hurry conveys the impression that the situation is not one in which feelings or ideas are to be explored, but one in which a particular purpose or task is to be accomplished.

The slogans and symbols displayed also communicate. A supervisor needs to look at his office to see what its contents say to the person who enters. How many books does he have? What topics do they deal with? How are the materials organized? What art objects are present? What do they show about the taste and sensitivity of the inhabitant? What do the pictures reveal? What does the prominence given certain items say? What does the type of furniture and its positioning say? Is it an office that looks hard and business-like, or is it a place that seems to suggest that there is time and desire to explore ideas? The same type of questions can be asked about a conference room. The symbols and slogans that are present help to set the tone that fosters or inhibits communication.

Communication is affected also by the perceptions of roles held by the people involved and the ideas of authority that individuals associate with these roles. A professor commented to a former administrator, "You know, I can talk to you more openly and honestly this year." When asked why this was true, the professor replied, "You were in a position of authority last year." The stereotype that an individual carries in his mind of the role of the other person affects how he can talk with him. Also, a person's perception of himself and his role determines how free he is to communicate. If he sees himself as inferior or superior, rather than seeing himself playing a different but equal role, he will be unable to share openly.

When one person sees another as having the power to affect his future, the communication is restricted. The person seen as having the authority to apply sanctions or give rewards may try as hard as he can to increase the depth and openness of the communication and make no progress. All his verbal and nonverbal messages are disregarded or misinterpreted, because the other person is fearful of the consequences of self-disclosure. The subordinate will share only those facts and feelings he believes the power figure will approve. Supervisors who wish to communicate at a level that will affect teaching behavior should avoid even the appearance of being a part of the chain of command.

The supervisor needs to realize that all the nonverbal elements of the communication situation determine the effectiveness of his work with the people with whom he seeks to communicate.

The Role of Emotions in Communication

The emotional element of a situation affects the quality of the communication. Emotional disturbances of individuals and lack of trust among members of the group restrict the communication. Dan Prescott stated, "Emotional disturbances decrease the range of facts that a person considers significant." If a person is deeply disturbed, only the facts that seem to him to bear upon his problem are important. He is unwilling to take the time to consider other ideas until his disturbance is decreased. Actually, he cannot consider other facts. Many research studies have tested the extent to which anxiety affects thinking, and the results always indicate that the greater the anxiety that exists, the less open an individual is to consider a range of alternatives or to engage in abstract thinking. If a supervisor wishes to have real communication in a conference, he will do all he can to decrease the anxiety of the other persons in the situation.

People hear what they want to hear. The human organism blocks out comments and actions that are destructive and seeks to preserve its own feeling of adequacy and competency. It is important to accentuate the positive during conversation with people. If they want help, they must trust the situation and reach for assistance, if they are to hear comments that will help them grow.

Nothing that a supervisor does will increase the communication if there is no trust between the people involved. The degree of trust determines the types of problems individuals are willing to examine. People do not reveal themselves to people they fear or people they do not trust. With people who are not trusted, a person will only share the thinking he wants the other person to hear. A supervisor who rates some people will not have the kind of relationship with these people that enables them to reveal their more serious problems, unless their past experiences with him prove that teachers are not adversely affected by the ratings.

The emotional element can be positive. If the persons attending a meeting have had many experiences together, trust and like each other, and enjoy their interaction, communication will be open and honest. If the participants expect to learn from each other, they share their fears, concerns, hopes, and insights. If previous conferences have been enjoyable happy occasions, the members will anticipate repetition of the experiences and take the steps they think will make the coming meeting even more productive.

Emotions are either an asset to successful communication or they represent the primary problem with which a supervisor must be concerned.

Social Organization Affects Communication

Kelley (1951) found that the more rigid a social structure, the less honest the members will be in their communication. If a person holds a high position in a rigid social structure, he does not reveal facts that will tend to lower his status. People who hold a low position in a rigid social structure engage in many extraneous and non-task-centered comments and actions. If a supervisor wants to have high quality communication with others, he does everything that he can to decrease an emphasis on status and difference.

In situations in which the social status lines are evident, the persons in the more unpleasant positions in the hierarchy have task-irrelevant content in their communication, and the high-status persons tend to restrict the transmission of content that would lower their own status or that would make them appear incompetent. The existence of a hierarchy produces restricting forces against communicating criticisms of persons at another level, and hostility develops as a result of perceiving persons at another level as threats to one's own desirable position or as occupants of a coveted but unattainable position. People within faculties who are without status and can't find a way of rising, socially or professionally, are the people who aren't sincerely concerned about any kind of project that's undertaken as a faculty task.

If a supervisor hopes to facilitate communication, he will work to decrease status lines.

Sources of Distortion in Communication

Ryans has postulated an information system that includes the sender, the receiver, and the message. In his model, the message is distorted by what he calls noise. The noise may be due to many factors. One of the sources of difficulty is semantic. The words used by the sender may not have the same meaning to the receiver. Each person's interpretation depends upon his past experiences and the way he has heard the word used before. Further, the meanings of words differ in different contexts and with different usages.

Another producer of noise is the sender himself. He may be using a message for a definite purpose that is not related to the desires of the receiver. He may be seeking to cover up certain kinds of information that he does not want to disclose as he sends the message. He may lack an understanding of the background of the receiver and unknowingly use words that have little meaning to the receiver. He may be inaccurate in his choice of terms. He may be seeking to convince or control. If the sender is not willing to engage in a process of self-disclosure with complete honesty in the situation, the message may become garbled.

The receiver may be the origin of the noise. He may not be ready to hear what the sender is saying. He may not want to hear what the sender is saying. He may deliberately misinterpret the message because of certain motivations that he has. He may lack the background to understand the message that is sent.

The situation may cause distortion of the message. For example, messages may be garbled by the nature of the group organization, insistence on conformity, or inadequate channels of communication.

Ryans' model is helpful in examining the barriers to communication in a school system and the ways they can be reduced.

Barriers to Communication

A person can be more effective in communication if he recognizes some of the most common difficulties people encounter in seeking to understand each other.

1. People use symbols or words that have different meanings. Each person interprets each word in terms of his background, needs, and purposes. Words also differ in meaning in different contexts and situations. A friend may call another friend by a derogatory name if both interpret the situation as a humorous one. The same word used between the same people in a threatening situation could lead to combat.

2. Members of the group have different values. People may be so closely identified with their own values that they do not want to consider any others. They may not recognize that anyone could possibly hold another value. They want to hold to their own values and not have them threatened. They refuse to try to understand other people's viewpoints. Deep commitment on the part of individuals to a certain set of values that are in conflict with the values held by other people will interfere with communication in a group; so will ignorance that causes misinterpretation of the situation.

3. Different perceptions of the problem. If different interpretations of the problem exist, and no attempt is made to resolve them, people will propose and argue for a variety of solutions without reaching agreement. They will begin to belittle or mistrust their fellows, because they cannot see logic or reason in their disagreements and alternate proposals. They will cease to attempt to understand anyone who could possibly argue for such a stupid proposal.

4. Emphasis on status. If certain people have superior knowledge, status, or experience, it can block communication if the superiority is emphasized. For example, if in a study group, the leader and resource people are sitting behind a table in the front of the room and the other people are sitting in a semi-circle on the other side, communication is hindered. Communication is more valid and accurate if resource persons are dispersed through the group. An individual hesitates to disagree with a person presumed to be an authority. He is less honest about what he believes. He may hesitate to present contradictory evidence.

5. Conflict in interest. When certain individuals are afraid that a decision will be made that will hurt their empire or take away some of the advantages they have, they try to block communication. They don't share all the facts. They try to use parliamentary procedures to divert attention from the real issues.

6. Making decisions by the majority vote rather than seeking consensus. Whenever a group seeks to make a decision by majority the members attempt to convince, to win, and to score points, rather than to try to understand the other person or to find out what beliefs are held in common. When consensus is sought, it is necessary to try to find out what the other person believes, too, so areas of common agreement can be determined.

7. Attempts to keep feelings out of the discussion. Some people believe that if feelings come into a discussion, communication doesn't occur. Yet feelings are as important to communication as facts. Feelings are facts, and to attempt to keep them out of a discussion is an attempt to limit the degree of communication. If a leader of a group views personal feelings as important data, then the expression of them by other people doesn't threaten him.

8. Use of words to prevent thinking. This practice is common. Advertisers use it. They are not trying to communicate but are trying to control action. It happens in many groups. Individuals use words and symbols that most members don't feel free to question. They seek to associate their argument or proposals with sacred symbols and shut off discussion. Some teachers use this technique in an attempt to control action of classes rather than explore the real issue. They attempt to get people to accept their ideas by the use of banner words — words that people line up behind.

9. Lack of desire to understand the other person's point of view or his feelings or his values or his purposes. If a person sees his role as getting people to accept his viewpoint or his values or his perceptions, he hunts ways to convince rather than seeking to understand.

10. Lack of acceptance of diversity. Unless group members value their differences, they don't really attempt to use differences to grow. The tendency of the individual to defend himself is a block to communication. When anyone attempts to protect his position and avoid being exposed as weak, he blocks any kind of attempt by the other person to understand his viewpoint. Whenever there is insistence on conformity there is a distortion of communication. If a person of superior status refuses to allow differences in opinion among the members of a staff, persons without power or authority will reveal only the information that they feel the high-status person will accept.

11. A one-way concept of cooperation. If the person with superior status believes that people cooperate by going along with his program or idea, other members of the group will not be honest in the messages they send. They will hunt ways of protecting themselves or of convincing the high-status person that they really understand and will do what he wants, even though they are engaging in a program of resistance. When the receiver feels that resistance is necessary, he will break or distort the communication.

12. Feelings of superiority.   The sender who has superior feelings does not communicate freely and openly with the receiver. He feels it is unnecessary. The receiver who feels superior does not hear accurately, because he does not believe the words of the sender are important. Any emphasis upon status interferes with the accuracy of the communication. When one member of the communication system insists upon being called by a given title that is an indication of status, or when he insists upon certain privileges, the receiver's reaction distorts the communication.

13. Vested interests.   The person who wants to protect his interests will not be completely open and honest in his communication. The others constantly wonder what he is not revealing, and the message that is communicated is the receiver's perception of the nonspoken motives rather than an interpretation of the spoken words.

14. Feelings of personal insecurity.   If the sender has feelings of insecurity, he will not reveal any type of information that will lower his status in the eyes of the receiver. He will not admit feelings of inadequacy. He will withhold the kind of comments that might reveal some of his reasons for being insecure. If the receiver feels insecure, he will hear only those things that he wants to hear. He will ignore comments that tend to accentuate his feelings of inadequacy or will interpret them as a personal attack. If he interprets them as an attack, he will immediately move to the defensive and hunt ways of further protecting himself or launching a counterattack. In either case, the original message is lost, and the purpose of the conversation becomes clouded.

15. An obvious attempt to sell.   When the sender attempts to convince or to convert the receiver, the receiver is forced to protect his integrity by belittling the communication of the sender or by hunting ways of refuting the message.

16. The concepts that the sender and the receiver have of their roles.   If they see themselves as coworkers and people with common purposes who play complementary and supplementary roles, they will communicate more accurately. If they see themselves as opponents or as persons with different degrees of responsibility for the successful outcome of the venture, the distortion will be increased.

17. Negative feelings about the situation.   If people fear that the situation is one in which they are not respected or their contribution is not valued, they will not attempt to make a real contribution. If they feel that the other person cannot be trusted, they will send messages designed to deceive rather than be honest.

An Individual Can Improve Communication

The perception a person has of himself as a sender and a receiver in a communication system determines his effectiveness as a communicator. As a sender, the individual should:

1. See himself as sharing, not telling. If he is there to tell and convince, he will not really hear the other person. He will hear only things to refute. He will concentrate so much on what he has to get across that he will not understand what is happening.

2. See himself as seeking to relate to other people, not to control them. If he sees himself as attempting to control, he hunts ways of blocking communication that will decrease his control. He also attempts to ignore messages from the other person, which contradict his purposes. If he seeks to relate, he will be constantly testing his own ideas and values by those of others. He will become more sensitive to others.

3. See his task as seeking truth rather than convincing others. If his purpose is to seek truth, he will increase his data by becoming aware of the facts known and values held by others. If he seeks to convince, he will refuse to hear the other person.

4. Judge his own contribution by the feedback he gets from others rather than his personal judgment. If he depends on personal judgment, he cannot be sure what others hear, or what he is really saying; neither can he clarify his points for others. He does not know the areas in which he is not communicating effectively. If real communication is to occur, the feedback from the listeners is as important to the sender as the statements that he makes.

5. Look for agreement and any disagreement and seek the meaning the other person intends in the areas of difference. He should value disagreement as much as agreement, because it indicates the portions of topics that need further analysis.

6. Seek to be empathetic. If he tries to be empathetic, he may find that reality in a situation is far from what he considers to be the objective interpretation.

7. Seek words with common meanings. He will use more than one word to explain a point to see if the other person makes a more accurate interpretation with one set of symbols than he does with another. He will be willing to be questioned. He will want the receiver to raise questions about any point that is not clear or about words he does not understand. He will value differences of interpretation and the exploration of meaning. If difference of interpretation is valued and seen as a way of increasing clarity, the receiver will not hesitate to make clear his lack of certainty about the intent of the other. He will recognize that each action affects the communication.

8. Seek to eliminate from his behavior actions that threaten. The sender will recognize that resistance is a part of communication. He will be listening with a "third ear" to discover what is not being said. He will attempt empathy to see how what he is saying sounds to the listener. He will use nonverbal cues consistent with the verbal statements that he is making.

As a receiver the individual should:

1. Seek to help the sender clarify his meaning. He should even raise questions from time to time about meaning that appear perfectly clear to him, because he may be interpreting in a way that the sender did not intend. Much distortion in communication is produced by people thinking they are in agreement when they are not. He will ask, "Is this another way of saying what you said?" He can understand that his experience determines what he can hear and will seek to discover the background of experience that causes the sender to make the statements that he does. He will recognize that he is interpreting in terms of his own needs and purposes and seek clarification. He will try to eliminate stereotypes from his own thinking and ask for specifics.

2. Seek understanding. His first emphasis is on attempting to discover what the other person is saying, rather than evaluating it. He can look for agreement in areas where it exists and seek to isolate the areas of difference that he will want to explore later. If he argues, he doesn't attempt to hear. He seeks to win the argument. If he accepts, he increases the range of factors he is able to consider.

3. Seek to identify what is not being said as much as he tries to understand what is being said. The ideas that are not expressed, perhaps deliberately withheld, are as important as the statements made. If the listener can react in such a way that he helps the sender move into areas that are not being verbalized, he has a better chance of achieving a real communication with the sender. An individual in his roles as sender and receiver will improve communication as he decreases emphasis upon status, removes fear and distrust as far as possible from the situation, remembers that honesty begets honesty, avoids evaluating the other person's contributions, gives attention to the same degree that he demands it, avoids attacking or becoming defensive, and supports the person who is venturing into areas where he is testing the situation to see how open he can be.

If he is effective in improving the communication, the agreements will be understood, the disagreements will be clearer, people will value each other more or less, and the open interpretations will be more nearly similar to private ones.

Extra Communication Tasks of the Supervisor

As an individual with a special responsibility for increasing communication, the supervisor adds another dimension to the Ryans model. He is a sender and a receiver, but he is also a facilitator. He is a developer and maintenance man for the communication system as well as a participant. As a supervisor, he should:

1. Encourage people to know and value each other. He provides opportunities for social interaction. He helps people to become informed about the backgrounds and achievements of others.

2. Provide the physical arrangements that contribute to better communication. When conferences and meetings are planned, he makes sure that the location is the best available and that the furniture is arranged in a manner that encourages maximum interaction.

3. Seek to develop a permissive atmosphere. Permissiveness, as used by psychologists, means personal freedom to express a point of view or an idea without fear of recrimination because it is in opposition to one held by someone with power or authority. If the atmosphere is really permissive, the members of the staff value the person who is different rather than attempt to force him to conform. The person who is different is encouraged to challenge, because out of this challenge comes more insight for all. Achieving this attitude is not easy. In some staffs, the person who is different threatens other people, and they hunt ways of quieting him.

4. Seek to identify areas of agreement and areas of disagreement. Areas of disagreement are just as important to a group as the areas of agreement. Good communication does not result in consensus. Consensus on all phases of a problem cannot usually be reached. The supervisor does what he can to help the group value areas of difference because they indicate the points that need to be explored further. Individuals grow to the extent to which the group is able to explore its differences without fear of coercion.

5. Reflect to the group what he thinks the group has said. He may say, "This is what I have heard you say," or "Is this what you said?" This action helps the group summarize and move to the next point. By reflecting and asking if he is correct, the supervisor also makes it possible for the sender to clarify what he really meant or help the group understand a member who apparently differs. Many times an individual is not sure what the other person has said and begins to bristle because he does not understand. When a supervisor reflects ideas, he helps people understand each other and decreases conflict. If the supervisor or another member of the group feels free to state a third person's position in other words and asks if the interpretation is correct, the spokesman has a chance to say, "No, I did not mean that. I meant to say . . ."

Another clarifying technique that can be used by supervisors or by other group members is to make an application of an idea and say, "Is this what you meant?" For example, if someone says the teacher should be permissive, another group member may ask, "Does this mean then that I should not question the little boy who said, 'Let's spend one-half of our time writing and the rest of the time playing.' " As a listener states an implication of a remark and asks if the person meant to make such an application, a chance is provided for the sender to clarify his remarks and to improve communication.

A supervisor has a better chance of being effective if he remembers that: communication is a process in which people attempt to share personal feelings and ideas and to understand the other person's feelings and ideas; it is part self-disclosure and part seeking to understand the other; it is decreased by feelings of superiority and inferiority, by fear and anxiety, by rigid social organizations, by attempts to pressure or control, and by pressure to achieve, produce, or conform; it is increased as trust is developed, when people feel they have common values and goals, when diversity is valued, when the wish to explore differences is present, when each person is free to make his own interpretation and form his own values, when consensus is sought without coercion or manipulation, when individuals like and accept each other, and when people support each other in sharing emotion.

If the communication is good, agreements will be understood, disagreements will be clearer, people will value each other more or less, public comments and private comments will be more similar, and the formal and informal norms of a working group will be more alike.

For the supervisor this means: that he will work to build group acceptance and trust; that he will support the right of individuals to differ; that he will de-emphasize social status; that he will provide time for group members to interact; that he will seek uncoerced consensus in decision making; and that he will see his role as a helping and service function rather than a directing, rating, and controlling operation.

6 Application of Communication Theory to Supervisory Practices

As a school system grows larger, the problems of communication become more and more acute. When all staff members know each other and see each other frequently, communication may become distorted, but difficulties can be solved if the individuals involved make the effort. However, when the staff grows to the size where no one can know all his fellow workers, the task of communication becomes increasingly difficult. The process of developing trust, a willingness to share, a common language, and adequate channels for communication among hundreds of strangers requires a high degree of competency and careful planning.

Communication Through Customary Channels

Typical communication methods in large systems include curriculum bulletins, policy bulletins, administrative and supervisory staff meetings, teachers' meetings, and reports. Many times these procedures fail to provide adequate communication.

Curriculum bulletins are prepared by the central office staff or a committee and distributed to the entire staff. Few persons read them, and those who do find little meaning in them unless they have had a part in producing them. They do not fill a need and were not prepared in response to a request from teachers. They are sent, but no message is received. Teachers do not see themselves as a part of the communication system or see the curriculum bulletins as their communication channel.

The curriculum bulletins are used primarily for communication among supervisors in different school systems who wish to exchange information and by new teachers in a system who feel the need to become informed about the organization to which they belong.

If curriculum bulletins are to become better channels of communication, efforts must be expended to bring teachers into the communication system. Teachers must have a voice in deciding what bulletins will be prepared and have opportunities for input of ideas and reaction to preliminary drafts. Frequently, teachers are never consulted about the form and format of the curriculum bulletin. Who knows better what material teachers will read?

Policy bulletins are no more effective as communication channels. Decisions are made somewhere concerning the distribution of policy bulletins. Some are restricted to administrators and supervisors. Although restricted bulletins help to keep the supervisory group informed, the information may or may not be spread throughout the teaching force, and the peripheral membership of teachers in the group is emphasized. Other policy bulletins are "made available" to the entire staff. Notice the use of the term "made available." The effect is not to communicate with the entire staff but only to permit everyone to know what's happening. Sometimes the policy statements are posted on the bulletin boards where teachers may read them, and teachers are asked on occasion to initial the notice to prove they have read it. Could the surroundings be worse for receiving a message accurately than standing amid milling teachers and children whose necks are stretched up to read? Think of the messages sent back as the hand is raised to initial the policy bulletin. Quite obviously the overt message travels one way – down. And no one at the top knows the *covert* response. It is difficult to know how much information teachers want, and the administration does not want to burden them with unnecessary items.

If policy bulletins are to be effective as communication channels, they must be seen as a part of a system in which teachers may send messages. Ideally, the policy bulletins would be responses to questions and proposals. At a minimum level, the bulletins should be official statements of decisions resulting from deliberation about problems that teachers have had a part in identifying. Also, a wise administration will seek teacher evaluation of the form and distribution of the bulletins. The basic ingredient in communication about policy is to create an organization through which each person in the staff can have representation in its formulation. And certainly it is "penny-wise and pound-foolish" not to issue a copy of a policy to each teacher who will be affected. The critical factor is to provide an easy flow of communication up, down, and sideways.

Supervisory staff meetings are not always pretty when viewed in terms of communication and group development theories. Sometimes they are announcement sessions. Sometimes they are occasions when the highest official talks. The meeting leader suffers a case of communication isolation. People don't tell him what they think or show him how they react to his statements or proposals. All the reactions are covert. If the leader could hear the muttered comments as people leave the meeting, he would not be so smug about the accomplishments of the session.

Teachers' meetings in large school systems are typically poor attempts at communication. Teachers are informed that they must assemble to hear someone they do not know talk about a topic they have not selected. They go with resentment. They listen with resistance. They forget without remorse. They have no opportunity to evaluate, talk back, or ask for further clarification.

When teachers' meetings are seen as efforts to communicate, it is evident that teachers must have a part in planning them and have opportunities to evaluate them. The meeting must be so structured that there is time for teachers to talk together about the input the speaker has made. The minimum type of interaction should be a program with a presentation, discussion groups, and reaction panel or question-clarification period.

Probably the worst form of communication in any system is a report. No matter how beautifully prepared and expensively printed, it is like a burial: everyone receives a copy and lays it away. Seldom is it read unless the recipient wants to see if he has been given credit for a contribution he made. Reports are more likely to be attempts to communicate with persons outside the system.

If reports are to be used as communication channels within the system, a distinction should be made between outside reports and reports for home usage. "Inside" reports should be attempts to share failures as well as triumphs, should include questions as well as answers. All extraneous information should be deleted. Responses should be encouraged. In its best form, it will include a proposal of next steps, which the staff is invited to consider.

It is true that schools rely heavily on face-to-face communications and various kinds of written communication (McCleary, 1968). Certainly, these are important approaches to communication and every effort should be made to improve their effectiveness. But, there are certain technological developments that have important implications for communications in schools. Closed circuit television can be used for mass communication from the central office to local schools. Consultants can be used in small groups to answer questions and get feedback from teachers. It is also possible to have a telephone hook-up so that teachers can raise questions with the communication from the central office. Video tapes and sound tapes can be used in many ways to promote communication. It is possible for authorities from distant places to put presentations on video tape which can be played back for small groups in the school system. The telephone hook-up can provide for interaction between participants and speaker. Video tapes and television can be used to share teaching procedures and innovations among staff members. Staff members can also use video tapes to describe and analyze their own teaching. With the advent of larger and more complicated school systems it will become increasingly important to use technological advances in communication to improve the quality of communication in schools.

Organization and Operation of a Meeting

The most common attempt at communication in a school system is a meeting—committee, faculty, department, administrators, or teachers. If the meetings are successful, failure in other forms of communication is overlooked. If the meetings are unsatisfactory, it is difficult to develop cohesiveness and commitment within the staff.

Since many meetings are planned and conducted by supervisors, it is important that they know how a meeting can be conducted to facilitate communication. A skilled leader can conduct a discussion in such a way as to develop a quality of problem-solving that surpasses that of a group working with a less skilled leader, and he can obtain a higher degree of group acceptance than a less skilled person. The most skilled leader obtains agreement on the desired solution; his contributions consist of summarizing, encouraging analysis, supplying information, sharing ideas, and preventing hurt feelings. The amount of consensus and the change in consensus is positively correlated with the skill of the discussion leader (Hare, 1952).

The success of a group meeting depends to a great degree upon the skill with which the discussion is handled. If a group is unaccustomed to working together, it may be well for the supervisor who has skill in discussion leadership to preside at meetings. The discussion leader sets the mood of a meeting, and his skill determines the flow of the discussion. He has many responsibilities.

The first function of a discussion leader is to create an atmosphere that is easy, yet businesslike. He must be friendly, exhibit a sincere welcome to all group members, and accept their comments and participation. He must encourage all members to accept as worthy of consideration the comments of every other member. He helps new members to become acquainted. He watches to see that the timid person who has an idea has the opportunity to bring it into the discussion. He prevents a few persons from dominating the meeting.

A second function is to guide the flow of discussion. It is his job to see that all who have comments or questions are recognized and to refer questions to the proper source in the group for an answer. To do this properly, he must keep the total flow of the discussion in mind and must remember the types of comments that each member of the group has made. With these points in mind, he is ready to shift a question to the proper person, or he can place two comments or two questions in opposition to each other or show their relatedness. He provides the transition from one question to another.

A third function of the chairman is to clarify questions. Many times, a question will be in such abstract form or will be so long or unwieldy that the discussion will be hampered by it. In such cases, the chairman must step in. He may ask the questioner to define certain words used or to state the question another way. Or the chairman may short-cut the process and restate the question in a brief, direct form. In any case, as he finishes clarifying the question, he must get the acceptance of the questioner that the rephrasing has not changed the original meaning of the question.

A fourth function of the chairman is to keep the group on the topic. He must constantly watch to see whether comments and questions further illuminate the issue under discussion or whether they lead the group away from the point. Many times he will be forced to make judgments concerning the degree of deviation from the issue that will be allowed. In bringing the group back to the issue, the chairman must act in such a manner that even the person taking the group away is not made to feel that he is disrupting the discussion or making an unsatisfactory contribution to it. Some ways of doing this are: to restate the issue after the participant has concluded his contribution; to state the points that have been made on both sides of the issue; to point out how the last comment bears on the issue and ignore the portions of the contribution that were leading the group away; or to state that the last comment opens up other issues or ramifications of the present issue that the group may wish to explore and ask the group whether they want to stay with the original issue or pursue these new possibilities further.

Summarizing the discussion is one of the most valuable functions that the chairman can perform. Through this process, he gives order to the discussion. He outlines the flow of the discussion for the group at various times during the meeting. In situations in which a blackboard is not used to keep a running outline of the meeting, this function is essential.

The number of times that the chairman summarizes depends upon the way in which the group is moving. If the discussion gets under way quickly, if the progress is rapid, and if all members of the group are keeping the issue clearly in mind, the chairman can let the summarizing go for long periods of time. If the group does not have its purpose clearly in mind and is moving slowly, the frequent summaries will help to stimulate more rapid progress. It is especially important for the chairman to summarize or to have some member of the group summarize as the meeting closes. Unless this is done, many people who are not too skilled in group discussion feel that nothing has been accomplished and that the period has been only a bull session. The morale of the group will be strengthened if the chairman points out the specific accomplishments of the meeting.

The chairman has the responsibility for keeping order in the discussion. He must step in when several people attempt to speak at the same time. He must raise the type of questions that will pull back into the main group a small subgroup that starts a discussion within itself. He must watch for outside distracting influences, such as street noises, people walking in and out of the meeting, and scraping of chairs. He must take appropriate action to eliminate these disturbing factors as far as possible.

The chairman must watch all members of the discussion group he is leading. As he glances at the faces of participants, he can see whether or not they believe the meeting is moving satisfactorily, detect the glances that indicate that a person has a contribution to make, note the frowns that mean that a member of the group disagrees or questions what has been said, perceive indications of restlessness such as doodling, crossing of legs, and squirming in chairs, see which members of the group agree with other members of the group, obtain a picture of the development of consensus, and know when it is time to raise the question of whether or not the group is ready to make a decision. The signs are small, but they are the cues by which a leader of a discussion group must operate. Someone has aptly called leading a discussion group "playing by ear." And close observation of the group is the only way this playing by ear can be successful.

Participation in a discussion group depends upon the nature of the individual. A discussion leader has responsibility for giving individualized attention. He must particularly watch the timid members of the group; when they give the slightest indication that they have a contribution to make, he must call on them. He must keep the overly talkative person from participating too much. He can do this by watching for over-participation in the first part of the meeting, by not gazing directly at the offending participant as the meeting goes along, by referring specific questions to the less aggressive members of the group, and, with groups in which the discussion leader has worked many times, by asking the talkative members to help bring out the less articulate members.

The discussion leader must also watch for persons in the group who have leadership qualities. Such persons can be detected by watching the attention the group gives to various speakers. When they are recognized, they can be used in helping the meeting to progress. After they have finished the statement of the point of view that they espouse, the discussion leader can ask the other members of the group whether that is the position they want to take.

Leaders in the group who disagree with each other can be used to help clarify a position. But a danger against which the discussion leader must be constantly on guard is the alignment of people in camps behind the opposing leaders, so that the discussion group becomes two groups instead of one. The discussion leader's responsibility after the issue has been made clear is to ask the type of questions that get members of the group to state the areas of agreement and then center the discussion on seeking more agreement in areas where it has not yet been achieved.

It is extremely helpful to a discussion leader in improving his techniques to have certain types of analyses made of the meeting and of his work. A common form of analysis is the use of a flow chart by which the flow of the discussion from one member to another within the group is charted. Such a chart shows whether the participation was widespread or was restricted to a few. The flow chart will also indicate the number of times the discussion leader stepped into the picture. The more skilled the leader becomes, the fewer times he will have to participate to keep the group on the issue, to summarize, and to maintain feelings of group unity. A flow chart will also tell whether or not the center of focus stayed within a certain part of the discussion group. If a flow chart of the first part of the meeting indicates that the leaders are all in one section of the group, some members of that section may be asked to shift positions before the next session starts. Or the flow chart may indicate that the seating plan of the whole group should be changed.

Another type of analysis that proves helpful to the discussion leaders is to have someone make a verbatim listing of the comments the chairman makes. In this way he can see whether his questions are the type that bring all members into the discussion or whether they encourage the discussion to become dialogues between the chairman and a single member of the group. For example, one of the questions that stimulates dialogue is, "Don't you think our purpose should be to win community support, Bart?" Putting the name of the individual at the end of the question excludes all the other members of the group and makes that individual feel a responsibility for replying directly to the chairman.

Some pertinent questions for the official leader to ask himself in evaluating his discussion leadership are:

Do I listen more intently to some members of the staff?

Do I recognize certain persons more quickly, because their thinking is closer to mine?

Do I tend to discredit thinking that is not in agreement with my own?

Do I pass value judgments on contributions as they are made?

Do I expect the staff to give me the floor before anyone else?

Do I expect people to agree with me because of my status?

Probably the best form of in-service training for a discussion leader is to make a video tape recording of meetings that he conducts. The discussion leader can hear and see the mistakes that kept the group from making progress.

In summary, the discussion leader secures group agreement on the agenda, maintains an atmosphere that encourages full participation, is impartial toward ideas, helps the group establish its own rules of procedure, keeps discussion centered on the problem, summarizes as necessary, brings out issues and agreements, and makes or provides for final summary.

In the beginning of group work, it may be necessary to spend some time thinking about the various roles of members of the group. Definition of function through thinking together will relieve a sense of insecurity on the part of some staff members who have not participated in decision-making groups. Each participant has a responsibility to contribute ideas and suggestions, to listen to what others say and relate it to the problem, to think for himself, and to state points clearly and briefly without wrangling over details and technicalities.

As a member of the group each person has, along with the discussion leader, a responsibility for the direction and speed of the meeting. He needs to assume an active role. He may take action to change procedures when he thinks satisfactory progress is not being made. He may request clarification when it is needed. He may summarize and state what he believes the next steps should be. He may ask that certain persons be recognized. In short, he may assume any of the functions of the discussion leader with the understanding that he is attempting to assist the discussion leader to coordinate and move the group forward.

In some meetings, the supervisor serves as a consultant. His role should be understood by him and by the group. He is brought to the meeting to help the group solve its problems. He is not there to express his concerns or to sell the faculty a bill of goods. During the meeting, his function is to participate as a member of the group. He should not expect or be given preferential treatment. Like any other member of the group, he will supply special information that bears on the problem. This information may be volunteered when pertinent or it may be requested by the discussion leader. As a consultant he will receive his guidance from the discussion leader. The discussion leader is in charge of the meeting, and the consultant is there to assist him in keeping the group on the topic and moving toward a solution.

On occasion, a supervisor will speak to the faculty. Such a situation should not be considered a group activity. It should be recognized and used as a straight lecture. It will help in the total group growth of the staff, however, if these talks grow out of problems that have emerged in group sessions and are looked upon as data-collecting activities. The information obtained should be taken back into the group for evaluation, rejection, or use.

Each meeting should have a central purpose that all participants recognize. Although a portion of the meeting may be used for announcements and the exploration of new ideas, most of the time should be devoted to seeking consensus on the central question. The chances of focusing attention and reaching agreement are greater if the meeting is used to consider a proposed solution to a school problem or a proposed improvement in policy or program. Meetings should be devoted in large part to discussion of the definition of a problem or to reports of study committees that are ready to make definite proposals. Meetings built around the consideration of proposals become definite and important. Members of the group know that time is being spent in making decisions that will affect them.

Meetings should not close without reaching conclusions. These conclusions may be decisions to accept proposals or to refer them back to a committee for further study of a specific nature. It should be pointed out that reaching conclusions involves clear indication of the responsibility of individual members for the execution of the decisions. Meetings that end without any feeling of accomplishment soon break the spirit of a group and their belief in the value of time spent in meetings.

During the meeting, the group needs all the assistance that can be provided to help it know its progress. It proves helpful in many meetings to have a person record on a blackboard or chart the issues being discussed, the points made, and the agreements reached. Some groups have found it helpful to use large sheets of paper that can be taped to the wall to record the progress of the meeting. Then there is no problem of running out of board space and having to erase, and the running account of the meeting preserved on these sheets serves as the basis for the minutes and as data for study by any persons interested in increasing the achievement in meetings. Time should be taken at the end of the meeting to check with the total group to see if the record that has been kept is an accurate account of the meeting.

A permanent record should be kept of every meeting. It should include the name of the group, date, meeting place, members present, members absent, problems discussed, suggestions made, problems referred, decisions reached, responsibilities accepted or assigned, and plans for the next meeting.

The record is essential for securing continuity of planning and avoiding waste of time through repetition. The record should be circulated to all who have participated in or are affected by actions taken or being considered. It keeps everyone in touch with the work of the group and serves to give a sense of direction and achievement.

Meetings can be improved by evaluation. One technique is the use of a process observer, whose function is to keep a record of the interaction among members of the group. He is an evidence-collector. He is not an evaluator. On the basis of the evidence presented, an evaluation can be made of the process and progress of the meeting.

Guide sheets have been worked out to help process observers. Listed below are questions culled from many such forms.

> Was the meeting slow in getting started?
> Was the atmosphere easy, relaxed, and comfortable?
> Was the tempo slow, hurried, or satisfactory?
> Was the interest level high?
> Was the purpose clear to all?
> Were members cooperative?
> Was information shared?
> Were members sensitive to each other?
> Were tensions brought out into the open?
> Was there evidence of feelings of superiority?
> Were ideas forced on the group?
> Was the group able to accept differences?
> Was the group able to discipline itself?
> Was any decision reached?
> Was there resistance to group decisions?
> Was participation spread throughout the group?
> Was discussion centered for a long period in one portion of the group?
> Was the discussion initiated by group members?

Were there difficulties in communication?
Was there a feeling of give and take?
Were members eager to speak?
Were certain members taking more than their share of the time?
Were members showing aggression?·
Was the discussion limited to the topic?
Were members assuming responsibility for the success of the meeting?
Were members attempting to draw out each other?
Did the leader help the group to establish a direction?
Did the leader give encouragement?
Did the leader attempt to include nonparticipating members?
Did the leader volunteer more help than was needed?
Did the leader recognize those who wished to speak?
Did the leader dominate the meeting?
Did the leader manifest feelings of superiority?
Did the leader keep things going?
Did the leader bring the specialized skills of members to bear on the problem?
Did the leader summarize as necessary?
Did the leader try to give answers for the group?
Did the leader get a consensus?

The study of a check list for the process observer helps members of the group to become more effective participants in that group.

Out of the study of group dynamics has emerged the beginnings of a classification of certain types of participation in groups. Although the definitions of various roles such as coordinator, clarifier, critic, protagonist, manager, arbitrator, reality tester, group conscience, encourager, and boss are still hazy, discussion of these terms as related to the group operation serves to help supervisors mature in their thinking about effective group communication.

Communication in a Person-to-Person Conference

Much of a supervisor's work is done in person-to-person interviews. Planning a program, planning with a teacher for the description and analysis of his teaching behavior, considering a proposal or request, and interpreting a policy are only samples of the constant use the supervisor makes of the interview. Much of his success depends upon his effectiveness in the person-to-person conference.

No pat formula can be established for an interview. If there is too close adherence to a set pattern, the supervisor's interview is likely to be ineffective. A supervisor in one of the important school systems of the country had read books on the psychology of managing people. In conferences he used flattery, promised rewards, fear, and anger in the proper proportion and at just the right time to obtain his ends. With some personnel this technique might have been successful. With the group he supervised it did not work. They had read the same books. They could predict the trend of the conference and block it if they wished.

The difficulty this man experienced was due to a false concept of the purpose of the conference. He felt a conference was the place to influence a subordinate to accept a decision he had made in advance. He conceived of supervision as making decisions and getting others to accept them.

All his difficulties and dissatisfaction would have disappeared if he had learned that the supervisor's function in education is to create situations in which planning can occur, not to make the plans. A conference between supervisor and supervised is designed to produce cooperative planning, not to impose a plan on the subordinate.

Using the conference for cooperative planning does not mean that the supervisor will not plan in advance. He will. But it will be a special kind of planning. During World War II, the writer had an opportunity to observe a consulting firm at work. Their business was to guide the planning of industrial concerns over which they had no control. Their most important technique was the individual conference. Before each conference, the consultant spent about half the time in getting ready. He reviewed all the information he had about the person with whom the conference was scheduled. He decided upon the *pivotal* questions for the talk. He determined additional information to be secured. He thought through possible solutions that might emerge from the conference. Under no circumstances would one of these consultants allow himself to be drawn into a conference without pre-planning.

No conference was scheduled without a definite purpose. It might be an exploratory conference to establish facts, or a conference to reach a solution to a problem. In any case, the conference had a purpose. It should be emphasized again that the consulting firm did not conceive of the man-to-man conference as a selling proposition. The purpose was not to convince anyone of the rightness of the firm's thinking, but to reach answers through thinking together.

The purpose of an interview should be clear to all parties. A man kept in the dark is afraid and insecure. He plays his cards cautiously, until he knows where the conference is going and what is expected of him. If the supervisor does not want to waste time, he should state the purpose early in the conference or announce it beforehand. Of course, if the conference is requested by the teacher, the supervisor has an equal right to know the purpose. In either case, the person invited to the conference has a right to ask what it is to accomplish.

If the conference is to be successful, it helps to hold it in a quiet place where the participants will not be interrupted. A conference is an attempt to reach a union of minds and purposes. It is a delicate procedure. Most people maintain a front, composed of certain mannerisms, points of view, and positions that they believe their role in life demands of them. If the participants do not declare their positions openly, the conference becomes nothing more than a sparring session. They may win each other's respect for skill in offensive and defensive warfare, but they do little to win each other's confidence.

A quiet, uninterrupted atmosphere is necessary to facilitate the lowering of "fronts." As long as a man feels he may regret letting the other person know what he is really like, he will not take the chance. He does not reveal the way he really feels if he does not trust the other person or if he fears that the information he offers may be used against him. No one tells his secret desires or plans on a street corner or at a party where all may hear. Nor will a person express himself openly if the conference is being constantly interrupted by people entering the conference room or by the ringing of the telephone. No skilled psychiatrist or counselor holds a consultation where interruptions may occur that will break the trend of thought or that will destroy the atmosphere of mutual confidence. If the need for an interview arises in a crowded, noisy situation, the supervisor should suggest retiring to a quiet location for the discussion.

Interruptions do not matter, however, if rapport has not been established—neither does the conference! The building of rapport depends upon putting the other person at ease. If the supervisor has known the teacher for years, and if their work together has produced respect and trust, rapport has already been established, and this phase of the conference is taken care of automatically. If the supervisor has built a reputation for helpfulness, honesty, and trustworthiness, rapport is more easily established. He is a respected person until proved otherwise.

But even with the persons who trust him, certain actions can destroy a supervisor's effectiveness. Emphasizing superiority is fatal. Some supervisors arrange their office in such a way that their chair is in front of the window. Any person talking to them is at a disadvantage. Superiority feelings can be displayed by voice, by insisting on fitting the conference into the supervisor's schedule, and by not giving the teacher a part in determining the length of the interview. The surest way of guarding against such behavior is to remind oneself constantly that supervision is a service operation, and that supervisors exist only to help the teacher.

Barriers can be built in other ways. Always getting the desk between the supervisor and the supervised is one technique. Sticking to Mr., Miss, Mrs., or Dr. is another. When a supervisor keeps his shield high, he cannot expect a teacher to lower his.

Informality is of great importance in conferences. Many supervisors fail to achieve it because they believe they must impress the persons with whom they work. They fail to realize that the only way people are impressed is by real value. If a supervisor has worth, it will make itself evident. Teachers will say, "He grows on you." Sham is equally easy for teachers to detect. A good show is recognized for what it is worth.

A successful conference cannot be rushed. When understandings are to be reached upon which future action will be based, both parties must have ample opportunity to clear up any hazy points. Neither must the conference lag. A sense of constant progress must exist. Progress, however, can be in the direction of establishing better relations, as well as in logical movement to a conclusion. Signs of impatience or dissatisfaction or confusion are an indication of a need for readjusting the speed of the conference.

It is not always possible to start a conference at a fast pace even with an old and trusted friend. He may be laboring under some emotional stress resulting from an immediate conflict with another teacher or with a member of his family. Financial problems or other personal matters may cause him to be less acute than usual. Paying attention to the emotional status of the teacher and adjusting to suit his mood will pay dividends in successful conferences.

A conference should end with a definite conclusion. It may be nothing more than the statement, "These are the facts we agreed on, aren't they?" Or it may be, "It is my understanding that we agree to try this solution." If the conference has not gone as far as the supervisor had hoped, he should try to plan with the teacher what steps should be taken next.

A conference should end with an outline of the next steps, and the teacher should be made to feel that he is capable of taking them. If he leaves with a fear of failure, the agreement will have been futile. Such a situation is worse than no agreement at all, because confidence in the supervisor will be lost when the procedure agreed upon fails, as it most certainly will if the participants lack confidence in it.

The supervisor has a responsibility for believing in a plan before it is accepted and for conveying his belief to the teacher. If doubts have not been eliminated in the minds of both persons, the planning period has not been adequate.

After the conference is over, the supervisor should make a record of the agreements and of his own commitments. Failure to remember or to live up to agreements is a violation of the teacher's confidence and will result in the destruction of future effectiveness with him. Few people have memories good enough to keep all the agreements made in a busy schedule. Memories must be supplemented by written records.

Finally, it is helpful if both participants work hard for authenticity. This will facilitate credibility of agreements reached and attempts to carry out those agreements. It also helps to maintain and improve a relationship of trust, mutual understanding, and effectiveness.

Organization and Operation of a Workshop

The purpose of a workshop is to give the participants a chance to work on their problems with the assistance of a staff of resource people. Participants and staff members work on a peer relationship.

The form of the workshop that evolves in a system depends on the schedule of the staff and on the availability of time. Some school systems have established a two- to five-week workshop in the summer; others have attempted to approximate a workshop program by weekly meetings held throughout the school year. Where it has been necessary to spread out the workshop over the year, the leaders have attempted to schedule it in such a way that long blocks of time are available.

There are many ways of getting a workshop started in a local school system. One is to have staff members attend out-of-town workshops, held under the sponsorship of a university or a national organization, or to attend workshops in other school systems. The reports of their outside experience serve to stimulate the inerest of other staff members. Another method is to get a small group of the staff together, not all status leaders, and discuss the workshop idea. Out of such meetings may grow the nucleus of a workshop.

Any movement into a workshop plan should be made with the understanding that it is done on an experimental basis and that it will be evaluated by the staff, the community, and the board of education. It has proved wise in some schools to include members of the community and members of the board of education in the workshop as a way of insuring that an accurate evaluation of the workshop reaches these groups. When such persons attend the workshop, the program often becomes more dynamic, and the results are far-reaching.

When it has been decided that a workshop will be held, it is desirable to choose part of the staff from the leaders in the local system. Such a choice will guarantee to the teachers that the approach will be a practical one and that it will have the support of these leaders. However, no staff member should be chosen who is not enthusiastic both about working in the workshop and about the workshop technique. A misguided or disgruntled staff member can do much to disrupt the workshop activity. The ideal situation is, of course, to have the total school staff in a workshop, with all the official leaders filling their customary roles.

In addition to the local staff members, outside consultants should be provided. They will increase the variety of ideas and will give teachers in the system a feeling that the workshop is a different experience from the ordinary teachers' meeting. Teachers will have a chance to come into contact with persons working in another locality or with an authority they respect. Two types of outside resource people are helpful: the first serves as a continuing staff member throughout the workshop; the second, who has a special contribution to make to the planned program, can be brought to the workshop for a day for a presentation at a general session and can work with small groups that will best utilize his talents. The selection of the outside staff members should be determined by their competency to contribute to the solution of the major problems identified during the pre-planning.

The ideal plan is for the entire staff of a local school to work together in a workshop. This makes it possible to plan new engagement opportunities for students and plan for the implementation of the ideas. It also makes it possible for teachers to understand and support innovative efforts of their fellow teachers. Further, it can open the door for continuous interaction, shared learning, and cooperative effort among the teachers and official leaders of a particular school.

If total staff membership is not possible, attendance should be placed on an optional basis. All staff members should be invited to attend, but admission should be only by application. The three major factors in making the final selections should be the enthusiasm of the applicant, the carefulness with which he defines the problem on which he wishes to work, and his need for the experience.

School team possibilities should be another major consideration. The possibility of implementing workshop planning is much greater when a team from a school, including an official leader, comes to the workshop, plans a proposal to take back to the faculty, and carries it through the faculty organization. It is important for these leadership teams to involve the rest of the faculty in planning for the workshop. The identification of problems and procedures for working on them in workshop could be identified and discussed. This would facilitate follow-up and implementation when it is taken back to the faculty.

In addition to arranging budget and location of space, it is necessary for the staff to meet together, to agree on a method of operation, to study the problems listed by applicants, to select materials, and to draw up a temporary schedule.

In the organization of the workshop, most staffs have found it desirable to plan a time for the total workshop group to meet together. This phase of the program, including presentations by special authorities and sharing of the products of the work groups, gives the group a feeling of unity.

The workshop has certain definite characteristics. It is a place where teachers go to work on their own problems or the problems of their school. The work is based on the problems of the individuals enrolled. All participants in the workshop follow individual programs. A plan of operation, organized to provide the types of experiences that will enable the members to fulfill their own goals, is developed after the participants arrive. It is a flexible plan. It may be changed many times during a workshop. Preliminary planning by the staff is usually restricted to collecting equipment and devising a plan for getting under way. In some cases, the staff goes further and establishes a general pattern for the work, which includes some general sessions and provisions for work groups. The staff may suggest a preliminary daily schedule to be followed the first few days, but this plan is only temporary until members of the workshop, including the staff, can devise a more effective way of working. Unsatisfactory procedures are eliminated and new provisions are made for unanticipated activities.

Cooperative work is encouraged. If members of the workshop have problems in common, they are encouraged to plan together and to share the results of their work.

No group assignments are made. Each participant has an adviser to help him plan his work during the workshop period. With the adviser, the participant works out his schedule and the method of attack that he will follow in solving his problem.

Many types of creative activity are made possible. Recognizing that the teachers are stimulated by the opportunity to work in many media, provision is made in workshops for experience in dramatics, dancing, and a multitude of art forms.

An all-pervading aspect of the workshop is evaluation. All the activities of the workshop and of the individual are subject to joint evaluation by the workshop members, the staff, and the individual participants. Each member of the workshop is encouraged to evaluate the group's progress and his own.

An important characteristic is the stress on social interchange. In the preliminary planning, provision is made for social activites, and as soon as the group gathers, a social committee is organized that has the responsibility for planning and conducting a wide variety of social activities.

Committee work is also an essential element of a workshop. The major committee is the planning committee, which has overall responsibility for planning, organization of the workshop, and revision of the program. Other committees, established as needed, are the social, library, evaluation, visitors and hospitality, publicity, publications, bulletin board, and decorations committees.

But the real center of life in the workshop is small work groups, organized around the common interests of a number of the participants, for cooperative attack on common problems. Each small group needs one or more staff members to maintain a continuing relationship with that group in the solving of the problem it undertakes.

Another type of planning needed is for ways to provide individual counseling. Much of the benefit of the workshop situation comes from this person-to-person relationship between adviser and advisee. The adviser has the special role of helping the workshop members to tap fully the resources of the workshop. He informs the participant about staff members or other workshop members who have information and knowledge bearing upon the problem the student is undertaking to solve. One adviser should not attempt to guide more than ten to twenty participants.

In the planning of a workshop, provision is made for great emphasis on evaluation—evaluation of the process, the ways of working together and the learning outcomes. During the entire program the evaluation is a continuous process in which all members of the group participate. It is unusual in most workshops to establish an evaluation committee that has the responsibility of recommending evaluation procedures to the total group and of organizing and carrying out the evaluation procedures the workshop group accepts. Evaluation periods with the discussion under the leadership of a panel composed of members of the various work groups have proved to be an effective way of improving the workshop process. Almost all workshops have found it advisable to use, in addition, a formal check sheet to focus the attention of the workshop members on the important phases of the workshop experience and to help everyone to strengthen weak points. Workshop members grow in teaching skill through opportunities to analyze why group activities are productive or unsatisfactory.

Throughout the workshop program, emphasis is placed on sharing leadership. Even in the large sessions, participation by as many members of the audience as possible is encouraged. In the small work groups, the staff leader immediately gets the group into the planning and the carrying on of the work. As soon as he can, he moves into the background and serves as counselor and resource person rather than as chairman of the group.

An important step in obtaining involvement of participants in the operation of the workshop is the formation of a planning committee. This committee is composed of representatives of each work group and the staff. It has responsibility for scheduling and revising the program to meet the needs of participants and for establishing policy and procedures. This committee seeks the recommendations of each workshop member concerning needed changes.

In forming a schedule, each work group and workshop committee submits to the planning committee the activities it wants scheduled. The planning committee coordinates the requests and formulates a schedule, which is distributed to each workshop member. By this process it is possible to maintain flexibility in the program and at the same time to give each workshop member the security of a definite schedule around which he can plan his individual actions. The schedule usually includes a variety of activities: general sessions, coffee hours, work groups, social activities, arts and crafts, and excursions. Time for informal conversation and social activities pays handsome dividends.

Means of communication among work groups must be maintained by sharing the products of work groups, by using general sessions to exchange ideas among work groups, and by joining work groups together for meetings where they have common interests or can use the same resource people. The planning committee provides the machinery through which such coordination is made possible.

Before a workshop ends, the members will want to insure that the results of the workshop will be implemented. One way is to establish a method of maintaining communication by arranging for an exchange of resource material developed during the year, or to establish meeting times at which persons doing the same type of work can gather to exchange ideas and results. The official leader can assist in this follow-up by making sure that resource people will be available to assist workshop participants to carry on the work they have planned at the workshop.

There are many factors that affect the possibility that the plans generated in the workshop will be implemented at the local school. Was the activity of the workshop closely related to the needs of the teachers? Were official leaders and other teachers in the local school sensitized to the plans of the teachers in such a way that they can provide psychological and logistical support on a continuing basis?

The most important means of implementation will be the changes that take place in individuals during the workshop. A principal, whose seventh- and ninth-grade teachers had attended a workshop, writes:

> The workshop group of both seventh- and ninth-grade teachers gained such an insight into the experience curricula that now they not only check their practices against their philosophy, but they evidence conviction for, and confidence in, what they are attempting to do. I observe growth in self-direction, in planning ability, and in ability to work together in groups on the part of both teachers and pupils. We have, however, much yet to be achieved.
>
> The school is planning parent meetings. The difference in attitude and in eagerness to include parents between those who attended the workshop and those who did not is very noticeable. The workshop teachers evidence more security in talking with the parents and asking for their participation in discussion of such subjects as evaluation, characteristics, and needs of the age groups.
>
> The enthusiasm of the workshoppers has extended to other members of the faculty. The Spanish teacher is introducing an activity program in Spanish. The tenth-grade teachers have begun studying characteristics of tenth graders and are discussing adjustments to make to meet the pupil needs more effectively.

The official leader's functions in a workshop program are: to stimulate the original interest in a workshop; to pull together people who will be interested in planning a workshop; to secure facilities and staff members with whom to carry out plans; to serve as troubleshooter and coordinator during the workshop program; and to provide all the help and encouragement possible to those who implement ideas in their schools after the workshop is over.

A variation of the workshop that has been developed in some schools is the two- or three-day retreat or camp, which permits the faculty to get away from the school and other regular routines to think and plan together. In such meetings, the group process steps consist of isolating the concerns of the group, getting agreement on agenda, exploring problems under skillful discussion leadership, and arriving at consensus on steps that need to be taken. Retreats are used more for exploration, long-term planning, and agreement on point of view than for intensive work in the solution of simple problems.

The Pre-School Planning Conference

A supervisory procedure that is gaining widespread acceptance is the pre-school conference. Unlike its predecessor, the institute, it is a work session. It provides an opportunity for the staff of a school to give full time to work on program improvement.

The amount of time made available for pre-school conferences varies from one month to one or two days. The time is used to: develop a feeling of belonging on the staff; evaluate the existing program; identify problems; plan curriculum innovations; formulate new policies; plan the in-service program; agree on routine procedures; orient new teachers; give teachers opportunity to organize instructional materials; study the cumulative folders of incoming students and provide the opportunity for teachers and supervisors to begin cooperative planning.

The pre-school conference closely parallels the workshop as a supervisory procedure, but it has certain advantages: all staff members are present; it is recognized as a part of the work of all staff members, and it deals with the real problems of getting school under way.

Any group operation, whether it is an individual faculty meeting or a workshop, must be studied and revised to increase the quality and contribution of communication to the improvement of the school program.

Informal Communication Centers

Not all communication takes place through official channels. In fact, the formal communication may not be the real communication. The bulletins and the discussions in faculty meetings are the overt and approved communication. But the communication that determines action is the covert and informal communication in the cafeteria or at the bowling alley after school.

Supervisors should not try to combat or ignore informal communication. Rather, the informal system should be recognized, understood, and used to improve the educational situation for children. It is important to work in such a way that the formal communication more closely approximates the message of the informal. If administration and supervision have created a permissive atmosphere in which diversity is valued and used, the covert communication will be more like the overt. For this condition to be obtained, it is essential to build trust and the freedom to differ.

The informal communication is the real communication. It will exist whether the formal occurs or not. It will determine the group's norms and its goals. Informal communication should be recognized and cultivated. If it is hoped the staff will become a cohesive group with common values, steps should be taken to foster informal interaction. Social activities, attractive teacher lounges, and teacher work rooms are all efforts to provide situations for teachers to discuss problems informally. The ideas and agreements reached will be brought into the official channels if supervision operates in a manner that makes the informal interaction respectable. If the administration tries to repress the informal communication, it will find that it is unable to progress, because people listen to official statements and then act in terms of informal agreements.

The success of a school system is dependent upon the quality of communication in it. It is necessary to examine bulletins, meetings, conferences, and the social climate to determine whether they facilitate open and honest discussion and decisions by all or whether they lead to isolation, indifference, and covert resistance.

THE FUNCTIONS OF
SUPERVISION

Instructional supervision is assumed to have the functions (anticipated outcomes) of curriculum development and instructional improvement. Accordingly, Chapter 7 discusses curriculum development. Instructional improvement is developed as a function of supervisory action in Chapter 8.

7 Supervision Is Curriculum Development

The assumption that supervision is curriculum development demands not only a definition of curriculum, but a consideration of it as an important function of instructional supervisory behavior. Accordingly, in Chapter 7 a brief conceptualization of curriculum will be presented and followed by a discussion of the sources, forces, pressures, processes, decisions, and behaviors out of which the curriculum is wrought. The development and utilization of power including both authority and persuasion will be examined.

Curriculum

Lewis and Miel (1972) recently discussed the evolvement of a concept of curriculum. The author was influenced by the work of these authors in developing the section on curriculum.

One lingering definition of curriculum has been that it is the subject to be studied. This became the textbook, the course of study, or subject outline which was to serve as a guide to teachers. Often such materials were developed by the State Department of Education and became the official course of study. Sometimes these materials were prepared by committees of teachers and curriculum workers for a school system or a local school with great care and elaboration. Objectives were developed along with statements of the activities, materials, and procedures to be used to achieve the objectives. Methods and procedures for evaluation were also included. In some instances the materials were tried out and polished before they became the official curriculum of the school. But in all cases the curriculum was thought of as the subject matter to be learned and the proposed conditions for learning it.

In the early thirties Caswell and Campbell (1935) proposed a new way of thinking about the curriculum. They had observed the great efforts that had been made to develop curriculum guides but had also noticed that there was a lack of congruence between the guides and what they saw happening in the classroom. They also were impressed by the fact that teachers who participated in the development of these curriculum materials were more likely to utilize them in their teaching. As a result of these observations and others, they began to think of curriculum as what happens to students in school.

This kind of definition of curriculum shifts the emphasis to the student and what is actually happening to him rather than a course of study. Later curriculum writers defined the curriculum as engagement opportunities provided by the school. Gordon Mackenzie (1964, p. 402) defined the curriculum as follows:

> It appeared to be more fruitful, therefore, to define the curriculum as the learner's engagements with various aspects of the environment which have been planned under the direction of school. The assumption here is that engagements can be observed and to some extent controlled.

It is apparent that Mackenzie is moving toward a definition that will make it possible to study the curriculum since he shifts the emphasis from what happens to the child (very difficult to study) to the conditions with which the child interacts.

Art Lewis and Alice Miel (1972, p. 27) have recently defined curriculum:

> The curriculum is taken to be a set of intentions about opportunities for engagement of persons-to-be-educated with other persons and with things (all bearers of information, processes, techniques, and values) in certain arrangements of time and space.

Lewis and Miel's definition is consistent with Mackenzie's except that it adds the concept of "intent." Mackenzie speaks of engagement opportunities with which the learner interacts, and Lewis and Miel are defining planned engagement opportunities with which it is anticipated that learners will engage. This is a useful distinction. Therefore, in this book supervisory behavior directed toward the planning and development of intended engagement opportunities for learners is discussed under curriculum development. Activities which focus on the actualization and improvement of engagement opportunities will be examined in Chapter 8, "Supervision Is Improving Instruction."

Curriculum means many things: the design and structure of the curriculum plan; the organization of the curriculum that is described in curriculum bulletins and teachers' guides, the instructional materials that are approved and supplied by the school system, the beliefs about the educational process that represent the consensus of the teaching staff, the course syllabi, the engagement opportunities that the teacher organizes for pupils, the school environment, both intellectual and physical, and many others. Together, all these factors constitute the program that the learner experiences as he attends a school. Supervision has the responsibility for effecting continuous improvement in the curriculum. The approach to change may focus on any of these facets as well as many others.

Rationale for the Curriculum

Dr. Ralph Tyler (1950, pp. 1-2) has suggested four fundamental questions which need to be answered in order to develop a curriculum and plan of study:

1. What educational purposes should the school seek to attain?
2. What educational experiences can be provided that are likely to attain these purposes?
3. How can these educational experiences be effectively organized?
4. How can we determine whether these purposes are being attained?

It is not our purpose to attempt to answer these questions. This needs to be done at the teacher, school, system, state, and national level in terms of the demands of a particular situation. It is not even our purpose to discuss the study of these questions in great depth since this has been done by scholars who specialize in the study of curriculum planning. Rather, it is the purpose of this section to identify the questions, define the process of answering them, and discuss instructional supervisory behavior as it relates to this process.

PURPOSES OF EDUCATION

The institution of public education is a sub-system of a larger society and, therefore, receives certain input from the society. Examples of input from the society would include students (clients), professional personnel, financial resources, and specification of educational objectives. The society establishes and supports a number of sub-systems on the assumption that these sub-systems contribute to the well-being of the society. When the society perceives that a particular sub-system is not meeting its expectations, the support system is likely to be challenged. The system of education is no exception. Societal expectations are one important source of educational objectives. But our society is pluralistic; therefore it is characterized by conflicting values, power thrusts, and expectations for education. It is also true that societal expectations are nebulous and very general and, therefore, require constant study, definition, and interpretation on the part of the educational institution at the school, system, state, and national levels.

The students constitute another important source of educational objectives. Student needs, hopes, aspirations, interests, achievement levels, and attitudes are important sources of data for developing educational goals and need to be studied on a comprehensive, intensive, and continuous basis. Such study needs to be done at the classroom, school, system, state, and national level and serves as input for the development of educational goals and behavioral objectives. Since students are a part of society, the study of students contributes to the understanding of societal expectations and the study of society contributes to the understanding of student needs.

The organized disciplines of study have been an important source of subject matter content and educational objectives. For many years the organized "learnings" of the disciplines were "translated" by subject matter specialists into subject matter for the school curriculum. But in recent years there has been a shift from this approach to an attempt to provide learning experiences for students that will help them develop a grasp of the structure and methodology of the discipline. In other words, the idea is to let the student experience the theoretical formulations, hypothesis testing, and synthesizing process as the scientist experiences it. There is little question that this is one of the important sources of educational objectives.

There are legally constituted bodies such as school boards and state boards of education that have the responsibility to study, define, and interpret from these sources the general goals of education. This is a continuous process which requires the services of professional educators, including teachers, supervisors, and administrators. It is necessary to develop general educational objectives from the statements of terminal goals. This is a professional job which requires the participation of administrators, supervisors, teachers, and students. Instructional supervisors not only participate in this operation, but also have special responsibility to facilitate both the process and the diffusion of the product at the next level of specification.

The general statement of objectives at the national, state, system, and school level provides a framework within which more specific objectives can be developed for specific students. It is necessary for teachers, students, and supervisors to work together in the development of teaching objectives in order to assure some congruence among teacher, student, and system expectations. This process will be discussed in the chapter on the improvement of instruction.

INTENDED ENGAGEMENT OPPORTUNITIES

Intended engagement opportunities are the conditions which are developed in anticipation of the instructional process. The assumption is that the student can achieve certain behavioral objectives through a particular engagement. Examples of engagement opportunities could include packaged materials, films, and activities. Such materials could be developed within or outside the school system. The planning and implementation for the development of such materials is an important function of instructional supervision which should involve students, teachers, and administrators. The selection and actualization of engagement opportunities is a teacher responsibility with special levels of support available as needed. The process of instruction and the function of supervision in this process will be discussed in the chapter on instructional improvement.

EVALUATION OF BEHAVIORAL OUTCOMES

As a sub-system of the society the institution of public education is accountable to the society for the achievement of educational goals and objectives. This fact necessitates a rigorous system for evaluation of the objectives.

Evaluation is a process not only for determining the extent to which educational objectives are being achieved, but for clarifying the conditions of learning and therefore, possible relations between learning conditions and learning outcomes. It therefore provides the basis for a continuous program of curriculum and instructional improvement. Local schools can evaluate engagement opportunities that are being provided and actualized. Individual teachers can become sensitive to the outcomes of their own teaching efforts and develop new approaches based on continuous evaluation. An adequate system of evaluation requires that objectives be stated in a form which defines the performance that it is hoped the student will achieve. This makes it possible to design a program to determine the extent to which students can demonstrate the appropriate behavior. This kind of data provides feedback for teachers as they continue to develop and actualize engagement opportunities for learners.

Sources of Pressure for Curriculum Change

Curriculum change is attempted by many people. The national government seeks to bring about curriculum change by making available federal funds for special projects. One example is the National Defense Education Act of 1958. The legislative body of the national government decided that public schools should put greater emphasis on science, mathematics, foreign languages, and guidance. Funds were made available to support curriculum development and teacher education activities in these areas and to supply resource persons who would exert leadership in improving the curricula. Pressure for change resulted. In the mid 1960s additional federal funds were supplied for other kinds of curriculum improvement, especially improvement of the program for the underprivileged. In the early 1970s there has been support for career education.

Curriculum change may also be initiated by foundations that make available funds to enable schools to undertake innovations in certain areas. For example, during the 1950s, the Ford Foundation made contributions to experimentation with education by television.

Community dissatisfaction with the existing program may lead to curriculum change. If a large segment of the community believes that reading can be taught more effectively, it can exert pressure on the board of education that results in efforts to change the program of teaching reading.

Associations of scholars that believe that more attention should be given to their discipline in the public schools can exert pressure to secure the addition of more courses in their field to a public school curriculum.

Persons who have access to the mass media can advocate a point of view that may influence boards of education to underwrite curriculum development in certain areas.

Accrediting associations may establish standards that must be met if schools are to be accredited, and these requirements lead to the initiation of curriculum change.

The impetus for curriculum change can also come from student dissatisfaction and frustration. In the early 1970s students have been pushing for relevance in the curriculum and a more meaningful role in curriculum decisions.

Curriculum change can come about as a result of study of students and educational outcomes by the professional staff. Data from this kind of study can create dissatisfaction on the part of the professional staff and a motivation to change.

Finally, the board of education may decide that curriculum change is needed; the administration may recommend to the board of education that support be given to certain curriculum innovations; a curriculum council may decide to bring about a curriculum change; the faculty of a given school may decide that certain changes should be made; an individual teacher may recommend changes and, if he is able to influence enough members of the staff, secure the change; or he may, within existing policies, carry on innovations within his own classroom. The responsibility for the initiation of curriculum change has no preassigned location.

The Changed Role of Supervision in Curriculum Development

When the first edition of *Supervision for Better Schools* was written, the major impetus for curriculum change lay in the supervisory staff. For the most part, the public, the national government, the mass media, and associations of scholars ignored the need for change in the curriculum of the public schools. Persons designated as curriculum directors, supervisors, and teachers with a professional dedication assumed the role of change agents. The point of view underlying the first two editions of *Supervision for Better Schools* was that the supervisor had to carry the major responsibility for the initiation of change.

By the mid 1960s this condition had changed completely. Persons in the national government, foundations, scholars, students, and the general public had come to realize that the type of education provided determines the future of our society. Each group with its own vision of what the society should become had begun to exert effort to secure the kind of educational program that would realize their dreams. Public school administrators found themselves confronted by many different demands for curriculum change. The task had become that of deciding *which* change was to be made rather than *whether* change should be made.

The supervisory staff in a school system found itself in a different role. Instead of devoting a major portion of its effort to the development of ideas for change, it found itself confronted with the task of assisting in the decision as to desirable changes, assisting in innovation, supplying the many types of resource help necessary in innovation, coordinating the incorporation of innovations into the program in such a way that student programs would have continuity, assisting in the evaluation of innovation, helping the staff become aware of the variety of alternatives being proposed, assisting in the choice of the alternative that seemed most appropriate in the system, and developing a plan and design that would determine the types of innovations to be supported financially.

Two Approaches to Curriculum Change

Many people during the late 1950s and early 1960s decided that the local school system could no longer serve as the unit for curriculum development. It was felt that curriculum development was so important that it could not be left to the kind of efforts that could be mounted with the monetary and personnel resources available to the local school level.

In many respects, it would seem that 1957, the year of Sputnik, was an important dividing line in proposals of strategy for curriculum change. During the previous three or four decades, when curriculum making was changing from textbook writing to program planning, most proposals were rooted to a philosophy of pragmatic evolution. Beginning in the early 1930s it was believed that the best educational program would be produced by curriculum changes made by individual teachers, faculties of a given building, the staff of a system, and, in a few cases, by the state department of education. Since 1957, there has been a shift on the part of many to a belief in a strategy of directed change. Persons, often those outside of public education, assume that they know the change that is desirable and then use the best strategy they can devise to bring about the desired change.

ASSUMPTIONS IN THE PRAGMATIC APPROACH

During the pragmatic period, there were certain assumptions that were made about the strategy of change. Some of these, stated perhaps in over-simplified terms, are the following:

Change in the curriculum is effected most efficiently at the local school building level. Koopman, Miel, and Misner (1943), among others, enunciated this assumption in *Democracy in School Administration.* It was their belief that if the curriculum is to change, the teachers must change, and the teachers must change through their involvement in curriculum development. Since it is almost impossible to involve all teachers in system-wide planning, the planning and involvement should be at the local building level.

Change in the curriculum occurs as people change through their participation in decision-making related to the curriculum. With the emphasis on curriculum change at the local building level during the late 1940s and early 1950s, a number of persons (Koopman, 1943 and Spears, 1957) including many curriculum leaders, attempted to describe the process through which involvement could be deepened by participation in decision-making.

Change in the curriculum is produced through in-service education that develops new teacher perceptions and skills. Spears (1957) in his book, *Curriculum Planning Through In-Service Programs,* described the ramifications of this assumption.

Change in the curriculum is effected by in-service education of the principal, which produces a change in his work style. Sugg (1955) found a vast difference in the amount and kind of curriculum changes in schools where principals followed one type of work style as opposed to curriculum changes in buildings with principals who followed a different work style. Grobman (1958) reported that in-service education can be effective in changing the work style of principals.

Change in the curriculum is effected by supplying teachers with consultants who assist them with innovation. From the time of the Eight-Year-Study through curriculum movements of the early 1950s, such as intergroup education and economic education, attempts were made to bring about change by using consultants to support those who were doing the experimenting.

Change in the curriculum is effected by providing workshop opportunities for key teachers in a building who then become resource persons and leaders for other teachers on the staff. This assumption has guided the thinking of most of the organizations attempting to influence the curriculum from outside the regular administrative channel during the two decades prior to 1957. Workshops in economic education, family finance, intergroup education, and human relations are examples of the implementation of this assumption.

A Rethinking of Assumptions

Even before 1957, some observers of the process of curriculum change had reached the conclusion that some of the assumptions of the 1930s, 1940s, and 1950s needed rethinking. Teacher turnover during and after World War II was so great (from 10 to 50 percent a year), depending on the location of the school, that changes produced in teachers by in-service education failed to provide lasting curriculum changes. The in-service experiences provided modification in the perceptions of the teachers with regard to themselves, their role, and the situation; so the teachers made changes. But then they moved to another school system, and the residue left in the locality that had provided the in-service education was not as great as anticipated or as the situation demanded. With rapid teacher turnover, the process of changing curriculum design and structure needed to be modified if the changes made were to have any lasting effect.

Second, it was seen that changes in curriculum produced by the supplying of funds for a specific innovation were quickly dissipated when the funds were exhausted or when newer innovations received the extra financial support. An innovation that was not discarded or supplanted in a five- to ten-year period was unusual. In many schools, instead of innovation's being a sincere effort to produce major change in the program, it became a process of keeping up with the Joneses, and there was no integration of the innovations into the curriculum structure.

Third, change in the curriculum that was initiated by or identified with a forceful leader was modified when he was removed from the situation. If he left the situation for a better job, the administrator who followed him often lacked the same vision or had another vision and allowed the innovations of his predecessor to erode. If the forceful leader was fired because he had created opposition, innovations that he had brought about were eradicated as quickly as possible. Such programs seemed to relate closely to the personality and values of the leader, and the quick turnover in school administrators made lasting impact unlikely.

Fourth, changes in the curriculum that aroused the opposition of the community power structure were soon curtailed or modified. Strategies for making major curriculum changes proved ineffective if laymen had not involved the community power structure leaders directly or indirectly in thinking through what should be done.

Assumptions in Directed Change

In 1957, many persons were caused to rethink the question of who should make decisions concerning curriculum change. How free should a professional teacher be to decide what he would teach and how he would teach it? Should he be free to ignore new knowledge if he so wishes? Should he be free to use less effective instructional techniques? Is the faculty of a local school free to refuse to consider curriculum improvements or to ignore the necessity for promoting types of growth that may be needed in the community and in the nation?

Since the fifties, some persons concerned with the national welfare have advocated directed change. They believe that change should not be equated with chance, but with development; and that innovation should be linked to long-term goals. The advocates of this position make the following assumptions:

Some persons in government, foundations, universities, public schools, or somewhere else must decide on the desired goals and plan innovations designed to promote them. How the decision-makers will be selected is usually not discussed.

Basic research, program design, and field testing should be done by well-defined curriculum development projects. The best experts possible should be brought together to design a program based on the best available research, and it should be tested in many field situations to determine its quality and its adaptability. Huge sums of money and expert personnel are needed for the design and the testing, and the procedure is more expensive than a single system can underwrite.

Major instructional innovations should be introduced by the administration, because it can marshal the necessary authority and precipitate the decisions necessary for adoption. Each local school system should choose the prepackaged instructional systems that are appropriate for it. After a system has been developed, boards of education and staffs must be informed that such a system exists, must be convinced of its desirability, and must make the decision that it will be adopted.

The prepackaged instructional system can be introduced despite original opposition or apathy on the part of the teachers. Although some may oppose it, they will soon begin to accept it. It is stated that faculty members begin to prefer new methods within four months to a year after the introduction. They develop a sense of commitment to the new methods, because these are the ones they are using.

The informal communication system determines whether formal presentations will be heard. It is important for the innovator to recognize that the formal organization is not necessarily the real power in the organization; he must seek to know and work through the informal system.

The earlier acceptors of the innovation, according to Barnett (1962) will be the dissident, the indifferent, the resentful, and the disaffected. They have nothing to lose and will readily accept the new. The later acceptors will be influenced by the prestige of those who sponsor and create.

Real or assumed knowledge of the innovator's identity is a major variable in the acceptance of a particular innovation. Teachers will be willing to try an innovation that is advocated by someone whose reputation they respect or who is associated with an organization or institution that they revere. To secure a change, many authorities must be ready to lend their prestige and their personalities to the cause of directed change.

The key to successful innovation is providing assistance to teachers as they begin to implement the adopted program. If attention is given to the teachers by the principals or other persons provided to assist them, it gives the teachers an exhilarating effect that enables them to be more successful with and become more enthusiastic about the innovation.

The most persuasive experience that can be provided to convince staffs of the value of an innovation is to make provision for them to visit a successful new program and see it in action. No matter how much is said or written about a new program, it is not as effective in convincing teachers of its value as their seeing it in successful operation in a situation that they can identify as being similar to their own.

Because of teacher turnover, a continuous program of in-service education in the skills necessary to implement the innovation must be available for new teachers brought into the system. It is not possible to think of providing a program of in-service education on a one-shot basis. Each new teacher must be inducted into the instructional system.

The process of curriculum change contains three steps—innovation, diffusion, and integration. According to the advocates of directed change, innovation is developed on the outside, and the process described in the preceding paragraphs leads to diffusion and integration.

Changes in social systems are much more difficult than changes in individuals or groups. An individual changes in terms of his needs and purposes or his motivation. Groups change through interaction, but there is greater fear of a change in the organization, because of the results of structural alteration.

Some Second Thoughts

The period of the sixties was a time of great effort for educational innovation. Proposals for change came from a variety of sources including foundations, federal government, scholars, private enterprise, and many others. Examples of proposed changes included: team teaching, nongraded program, informal education, computer assisted instruction, curriculum changes proposed by the "scholars," programmed learning and a wide variety of packaged materials. The "directed change" approach was utilized and the call and thrust for educational change was heard and seen around the nation. What has happened as a result of this great effort?

In a study by John Goodlad, Francis Klein, and others (1970), a major conclusion was that nothing much had changed in educational institutions. There was little evidence that teachers were guided by clear understanding of the behavioral outcomes for children which they taught. "Telling" and "questioning" were still the dominant "techniques" used by teachers. Students were not found to be discovering for themselves through inquiry. The textbook was still the prime medium of instruction, and the use of a variety of media was not observed. The organization and presentation of subject matter did not provide for individual differences. Teachers were in general unaware or unable to develop practices consistent with modern principles of learning. School buildings were still drab with egg-crate designs and self-contained classrooms. In short, schools and teaching were found not to have changed very much in spite of the innovations of the sixties (Goodlad and Klein, 1970, pp. 77-94). More study and research is needed to determine the success and failure of attempts to change before and since 1957.

It is obvious that the contrast of the two approaches, *prior-* and *post-*1957, is sharply drawn to highlight the issues. Obviously, some innovations before 1957 were characterized by the second group of assumptions, and many current approaches to curriculum change still rely on pragmatic evolution.

It is also obvious that in the years ahead, there will be many sources of change in the curriculum. Many organizations and individuals will attempt to bring about the changes that they deem desirable. Each school system will be forced to make decisions from among conflicting proposals. Even if the board of education and the educators in charge of a system wanted to abdicate, they could not. The competing pressure groups from the outside will not allow it. Each system must devise a procedure for deciding the curriculum changes that it will make. It cannot simply abdicate and let others make the decision, because there are competing pressures from the outside to determine the curriculum. Decisions must be made ultimately by the local school system, the local school, and the teacher.

THE COMPLEXITY OF THE PROCESS

The legal decision concerning curriculum change is a decision by the board of education and the superintendent. How a system gets to the place where this decision is reached depends upon the theory of change that is being followed in that system.

One theory of change would postulate that the administrator can make a decision and then, by manipulation and influence, secure the adoption of that change by the members of the staff. The authority of the administrator will be used to insure that people follow the directives that originate from the administrative office. The supervisory staff will be used to make sure that teachers implement the change and to assist them in developing the skills to carry out the change.

The theory of change recommended here is based on the postulate that a lasting change occurs only as the people who must implement it are convinced of its worth. The strategy becomes a question of how to involve people in the process of making intelligent decisions.

It is recognized that each group develops some common goals and norms. These norms are the products of interaction and govern behavior of the members of the group. Any member of the group may advance the ideas that ultimately become the goals. But each idea stands in the open marketplace and is accepted or rejected in terms of its merits as judged by the purposes of individuals and the total group.

It is important to recognize that in a large school system there are many groups. One group will be the central office staff, and it will be composed of a number of small psychological groups. Each faculty also constitutes a group and it is composed of small psychological groups. The school system staff is composed of many groups; and if the system is large, there is little development of groupness in the total staff. It is much more likely that departments and faculties will have goals than it is that the total system staff will have common goals. It is also more likely that the teachers of a given subject matter or given grade level will have common goals and norms than it is that the total system staff will have common goals and norms.

When anyone gets an idea of change that he hopes will occur, he faces the task of planning a strategy that will help various groups in the system staff have the opportunity to examine the idea and perhaps to adopt it.

There are at least three stages in the process from the idea to the adoption. First, there must be dissemination of the idea among all the groups that it is hoped will consider it. Second, when individuals or groups within the total staff become convinced of its worth, they will need to have the opportunity to demonstrate it. The demonstrations themselves become a part of the dissemination process because they give concrete illustrations of the idea. Persons who have been unaffected by the verbal description of the idea will have opportunity to see merit in it for themselves when they see the demonstration process. Seeing an idea in action increases the possibility that people will be able to examine it. The demonstrations provide a basis for discussion that enter into the forming of norms which permit other people to experiment with the idea or lead to their rejection and elimination of it. If norms are developed which make possible individuals and schools joining in the demonstration, much of the process of adoption of the program into the system is already accomplished. The remaining step is merely sharing the skills which enable teachers to conduct their programs in the demonstrated manner.

Refereeing Curriculum Issues

When a proposal for curriculum change is brought to the school by an outside agency, the school staff must exercise its responsibility for decisions concerning the educational program that will be offered. A project is not more worthy because the preparation of instructional material was underwritten by some foundation rather than having been prepared with the backing of a publishing company. The authors in either case should have their wares evaluated in the open marketplace.

A project director has no more right to use classrooms of children for experimentation than any other author who wants a tryout of his materials. School people have the same responsibility for judging whether they should allow such an experimenter to use their pupils.

One curriculum project director of the early 1960s stated, "I get my directives from the world of mathematics. The hell with mental health." School officials have a responsibility to decide whether or not the products of a person who gets his directives from a discipline are suitable materials for use in their schools; they must decide whether the materials produced will be more harmful than helpful to most children.

A curriculum project product must be judged by the contribution that it can make to a given school situation. Simply being the producer of something new does not mean that a person is entitled to have access to the facilities of a school system, or that the new product is better than existing ones. Also, the responsibility for attaining a sequence and a balance in the curriculum rests with the curriculum workers of a given school system. The curriculum innovators are working with only parts of the curriculum. They are producing segments, which can be inserted into the curriculum at appropriate places. To date, no sequence has been developed in any field from kindergarten through twelfth grade. No producers of new curricula in subject matter fields seem to be thinking seriously of the pattern the total curriculum should have.

In a period in which many forces are attempting to bring about curriculum change, the assistant superintendent for curriculum and instruction, who represents the superintendent, must serve as the referee in many struggles for control of the curriculum. Representatives of curriculum projects or lay groups that become convinced of the importance of particular projects attempt to influence the board of education and the superintendent to install a particular instructional package in the school program. Although the proposed innovation may have merit, it may not be as desirable for a given community as some other alternatives.

The head of the supervisory staff must not be stampeded. While he should encourage desirable change, the decision to move in a given direction should not be made without consideration of a variety of alternatives evaluated in terms of the needs of the local situation. He should insist that there be a hearing for any proposal that is being considered. If there are other programs in the same field that have been developed by other groups, representatives of the competing projects should be asked to describe their product and its special features. Opportunities should be provided for members of the supervisory staff, interested principals, and teachers to study the various curriculum materials. Not only will much valuable in-service growth take place for the staff members who are involved in the consideration, but the choice can be made with full knowledge of all the staff and in terms of the needs of the particular population being served by the system.

The important principle involved is that the administrator should not make the decision without thorough consideration by the people who will be involved in its implementation. If proponents know that any particular curriculum package will be evaluated by many people in the system before it is accepted, they will operate in a different manner. Their contacts will not be with boards of education or superintendents alone. They will want to discuss their program with the teachers, principals, and supervisors in the system.

Struggles for the adoption of particular curriculum projects will be decreased if the school system has an energetic curriculum development program in progress. In such a school, the members of the supervisory staff will be searching throughout the state, region, and nation for projects that seem to be preparing worthwhile materials. They will present these developments for study and consideration before anyone attempts to sell the board of education on a particular project. If members of the community and proponents of a particular project know that a school system conducts a regular and consistent program of study and development, their actions will be guided by this knowledge. They will know that this is a school system that does not buy a pig in a poke, that no particular pattern will be accepted without study, tryout, and evaluation, and that the system is applying criteria in its judgment of curriculum materials that prevent the adoption of an inappropriate product. With such an understanding of the situation, only the most foolhardy proponent would attempt to "sell" the superintendent or the board of education without submitting his plan to the unit that is studying all the materials that are available.

The Curriculum Policy Decision-Makers

But who in the local system will make the decision? Should it be the superintendent? the board of education? the supervisory staff? the school faculty? the individual teacher?

Obviously, the board of education makes the official decision. But the board of education does not usually make the decision on its own. It turns to its professional staff for recommendations. Who in the professional staff will make the decision?

Ultimately, the decision must be implemented by the classroom teacher. If the perceptions and motivations of the classroom teacher are ignored, any decision will not be successfully implemented either through ignorance on the part of the classroom teacher or through subtle resistance. In deciding upon who will be included in the decision-making process, the supervisory staff must decide whether it believes that it can influence and manipulate classroom teachers so that they will do what the supervisory staff decides, or whether it must bring the classroom teacher into the decision-making process.

The decision, in the opinion of the writer, will depend primarily on the assumption that the central office staff makes regarding the professional nature of the classroom teacher. If it believes that the classroom teacher is a professional person operating in terms of principles and commitment, it will seek ways of involving the teacher in the decision. If it believes that the classroom teacher is a technician whose function is to carry out directives without professional integrity, the decision will be restricted to those persons who are designated as curriculum planners.

The decision about inclusion of teachers becomes more difficult when the staff of a system is one in which there is rapid turnover. If the tenure of a teacher in a system is of short duration can that teacher be allowed to participate in the decisions? Should the assumption be made that any person who accepts a job in a given school system accepts the responsibility for carrying out the policies and program that were established before he came? Or should it be assumed that professional teachers have learned to make intelligent decisions in other systems and can in this one?

If the staff assumes that teachers should participate in the decision-making with regard to curriculum change, the question becomes what types of decisions should be open to all members of the teaching staff? What types of decisions are appropriate for the faculty of a single school? What questions must be decided at the system-wide level? How can individual teachers participate in system-wide decisions?

Certain guidelines can be established.   All teachers should have the right to identify the types of problems that they see in the curriculum of the school in which they teach. These teacher concerns should be fed into the decision-making channels. Teachers should have the opportunity to react to innovations that are being considered for system-wide adoption. Within these restrictions, the supervisory staff should feel free to move ahead to innovation and change.

Teachers should also know the limitations within which they are free to make decisions about change without consulting the faculty of which they are a member or the supervisory staff of the school system.

Principals should be informed of innovations that individual teachers are attempting, and if these innovations will affect the rest of the school, the principal should be consulted before they are undertaken. The principal should be a major force in the decisions concerning curriculum changes that will affect the entire school. If the local school has a curriculum committee, the principal will undoubtedly function as the executive secretary or as a very active member. Certainly, he should be aware of proposals that are being considered and help the faculty examine them in the light of other alternatives. He also has the responsibility for implementing the decisions that are reached by the local faculty.

Beyond the local school, the principals should be represented in the curriculum decisions by a representative chosen by the principals' group. Principals as a group should have an opportunity to discuss changes that are contemplated in system-wide curriculum policy. The results of their deliberation should be fed into the curriculum council.

Some representative body of teachers, supervisors, and principals should have the final decision concerning the recommendations that will be made to the superintendent and board of education. This group may be called a curriculum council, a planning committee, or a program development committee, but it serves the function of being the official policy recommending agency. Its membership should include a representative of each faculty, a representative of the principals, and a representative of the supervisory staff.

If these principles are followed, each member of the professional staff is represented in decisions related to curriculum policy.

The Organization for Curriculum Development

The curriculum council should establish the framework within which local schools operate. It should recommend to the superintendent and the board of education those changes in policy that affect system-wide curriculum and instruction, including the development and evaluation of system-wide goals. It should have responsibility for recommending innovations that the council believes should be tried out in the schools. It should encourage the supervisory staff to establish and conduct the in-service program that will enable the system to implement the decisions that have been made with regard to system-wide change, be on the lookout for innovations that are proving effective in other systems and bring information about these innovations to the council for consideration, support and assist individual teachers and schools with innovations that are being tried out on a demonstration basis.

The curriculum council serves as the nucleus for the formation of curriculum policy, but it will be relatively useless without an organization for initiating and implementing curriculum decisions at the building level. Each school in the system needs an extension of the curriculum council. It may be called what the system prefers, but there should be a curriculum committee in each building which is responsible for interpreting the system structure of goals and curriculum policies and developing and evaluating the local school structure of educational goals and curriculum policies for consideration by the faculty. The curriculum committee in each building should be composed of representative selected teachers and the principal. It should identify problems it thinks the curriculum council should investigate and make decisions concerning the type of in-service opportunities needed by the faculty. Where possible, the chairman of the curriculum committee should serve as the building representative on the curriculum council. The organization described can do much to coordinate the curriculum development program of the system.

The executive officer of the curriculum council should be the assistant superintendent for curriculum and instruction. All proposals for innovation from outside the system come to him directly, through the board of education, or from the superintendent. The supervisory staff works with him and keeps him informed of new curriculum developments within and without the system. His relationship with principals provides sources of information. In addition to knowing what is going on, he is in a position to implement the decisions of the council. He can recommend to the superintendent and to the board. He has the staff to act. He can work with the principals to secure needed cooperation.

The supervisory staff carries the primary responsibility for the development and implementation of curriculum policy. Its members are a source of information and initiation. As individual supervisors become aware of demonstrations that are available in other school systems, they should visit them and bring back to the local system descriptions of practices that should be considered there. They should feel free to form study groups that will investigate new programs developed by massive curriculum projects or state groups, to secure ideas that individual teachers or individual schools within the system may wish to try out. They should assume the responsibility of keeping fully informed about all experimental efforts in the local system and making information about these available to the total administrative and teaching staff. They are the executive officers assigned to implement a program recommended by curriculum council and approved by the board of education.

Executive action by a staff member may consist of locating teachers or schools that wish to experiment with a hypothesis, serving as consultant to the teachers and administrators who are experimenting, assisting in evaluating an innovation, conducting in-service education related to a project, and preparing a report of recommendations growing out of a specific demonstration.

The Organization and Operation of the Central Office Supervisory Staff

The central supervisory staff has four kinds of responsibilities: to project a blueprint of what the curriculum in that school may look like five years in the future; to develop hypotheses that are important ones to explore either through research or demonstration; to support and assist in research and demonstration; and to facilitate the maintenance of the quality of the on-going program.

These responsibilities require that the supervisory staff include persons with different competencies and responsibilities. In a school system of any size, a general supervisor is no longer sufficient. Specialists in subject matter, media, evaluation, research, and dissemination are also required. This need for specialists has led some people to assume that general supervisors are no longer needed. These people have failed to recognize the necessity of a supervisory team composed of both specialists and generalists rather than a generalist who tries to be all things to all people.

Curriculum development for the supervisory staff consists of research, demonstration, and dissemination. The first responsibility of the staff is the collection and evaluation of existing research to insure that the system has available the data pertinent to the issue under consideration.

A wonderful period for supervisors has arrived. Much of the frustration many have felt with regard to collecting information about research has been alleviated. The U.S. Office of Education has set up E.R.I.C., Educational Research Information Center, which makes it possible to secure existing research that relates to a given problem. Research and Development Centers have been established at various major universities throughout the country, which have a responsibility for doing research on a basic educational problem. Local school districts can turn to E.R.I.C. or a Research and Development Center and request information that will help form hypotheses or make decisions.

Further, new regional educational laboratories assist in curriculum development in local school systems. No longer must local supervisors work alone. The laboratories make it possible for education departments, institutions of higher learning, public school systems, and lay people of a geographic area to work together on the problems of curriculum improvement. The regional laboratories also make possible the funding of demonstrations and research in local school systems. They add one more dimension to the possibility for curriculum experimentation and dissemination. The regional educational laboratories have experienced some difficulty in getting support, but it is our feeling that the idea is valid and that some form of regional educational planning and support will survive.

Another factor that affects what supervisors do is the participation of the national government through various programs of education. When historians of the year 2000 look back to 1965, they are going to say that it was the year that the federal government said by legal action that it could no longer be content for any youngster to have less than a quality education. It was the beginning of a major federal government support for program development.

A basic function of the supervisory staff is carrying on curriculum planning activities. There are very few supervisory staffs with a person who has a clear picture of the hypotheses being tried out and who knows how these relate to one another or how experimental programs are being used to develop a new program for the future. This condition must be improved if satisfactory progress is to be made with the available resources. The supervisory staff must include persons who can state the present structure of the curriculum, project a blueprint for the future, and identify the hypotheses that need to be tested.

In addition to its responsibility for developing a curriculum design and for clarifying hypotheses to be tested, the supervisory staff is also responsible for developing proposals for desired research, demonstration and dissemination activites, and for consultation and leadership in experimental activities.

The transition from the present to a blueprint for the future is accomplished by following a process that will involve approval by the curriculum council and implementation by the supervisory staff.

1. Certain hypotheses are formed concerning desirable practices or curriculum design based on information secured from research or demonstration in another situation. Or the hypothesis might be formed by a member of the staff based on his experimentation and experience.

2. The promising hypotheses are investigated by research conducted in the system. This experimentation consists of finding someone or some staff that is willing to try out the hypothesis and have the results evaluated. The research personnel of the supervisory unit are made available to assist in the design and the execution of the experiment. Any school system that is seriously concerned with improving its program will have a number of experimental activities under way at all times. These activities are ways of collecting evidence concerning the value of hypotheses and determining which ones should be given further tryout.

3. When the research has been completed, the results will be presented to the total supervisory staff. If the results seem promising, the staff will secure permission from the curriculum council for experimentation with the idea in demonstration centers within the system, staffed by teachers and school staffs that are in agreement with the idea and are willing to try it. Announcements concerning these demonstration centers are made to the total staff with invitations to staff members who are interested to visit the demonstrations. Opportunities should be provided for visitors to discuss what is being tried and to discuss results as they become available.

4. On the basis of the results of the demonstration and the sentiments for further expansion of the idea throughout the system, proposals for change in curriculum policies are made to the curriculum council.

5. Information concerning the proposal will be made available to the total staff, and local faculties will have opportunities to discuss ramifications of the proposed change. Through these discussions, pitfalls and needed modifications will be identified. Representatives of the faculty will carry back to the curriculum council the reactions of their staffs.

6. If the reaction of the various faculties is positive, the policy will be adopted for the entire system. If it is not, further investigation and experimentation will be necessary. Perhaps options should be given to certain schools to move to the new policy while other schools retain present practices. A variation of this plan may be the establishment of a work group employed to spend a portion of the summer in revising and improving the programs that have been developed. The revision should then be resubmitted to the faculties for discussion and reaction.

The procedure outlined calls for securing new ideas, making them available to the total staff, providing demonstrations which enable people to evaluate the proposal more effectively, and thinking together, which leads to a consensus to adopt a new policy. The process depends on the principle of infection. As the central staff gives support and assistance to the teachers engaging in experimental effort, other teachers around them will look at what the experimental teachers are doing. Changes in other teachers come through their interactions with the teachers of classes involved in an experiment.

The process of curriculum development provides for initiation of innovation from many sources; establishment of an organization that provides for coordination and involvement; continuous experimentation based on the best hypotheses that can be formed from research and world-wide curriculum activities; multiple curricular innovations to permit many teachers to find curriculum improvement activities that they deem important; establishment of experiments and demonstrations in schools and classrooms, where the staff members involved believe in the hypothesis being tested; opportunities for other staff members to visit and discuss experiments and demonstrations; careful collection of evidence; and encouragement of continued questions and proposals for modification of the blueprint for the curriculum.

The supervisor's role is one of continuous studying of new ideas, encouraging teachers to be creative, assisting teachers in their attempts to implement a hypothesis, conducting in-service activities organized around the study of a demonstration, and aiding in the collecting of evidence concerning the success of an experimental effort. It is the role of a student and coworker—not that of a proponent or advocate.

The Community Power Structure and Curriculum Development

The school system has been described as a sub-system of a larger community system. As a sub-system the school receives financial support, goal specification, and some control over activities. Therefore, the changes that may be made in a school program are limited by the beliefs and decisions of the community power structure. If the changes are small and will not adversely affect any vested interests the power structure wants to protect, no interference will be felt. If, however, the change is major and will drastically modify the curriculum content or program organization, then consideration of the power structure may be needed.

All communities have a power structure which, according to Kimbrough's (1964) classification, may be monopolistic, competitive, or fragmented pluralistic. A monopolistic power structure is characterized by a unitary system of dominance over community decision-making. A competitive power structure exists when two or more power groups engage in competition that transcends more than one election. A fragmented pluralistic structure exists when there are several fragmented centers of power. Each school district exists within a community power structure, and lack of knowledge about its existence or shape may lead to unexpected and unnecessary difficulties for educational leaders attempting curriculum improvement.

The knowledge that a community power structure exists and operates does not decrease the need for informing and involving the rest of the community. The power structure will be affected and influenced by the way the community sees and supports the school.

A school cannot move too far ahead of the community. If it does, its program will be criticized, and as soon as the community gathers its forces, action will be taken to eliminate the phases of the school program the community does not accept or understand.

It is essential that a school program include a public relations activity that keeps all community members informed of what is going on in the school. Keeping the community informed includes such customary activities as columns in the local newspapers, radio programs, annual reports to parents, open meetings of the board of education, open-house days or visits to classes, fathers' clubs, and P.T.A. meetings. It also includes supplying teachers and pupils to talk at service and women's club meetings. But these are not enough. New methods should be sought.

Student participation in thinking out problems of classroom operation, school policy, and program increases the possibility of effective relationships with the various community groups. As pupils understand the school purposes and programs by participating in the processes through which they are formed, the student body becomes a public relations unit. Pupils explain and interpret the school to the community.

But informing the community is not enough. School personnel must become involved in community activities if the work of the faculty is to be coordinated with community groups. One of the functions of the school group and the supervisor is to establish channels of communication with the community. These must not be one-way channels. If they are, the staff operates in a vacuum and does not know how well it is communicating or how well its ideas are being received. If the supervisor wants to bring about a receptive frame of mind for the constant improvement of the school program, he must establish a situation in which there is an exchange of ideas between community leaders and the members of the staff.

In some communities, one channel that exists for the exchange of ideas is the community coordinating council. In such a council, representatives of business, service clubs, unions, and welfare agencies discuss the problems of the community and ways of solving them. If the school is represented on the council, the school staff has a way of sharing its thinking with other community leaders. If the school is not represented on the council, it should take steps to join.

Other groups in the community are working on community problems. The school leaders should encourage the community to invite school representatives to join these groups and should encourage teachers to accept such invitations. In this way, the thinking of the school staff can be shared with various segments of the community. The greater the number of faculty members that can be involved in community activities, the easier it will be to maintain a two-way flow of communication.

A false assumption that prevents many school staffs from working effectively with their communities is their belief that the only problems that should receive school attention are school problems. A much sounder attitude for establishing communication with the community is that community problems are school problems, that the frontiers of development in the community are the most fruitful areas for the thinking and learning of children. Some of the more advanced school curriculum programs are built around the solution of community problems. Studies of effective ways of learning have indicated that children learn more adequate skills through the problem-solving approach than through other approaches. No school leader need be concerned that putting emphasis on the solving of community problems will decrease the effectiveness of the school as a learning situation.

It is important to recognize that coordination with community groups of the nature described above is hindered when school regulations prohibit participation in political affairs. An official leader must work for political freedom for teachers so that they can be first-class citizens of the community.

Another phase of coordination with community groups is to have the community participate in planning the school program. When community members have a part in determining policy and program, they become valuable supporters. When they are kept out, they become suspicious and potentially hostile. The community's participation in school planning must be continuous. If members of the community are asked to think with the school staff only when a bond issue is at stake, or when the administration is on the defensive, they realize they are being manipulated. But when they are regularly consulted, before action affecting them and their children is taken, they recognize the good faith of the school staff, and cooperative responsibility results.

Specific ways the community can be brought into planning are:

1. Having individual teachers meet with the parents of the children they teach to discuss the program and the growth parents want their children to make.
2. Establishment of a citizens' advisory council on education.
3. Formation of curriculum committees that include teachers, parents, and pupils.
4. Creation of lay advisory boards to provide consultation services for special phases of the curriculum.
5. Bringing community members into the discussion of the school budget or other special proposals before the proposals are submitted to the board.

Planning with the community does not in any way relieve the school staff of the responsibility of formulating policy for the school. In the final analysis, the school administration and staff must take responsibility for major curriculum changes. And the challenge again becomes one of working with the power structure.

It should not be assumed that the power structure does not want curriculum change. The members may want and support it. They may be pushing the educational leadership to get moving. Callahan (1962) points out that the businessmen usually have undue representation in the power structure, and the innovations proposed will likely be made on the basis of business principles rather than upon educational principles. But the power structure cannot be assumed to be against curriculum change. At the present time, the chances are that the power structure will want change if they can become informed concerning the effect the change will have on the economic welfare of the community.

Kimbrough suggests that effective work with the power structure requires realistic understanding of the power structure, close communication with power wielders, and action proposals that are supported with a comprehensive rationale. The decisions on important policy, according to Kimbrough, are made before meetings take place. The official session is a democratic ritual. To wait until the meeting is to court disaster for a proposal.

All the information available about community power structures emphasizes the desirability of the school leadership establishing and maintaining channels of communication with the membership of the power structure. Otherwise all of the curriculum development efforts may be wasted, and the staff becomes disillusioned and disheartened when a major curriculum change is blocked by the informal power structure.

The preceding paragraphs should not be interpreted to mean that an educational leader should be a pawn. He should not, in an effort to influence the power structure or to retain his leadership in the staff, make statements or take actions contrary to his basic beliefs. If he does, his integrity will be so impaired that it will only be a matter of time before he is discovered, rejected, or ousted, and new leadership is sought.

It is necessary for an educational leader to be willing to be expendable. If he wants a leadership role so much that he is willing to compromise on his basic values, he loses his leadership. He must, if necessary, be willing to relinquish his position and seek another in a community whose values more nearly coincide with his own. Being willing to be expendable makes him fearless, able to go beyond the present status and stand for unfilled hopes and desires, and thus increase the number for whom he exerts leadership.

8 Supervision Is Improving Instruction

Improvement of instruction was earlier defined as the improvement of the development and actualization of engagement opportunities for students. In this chapter there will be two major approaches. First, consideration will be given to the process through which instructional supervisory behavior directly interacts with the teaching behavior system. This represents an attempt to influence the quality of education for children through direct participation in the processes of planning, actualizing, and evaluating the "teaching act."

Second, supervisory behavior which interacts directly with teachers but only indirectly influences the teaching situation for students will be discussed under the general heading, "continuing staff development."

Direct Interaction with Teaching Behavior

THE FUNCTIONS OF DIRECT INTERACTION

In Chapter 2 the earliest function of supervision was described as inspection. Committees of citizens had the responsibility of visiting teachers to determine whether they were doing the job. This became the basis for making decisions about retention and other kinds of rewards. There was no effort to improve the teachers or the teaching.

By the latter part of the nineteenth century and the early part of the twentieth century professional superintendents, principals, and supervisors had responsibility for the leadership in the schools. Supervisors and to some extent building principals did visit classrooms for the purpose of inspecting, rating, and monitoring. With the period of scientific management there was an attempt to use the method of science to determine the best method of teaching to achieve certain goals, and supervision saw to it that teachers carried out the specifications and achieved the desired results. This was accomplished through classroom visits which included the utilization of techniques such as telling, demonstrating, and rating. The data from such visits were also used for the purpose of making personnel decisions.

With the growing concern for the nature and needs of teachers which had its roots in the human relations movement, questions were raised about the compatibility of the twin functions of supervisory classroom visits: first, the rating of teachers for making personnel decisions and second, helping or assisting of teachers to become more effective in their teaching behavior. School systems do need data on the outcomes of teaching efforts to use as a basis for making personnel decisions and teachers do need an external source of individual help and assistance in their efforts to improve their teaching. However, it is our assumption that these two functions are not totally compatible in the same behavior system. Therefore, the fact that a supervisor is called on to participate both in program evaluation and the evaluation of the contributions of individuals to that program is recognized as a limiting factor in the supervisor's potential effectiveness in the psychological and technical support system. It does not mean the supervisor cannot be effective in providing support; he can. But it does mean that certain factors will need to be considered.

For example, a principal who is called on to evaluate teacher effectiveness and make personnel recommendations needs to be sensitive to the possibility that this will affect his participation in the support system. Teachers may not be willing to share their concerns and problems. Attempts may be made to hide weakness and avoid the "airing" of real difficulties. But, it is also true that the principal is probably in the best position to provide psychological support since he does make personnel recommendations. It is also true that principals and teachers can build mutual trust and esteem and help each other in spite of these possible difficulties.

It is also proposed that a separate and discrete supervisory behavior system be established with the function of direct participation in the teaching behavior system for the purpose of providing a technical and psychological support system for teachers.

THE TECHNICAL AND PSYCHOLOGICAL SUPPORT SYSTEM

The technical and psychological support system is provided on the assumption that it is possible to improve the quality of teaching and learning in the teacher-student systems if teachers have available an expert source of help. It is proposed here that the nature of that service can be defined by an examination of the process of teaching. It is possible to think of teaching as consisting of the following interdependent parts: planning, actualizing the plans, describing what was actualized, analyzing what happened, and generalizing in terms of future planning. These processes appear to be the crucial points at which supervisors and teachers can work together to improve the learning environment.

THE PLANNING PROCESS

This process involves the specification of anticipated learning output, learning conditions, and criteria for evaluating results. It also requires a design for verifying learning results and learning conditions. How will the teacher really know whether or not the planned learning conditions were in fact actualized? It is important for teachers to have access to a variety of resource persons during planning activities. Supervisors have a broader understanding of the goals of the school system and the local school and can help teachers develop and evaluate the specification of the anticipated learning outcomes of their teaching. It is also possible for supervisors to facilitate the process through which teachers can share planned learning activities. It is always helpful to have a "sounding board" or an outside opinion. But, it is crucial that this outside opinion does not carry official authority. The teacher must have the final authority for the plans if she is to be held responsible. The assumption is that teachers need to become more self-directing and self-supervising.

If teachers are to have feedback about what actually happened in the classroom it is necessary to provide for a procedure that will describe the particular learning condition. Interaction analysis, audio taping and video taping are examples of procedures for getting feedback. Such procedures require a certain amount of skill that teachers may or may not have. Supervisors can often provide the necessary help.

Effective supervisor-teacher cooperation in the planning process requires that a number of interdependent conditions be met. First, there is a need for mutual esteem and trust. This requires contact and interaction over time so that all parties have a chance to test each other's behavior. It means that time must be provided and devoted to the process. It also means that supervisors need to have and be willing to share relevant knowledge and skill in the planning process. If the teacher does not perceive the supervisor as a person who has the ability to help and as a person with whom weaknesses and concerns as well as strengths can be shared, then there is little chance that the planning can be effective.

The task of assisting others is more than a matter of wanting to do so. If a supervisor is to be effective, he must work in a way that makes it possible for the teachers to accept support and encouragement and to trust him.

The supervisor must function in a way that makes it possible for individuals to accept assistance. If a supervisor interprets his role as telling, the teacher can't accept it. If he interprets his role as being superior, the other can't accept it. If he exhibits obnoxious personal behavior, the other can't accept any assistance from him. If the supervisor does not encourage cooperation as a way of life, then accepting assistance is an indication of weakness, and his actions make it extremely difficult for anyone to accept his assistance.

If two people have some common goals, it is easier to provide and accept assistance. If two people see themselves as working on a common task, one can help the other without either being ashamed or resentful. The supervisor must be sure that his role is one of assistance, not of direction. He must recognize that the initiative belongs to the person requesting assistance, not to him. He must see himself making counsel available, not forcing advice on the teacher.

If a supervisor wants staff members to grow, he must help them to feel important. In every way he can, the supervisor should build his staff's feeling of self-worth. Showing respect for the other person's opinion, giving explanations for decisions, and saying those things that enhance, rather than detract, are tools of the supervisor.

Comments by the supervisor are belittling if they indicate that the supervisor thinks he could equal or surpass the achievements of his staff. Praise for a previous staff, or a recitation of personal successes in a previous situation, imply a dissatisfaction with, or lack of appreciation of, the present group. Freedom to think, to express an opinion, to make decisions, and to take action all contribute to the development of a belief in one's self. The supervisor who trusts a teacher and is willing to think with him further helps to build the self-confidence of that teacher.

A supervisor's behavior in conferences reveals his belief in the worth of others. When he shows respect for a teacher by listening to the teacher's comments and opinions, he builds the teacher's belief in himself. When the supervisor refuses to listen, he indicates that he thinks his ability is so superior that he does not expect any worthwhile contribution from any teacher, and thus decreases the teacher's belief in himself.

Actions that imply distrust decrease the sense of self-worth. When a supervisor requires that a teacher must check with him before any step can be taken, the supervisor shows lack of faith. When a supervisor forces people to give him detailed reports of their activities, he tells them they are not able to assume self-direction. When he establishes regulations that cover in minute detail the instructional procedures, he is denying the value of the persons involved.

Here is how one beginning teacher described her supervisor's positive faith:

> From the very first day I met him, I felt very much at ease with him and felt as though he were really interested, not only in me as a teacher, but also as a human being. All of the teachers felt that at any time they could go to talk with him about any matter, big or little, and he would always seem as though he had nothing else to do and as though what you felt was important, he felt was important, too . . . He was interested in what I was doing and in how *we* could help *me* to do a better job.

A second condition of effective participation in the planning process requires that teacher and supervisor reach some common understandings about the particular phase of teaching that is being planned. Teachers need to understand the plans since they are responsible and must actualize them. Supervisors must understand in order to contribute and also to make plans for describing what was actualized. Techniques that will be used, such as interaction analysis, need to be identified and teacher and supervisor need to agree that the techniques are valid and appropriate for describing the particular phase of teaching and/or learning behavior on which agreement had been reached.

Rogers (1962) has developed a conceptualization of the change process that has important implications for supervisors' participation in the teachers' planning behavior. Rogers describes three interdependent parts of the change process: (1) Antecedents; (2) Process; (3) Results. The antecedents are defined as the psychological dynamics of the innovator and the innovator's perception of the situation. Such factors as the teacher's anxiety or security, openness or defensiveness, mental ability, and skill development would be important contributors to teachers' and supervisors' readiness for change.

The teachers' and supervisors' perception of the situation is an important factor. Are the norms of the situation conducive to change in general and to this change in particular? Is the reward system designed to "pay off" for change attempts that succeed or fail?

The supervisor can be an important factor in the antecedents of change. He can support teachers' ideas for change, and provide needed security in failure. He can also communicate situational norms that support change and communicate recognition and deep concern for teacher's change efforts.

The process of change is defined by Rogers as having five interdependent stages: awareness, interest, evaluation, trial, and adoption. There is a wide variety of sources of information for these various stages such as professional meetings, fellow teachers, students, summer workshop, and many others. But it is clear that it is possible for the supervisory behavior system to serve as an important source of information. Feedback from student learning, new curriculum materials, new approaches that are being used in other schools are examples of sources of information that could contribute to teacher awareness and interest in planning new approaches in teaching.

Guba (1968, pp. 292-295) defined the following diffusion techniques: telling, showing, helping, involving, training, and intervening. He suggested that the change agent will have to select from these six the appropriate techniques or combination of techniques. He explains that the appropriateness of a particular diffusion technique is a function of the assumptions that are made about the adopter, the hoped-for effect on the adopter, the innovator, and the substance of the invention.

If the teacher is assumed to be a rational and competent professional, then the supervisor might first work to supply the necessary information. If the teacher is assumed to be inferior or subordinate to the supervisor, then it would be appropriate to sell or persuade, use politics, or reward or punish. In this book it is our assumption that teachers and supervisors work together as colleagues and therefore, share information, tell each other, and persuade each other, but in the final analysis the teacher makes the decision and is held responsible for the consequences. It is hoped that the teacher will become increasingly independent of the supervisor and therefore, more autonomous and self-supervising. The emphasis is on providing information systems, shared analysis, and shared decision making and problem solving.

THE INSTRUCTIONAL PROCESS

The instructional process is the actualization of engagement opportunities for students. Certainly, this is a realm of responsibility for teachers with commensurate authority provided. But it is also a dimension in which supervisors and teachers can work together. For example, teachers and supervisors may plan to cooperate on certain aspects of the teaching process. At the request of the teachers, the supervisor might react to certain activities or procedures. The teacher and supervisor could decide to change roles with the supervisor serving as actualizer of student encounters and the teacher serving as observer and analyzer. It is also possible that the supervisor would have a special competence in some area of teaching and the teacher would just like to see how someone else approaches the process. It has also worked well for teachers and supervisors to teach as a team in certain phases of the instructional process. This not only provides for utilization of the specialized expertise of each, but also provides a basis for shared experience and can facilitate the process of working together.

These procedures require a certain level of mutual trust and esteem, but they can also contribute to a growing depth of teacher-supervisor understanding and effectiveness. The possibilities for sharing ideas and learning from each other can be extended and thereby contribute to the improvement process.

DESCRIBING THE INSTRUCTIONAL PROCESS

The instructional process can be thought of as the actualization of conditions which it is hypothesized will result in certain learning outcomes for students. Without a valid determination of the instructional methods and content that were utilized, it is impossible to know to what one can attribute certain learning results. Without this kind of information, the teacher cannot make meaningful judgments about what procedures to continue or discontinue.

It was precisely at this point that the traditional approach to "classroom visitation" often failed. The supervisor would visit the classroom, but the main focus was on evaluation. How well was the teacher doing? An evaluative check list was often used. Then, if there was a follow-up conference, the supervisor would attempt to start off with something positive, "sandwich" in the negative criticism, and end the conference on a positive note. Normally little effort was made to verify what had actually happened, and the effort that was made was just based on the supervisor's "off-hand" observations.

It is proposed here that emphasis be placed on the description of the actualization process and that this be planned during the planning process. The specific nature of the observational techniques will be a function of the phase of instruction that is to be observed, the expertise of the teacher and supervisor, and the readiness of the teacher to be observed. If there is a desire to describe the intellectual content of student interaction and the teacher is willing, an audio-tape could be used or one of the interaction analysis systems (Bellack, Davitz and others, 1968, pp. 84-97).

A description of the emotional content of the interaction can be obtained from student reaction sheets or interaction analysis systems such as the Amidon and Hunter system. (Amidon and Hunter, 1966).

Video taping can be used for all of these purposes and is very effective for describing the total picture and non-verbal communcation.

There are many systems and techniques that can be used to describe instruction. However, it is not only crucial that a technique describe the thing to be described, but that both the teacher and supervisor agree that it will. This agreement is necessary before the process of analysis can begin.

It is desirable but not essential for the supervisor to participate in the observation process. The supervisor can provide an "outside" opinion, an extra set of eyes, and a more objective view. It is also possible that the supervisor would have special skills for the description or that the teacher would be so involved in the teaching that he would not have the time to manipulate the observation devices.

But, it is also possible that the teacher is not yet ready to share her teaching to this extent. In such cases, supervisors can facilitate the process through which teachers develop and utilize their own descriptions. Experience in working with both student teachers and teachers has demonstrated almost all teachers will eventually *want* to share their teaching with their fellow colleagues and will not only learn from the experience, but will also experience certain satisfactions from the recognition and just knowing that someone cares.

ANALYSIS OF INSTRUCTION

Analysis involves the process of trying to understand and make sense out of the description data. It is listening and looking at tapes. It is examining the results of interaction analysis in terms of the hoped for interaction. It is a chance for the teacher to examine his behavior in terms of his preconceived frame of reference. It is even a chance to evaluate the frame of reference.

Recently a video tape was made of a student teacher conducting a reading group of second grade students. During the course of the lesson the teacher became very intense in helping certain children who were having difficulty with certain words. She was so intense that she frowned and spoke in a high pitched voice. The children were observed to cringe and back off from the teacher. What does this raw data mean? What was the teacher communicating? Was this exceptional behavior or did it occur frequently? Is this data consistent with other data? Are there any general patterns that can be defined? These are the kind of questions that are dealt with in analysis.

It would be possible for a supervisor to do the analysis and report it to the teacher. We feel it is more appropriate for the teacher and supervisor to do the analysis together so that mutual interpretations and understandings can be developed in the process.

GENERALIZING FROM THE ANALYSIS

This is the process through which the analyzed data are studied in terms of their possible implication for future planning and actualization of plans. It is the "pay off" phase since it completes the "feedback belt" and makes it possible for the teaching behavior system to continuously profit from past experience and grow in its ability to predict and control future teaching plans. It not only provides the basis for change, but also gives direction for change attempts. Teachers and supervisors are sensitized to the need for change and have a basis and reason for continuing to work together.

Since the different phases of instruction were pulled apart and discussed in a certain order, it may appear that this is a suggested approach. Actually, these phases often function together in actual experience with planning, actualizing, describing, analyzing, and generalizing occurring at the same time. The process is "on-going" and continuous and no effort should be made to pull them apart as distinct steps or phases. Rather, they need to be treated as distinctive features of an harmonious whole.

Figure 5 may help explain the various phases of teaching behavior that have been used to identify points of interaction between supervisors and teachers.

Teaching behavior is assumed to have five distinctive but interdependent parts: planning, actualizing, describing, analyzing, and generalizing. It is at these points that the instructional supervisory behavior system and the teaching behavior system interact for the purpose of improving the quality of learning for students.

THE EVALUATION BEHAVIOR SYSTEM

The evaluation behavior system has been conceptualized as a separate system from the technological and psychological support system. It has the

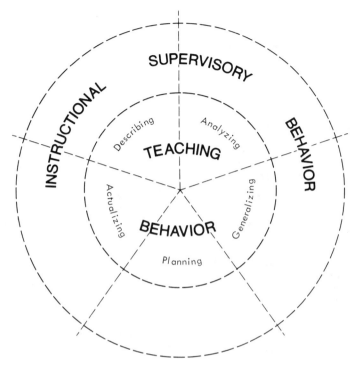

FIGURE 5

function of evaluating the effectiveness of the professional staff. The purpose of the evaluation system is to provide input for personnel decisions such as merit pay, tenure, promotion, and retention as well as to provide another source of feedback to teachers.

It is essential that the supervisory personnel who are assigned to this behavior system work closely with other supervisors and teachers in order to establish a comprehensive, valid, and acceptable program. There is a need to capitalize on the broad base of expertise and creativeness in the total staff. It is also necessary to have staff acceptance of the methods and procedures that are finally agreed on. Staff involvement in the process will increase the probability of staff acceptance.

There are many approaches to the evaluation of learning outcomes. Examples include standardized tests, student reaction procedures, student performance in school and community, specially designed tests to measure specific things, and expert observation. It is not our purpose to discuss these procedures in depth. It is our purpose to identify the need for evaluation as the major concern of a specific behavior system which is a part of the instructional supervisory behavior system.

Procedures for the Improvement of Instruction

COLLEGIAL SUPERVISION

Collegial supervision has been defined as a process for involving teachers in the supervision of each other. It makes it possible to broaden the base of expertise and creativeness that is available as a source of psychological and technical support. It also can reduce the amount of threat and stress that can be generated in a relationship that is perceived by the participants as subordinate to superordinate. Colleagues work together to help each other; and since colleagues that can help each other often work in close proximity, the help is available when it is needed. It is also assumed that the process of helping other teachers provides a source of recognition and sense of achievement and that this can contribute to the level of satisfaction and motivation that teachers experience in their work.

It is recognized that a great amount of teacher-teacher help occurs informally. Teachers ask each other questions, share materials, exchange procedures. This is beneficial and certainly supervisors can work to facilitate this process. But, it would be possible and productive to release a teacher with appropriate expertise on an ad hoc basis to participate in the supervisory behavior system. Teachers could be released to visit other teachers to help describe, analyze, and generalize about certain teaching behavior. It might even be appropriate to release teachers who need help so that they can visit a colleague for the purpose of sharing what that teacher is doing. Teachers could work together, each in turn acting as supervisor. For example, the teacher acting as supervisor would help with describing the teaching through the use of video tapes, audio tape or interaction analysis. Then the teachers could work together on the analysis and the process of generalizing the implications for future teaching. The next day the process could be reversed.

There are many ways of releasing teachers for activities of this sort. For example, it would be possible to use substitute teachers, parent groups, team teaching together with large group instruction or student self-directed activities. One idea that the authors like is the possibility of a group of specially prepared "floating" teachers that could be used to "fill in" for teachers who had been released for supervisory activities. Obviously, the "floating teachers" could be selected not only for their competence to "fill in" effectively, but also for their capacity to serve as part of the instructional supervisory behavior team.

CLINICAL SUPERVISION

Goldhammer (1969) has developed a sequence of five stages of the "supervisory act." He has identified the preobservation conference, the observation, analysis and strategy, supervision conference, post-conference analysis.' These five constitute the stages of clinical supervision. The stages are well defined with elaborate rationales for each. The author does an excellent job of discussing the processes of clinical supervision at each stage.

The need for observation, analysis, and follow-up is continuously stressed throughout the book. Rather than the traditional, superficial observation followed by evaluation, the focus is on meticulous observation to describe what is happening in the classroom. An effort to obtain teacher-supervisor agreement at this stage is advocated. Then, the supervisor analyzes the data and works with the teacher to improve instruction. The book is an excellent description and analysis of the process of direct interaction with the teaching behavior system.

THE "RIFLE APPROACH"

The size of the job of working with each individual teacher in each school is so overwhelming to some supervisors that it often results in very short and superficial visits or no visits at all. Therefore, the "rifle approach" is recommended for consideration. In this approach a school that has an interest and readiness for "direct supervision" would be identified. The teacher or teachers who would like to participate in cooperative supervision, action research, micro-teaching, or some form of simulation activity would be identified. Then, a great effort would be expended to provide the necessary support system to develop and maintain the action. This would be done on the assumption of a "spread" or "multiplier effect." It would be hoped that as the teachers get involved in the project that other teachers would become secure and interested enough to try it. The original strength of the support system could be reduced since the teachers who had become involved could serve to help other teachers develop the needed skills and understandings. Skills in interaction analysis, video taping and analysis could be learned and disseminated in this way.

MICRO-TEACHING

The Teacher Education Center of the University of Chicago has developed a model for micro-teaching that is consistent with the Stanford model but adds five stages (Guelcher, Jackson and Necheles, 1970).

Micro-teaching is a process that makes it possible for a teacher to participate in an actual teaching situation with immediate feedback available. The teaching situation is "cut down to size" in terms of content, number of students, and time in order to facilitate its manageability. Teaching behavior is defined in terms of specific skills or techniques so that a specific lesson focuses on a specific skill. It is assumed that it is possible to improve the execution of these skills and procedures.

The Stanford model had three stages. The first stage consisted of an introduction to micro-teaching including a film which explained the rationale.

The second stage provided small groups of students with an opportunity to view skill films for the purpose of becoming acquainted with specific teaching skills such as effective use of questions, establishing a set, reinforcement. The third stage was the teach-supervision-reteach cycles. Little attention was given to the content of the lesson. Rather, the major focus was centered on studying, analyzing, and improving the teaching behavior.

The Chicago model added several new dimensions to the micro-teaching process. For example, more emphasis was placed on the content and procedures of the lesson. Reinforcement and questioning were logically related to the lesson. It was also found helpful to give prospective teachers a chance to practice on peers before encountering students. This had the effect of reducing stress and providing a chance for "trying out" the lesson. The practice of providing seminars to train students to supervise their peers was also tried and proved to be effective. Out of the micro-teaching teaching cycle the concept of the "nuclear lesson" was developed. They found that a truly adequate lesson provides a "set" out of which numerous other "lessons" can emerge. This is a concept of continuity and provides an effective way of relating micro-teaching to "real" teaching.

Micro-teaching is a procedure which provides an opportunity for supervisors and teachers to identify, define, try out, describe, analyze, and retry certain teaching skills without the risk of an actual teaching situation. Teachers can try out lessons on peers or groups of teachers and supervisors. Or teachers can exchange positions in the "teach-supervise-reteach" cycle. Techniques such as films, video tapes, and interaction analysis can add greatly to the process but are not absolutely essential.

Promotion of Creative Teaching

Supervisors are coming to realize that change in the school program must have the individual teacher as its basis. If a better school program is desired, an environment in which the classroom teacher can be creative and can improve his teaching, must be established. Unless the supervisor sees his task as encouraging creativity in teachers, his function becomes restrictive. He sees his work as an attempt to discover what is going on and to bring about conformity to the existing instructional pattern. Emphasis on creativity is the threshold to improvement; stressing conformity means, at best, preserving the status quo.

In instructional improvement, final decision must be in the hands of the teacher. Although certain common principles operate in all good learning situations, it is impossible to say what good teaching will be, except in a particular situation. Judgment concerning that situation must be made by someone who knows all the factors and has the ability and freedom to take the action that will meet the specific requirements of the situation. No one has as much knowledge about his classroom as the teacher.

Creative teaching involves being dissatisfied with the results obtained from present procedures, feeling that perfection is something never quite attained but constantly sought, having new ideas, and being willing to try the new ideas and evaluate the results produced. Creativeness is really a constant state of experimentation. This experimentation has three phases: planning, testing, and revising.

Courage is needed to try new procedures, and many teachers will not depart from the methods with which they feel at home unless the supervisor helps them. For the supervisor, promoting creativeness in teachers involves solving three problems:

How can teachers be helped to obtain a clear sense of direction?
How can the willingness of teachers to try new procedures be increased?
How can the teachers be given greater security during the process of change?

If teachers have a part in the establishment of the purposes of the school program, their sense of direction becomes clear. Therefore, a primary step in helping teachers to become more creative, just as in encouraging teachers to assume responsibility, is to spend time with the staff to examine the purposes of the school and revise these purposes in terms of the basic values that the staff holds. Time is not wasted if it is spent in arriving at the common philosophy. This step is essential.

Once agreement has been reached on the purposes of the program, the next responsibility of the supervisor is to increase willingness to try new procedures by providing a permissive atmosphere and a secure relationship with the supervisor, plus removing the factors in the situation that encourage conformity to a pattern.

Teachers cannot be expected to be creative if the supervisor believes that there is one best method of teaching. If such is the case, teachers bend their efforts to discovering and following the method the supervisor accepts. But creativeness is encouraged by the supervisor's frank admission that the best procedure for any given group must be developed by that group in terms of its personnel and the limiting factors of the situation. Also, that the best method for any individual teacher will be an adaptation of the basic laws of learning to his own personality and particular skills. Much has been learned from research and experience, but teachers must continue to experiment to increase their effectiveness.

An essential step in promoting creativeness in teachers is to remove as many city-wide or school-wide restrictions as possible.

In a California city, a typing teacher returned from a summer of graduate work with the idea that his method could be improved by putting the markings on the keys of the typewriters. Before he could make this change, he had to submit a written request to the city curriculum committee for permission to deviate from the method used in other typing classes. When the committee did not act on the request within a reasonable time, the principal of the school sent through a purchase order for the necessary key caps. But the curriculum committee, which had worked out a relationship with the purchasing department whereby it passed on all orders relating to materials of instruction, stopped the purchase order. The teacher was thus unable to try out a method of whose value he had become convinced after much study. It is easy to imagine the lack of enthusiasm of that typing teacher for his job and his school system.

If teachers are to show creativeness, they must be accepted as people who have ability, understanding, and sufficient knowledge to prepare the best type of learning experience for their students. If teachers are not so accepted, creativity is easily stifled.

A way of increasing the teacher's willingness to advance new ideas and procedures is by supervisors being receptive to new ideas about teaching. If supervisors insist that their own answers are the only correct ones, teachers will turn from attempts to create for themselves to efforts to learn what the supervisor's answers are. By keeping his answers in the background, the supervisor encourages teachers to think, try, and evaluate for themselves. Discussions in which teachers' opinions are accepted on equal terms with those of the supervisor promote self-reliance, which is basic to creativeness.

One of the most effective ways to promote creativeness is to shift the emphasis on proof. Too many times, proof of the value of a new method is required before it can be tried. Too many supervisors feel that their chief function is to raise questions about teacher proposals in order to compel teachers to think through their ideas carefully and to leave out those ideas that are not worthwhile. Although this is a valuable and important function, it can be carried to such an extreme that teachers find it easier to follow customary procedures than to attempt to convince the supervisor that something new is worth doing. If supervisors put as much emphasis on proof that new procedures should not be tried as on proof that they should, creativeness will be greatly encouraged, and many more new things will be tried. In either case, the supervisor should not feel that the teacher's job is to give answers or proof that satisfy the supervisor. The supervisor's questions are only for the purpose of helping the teacher evaluate his own work.

One concept that has held back the development of creative teaching has been the idea that there is a model that should be emulated. Teachers should be encouraged to develop rooms that reflect the character of their work, the personality of their group, and their own best thinking. Not only does this practice add variety and color to the experience provided for children in school, but it leads to the emergence of more effective techniques of classroom organization.

Promoting a willingness to try new things is only the first step in developing creativeness in teachers. When this willingness is put into action, the supervisor must then give the security that makes any venture into new types of work satisfying.

A further way of promoting creativeness in the teaching staff is by giving recognition to those people who are trying new procedures. This recognition may consist of nothing more than having the people who are doing the experimental work tell the staff what they are trying to achieve and the results they are getting.

Experimentation should not be limited to a few members of the staff. All should be encouraged to experiment when they have an idea they want to test. If creative activity is limited to a few members of the staff, the status of those who are denied the privilege will be jeopardized; interstaff jealousy and diminution of creative endeavor will develop.

A second form of recognition is the commissioning of certain staff members to attend summer workshops on scholarships to develop new ways of working and of using materials in a given area. The choosing of the teachers to receive the scholarships should be made on the basis of expressed desire to attend, the extent to which the teachers involved have demonstrated willingness to try new procedures, and the need for spreading such experiences through the entire faculty.

Another way of giving the creative teacher recognition is by encouraging him to discuss new procedures with parent groups and by having the parents plan with him ways of making the procedures more worthwhile. Monthly planning meetings of parents and teachers, a practice that is becoming more widespread, make this type of recognition possible.

One of the big handicaps that many teachers feel as they attempt new things is the difficulty in obtaining evidence of results. School officials and teachers have become accustomed to determining pupil progress by the amount of subject matter acquired. Tests of subject matter information are seldom questioned by supervisors, parents, or pupils. On the other hand, attempts to measure other types of growth have been so infrequent in the past that they are viewed with suspicion by parents and students. A supervisor can help his teachers feel more secure by working with them to develop types of evaluation procedures that will measure a wider variety of types of pupil growth. As teachers learn how to evaluate additional types of pupil growth, and to see the results of the procedures used, they become freer in their attempts to develop newer methods of teaching that promote the so-called "intangible" types of pupil growth.

Creativeness in teaching is not something that can be bought or commanded. It can only be encouraged. It is encouraged by the attitude of the supervisor, by the removal of unnecessary restrictions, by demonstrations of belief in the ability of teachers to make intelligent decisions, by providing a wide range of materials and the financial means of securing those materials not available, and by placing the emphasis on proving why improvement should not be attempted rather than on proving why any new procedure should be tried.

The task of the helping teacher working with beginning teachers is easier, because the neophyte expects to receive help and is not ashamed. He feels a need of support and of a source of assistance in time of trouble. He knows his range of techniques is limited, and he wants more information than he has. But even in the case of first-year teachers, the length of time they maintain freedom within themselves to utilize the resources of the helping teacher will depend upon the extent to which the relationship is one that permits questioning, admission of difference, and independence of action.

Continuing Staff Development

Continuing staff development is an attempt to increase the competency of the present staff through courses, workshops, conferences, study groups, interschool visitations, lectures, and staff improvement days. Some large schools have elaborate operations with many offerings, and teachers are required to attend a given number of sessions. Some present their in-service education by television. Almost all school systems make some effort to upgrade their staff. Many state departments of education require that teachers take an additional college course every three or four years if they wish to have a certificate renewed.

Although the motives are good, the results satisfy almost no one. Courses are selected because of easy accessibility or a convenient schedule. Many teachers view the activities as unimportant and resist attending. Too frequently the sessions are compulsory, and the presentations are made to people who don't want to hear them.

Goodlad and Klein (1970, pp. 108-109) reported that they observed that teachers were heavily engaged in in-service activities, but that they were not improving their ability as teachers and were not solving school problems as they (the teachers) perceived it. Further, they observed that teachers had little opportunity to visit, observe, and participate in exemplary models. This was explained by the paucity of exemplary models and the lack of opportunity to be relieved from on-going teaching activities.

If educators would look at some experiences in agriculture, they would question the attempt to spend the same amount of in-service dollars on each teacher. Agricultural exchange agents found that the way to change farming practices was to place demonstration farms, also called experimental farms, where farmers could see them in operation and to recognize that some farmers (local influentials, adoption leaders, and opinion leaders) were turned to for ideas about new procedures more frequently than others.

Although the social organization and structure in education and agriculture are different, the results of in-service education activities are so disconcerting that consideration should be given to an educational demonstration model.

In Chapter 7, "Supervision Is Curriculum Development," it was recommended that the supervisory staff collect the available research concerning the educational problems confronting the school system. It was pointed out that the E.R.I.C. and the Research and Development Centers would make this collection easier than in the past. It was further recommended that additional research be done if needed and that the curriculum council serve the role of legitimatizing agent. Implementation based on research would be tried out before being legitimatized and made curriculum policy by recommendation of the curriculum council and approval by the board of education.

Allen (1971, pp. 109-131) has suggested that in-service education should focus in on the specific performances of teachers that are required to achieve certain kinds of outcomes for students. Specific performance criteria should be established which would specify the things the teacher needs to know and be able to do and would provide a basis for making judgments about teacher achievement in these areas. Thus, teachers could work in the in-service program to improve their competence according to specific performance criteria.

The in-service education activities of the school system constitute the dissemination and development phases of change. Viewed from this perspective, the in-service dollar should not be distributed equally throughout the staff. Instead, it should be spent on the ones who want it, the demonstrators, the inquirers, and the influentials. It should be spent on the horses who are on the track, not those who are sleeping in the stable.

If supervisors really believe the research that says that leadership is widespread and diffused, then they also believe that the main portion of the influencing of teachers in a school will be done by other teachers, and not by the resource people from the central office.

The money spent on the people who will really lead the thought and the effort in a school is the money that pays the biggest return. Following this hypothesis, the in-service money would be spent to support the following activities:

1. Opportunities for staff members to visit, observe and participate in outstanding education programs.

2. Seminars built around the study of research on a given topic.   If some very significant research has been found, for example, on education of the disadvantaged in language arts, a seminar on the topic is announced, and the people who are interested have an opportunity to become a part of the study group and to examine the findings. Only those who are interested enough to apply are in the seminar. If the study group is successful, some ideas for implementation will be formed as the people in this group look at the evidence.

3. Experiments that are an outgrowth of the seminar.   Certain teachers who participate in the seminar will develop ideas that they wish to try. These experiments may be with content or instruction procedures. Money will be made available to cover any additional expense. Members of the supervisory staff, perhaps the leader of the seminar, and a research worker will be made available to assist. The research worker's function will be to aid in the collection and interpretation of evidence.

4. *Seminars to consider the evidence obtained from the experiments.* The members of the seminar will include the experimenters, supervisors who are interested, researchers, and other teachers who have become excited about the experimentation. On the basis of study, the seminar group may make a proposal to the curriculum council.

5. *Open hearings on proposals.* The purpose of the open hearings is to inform as many teachers as are interested about the experiment and the results. In large systems, this open hearing can be presented by television and include samples of the classroom operation.

6. *Demonstration of practices that have been perfected.* If the council believes there is merit to the proposal, demonstration centers will be established in as many schools as possible. Teachers who are in sympathy with the proposal will be selected, brought together for training, and then identified as demonstration teachers. Supervisors will be assigned to support and work with the demonstration teachers.

7. *Clinics held as adjuncts to the demonstrations.* Opportunity will be provided for interested teachers to study the demonstrations through clinics. Each clinic will operate on a schedule that includes observation and discussion throughout several weeks. The plan will enable the observers to see progress and perhaps to do some try-outs on their own. The discussions will include the demonstration teacher, who will profit by the chance to get feedback from fellow leaders; the supervisor; and the observers. One of the things that the supervisor has to do is to help the group think through the concept that the improvement of the profession comes from people who are professionals questioning each other's assumption.

When a person or a committee prepares a project, he brings to it all the data he had been able to collect and the data of his past experience. He does not bring to it the data that the total group looking at a project is able to provide. This is the kind of data that might produce an improvement. A supervisor gets assurance out of questions because he knows that the real in-service growth takes place as people redefine the problem together, look at the differences in interpretation of the problem, and anticipate the consequences of various alternatives. If a staff doesn't disagree with each other, doesn't look look at different interpretations of the problem or the data or the anticipated consequences, no large faculty discussion is needed, and no new insight will be attained.

8. *Classes to develop skills and concepts.* After demonstrations have been held throughout the system, the results may be so satisfactory that the curriculum council will legitimatize the procedure and recommend it or make it

system-wide curriculum policy. In this case, classes will need to be established in which other teachers have the opportunity to develop the skills and concepts needed to implement the policy.

9. *Large group presentations.* Some large group presentations, many fewer than at present, will be needed to assist in the development of total staff identification, if not cohesiveness. No one should expect large group sessions to change a program. A session may be used for one of two purposes: either as an attempt to provide inspiration through support of existing norms or to bring to the total group a challenge of some existing norms. Although the impact will depend upon the quality of the presentation, any continuing result will come about through the staff's interpretations of what is said.

Continuing professional growth in a school system is to a large extent the intellectual atmosphere of the system. If many in the staff are excited about making improvements, individual teachers will become more professional and creative. They will be infected by the belief that the educational process can become better, and they can make a contribution.

When the administration is committed to experimentation, development and diffusion; when financial and supervisory support is given to innovators; when opportunities are provided for all to explore and experiment, then serving as a member of the staff is an in-service experience. When courses and workshops brought to the system are organized as a way of implementing the ideas people have accepted, the courses are meaningful. When persons seeking admission to in-service activities must make application and be accepted, then the efforts are being expended to help those who are ready to hear. The others, who are slow starters, will be affected through informal communication by the influential persons whom they accept as leaders.

Continuing Development for the Supervisory Staff

It is important for the members of the supervisory staff to have a program designed to sharpen their understanding of curriculum design and the strategy of curriculum design and of curriculum change. The curriculum generalists will need the opportunity to participate in regional and state seminars that increase their understanding of curriculum design and that help them develop models of desirable curricula. Through their interaction with others from school systems throughout the region, curriculum generalists will bring back to their own system new ideas with regard to desirable innovations and organization of the existing program.

It is particularly important for members of the supervisory staff to visit and get involved in exemplary and experimental programs in different parts of the country. Such activities provide a way for raising the aspiration level of supervisors and form a basis for the supervisor's contribution to new idea development in the system. It also helps the supervisor give leadership to the program of teacher participation in outstanding programs both locally and nationally.

In-service experiences will be especially important for the subject specialists who are brought to the supervisory staff. Many of them will only have a background in a single subject matter field and will need help in getting a picture of the total curriculum and the place that their subject plays in it. They will learn the language of the general curriculum workers and of specialists in other fields. Through staff discussions, they will discover the kinds of pupil growth being sought by other fields and determine the degree to which the goals of their field coincide with types of pupil growths sought in other areas. It is to be hoped that they will discover cooperative approaches with specialists of other fields as well as with the curriculum generalists. Most of all, they will gain greater understanding of the strategy of curriculum change. Since their background has been in the development of structure and design of their field, with little background in strategy of change and curriculum development, they will gain increased understanding and skills in this phase of their work.

All members of the supervisory staff will need help in becoming more effective in communication. The types of growth that will be required for the members of the supervisory staff give an indication of the type of outside consultant help that will be needed. Not only should the subject specialists have contact with the scholars in their fields who will aid them in looking at the offerings in their disciplines in the school system, but specialists in the fields of group development, strategy of change, communication, and curriculum design should also be brought to the staff for special seminars and consultation.

Much of the growth of the members of the supervisory staff can be secured by participation in national conferences and through fellowships that enable them to attend summar institutes. A part of each member's annual program should be participation in conferences, institutes, and special seminars designed to increase competency either in their subject field or in becoming more effective supervisors and curriculum workers. The head of the supervisory staff should work individually with each staff member to develop a plan of study that will help the member become increasingly competent.

Provision of Materials of Instruction

Teaching can be improved by supplying the teacher with better materials of instruction. A part of the task is production or selection of better materials. Another is the increasing of readiness to use a range of materials. A third is the provision of a rapid distribution system that enables the staff to get materials when they are needed. All three facets of supply are a responsibility of the supervisory staff.

The supervisory staff should have one media center, or several, that can be used by teachers to produce their own instructional materials. Consultant help to advise on instructional programming and the construction of specific pieces of material should be provided. The information and aid given to the teachers who come to the media center for help is probably the major contribution to improvement of instruction that a media supervisor makes.

He will also need to work with committees and faculties to help them know the range of materials available. Some teachers who are seeking better methods of teaching will know about audio-visual aids but will not be knowledgeable about programmed instruction, individualized instruction with computers, or ways of learning instantly what percentage of the pupils have gained the concept being taught. The media supervisor will need to arrange demonstrations and guided visits to schools where a fuller use is being made of a range of materials.

He will need to be the supervisor, more than any other, who encourages teachers to secure materials with a range of difficulty and content for each class. He should disseminate information about the spread of achievement, ability, and communication skills in each class.

The supply system for materials is a weak point in many supervisory systems. Teachers cannot get materials except by written requests months in advance of the desired date. Some schools even want the teacher to schedule films for the entire years. If materials are supplied on this basis, no teacher can adjust the curriculum to meet the needs of the class with which he is working. If this is the case, then the schedule of materials determines the curriculum structure that will be followed instead of the readiness and learning rate of the class.

A supply system should be responsive and flexible to permit a teacher to call and secure needed materials on a day's notice. The supply should be plentiful enough to prevent much delay because other classes are often working on the same topic. The budget provides the staple supplies and includes an item for experiments and development activities.

Not only the ordinary materials of instruction, but also programs supplied by television should be controlled by the administration that is responsible for curriculum and instruction. Television's only place in the schools is in supplying additional instruction or materials that teachers can use. Television materials should be a part of the regular curriculum and administered and supervised by the same persons.

It should be very clear that getting the right materials in the right place at the right time is an essential element of improving instruction, and supervision must have and accept responsibility for seeing that this service is performed well.

SUPERVISION AT
THE SCHOOL DISTRICT LEVEL

An instructional supervisory support system is provided at both the central office level and the local school level. Chapter 9 discusses the allocation and organization of the support system at the central office level.

9 The Supervisory Team at the School District Level: Its Organization and Functions

A basic assumption of this book is that the purpose of instructional supervision is to improve the quality of learning for students. This is done through the instructional supervisory behavior system which has the following functions: (1) technological and psychological support system for teachers, (2) improvement and development of curriculum, (3) continuing professional development of staff, (4) selection, procurement, allocation, and deployment of materials and equipment of instruction, (5) evaluation of teaching and learning, (6) development and evaluation of educational objectives, (7) coordination of educational programs, (8) research, (9) dissemination, (10) development, implementation, support and diffusion of new programs.

The activation of activities that have such a broad range of functions requires careful selection, allocation, and deployment of essential human resources. In the educational organization instructional supervision personnel are deployed at both the district level and local school level. Utilization of such personnel at the school district level necessarily requires a consideration of their function, allocation, organizational structure (including interdependence with structures at the local school level), roles, authority, needed specialization, and channels of communication. The purpose of Chapter 9 is to develop a discussion of these factors. No attempt will be made to prescribe specific organization structures, formula for allocation of personnel, specific role descriptions, or exact descriptions for district level functions. We assume such decisions are best made within the framework of the needs of a particular system. Rather, the discussion will focus on development of appropriate concepts and generalizations, the identification of crucial issues, and descriptions of representative examples.

The Functions

The central office instructional supervisory behavior team has many functions. It has responsibility for developing the curriculum design; coordinating the curriculum improvement efforts; stimulating innovation; developing demonstrations of new procedures and practices; keeping informed about new curriculum developments throughout the nation and making this information available throughout the school system; locating materials of instruction; developing new instructional media; outlining needed research; conducting research that is appropriate to the school system in which it works; providing technological and psychological support to individual schools and to individual teachers; cooperating with institutions of higher education in the effort to improve preparation programs for instructional leaders; studying, analyzing, interpreting and implementing community expectations of the educational program; communicating curriculum and instruction needs to the superintendent and board; providing a program of professional growth for the staff, evaluation of the effectiveness of the educational program; and the extension of school developed educational opportunities throughout the community. If the staff is fulfilling its mission, it will have a definite program in these areas.

GOALS AND OBJECTIVES

It is a function of the central office curriculum and instruction team to develop a continuous process of goal determination and evaluation for the total system. In order to do this community expectations must be studied, interpreted, and translated into educational goals for the total system. It is necessary to involve local schools and their communities in this process. The overall system goals provide the framework for the development of objectives at the system, local school and individual teacher level. The goals and objectives at these various levels provide the rationale for the overall design and coordination of the curriculum.

CURRICULUM DESIGN

The curriculum design function is an essential one that many school systems have neglected; so have state departments of education and the U.S. Office of Education. Individual schools or individual teachers have been encouraged to move ahead on their own in experimentation and innovation without much effort to develop a scope and sequence that gives coherence and continuity to the program. It has been assumed that a design will emerge.

It is essential that someone be responsible for looking at the total curriculum offering. This person needs to describe the typical pattern that is currently followed in the school system. He also needs to secure agreement on the types of developments that are desired and outline the steps that are necessary to achieve the desired goals. He needs to call to the attention of the persons with whom he works the resources that are available in terms of curriculum developments in other schools or curriculum packages that have been developed by some outside force, such as a foundation or the national government. He needs to help the local school staff develop a set of criteria by which they can judge whether curriculum material developed by an outside source will fit into the design of the curriculum in the school system in which he works. He needs to outline a strategy of change that involves the establishment of hypotheses to be tested and the development of innovative demonstrations that will permit the school system to field test a new curriculum program or new material in the school system for which he is planning. He needs to develop a pattern of research that will collect data as to the effectiveness of the existing program and any innovations.

In recent years, one of the functions of the supervisory staff in some school systems has been to become informed about governmental programs that make federal funds available to schools and to develop the proposals that will secure the funds to enable the system to engage in innovation. Too frequently, school systems have moved off in all directions without any coordination of efforts. Because funds were available, requests were made and projects were funded that had little relationship to the pressing curriculum needs of the system. In other school systems, a fund-seeking staff is not related to the supervisory staff and no attempt is made to coordinate federal programs with the rest of the curriculum.

Any satisfactory supervisory program includes a projection of curriculum development that makes it possible to know whether an action being considered is one that is progress or simply a diversion. A blueprint of curriculum development needs to be drawn. Although experience may reveal that revision is desirable, the original plan is essential. If money and effort are to be spent wisely, a plan and a strategy must be conceived. In a small system, the entire central office supervisory staff may develop the plan with the advice and consultation of teachers and principals. In a large system or a state department, it is important to have a designated curriculum planning group that assumes the responsibility of developing the master plan.

CURRICULUM COORDINATION

Curriculum coordination is a difficult task. It is important not to demand such strict adherence to a curriculum framework or a curriculum development plan that an individual school or teacher is not free to innovate. It is also necessary to have sufficient detail in mind that intelligent decisions can be made concerning the establishment of study groups, innovative undertakings, curricular materials, development groups, and diffusion activities. The coordination activities should include the development of goals for the system, the description of existing plans, the establishment of the organizational machinery that enables people to be kept fully informed about the present status of the program, the opportunities for innovation, the innovations and demonstrations that are being tried throughout the system, the collection of data concerning the results obtained by innovations, and the method for agreeing upon change in curriculum policies and programs. In addition, the coordinating unit must have the authority to encourage deviation from existing plans and the funds to support the implementation of promising ideas.

An effective coordinating effort will also include the bringing together of individuals and faculties that have common concerns and want to engage in similar innovative efforts. Members of the central office supervisory staff can assist the innovative groups by providing support, consultation, and opportunities to exchange ideas and results.

In some systems, the coordination will be carried on through curriculum councils. In others, the central office supervisory staff itself provides the coordination. One of the tests of a given pattern of work will be the extent to which the teaching staff of the system feels that the coordination is their effort rather than a control imposed by the central office staff. The creation of an apparatus that encourages participation and facilitates communication is an essential part of the coordination effort.

Coordination can be fostered by the development of curriculum bulletins and descriptions of desirable curriculum procedures. These bulletins describe the program as it exists and in terms of its ideal form. They serve as a description of the status quo from which individuals should be able to depart through innovation.

INSTRUCTIONAL MATERIALS PROVIDED

The supervisory staff, including media specialists, has a responsibility for locating and making available the materials of instruction that are appropriate. Publishing companies, curriculum projects, and other school systems are constantly making available new materials. Teachers do not have time to become informed about them. The supervisory staff must survey what is available and recommend the desirable new materials.

A part of the selection of materials of instruction is choosing the correct textbooks. They may be chosen by the central office staff, but one of the best ways of acquainting teachers with the new instruction materials is to make provision for their participation in the selection of the new texts. Committees of teachers in each of the subject matter fields can work with the resource people on the supervisory staff to choose from among the available texts three or four that seem most satisfactory for the instructional program of the system. As teachers participate in establishing the criteria for use in the selection of texts and survey the texts that are on the market, they not only become better informed with regard to what is available, but they become more intelligent users of textbooks.

An important part of providing materials of instruction is arranging a distribution system that enables teachers to secure supplementary materials quickly. Whether the materials be films or pamphlets or pictures or illustrative materials, they should be quickly supplied to the schools and to the teachers upon their requests. Well-organized programs of supervision have developed a system that supplies materials from the central depository to the teachers after a few day's notice. This function of selecting materials, storing and maintaining materials, and supplying them to classrooms in which they are requested is part of the supervisory function.

Research

A neglected function of supervision has been the conducting of research into instructional procedures and curriculum design. In too many systems, the development of new content and procedures has been left to other school systems, to publishers, or to individual teachers. Little money has been spent in research and development. As systems increase in size and more money is made available to produce quality education, individual systems must assume responsibility for investigation of the educative process and the development of more effective practices. A well-developed supervisory staff will include research workers who are able to design and conduct research projects. Each system needs to determine its frontiers and organize appropriate research projects. In a given system, the research may consist entirely of investigations of new instructional practices. In other systems, different content and curriculum designs may be tested. Research is frequently being conducted at the universities and by the major curriculum projects, but local research efforts are also desirable.

The supervisory staff has a responsibility for securing information concerning research results in other locations and supplementing it. They should also investigate appropriateness of practices and instructional procedures, in the local situation. As ERIC (Educational Research Information Center) is more fully developed and information can be secured quickly from the national depository of research information, local school systems will be able to quickly obtain a summary of available research. If the research that is already available supplies the answer the system needs, the local system will be able to make its decision on this evidence. But when additional evidence is required, the local supervisory unit must take the leadership in securing it.

DISSEMINATION

Another function of the central office supervisory staff is the dissemination of research information. Appropriate methods of conducting this activity have not yet been developed. Research bulletins in their present form are not widely read. Research reports, for the most part, have been rather meaningless to teachers. Someone must engage in the process of translating and interpreting research results, and this responsibility falls to the supervisory staff. Once the translation has been made, the method of providing it to the teachers who need the data must be developed. Experimentation with presentation of materials by educational television, by bulletins, and by conferences must be conducted. The supervisory staff is faced with the task of determining which procedures work and which make a difference in the way that teachers practice.

One of the methods of dissemination that are being investigated is the development of demonstration. Title III of the Elementary and Secondary Education Act of 1965 makes provision for demonstration units supported by the federal government. Local school systems that wish to establish demonstration centers may submit proposals to the U.S. Office of Education for financial support. If the U.S.O.E. decides that a particular demonstration will have implications for a number of school systems, it will be funded.

But demonstrations supported by the U.S.O.E. are not sufficient. Each school system needs to have demonstration centers that are a regular part of the curriculum program of the school. Research in agriculture in the mid 1930s indicated that the most effective procedure for changing farming practices was having experimental farms located close to the farmers whose procedures the government hoped to influence. Farmers located too far from a demonstration farm were not affected by the practices demonstrated. It is the hypothesis of the author that the same result will be obtained through demonstrations in education. Upon this basis, it is recommended that supervisory staffs seek to establish demonstrations in each of the schools in a system. These demonstrations may be teachers in given classrooms who are demonstrating certain new practices. They may also be a single school demonstrating a new type of curriculum design that can be observed by teams of teachers from other schools in the system. Much experimentation needs to be conducted with the ways that the demonstrations can be used as a basis of clinics in which principals and teachers analyze what they observe in a given demonstration.

It is also crucial to improve dissemination of ideas that are developed at the local school level. This can be encouraged by a program of teacher-teacher visitation, principal groups that visit in different schools, workshops, and curriculum planning activities.

PSYCHOLOGICAL AND TECHNOLOGICAL ASSISTANCE TO PRINCIPALS AND TEACHERS

Historically the most important function served by the supervisory staff has been to provide resource help to teachers and principals; this function must continue. The administrative relationships between principals and the teachers in their faculty prevent the principal from being of service to certain teachers. The principal's requirement to make judgments concerning tenure and increases in salary prevents the kind of openness and honesty that is necessary for depth analysis of the teaching practice of teachers who are labeled less than satisfactory by the principal. Such teachers need the help that can be supplied by a consultant who does not engage in the rating practice. Each school system needs a reservoir of resource people who can be called upon by the principal or by a teacher to assist in a given instructional situation. These supervisors may work with a teacher who is having difficulty or may assist the teacher who is experimenting with new practices.

Further, no matter how adequate the principal may be, he will not have all the special competencies that given members of his staff may require. By having a number of supervisors with different competencies, it is possible to make available assistance of the specific type that is needed by a given teacher. And the principal himself needs resource people to call upon for advice and consultation about specific instructional and curriculum problems. A school system strengthens its administrative staff as it makes available to the principal the kind of support and assistance that it requires.

All staff members in a school system, whatever its size, need support and stimulation if their vision is to be enlarged and their growth nourished. In each system, there is a necessity for resource people who are not administrators. These people may be curriculum workers, supervisors, research workers, instructional material workers, and others who provide services designed to support and enrich the learning experiences of children.

In no sense is this statement a criticism of the competency of teachers or administrators. Instead, it is a recognition that school programs must be constantly improved if they are to meet the demand for an adequate educational program. In a period when knowledge is multiplying, when society is changing at an almost inconceivable rate, when new tools for teaching and learning are being developed, and the schools are attempting to serve an ever increasing range of pupil needs, teachers and administrators need encouragement, support, and assistance in developing new competencies required by the added dimensions of their role.

PROFESSIONAL DEVELOPMENT OF STAFF

Teachers, administrators, and supervisors need an opportunity for continuous professional development. The changing nature of what is to be taught and how it is to be taught demands the development of new understandings and skills on the part of teachers and administrators. It is also true that new approaches to staff differentiation make it possible for teachers and administrators to aspire to new positions of responsibility. It is through the program of professional development that teachers and administrators can maintain a readiness to meet the challenge of new programs and new responsibilities.

CONTINUOUS STUDY OF THE PROFESSIONAL STAFF

A prime function of the curriculum and instruction staff at the central office level is to know the special competencies and skills of the professional staff. A knowledge base of this sort is the starting point in the process of utilizing the special expertise of teachers, administrators, and supervisors in activities such as curriculum development, support for teachers, demonstrations, research, and dissemination. The challenge to the central staff is to get the person with the appropriate expertise in the right place at the right time.

EVALUATION

The central office staff is concerned with evaluation from two important perspectives: first, the school system needs data on the effectiveness of local schools and individual teachers in the achievement of educational goals. It is essential that the central office instructional team develop and implement a design for getting and making this kind of information available. It is recommended that the development of the design should be a function of broad participation of teachers and administrators. The process should be comprehensive and continuous and hopefully represent the best thinking of the system.

The focus of the evaluation should be on the outcomes of instruction and learning rather than the instructional process itself. The system needs to know the effectiveness of each school and each professional person in the system in order to make appropriate personnel decisions.

Second, there is a need to facilitate the process of self-evaluation of both individuals and school units. This process involves the technological and psychological support system and has the function of helping teachers explicate their objectives and program conditions, describe what happened, analyze what happened, and generalize for future planning.

The Organization

The supervisory staff, regardless of the size of the system, is the task force organized for curriculum development and instructional improvement. Its membership must supply the resources and leadership that are needed by teachers and administrators for continuous evaluation and innovation.

No formula has been developed for the number of supporting people that should be provided to assist teachers. The kinds of resources and resource people that should be made available in a school system will vary from community to community and from school system to school system. Each has its own needs and priorities. Each must define the type of supervisory unit that it needs in terms of its own priorities and available financial support. Each board of education should have a plan for adding resources that takes into account the state requirements, the community needs, the staff needs, and the needs of students.

THE ALLOCATION OF HUMAN RESOURCES

The rational allocation of personnel for the central office team requires consideration of the needed activities, the function of such activities in the achievement of the goals of the school, the specialized competence that is needed to conduct the activities, the size of the school system, and the organization of the school system.

As school systems have grown, become more complicated, and extended instructional services as well as other services for students, the need for central office personnel has expanded rapidly. In a study in New York it was revealed that the number of curriculum specialists and supervisors in the State of New York had doubled between 1948 and 1955 (Cooperative Development of Public School Administration, 1957).

The Educational Research Services of the American Assocation of School Administrators made a survey of three hundred school systems (AASA, 1971). A general trend was determined in the direction of increase in size of central office staff. It was reported that it was rare to find a central office staff that had decreased in size in the last five years. Chief causes for the increases in central staff were identified by school systems as:

1. Increase in educational services for all pupils.
2. Development of compensatory programs (financed by federal funds)
3. Growing school enrollments
4. Change in organizational structure.

Certainly, it is true that central office personnel in curriculum and instruction have increased and will continue to do so. Unfortunately, it is also true that such positions have often been added without careful consideration of the rationale for the position, description of the position, or the way the position would relate to other parts of the program. Positions have often been added to bring prestige or to get federal monies and not necessarily after careful consideration of school objectives, necessary activities to achieve the objectives and personnel and organizational structure that are needed to activate the activities.

The proposed list of functions for the supervisory staff requires a broad base of human specialization to carry on the necessary activities. The continuing development of knowledge and methodology in such content fields as mathematics, science, foreign language, social studies, language arts, reading, physical education and fine arts (to name a few) requires specialists to help keep teachers abreast of new developments. The schools have expanded programs in vocational and technical education and this requires specialized coordination at the central office level.

The supervisory team must also coordinate curriculum design, program evaluation, professional growth programs, and initiation, development, and support for innovative programs. Educational media resources have expanded dramatically in the last few years and it is up to the central office teams to make the ideas available to teachers as well as to provide teachers with an opportunity to develop necessary new skills.

To allocate human resources for the central office team requires not only a careful definition of each required specialization, but also the establishment of priorities within the framework of economic reality.

It is always difficult to decide whether or not a specialized service should be provided at the central office level, the local school level, or brought in on a temporary basis from a cooperative of which the school system is a member, a university, or various kinds of local community resources.

Activities which involve and require the support of the total organization need to be provided at the central office level. Curriculum development and design, overall planning for continuing education of staff, procurement, organization, dissemination of certain materials and other resources of teaching, experimentation, demonstration, development and application of education innovations are examples. Certain highly specialized subject matter consultants need to be stationed at the central office level. Naturally, needed expertise can often be provided from throughout the system on an ad hoc basis. For example: there may be a principal with special competence in early childhood education. Such a person could be temporarily assigned to head up a study of the needs, needed resources, and personnel to establish a kindergarten program in the school system. A person from the central office staff could be used to fill in for the principal while he is on special assignment.

The possibility of school systems joining together in educational cooperatives so as to make it possible to provide certain services that could not be provided otherwise is an idea that merits careful consideration. For example, a group of school systems in Northeast Tennessee feel that they need the services of an "educational planner." However, it is economically unfeasible for each system to employ such a person. Therefore, they are considering hiring the person through the "cooperative" and letting him provide services to all the systems.

There are also untapped community resources that can be studied, analyzed, and made available to the teaching behavior system. Professional and technical persons such as lawyers, medical doctors, physicists, geologists, and social workers are examples of people in the community that can provide support for the teachers and supervisors.

It is also crucial that the opportunities for student educational activities be extended to the community, and this needs to be coordinated at the central office level. Otherwise, there could be confusion among teachers, local schools, and the community that could lead to problems for the program.

We assume that the local school is the basic action agency for school improvement. Therefore, the central office team exists primarily as a support system and change agent for the local school. Appropriate specialists from the central office team, local schools, or outside agencies can be assigned to local schools on a temporary basis in order to achieve a change, develop an idea, help teachers develop new skills, or give needed support to a new curriculum development. It is not only the function of the central office team to provide a considerable amount of expertise from its own ranks but also to be sensitive to and able to deliver appropriate expertise from throughout the school system and community.

The size of the school system is an important factor in the allocation of central office personnel. In large school systems it is economically feasible to allocate more specialists with a broader range of specializations to the central office team. Smaller systems need to utilize "outside" resources such as educational cooperatives, nearby universities, nearby school systems or community resources. The assignment of an instructional supervisor to a particular school has a tendency to limit his services to that school. But, it is also true that an instructional supervisor who is assigned to a particular school has a greater chance to become an effective worker in that school. Certainly, there is a need for instructional supervisors at the local school level. Principals, assistant principals, and department heads often help to provide the needed support. The size of the school system, the size of the local schools, the physical proximity of local schools, and the organizational structure of the system are important factors in the allocation of human instructional resources at the system and local school level.

THE ORGANIZATIONAL STRUCTURE

The central office curriculum and instruction team is a sub-system of the organization. Organizations exist because certain human beings feel that certain objectives can be achieved more effectively through the organization than through individual effort. The central office team exists because it is assumed that as a unit it can achieve certain objectives which will contribute to the achievement of overall organizational goals. Therefore, the organization has certain expectations for the curriculum and instruction team and is willing to allocate material and human resources to it. But, it also holds the team accountable. The curriculum and instruction team must not only produce the desired ends but must be able to demonstrate the achievement of objectives.

If the curriculum and instruction team is to be an effective unit in the organization, there are certain factors or needs that should be given careful consideration:

1. The need for a unitary system of authority. (Van Miller, 1965, p. 507). There is a need for a single executive officer for the curriculum and instruction unit. He is responsible and accountable for the effectiveness of the unit and therefore, needs the appropriate authority to coordinate the activities of the unit toward the achievement of the unit's overall goals. Certain specialized individuals and subunits are necessarily concerned about their own special goals and might in the heat of operation fail to consider the overall goals and the way the sub-systems fit together. A unitary system of authority provides for the coordination and control of the sub-systems in the unit.

The official leader for curriculum and instruction also provides the formal connecting link between the team and the rest of the organization. He is directly responsible to the next echelon of authority and is probably a member of the superintendent of schools' executive team. This is a necessary communication and influence link that makes it possible for curriculum and instruction to hear and be heard and influence and be influenced by the rest of the organization.

2. The need for organizational members to participate in decision making and policy development according to expertise and achieved prestige and not just formal position in the organization.   It is essential for the organizational structure to provide enough flexibility, communication linkages, and cooperative endeavors so that human beings can assume certain leadership roles on an ad hoc basis and with responsibility and authority as needed. Historically, this has been difficult to do. People assigned to a unit worked in that unit. Not to do so could lead to disfavor by the leadership of the unit. It could also be threatening to the official leadership. Organizations need temporary systems with temporary leadership with temporary authority. Organizational members need to recognize and accept this.

3. The need for specialization and generalization.   The broad range of functions of the curriculum and instruction team underline the need for specialization. There is a need for people with highly specialized skills and understandings. This makes it possible to work on tasks and assignments where they have the greatest interest and competence. They can perfect their work and thus enhance their potential contribution to the goals of the organization.

But specialization can also narrow the interest and competence of an individual so that he may have more difficulty in seeing the relationship between his work and other segments of the organization. He may even have difficulty in understanding and appreciating the contributions of other specialists. The specialists may have a contribution to make but may not have the human skills necessary to put it into effect.

Therefore, there is also a need for a generalist. He needs to be sensitive to the total situation so he can see how the parts fit together to form a totality. It is also necessary to facilitate the process through which the specialized expertise can be delivered where and when it is needed. Human and technical skills are fundamental in this process.

4. The need for communication.   The communication process has been discussed in depth in another section of this book. Suffice it to say that it is crucial that the organizational structure facilitate communication in the curriculum and instruction team. Included is the need for communication between the instructional component and other central office teams such as planning, personnel, business, and others; the need for communication with local schools including both teachers and administrators; the need for communication with the superintendent and board of education; and the need for communication within the curriculum and instruction team. It is important that teachers and administrators in one school know and understand what is going on in other schools, and members of the central staff can facilitate this process.

Effective communication not only requires that people can be heard but that they are crucially involved. The organizational structure must provide for a deliberate plan of broad-based involvement in such areas as curriculum planning, planning for continuing education, planning the teacher support system. People need to get involved in crucial decision making and policy development in matters of curriculum and instruction. The organizational structure should provide for this on both a formal and informal basis. The formal should provide for both permanent and temporary systems of decision making and implementation. The informal channels should be supported by providing time, physical space, and human participation.

5. The need for control and conformity.   Organizations need a certain level of predictable behavior of organizational members. Certain people need to be at certain places at a certain time prepared to do certain things. Various segments of the curriculum and instruction teams are dependent on other sections for their proper functioning. For a "line of cooperation" between the central office curriculum and instruction team and local schools to work effectively requires reciprocal and predictable behavior on the part of both. The organizational structure must provide for a line of authority that can assure this kind of interaction and cooperation.

6. The need for flexibility, creative response, and non-threatening inter-personal influence.   It is true that there is a need for control, but it is equally true that there is a need for freedom of movement so that organizational members can exercise their expertise and creativeness in organizational work. Societal expectations for the educational organization change and organizations must change. Members need new understandings, new skills, and new attitudes. Too much control and too much conformity can lead to complacency and inability to change. Creative ideas for improvement can get smothered in the sands of complacency, defensiveness, and "put downism". The need is for a structure that not only provides but seeks out the release of the creativeness of organizational members. The reward system must recognize both creativeness and those who support it.

7. The need for human consideration. The most important part of any organization is the human membership. People have physiological, psychological, and sociological needs; and organizational structures should contribute to the satisfaction of these needs. The need for close and positive identification and acceptance in certain groups is well known. Studies reported earlier indicate that satisfaction of the need to be esteemed by colleagues, the need for recognition, and the need to know someone cares are crucial to the level of worker satisfaction. The structure of the organization can provide the setting and time in which organizational members can carry on a dialogue, come to know each other, share ideas, recognize each other, help each other gain esteem, gain affection, and become an important fully functioning part of the total operation.

8. The need for a broad base of leadership. Leadership can be thought of as the effort of one or more individuals to influence the behavior of other individuals. The assumption is that the capacity for creativeness, innovative ideas, intelligence, and influence is widely dispersed throughout the organization. The need is for an organizational structure that provides for the release of this potential leadership behavior. It would be possible to seek the leadership wherever it is found in the organization and apply it where the problem or decision situation exist. An important function of the permanent members of the curriculum and instruction team would be to seek out problems, places where help is needed, places seeking new ideas, places trying new ideas, and bring the needs and resources together. Potential leadership people could be released on a temporary basis and provided the appropriate authority for that particular task.

THE ASSISTANT SUPERINTENDENT FOR CURRICULUM AND INSTRUCTION

The paramount responsibility of the assistant superintendent for curriculum and instruction is to develop and implement decisions about "what should be taught?" and how it should be taught. More and more these decisions must be based on the changing needs of students and the changing expectations that society has for the schools. This requires close and continuing communication with the students, the local schools, the community and other segments of the superintendent's central office team. The assistant superintendent for instruction is the hub of this communication network, has the responsibility and must have the authority and resources to effectuate the process.

The facts of changing curriculum, differentiated staffing, open facilities, open curriculum, cooperative teaching, new roles and needed new skills and understanding for teachers complicate the responsibility of the position. The growth of schools, federal programs, and new services for pupils demand more specialized services from the central office team.

Someone must be responsible for charting the work of the supervisory staff and for developing a plan of action to implement the curriculum development goals of the school system. Someone must secure the personnel and the financial resources to conduct the activities listed. This person is usually designated as an assistant superintendent in charge of curriculum instruction or as the director of instruction.

It is important in the organization of a supervisory unit that the assistant superintendent in charge be responsible for the work of all the specialists within the unit. He must see that the unit works as a team without competitive and divisive programs being sponsored by it. He must insure that there is a clear and free communication within the division so that there is sufficient opportunity to resolve issues that may arise among the various specialists. The supervisory staff serves the total system. It is not fulfilling its function when it makes conflicting demands upon administrators and teachers within the system. The assistant superintendent must insure that the decisions, relationships, and activities affecting curriculum or instruction are in accordance with the established policy of the system. He must also see that any recommendations for policy change are formulated after consultation with persons who will be affected by any such decision. If conflicts of personality or interpretation arise within the staff or between resource people and teachers or administrators, they should be settled by the assistant superintendent directly or in consultation with the appropriate administrative authority. It should be clear, however, that the supervisory staff does not function as a separate entity within the system. It provides the apparatus through which the system works to formulate policy with regard to curriculum and instruction.

THE CURRICULUM AND INSTRUCTION STAFF

Griffiths and others (Griffiths, Clark, Wynn, and Iannaccone, 1962) have defined two kinds of positions which appear appropriate for the supervisory staff. The position of coordinator is recommended for systems where there is a need for the coordination of certain programs at the central office level. Examples of such programs would include vocational and technical, early childhood, middle school, elementary, secondary, special education, science, languages, and many others. The position involves the specification of objectives, program conditions, and evaluation of the outcomes for the program. The coordinator is also responsible for planning manpower needs, recruitment, selection, coordination and evaluation of specialized personnel. Naturally, he performs the activities in cooperation with other segments of the organization.

A program requires overall coordination since normally there are certain specialized services and consultants which have to be shared by different local schools. In some situations various parts of the program have to be provided in different schools but need to be available to all students. For example, in a vocational and technical education program, "School A" might offer automotive mechanics, cosmetology, and other subjects while "School B" offers electronics, building masonry, carpentry, and other subjects. Students from "School A" may need to take electronics at "School B" and vice versa. The sharing of resources, facilities, and students among local schools requires careful and continuous coordination at the central office level.

The coordinator of a program would normally be a specialist in his own right and would provide appropriate service and consultation to local schools and other segments of the school system within the limitations imposed by the overall demands of the position.

The position of consultant is provided to deliver specialized services and consultations to the teaching behavior systems and others such as local school administrators, personnel services, business, and school board. The service dimension indicates the provision of something that is used. For example, a media consultant may provide certain films, books, and audio-visual equipment. He may even make video tapes of teaching situations so that teachers can see themselves in action. Other services could include psychological and physiological examination of children, teaching certain specialized subjects, providing workshops, developing educational programs for the professional staff, serving as a coordinator of an experimental program.

Consultants also participate in the psychological and technological support system for teachers. They consult with teachers. They react. They make suggestions. They provide descriptive feedback. Hopefully, consultants can participate in this kind of work with teachers on a nonthreatening basis since they are not on the authority line and serve only on a cooperative basis. It is not recommended that they participate in the process of evaluating teachers for personnel purposes such as tenure, merit pay, and other. Rather, the assumption is that teachers need a source of nonthreatening help and support.

THE CURRICULUM PLANNING COUNCIL

As stated in preceding chapters, each school system needs some continuing body with responsibility for making recommendations and decisions within the framework of the overall policy of the system. In some school systems this group is called a curriculum council. It may have other names such as planning committee, development committee, or curriculum policy committee. In any case, it should be representative of students, classroom teachers, administrators, and curriculum specialists.

In a small school system, all teachers might participate in it directly. In a large system, it will be necessary to have representation. This body initiates, and is a clearing house for, studies, experiments, and innovations; it makes decisions; it formulates recommendations; and it advises the administration with regard to all curriculum and instruction policies and problems.

It is important to recognize that curriculum and instruction decisions are made at many levels. The pupil decides what his curriculum really is. The teacher makes certain choices about content and procedures that are within the framework of a given school. The principal and the faculty of the school make certain curriculum decisions within the policies of the total system. On the system-wide level, the curriculum council is the body in which are formulated the decisions that will be implemented by the supervisory staff.

The important principle to keep in mind is that a decision should be made as near the level of implementation as possible. If it is a decision that will not interfere with the sequence of pupils from year to year, or with the working relationship with other pupils in the building, the teacher should be able to make it. If it is a decision that can be implemented in one school without affecting the other schools in the system, the faculty of that school should be able to make it. If it does involve system-wide operation, the decision with regard to policy should be made at the curriculum council level. Throughout the entire process of policy development, groups and individuals should be guided by the principles of keeping available as much freedom of choice as possible. The place where a decision should be made and the people who should be involved in the study on which it is to be based are determined by the kind of policy or policy change that is proposed and by the nature and extent of its anticipated effects.

It is important also to keep open the channels by which requests for initiation or review of policy can be made. Any teacher, principal, faculty or resource person, as well as any board of education member or administrator, should be able to get consideration of a problem that may call for new policy or a redefinition of existing policy. If any staff member can secure consideration of a problem that is important to him, he feels that the system is responsive to his feelings and his needs. This belief is basic to good morale and the assumption of responsibility by all individuals.

A Possible Organizational Structure

It has been previously stated that each system is unique. Each has its own goals, priorities, human resources, and problems. Certainly, the organizational chart should reflect the individuality of the system. Therefore, Figure 6 is presented only as a possible structure and certainly not as a model.

It is assumed that the system is a medium-sized county system with about 25,000 students. Approximately one third of the students are in early childhood education (kindergarten through grade 4), one third are in middle school (grade 5-8) and one third are in high school (grade 9-12). The following chart represents the organizational structure of the superintendent's team and the way it relates

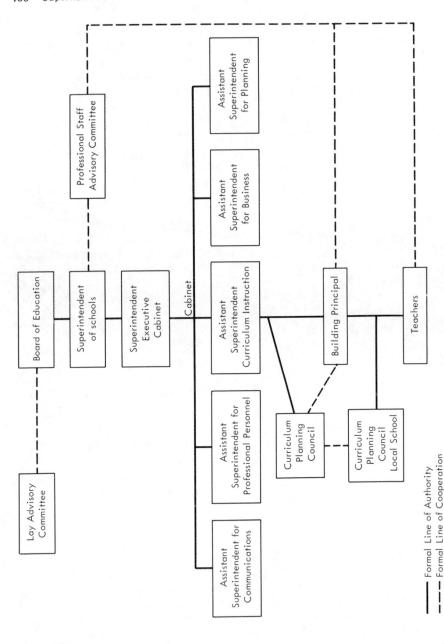

to the board of education, the community, the rest of the professional staff, and the students. The reader is referred to Griffiths, Clark, Wynn, and Iannaccone, *Organizing Schools for Effective Education,* for excellent representative charts on various sized school districts.

The organizational chart clearly shows the board of education as the basic source of formal authority in the organization. The superintendent acts on the authority of the board of education. The superintendent's executive committee, composed of the assistant superintendents, is an important policy-developing structure in the organization. The board of education has a lay advisory board that can be representative of the community and therefore could help keep the board sensitive to changing community educational expectations.

The superintendent has a professional staff advisory board that provides direct contact with teachers and local school administrators on a line of cooperation.

The assistant superintendent for instruction is on the direct line of authority with the superintendent, the principal, and the curriculum planning committee. This authority makes it possible for the assistant superintendent for instruction to provide for the necessary cooperation among members of the central office instructional team and the local school and for cooperation among local schools. The assistant superintendent is also in a position to communicate needs and expectations of local schools and the central office curriculum and instruction team to the superintendent's executive cabinet and conversely to communicate and coordinate central office expectations for local schools. Thus, the foundation is provided for communication and coordination of all the elements of the program of instruction. Figure 7 illustrates the organization of the central office curriculum and instruction team.

The responsibilities of the coordinators have already been defined. Each coordinator has a staff of specialized consultants that are on the authority line to the coordinator but on the line of cooperation to the curriculum planning committee, the principals, and teachers. Each local school has a curriculum planning committee that is represented on the system-wide curriculum planning committee. The crucial part of the system has to be the way the teachers, principals, supervisors, and assistant superintendent work together.

The Principal and the Central Office Supervisory Staff

Sometimes lack of harmony in a faculty exists because two supervisors, the principal and the general or special supervisor, do not have their working relationships clearly defined. Each believes he has responsibility for the success of the program and attempts to influence the direction it will take. Teachers are caught in the struggle for control.

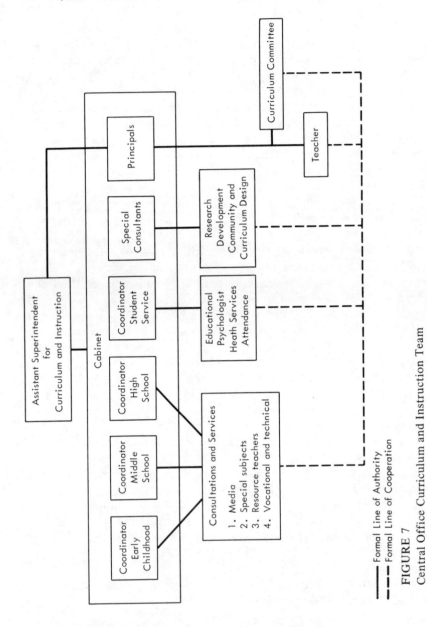

FIGURE 7

Central Office Curriculum and Instruction Team

The functions of all official leaders should be known to the staff. Where there is conflicting authority, the program and the morale of those involved will suffer.

The principal is responsible for the program in his building, and must abide by the goals that have been established for the system. Supervisors, general and special, are available as consultants and helpers, but they cannot direct the work of individual teachers in a manner contrary to the wishes of the principal. If they do, the principal cannot be held responsible for the program in his building.

If a superintendent told each principal how to operate his building, or told each teacher how to teach, he would be depriving them of their responsibilities. Instead, he should hold each principal responsible for developing a program in his building that produces the kinds of pupil growth sought.

To assist principals, the superintendent may make available supervisors with special skills and knowledge. The principal may draw on these supervisors for advice or ask them to assist teachers who are facing difficult problems. But the supervisors should not be made responsible for the program itself. If the program in a building is not getting desirable results, the superintendent should hold the principal accountable and should require him to demonstrate that he has taken steps to improve the situation and that he has used the available resources.

Supervisors should be present at the planning sessions of the superintendent and the principals. Otherwise, they will not feel that they have a vital part in the program and they will lack the information they need to be of assistance to the principals. If supervisors are to perform most effectively in improving instruction, they must be fully informed and included in the planning.

A major city of the United States employed forty supervisors. During a ten-year period, the superintendent did not hold a meeting with the supervisors. They were not included in the principal's meetings. At one time during the period, they were told to direct the programs in their areas. Again, they were told to serve as consultants and to stay in their offices until called. Difficulties arose with various principals, and personality and friendship determined the use made of the supervisors in each school. The supervisory positions became dead-end jobs in which people lost hope and faith.

The relationship between principals and supervisors needs careful examination and discussion. Supervisors are not errand boys for principals, nor are they the bosses of principals. Supervisors and principals are persons of comparable professional ability and skill performing different functions. Supervisors are consultants to be called in to help analyze problem situations, to try out remedial measures, and to assist in evaluation of results. They can be called upon for advice and suggestions, but they abandon their function when they try to sell or convince. The responsibility for decisions rests with the principal and his staff. When each principal is responsible for the program in his school, the general or subject-matter supervisor serves as a resource person for the principal and teachers.

> The principal of a high school in a southern city was concerned with the quality of the intramural program in the school. He asked the physical education specialist to come to his office to discuss intramural sports. During the conversation, he requested a set of criteria by which to judge a high-school intramural program, and the physical education supervisor agreed to prepare and send it.
>
> A week later, the principal called a meeting of the physical education staff and representatives of the student council and invited the physical education supervisor to be present. He submitted the proposed criteria to the meeting for analysis. Some objection was raised to some of the criteria. In the course of the meeting, some students and teachers began to apply the criteria to the intramural program in the school, and the head of the physical education department asked the supervisor to join a future department meeting in which an evaluation of the intramural program would be started.
>
> The physical education supervisor revised the proposed criteria for intramural programs and placed it in the system-wide curriculum bulletin in the hope that other principals or departments would be sufficiently challenged to request a meeting to discuss them.

The special subject supervisor's success depends upon his competency in his field and his way of working with people. If he does not show insight in his discussions with principals and staff, he will be ignored. He cannot succeed simply because he bears the label, supervisor. If he does not present his ideas in a friendly, relaxed manner, he will not be taken seriously or called again. We build defenses against someone who threatens us by his manner or by his use of knowledge. The supervisor's participation must convince others that his knowledge is a tool at their service rather than a club to force conformity to a pattern they cannot understand or accept.

Sometimes the supervisor has a delicate consultative function to perform. He may feel it necessary to call shortcomings of the school to the attention of the principal. Whatever his relationship with the principal, this task is dangerous. If he makes generalizations about the situation and then attempts to document them with specifics, he almost always fails. If he approaches the problem by proposing joint examination and evaluation, he has a better chance of succeeding. If he can make the study of the situation a part of action research designed to improve the program, he is less likely to fail than if he collects data by himself to use in making a judgment about another's work or to convince the other that he ought to change.

There may be times when a special subject supervisor is not used in a school. The principal may lack vision or may be antagonistic to the individual serving as supervisor. If the program in the school is excellent, the supervisor may not be needed and should be left free to use his time more effectively in another school. If the program is poor, the supervisor must depend upon the superintendent who is ultimately responsible and to whom the principal is accountable. If the supervisor is not able to report progress in a certain school, the superintendent is the individual who can and must open the door to improvement. He is the one to ask the principal for evidence of progress and for an accounting of how the available resources are being used. If the principal develops confidence in a supervisor, the supervisor feels free to help individual teachers.

A Kentucky supervisor spent fifty hours his first semester on the job talking with one principal who had some doubts and who apparently liked to talk. But as a result of this exploration of ideas and the mutual respect that resulted, the supervisor was able to work effectively in this school. The reputation he established for helping teachers in this school spread throughout the county and opened doors and invitations to help in other schools.

The supervisor finds it hard to be effective in working with a teacher when the principal resents his efforts. In the day-to-day contact in the school, the principal's casual belittling or slighting remarks about the supervisor's assumed importance can breed in teachers a feeling of insecurity and doubt, if not downright suspicion and hostility.

To secure the best results, the supervisor should visit a teacher only at the teacher's request. If the principal believes in the supervisor, if the teacher's contacts with the supervisor in group meetings have been easy and non-threatening, and if other teachers have testified to the supervisor's worth and friendliness, the chances are good that teachers will request his assistance. But if the supervisor shows aggression, a desire for power, feelings of superiority, or insecurity, teachers will hesitate to establish working relationships with him.

Occasions may arise when it is necessary for the supervisor to ask to visit a teacher. If the principal believes that an unsatisfactory teacher needs help or complaints of parents or pupils indicate that an inquiry is warranted, the supervisor may request permission to observe. The teacher has no choice but to issue an invitation. To refuse is to admit that something is not able to withstand scrutiny. What happens after the supervisor enters the classroom depends upon his skill in communication and analysis of the situation.

If the working relationship between principals and supervisors is not satisfactory, the superintendent must assume responsibility and take leadership in improving the situation. The superintendent is the only individual with the authority to make decisions in this area. When the superintendent uses his authority and is willing to share the decision-making process, a control exists that holds the group together until agreement is reached. When it is not clear that the superintendent is assuming responsibility for reaching a decision, persons without authority can only hope that cooperative impulses will prevail.

SUPERVISION AT
THE LOCAL SCHOOL LEVEL

Supervisory behavior emanates from the local school level as well as the central office level. Chapter 10, Chapter 11, and Chapter 12 deal with the functions, allocation, organization, and operation of supervisory services in the local community setting.

10 The Supervisory Team at the Local School

The local school is the basic action agency for the development and activation of learning opportunities for students. Certainly, teachers are the primary agents in this process. But, it has been a major thesis of this book that there is a need for a support system that interacts with the teaching behavior system for the purpose of improving learning opportunities for students. The local school instructional supervisory team is an important part of that process. The purpose of Chapter 10 is to discuss in some detail the work of this team, the allocation of personnel for the team, and the organization of the team.

The Work of the Instructional Supervisory Team

The tasks of the local school instructional supervisory team are quite similar to those of the central office team. For example, participation in and coordination of the continuous development and evaluation of educational goals at the local school level; provision for the psychological and technological support system for teachers; experimentation, development, and supervision of new programs; intersharing of educational ideas with other schools in the district; continuing education for the professional staff; curriculum design, coordination of various specialized sub-systems in the local school so as to maintain balance and common direction in the program; selection, procurement, allocation, and deployment of materials and equipment of instruction; educational planning; manpower planning, selection, induction, and utilization are all proposed as tasks of the local school instructional supervisory team.

GOAL DEVELOPMENT AND EVALUATION

It is essential that each local school provide a means for the continuous specification of projected outcomes of the instructional program. Such a projection is necessarily developed within the framework of system objectives, community expectations, teacher concerns, and the interest and needs of students in the school. One key to effectiveness in this task area is to provide a broad base of participation. In this way it is possible to increase the probability of having a program that reflects the needs, interests, and aspirations of students, teachers, administrators and members of the community. Broad participation also contributes to the level of understanding of, and support for, the program. Faculty awareness of overall school goals is an essential ingredient for motivation to achieve these goals.

It is also important to provide meaning for overall goals through the development of operational objectives or behavioral objectives. Such objectives provide direction in the design, development, and activation of engagement opportunities for students and also provide a basis for evaluation as well as the development of instruments and procedures for evaluation.

Teachers need to be closely involved in the development of the overall goals for the school, since they need to develop goals and objectives for their own instructional activities that are consistent with overall goals and that will contribute to their achievement.

PSYCHOLOGICAL AND TECHNOLOGICAL SUPPORT

Teachers need technological support. They need specialized service in the procurement and utilization of materials and equipment. They need expert consultation in specialized subject fields. They also need assistance in the development and activation of learning opportunities for students. There is a need for teachers to have a continuous source of feedback on the effectiveness of their own teaching efforts. They need sensitive and knowledgeable people who are nonthreatening and who are available for interactions about instructional plans, observation, analysis of instruction, and cooperative evaluation.

Obviously, much of this service and consultation can come from the central office. But there is also a need for support at the local school level. Such support has the advantage of constant visibility and availability. A teacher can get to know, like, and respect a local media specialist, helping teacher, department chairman, or curriculum specialist. These people eat, play, take duty, and drink coffee with teachers. They provide service and consultation for teachers when it is needed. Thus, the potential for an effective working relationship is there.

The local school instructional team not only has the advantage in the provision of services and consultations but also has the advantage in developing sensitivity to the needs of teachers. Since these local instructional leaders are in close contact with members of the local school faculty and instructional personnel at the central office level, they are in an excellent position to facilitate the process of bringing together personnel with needs and personnel with special competence to provide service.

Psychological support is a crucial need of teachers. When things are not going well, when a new idea failed to work, when there is insecurity in trying a new idea – these are times when members of the faculty need special support. The principal is the chief executive officer of the school; therefore he is in an excellent position to provide needed support. Since he has a formal position and some formal authority, it helps teachers to know that he understands, wants to help, and will stand behind them in failure as well as success. Other members of the instructional team can also provide the right kind of support at the right time. The need is for behavior that communicates sensitivity, understanding, and caring. Members of the local school instructional team are in the right place at the right time; they should have the competence to deliver this kind of support.

In a recent meeting of a group of principals, one principal told of an experience in which he had visited a teacher's class. During the course of the visit, he and the teacher chatted about several things that were going on. As the principal was leaving, the teacher began to tell him how much the visit had meant to her. He was curious and asked about it. She indicated that he was the first adult in six years that had visited her class, and that it was just wonderful to know that someone cared about what she was doing.

Teachers need to feel that what they are doing is important. Getting this feeling is at least partly a function of the recognition and support that they get from others who are important to them. The instructional leadership team at the local school is not only in an excellent position to provide this kind of support, but can also facilitate the process through which teachers can receive support from their fellow teachers, parents, and students.

EXPERIMENTATION WITH NEW PROGRAMS AND CURRICULUM DESIGN

Development of, experimentation with, and diffusion of new programs are crucial tasks of local school leadership teams. Naturally, this is an essential part of the on-going process of curriculum design. The local school is the place where the students interact with program conditions. It is necessary for the various segments of the program to have a common direction. They need to be interdependent parts, and this requires overall design and coordination. It is not only necessary to design engagement opportunities for students in terms of overall objectives, but it is also necessary to examine the way they fit together in the total program. This is curriculum design and it is a crucial function of the local school supervisory team.

Members of the supervisory team can be selected because of this special competence. They can be given the time to devote to curriculum planning and the opportunity to be aware of expectations from the central office. This does not mean that teachers do not participate in curriculum planning. They do. But it does mean that local school instructional leaders have a special part to play. One aspect of the role is to make sure that teachers are heavily involved.

Educational objectives change. The expectations of people in the community change. The needs of students change. There is constant development of knowledge out of which flow ideas for new programs. Programs must constantly change, and this requires the development of new ideas, evaluation of the ideas in terms of the overall curriculum design, trying out appropriate ideas, and evaluating the trial. The local school supervisory staff must provide the leadership for this process. When a decision is made to adopt, then leadership must be provided for the diffusion of the new program.

MATERIALS AND EQUIPMENT

Teachers need a broad base of materials and equipment of instruction. Such materials and equipment are in constant production and change. Programs change and require new materials and equipment, new knowledge and technology provide the basis for new media for education. New packaged programs, computer assisted programs, tapes, video taping equipment, overhead projectors, and films are examples of new materials and equipment that are becoming available. Teachers need to keep abreast of these developments. But their teaching responsibilities limit their opportunities. Therefore, it is proposed that the local school instructional leadership team provide these needed expert services and consultations. The teachers not only need to be made aware of the new developments but also need an opportunity to develop the understandings and skills that will assure their use in the activation of learning activities for students.

The local school instructional team is in a strategic position to provide these services. Since they are in constant interaction with teachers, they know their needs. They also are constantly available to give assistance and provide for follow-up activities. Certainly, some things need to be provided at the central office level. But, it is the function of local school specialists to keep informed of such services and facilitate their effective utilization at the local school level.

EDUCATIONAL PLANNING

Effective educational planning at the local school level requires a definition of goals to be reached in each program, an operational definition of the goals, projected target dates, and a clear statement of needs including new personnel, equipment, materials, and facilities. The process is continuous; it needs to be done on a long-range basis.

Planning is a comprehensive process and requires the participation of all personnel. But the supervisory team would be expected to provide much of the leadership and hard work required to get the job done.

STAFF SELECTION AND DEVELOPMENT

There is probably no function of the local school instructional supervisory team that affects the quality of education for children as much as staff selection and training. The educational program must constantly change to meet the changing needs of students. Teachers need new conceptual, technical, and human skills. Current staff must be provided an opportunity to develop these skills or new staff members must be employed that already have them. Both approaches must be used. The processes of staff development and selection at the local school level will be discussed in depth in a later chapter.

The Allocation of Personnel

The allocation of personnel for the supervisory team requires a consideration of the size of the school, the organizational structure, needed activities, and the specialized competence needed to conduct the activities. The size of the school is a crucial factor in decisions concerning whether to provide a needed service or consultative resources on a permanent basis or "on call" basis from the central office. The larger the school the easier it is to justify permanent assignments.

The size of the school is also a factor in the determination of the needs for coordination. For example, relatively large elementary schools may have as many as two or three teams of teachers that conduct learning activities for students in early childhood education. Such teams require official leadership to coordinate the activities of the team and the team's interaction with other teams in the schools. Department heads and program coordinators might serve similar functions in middle schools and secondary schools.

There is also a need for a broad range of specialized services. Teachers need help in the selection, procurement and utilization of materials and equipment. They need technological and psychological support and it needs to be available when it is needed. Certainly, every effort should be made to provide a team of specialists at the local school level that can give the broad range of services and consultations required. But economic realities make this impossible. Therefore, it is proposed that such services also be utilized from the central office level, fellow teachers, and members of the community at large.

The assumption is that teachers not only have a broad range of needs but also a broad range of specialized competence that can be utilized in providing needed services and consultations to other teachers. An important part of the job of the supervisory team is to locate available resources and develop procedures for their utilization. Therefore, it is proposed that in the allocation of human resources provision be made for the release of teachers on an *ad hoc* basis to participate in instructional supervision. This could be done by the allocation of personnel who participate both as teachers and instructional leaders. They could fill in for teachers who are needed to provide supervisory services as well as providing such services.

A broad range of specialized people is normally available in the community. Social workers, scientists, counselors, medical doctors, and business executives are examples of individuals who could be called on to provide needed services for teachers.

Specialized services and resource people are also available from the state and federal governments. Funds are constantly becoming available that can be used to support special programs and provide specialized services to teachers. Schools that are aware of such programs and that are effective in attracting them can improve the quantity and quality of support for teachers.

It is obvious that there is no single rule that can be used to allocate personnel for the supervisory team. Rational allocation requires study of the way the school operates; the need for services; resources available from the central office, community, and local instructional staff, and the particular activities of a school at a given time. For example, if the school is giving serious consideration to the development of a new program, certain resources may be needed. If a program has been adopted and teachers need to develop certain skills, other resources may be needed.

If the school operates according to a formal bureaucratic model, the need for supervisory services might be different than if the school is trying to get a broader base of involvement in decision making and problem solving. If the school is highly dynamic with a high thrust for improvement, the needs would be different than in a relatively stable situation. The need for study is apparent, and so is the need to provide for the uniqueness of each school.

The Organizational Structure

In Chapter 9 the following needs of organizations were identified and discussed as they applied to organizational structure at the central office level:

1. The need for a unitary system of authority.
2. The need for organizational members to participate in decision making and policy development according to expertise and achieved prestige and not just formal position in the organization.
3. The need for specialization and generalization.
4. The need for communication.
5. The need for control and conformity.
6. The need for flexibility, creative response, and nonthreatening interpersonal influence.

7. The need for human consideration.
8. The need for a broad base of leadership.

The reader is referred to Chapter 9 for a more detailed discussion of these factors. The assumption is made that they are equally appropriate as needs of the local school organization as they are for the organization of the school district.

In essence what is being recommended is an organizational structure that is characterized by "openness." Such an organization is responsive to external influences. It can evaluate the meaning of such "input" and develop decisions for future direction and action. It is willing to constantly evaluate ends and means in terms of constantly changing internal and external conditions.

The need for specialization and differentiated staffing is recognized and provided for, but so is the need for sharing, learning from each other, and recognizing and utilizing expertise wherever it exists. The need for constituted authority is assumed but the source of that authority is the human being who must be controlled in order to provide for the coordination of specialized parts to assure the achievement of overall goals. Organizational members understand each other and provide enough conformity to facilitate interdependence of parts and provide enough individual uniqueness to assure creative responses.

The emphasis is on a broad base of organizational member participation in goal setting, program developing, problem solving, evaluation, and planning. Formal position is utilized to facilitate these processes. The identification and release of faculty intelligence and creativeness are recommended as functions of the local school instructional team. The delivery of service and consultation wherever it is found and whenever it is needed to improve the quality of education for students is central to the work of the instructional team.

THE PRINCIPAL AS INSTRUCTIONAL LEADER

The principal is one official leader at the local school level that is primarily concerned with the overall goals of the school. The local school organization is a dynamic web of interdependent parts that are assumed to contribute to the realization of the overall goals. But the parts are sub-systems of the supra-system; they have their own goals which may or may not be congruent with local school goals. For example, a school may have a football team with a winning tradition that has become a powerful factor in the school. The need to win may precipitate certain practices that are detrimental to other parts of the school. The power of the sub-system (the football program) may make such practices possible. The need for coaches and assistant coaches may influence personnel selection in such a way that coaches are hired with the hope that they are competent teachers. Students may be pulled out of classes for football practice to the disadvantage of academic objectives. A "part" has gotten out of balance in terms of overall system goals. A major function of the principal is to weave these parts into a balanced, coordinated, and fully functioning whole that can maintain optimum goal achievement.

The principal is a central factor in the communication network. He has direct contact with the central office and thus responsibility to interpret and communicate central office expectations to the local school. He is also the chief communicator of local school needs and expectations to the central office. The local school internal network of communication is a major concern. It is crucial that local school curriculum specialists and resource people work as a team among themselves and with teachers. Teacher-teacher, teacher-curriculum worker, and teacher-administrator communications are paramount in the planning and actualization of learning activities for students. Communication with other schools in which new ideas, materials, equipment, and human resources are shared is largely dependent on the effectiveness of the principal.

The principal not only provides leadership to identify and utilize appropriate personnel to provide an adequate system of psychological and technological support for teachers, but he also participates in the process.

The goals and means for achieving goals are constantly changing. Open facilities, open curriculum, differentiated staffing, new programs, cooperative teaching all demand new understandings and new skills for organizational members. Schools must change and people must change. But, there is also a need for stability. The forces of change must be understood, utilized, and controlled. The principal is the chief instructional leader of the school; he is responsible for maintaining this delicate balance.

THE CURRICULUM AND INSTRUCTION STAFF

The positions of coordinator and consultant were recommended as appropriate positions for the supervisory staff at the district level. These same positions are recommended for members of the curriculum and instruction team at the local school level.

The position of coordinator is called for where there is a program with definable interdependent parts that need to be pulled together toward the achievement of certain goals. The position of coordinator could be used to designate a team leader of a group of kindergarten teachers, aids, technicians, and student teachers. A possible definition of the team coordinator's role follows:

1. To involve the team in the development of goals and behavioral objectives for students that are consistent with the expectations of the local school and school district.
2. To involve the team in designing and developing plans for the actualization of engagement opportunities for students in order to achieve the goals and operational objectives.
3. To involve the team in developing a plan for the evaluation of the achievement of student goals together with the actualization of the plan.

4. To involve the team in the planning and implementation of a design for staff selection and evaluation that is consistent with personnel policies in the organization.
5. To facilitate the provision of the psychological and technological support system for the team.
6. To facilitate the communication and actualization of team expectations of the system and system expectations of the team.
7. To participate in the process of helping and being helped by team members and to facilitate the process of team members helping each other.

The above role definition is not presented as a model, but rather as an example of a possible role definition. The role definition of a particular team leader would be a function of the organizational expectations, team member expectations, team leader expectations, and the way the team leader relates to these expectations.

Other examples of the need for coordinators at the local school level would include coordinators of content departments, athletics, guidance services, teaching resource centers, laboratories such as science, language, drama and many others. Coordinators exist to design, implement, and evaluate programs in cooperation with other specialists.

Consultants are used to render certain services or help through active participation in the teaching behavior system. Examples of the behavior of consultants would be helping a teacher use video taping equipment, helping a teacher use some system of interaction analysis to describe student-student interaction in her group, listening to a teacher talk about plans for actualizing certain engagement opportunities for students, making a suggestion to a group of teachers about using micro-teaching; demonstrating the use of micro-teaching; helping a group of teachers reach consensus on an approach to the teaching of reading.

It is important to recognize that coordinators participate in consultative behavior and consultants often become coordinators on an "ad hoc" basis. This is also true of teachers, teacher aids, technicians, and administrators.

POSSIBLE STRUCTURES FOR INSTRUCTIONAL SUPERVISION

The effectiveness of any system of instructional supervision is at least partly a function of the organizational structure. It has already been explained that each school has its own identity, needs, priorities, and human capabilities. Therefore, the possible structures described in this section are not necessarily recommended for a particular local school. Rather, it is hoped that various elements might be appropriate for a particular school, but, more importantly, that the use of actual models may help clarify the implications of assumptions, concepts, and principles discussed in this chapter.

The following example was developed for an early childhood school (kindergarten through third year). There are 150 children in the kindergarten program and 900 children about equally divided among first, second, and third year children. The school operates on a nongraded basis, and an attempt is made to provide each child with an opportunity to develop and explore interests, intellectual skills, human skills and creativeness in his own way and according to his special capacities. There is an assumption that children develop at different rates and have different interests in, and capacities for, learning and also that children need to interact with other children of different ages, interests, and capacities.

It is assumed that all the people in the school, including children, teachers, consultants, coordinators, custodians, aids, and administrators are important and, therefore, their needs are important. Needs for belonging, affection, stability of structure, change, recognition, and achievement are recognized, and an effort is made to provide a working environment in which those needs can be satisfied.

All the people in the school have a potential for making a contribution to school improvement and are therefore considered as important human resources. Every effort is made to provide a broad base of human involvement in problem solving and decision-making activities. Administrators, teachers, consultants, and coordinators can help and be helped by each other. There is also a broad base of human competence with focus on utilization of the competence in school improvement.

The need for coordination and control is recognized and utilized, but organizational members have a say in the development and continuous evaluation of that control system.

The system of instructional supervision is built on the notion that it is an organizationally sponsored behavior system that interacts with teaching behavior for the purpose of improving the quality of learning for students. Since teachers are assumed to be professionally competent and to represent a broad spectrum of specialization, it is recognized that teachers need to help and support each other. Therefore, an important task of administrators, coordinators, and consultants is to study the competence of the staff and to facilitate its utilization in the program of supervision.

It is known that the content, methodology, and materials and resources of teaching must constantly change along with the changing needs of students and new developments in knowledge and technology. A broad technological and psychological support system is provided for the teaching behavior system. Coordinators and consultants with special skills and knowledge are available to teachers at the local school level. Other specialists are utilized from the school district instructional team, institutions of higher education, local community, and other local schools.

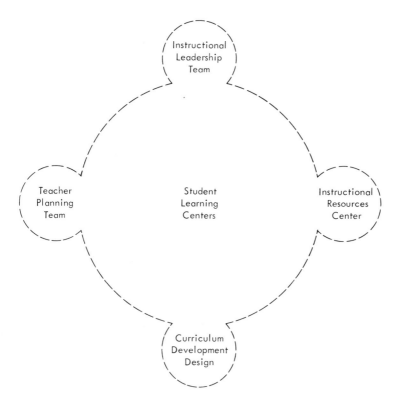

FIGURE 8
Supervision in a Local School

In summary, supervision in this elementary school is perceived as a dynamic web of interpersonal influence, help, support, and collaboration which is wrought out of communication based on human openness, trust, and authenticity. Figure 8 is a conceptual scheme for visualizing instructional supervision in this school.

The conceptual scheme clearly shows the "student learning centers" as the focus of the instructional supervisory behavior system. The four support systems are identified as the "teacher planning team," "instructional leadership team," "instructional resources center," and "curriculum development and design center." Each of these sub-systems is shown to have its own identity (reason for being) but is also shown to be interdependent with the student learning center, with each other and as a sub-system of the local school system.

The student learning centers are where the action is; that is, engagement opportunities for students are actualized. Programmed learning, computer-based instruction, packaged materials, taped cassettes, large group instruction and small discussion groups are examples of instructional techniques and ways of grouping children that might be utilized.

In the example school there is one student learning center for 150 kindergarten children. There are six learning centers for the children from first year through third year. Each unit is made up of 150 children who vary in age, interest, physical development, social development and intellectual development.

The "teacher planning team" for each learning center is composed of a teacher-team leader, two general teachers, two special teachers, a media technician and three aids. The situation is open in both social structure and physical facilities. Students and teachers have easy access to each other so that helping, providing feedback and demonstrating come easily and naturally. The team leader has the responsibility to involve the team in cooperative planning, teaching, and evaluation. Objectives of learning are defined, programs are designed, implemented, and evaluated on a cooperative basis. Quality control is explicit in the total process of goal development, program implementation and evaluation. The team leader is the crucial factor in facilitating the processes of teachers' planning together, observing each other, analyzing each other and generalizing from the analysis.

The team leaders, principal coordinators, and consultants along with other members of the team facilitate the process of person-to-person and team-to-team supervision within the school. This involves identification of special competence throughout the school that can be shared and identification of teachers with needs or problems and bringing them together.

Teachers are often released on a temporary basis to be helped or to share certain ideas or skills with other teams. Coordinators or consultants often "fill in" for teachers on such occasions. The same process can be utilized in school to school sharing.

As a sub-system of the school district, the student learning centers also have special consultants and services available from the central office instructional team. This service is used, and the team leader is in an excellent position to help in this endeavor. The doors remain open to other agencies such as special community resources including institutions of higher education.

The "instructional leadership team" is made up of the principal, student learning center team leaders, coordinators, and special consultants. The instructional leadership responsibilities of the principal have already been defined. It is through the instructional leadership team that the principal can implement his role. Objectives for the school can be hammered out. The various specialized parts of the school can be studied, analyzed, and evaluated according to their contribution to the achievement of overall goals. Long-term and short-term planning can be implemented, including a consideration of long-term goals, programs, personnel needs, and facility needs. Such planning needs to be coordinated with district level planning.

The "curriculum development and design center" is where the program of engagement opportunities for students is designed and tested. Each learning center is represented along with the various other sub-systems in the school. There is also a representative to the school district curriculum development and design center. The interlinkage of these centers facilitates curriculum coordination at both the local school and school district.

The instructional resources center is primarily a service center to the student learning centers. Materials and equipment are developed, collected and made available according to the needs of the learning centers. The function of the center is not just to make materials and equipment available, but rather to involve students and teachers in the process of development, procurement, and use. Examples of such involvement would include student made movies, slides, and pictures to share certain ideas; teacher developed instructional techniques; commercially developed programs. In a fundamental way the instructional resources center can contribute to the sharing of instructional materials, equipment, and "know how" among the student learning centers.

The local school is a dynamic system of interacting parts that fit together to achieve certain common goals. The instructional supervisory behavior system interacts with the teaching behavior system to improve the probability that these goals will be realized.

Leadership in the Local School

If it is recognized that leadership is any contribution to the establishment and achievement of goals by a group, it is easy to see that official leadership must be concerned with the fullest possible cultivation of the leadership potential of each member of the group. Merely apprenticing one member of the faculty for future status leadership is too limited a concept of the responsibility for developing leadership. It restricts the possible accomplishments of the group.

The development of leadership in group members involves getting them to assume responsibility for the planning and development of a program; it also involves creating the type of atmosphere in which they are encouraged and stimulated to exert their full native ability. Through helping staff members achieve leadership, the full power of the group is released. Each member makes his maximum contribution as he has the opportunity to lead, and he grows in strength and ability through the experience.

In a school faculty, leadership is fostered by creating a permissive atmosphere in which the individual feels secure enough to make his unique contribution; providing positive support for faculty members who attempt leadership; rewarding successful leadership attempts and providing psychological support and technical help for unsuccessful leadership attempts; offering individuals an opportunity to participate in decision-making and problem-solving activities according to their interest and expertise; and providing an opportunity for faculty members to assume responsibility with appropriate authority in program improvement, human development, staff selection, goal development, and other activities on a temporary basis.

DEVELOPMENT OF LEADERSHIP IN OTHERS

Why aren't teachers willing to exert their full leadership? In light of what has been said already about people wanting recognition and the feeling that they are making a contribution, it would seem that everyone would want to lead in any way he could. Some teachers are willing to lead; others are not. Much of the difference lies in the type of supervision they have had. If their official leaders have been reluctant to delegate authority and have attempted to control all teacher actions, only the unusual teachers will volunteer to assume responsibility. After teachers have been dominated and directed for years, they cannot be expected to rush to assume leadership. Any new principal will have to work with them a long time before they will lose their suspicions, feel that the program is theirs as well as the principal's, and become willing to exert initiative. If, however, teachers have experienced stimulating official supervision that has worked for teacher leadership, they exert leadership.

Official leaders must begin with people where they are. Members of the instructional leadership team must accept teachers for what they are, without condemning them for behavior that is the result of their past experiences, and attempt to create the type of environment that makes it possible and desirable for people to assume leadership.

Leadership involves pioneering. As people venture into the unknown, the chance of making errors is greatly increased. If supervisors want to encourage leadership, they must support teachers as they work out solutions to new problems. If a principal has a faculty that has never taken a field trip, and he wants it to begin to utilize community resources, he must make clear his backing of field trips, help arrange schedules and transportation that makes trips possible, and then give teachers freedom to experiment.

The first prerequisite for increasing a teacher's willingness to risk making a mistake is the establishment of an atmosphere in which mistakes during innovation are not penalized. Official leaders must recognize that teachers incur some insecurity through creative efforts; some mistakes will occur; advances and new learning come about as the result of mistakes as well as successes; and some sense of order may appear to be lost while new methods are being tested. They must understand that teachers who are attempting creative work need greater support from their supervisors. People are less willing to take chances when there is a possibility of being punished for mistakes made. The principal must let the staff know he understands that a teacher may make mistakes in attempting procedures for which no pattern has been set.

If team leaders want to foster leadership, they must recognize and respect the need of staff members for security. They must eliminate, as far as they can, the possibility of making reprisals. Because the principal exerts power over promotion and salary, some teachers will hesitate to place their ideas on an equal basis with his. Some schools have attempted to eliminate fear of supervision by creating consultants or resource teachers who assist but do not rate, by establishing a salary scale with automatic salary increases, and by holding workshops and camps where teachers and supervisors work together as equal members of a work team. All such efforts should be judged by their effect on the creation of a school environment in which teachers feel secure to make an error in judgment or to differ in opinion with the official leadership.

The principal must avoid stereotypes of what constitutes worthwhile contributions and good teaching. Otherwise, teachers learn not to assume leadership, because the person who does assume responsibility and carries it out in a way that differs from the principal's original idea is reprimanded. Teachers in such a situation quickly become afraid to "stick out their necks." They avoid any type of work that leads them beyond their customary routine into activities in which they are unsure of the principal's desires or their ability to meet them. As teachers find that the easiest way to be happy and safe from criticism is to stick to the regular job, it becomes more and more difficult to get them to assume leadership. A principal may repress growth without realizing it.

After twenty years of teaching, a junior-high-school English teacher had decided that teaching grammar for the full period each day was not the most effective teaching procedure or the most enjoyable. She searched and found a magazine published in London for British adolescents. She subscribed to the magazine, using money from her salary. The pupils enjoyed it. They took copies home and their parents approved and commented favorably to the teacher.

One day the principal came by and saw it. Reacting in light of public opinion that opposed UNESCO, he commented, without any attempt to discover the facts, "I'd get rid of those magazines. Someone might think we are teaching UNESCO." The teacher, who had begun to venture after twenty years of conforming put the magazines back in the closet.

Opposition to the ideas of principals, team leaders, department heads, and other members of the official leadership team must be accepted and recognized as a contribution to group growth and program improvement if leadership is not to be confined to areas the official leader has already explored and described. It is easier to accept the philosophic concept of valuing opposition than it is to practice it. It is difficult for an administrator to keep from ascribing unworthy motives to the person who opposes him. It is easy to believe that the opposition is seeking power or protecting a vested interest. It is more difficult to assume that he is as intellectually honest, or that he is acting because of a deep commitment to fundamental values.

It is especially hard to give due credit to the opposition when it adopts tactics that seem unfair. Occasions that test the administration are: a certain group always opposes him; it is obvious that there has been a decision before the meeting and that a plan has been developed for blocking consideration of an idea or for railroading one through; argument descends to name calling and appeals to emotion. At such times, the principal finds himself torn between the desire to utilize everyone's contribution and his responsibility to conduct the business of the school in such a manner that a unified, consistent program is developed. If unjustified and unfair opposition continues, the principal may have to discuss the decision-making process with the leaders of the opposition, but he should recognize such procedure as an act of desperation to be used after all his techniques for achieving group integration have been exhausted. If discussion does not secure positive results, the principal will be forced to use his authority to make sure that consideration is given to issues and possible solutions.

The Use of Authority

The principal who is seeking to develop more effective ways of using his authority can share it. As he gives others a part in determining how authority shall be used and who shall use it, he is currently sharing his authority and his responsibility. He does not relinquish either authority or responsibility, but the group acquires both by accepting the invitation to participate in decision-making. Of course, the principal is responsible to those who delegated authority to him for the way it is used. But so are the other members of the staff after they have shared it. They become co-advocates and defenders, if necessary, of the steps taken. The principal is never alone against the board or the community if he has shared his authority.

Sharing authority is not as familiar a concept as delegating authority. The right and necessity for an official leader to delegate authority are never questioned, but principals have not been equally clear about the possible results of sharing authority.

From the point of view of those who have granted the authority, the official leader is responsible. He cannot escape this responsibility. If he delegates authority, he is performing an administrative action. If he shares authority, he is using an administrative procedure. As far as the persons above are concerned, the principal has full authority and responsibility. He can exercise the authority as he sees best. He is free to share authority if he feels it will get better results.

From the point of view of the staff working beneath the principal in the line of authority, there is a vast difference between delegated and shared authority. Persons to whom authority is delegated assume responsibility for its use but not for the decision on how it will be used. They are responsible to their official leader, but not to anyone beyond him. The arguments of the lesser Nazis in the trials following World War II illustrate the refusal to accept responsibility for decisions concerning the use of authority. On the other hand, persons with whom authority is shared assume responsibility for decisions concerning its use as well as for the execution of decisions. All persons who accept a share in deciding how authority will be used become responsible to each other and to persons outside the group for the utilization of the authority.

The official leader's decision on whether to delegate certain authority to certain staff members or to share his authority with the total staff must be made on the basis of how the work of the staff will be affected. The autocratic leader can secure cooperation in carrying out his goals by using threats and rewards. If people are afraid, or if they wish to obtain what the leader has to offer, they will surrender their will to his and will cooperate in doing what he wants. If a leader chooses to operate democratically, his major source of control is sharing his authority to make decisions. He cannot force people to join in making decisions. If they are not willing to share voluntarily in the decision-making, he will be forced to use the same techniques of control that the authoritarian leader uses. If, however, the members of the group see value in sharing decisions and understand that in the process their purposes will be considered and utilized, their participation is voluntary, and it results in their assuming responsibility in the execution of the decisions. Cooperation is voluntary because the individual's purposes are included in the determination of the action to be undertaken.

The basic way a nonauthoritarian leader has of getting people to cooperate is to give them a share in deciding how the authority allocated to the group and its official leader will be used. As members of a group make decisions on how authority is to be used, they inescapably acquire a sense of responsibility for the success of their decision. If they are willing to live by the agreements reached, the decision-making process becomes the control, and authority is spread throughout the group. All become responsible for the decision and its enforcement.

Shared authority is contingent on the good faith of the members of the group. Unless individuals are willing to live up to an agreement, the principal has the responsibility to enforce the decisions of the group. He cannot avoid it.

Members of a staff have many ways of resisting an activity in which they do not believe. Passive resistance, such as forgetting, missing the point, coming late, getting simple arrangements confused, postponing, overemphasis on details, oversubmissiveness and glorification of the past, is not always recognized by official leaders. Active resistance, such as disagreement, counter-proposal, or refusal, is sometimes considered insubordination.

If the team leader is to be a real leader, he must: recognize manifestations of resistance; be able to facilitate and tolerate expressions of resentment, disappointment, and antagonism without becoming defensive; hear valid criticism; be sensitive to cues concerning the real dissatisfaction underlying negative expression; be willing to discard practices that do not contribute to group purposes; and be able to help groups find common purposes. In brief, he must be willing to accept the fact that another person's purposes and ways of reacting are as natural and valid as his own.

But the official leader cannot allow a program to disintegrate. He is hired to accomplish a mission. If he can move forward by a procedure that enables members of the staff to grow by assuming more and more responsibility, he is exerting leadership. If the level of staff morale is low, or if a portion of the staff is bitter and antagonistic as the result of previous experiences, it may be necessary for the official leader to use his authority to control the organization and to keep it functioning. When forced to use authoritarian measures, the principal should recognize that such measures may prevent him from ever becoming a successful leader in the situation. But he cannot, with any conscience, allow the program to disintegrate.

For effective group operation, official leaders must take steps that make clear their willingness to share authority and keep the lines of communications open so that all who wish may participate in the formulation of policies. But the group leader must also assume the responsibility for exercising the authority that forces individual members to live up to group agreements and system-wide policies. In any case, he must continue to believe in people and work for shared responsibility.

Acceptance of official responsibility by staff members means accepting and executing assignments. In the context of shared leadership, this acceptance is enlarged to include responsibility for contributing ideas, helping the group to reach cooperative agreements, joining in the establishment of plans, and accepting and executing assignments that grow out of group planning.

THE DECISION-MAKING PROCESS

If an official leader such as a team leader, committee chairman or principal is to use the decision-sharing procedure effectively, he must help the group identify the problems that it feels are important. A principal in a southern school system usually began his preschool conferences by listing the problems that he felt were important for the staff to work on. He changed procedures by sending a letter to each member of the staff prior to the preschool conference, asking the staff member to indicate the problems he felt should be studied in the conference that year. From responses to this inquiry, he drew up a list of problems, which was presented to the staff at the opening of preschool conference. The procedures used by this principal placed the emphasis on identifying the problems of the staff, rather than telling the staff to cooperate in the solution of the supervisor's problems.

As mentioned earlier, teachers who have not previously had a part in planning do not move easily into faculty planning sessions. In the beginning, the principal can only offer opportunities to participate in the planning. When certain members of the staff accept these opportunities, it is important to support them and carry out the plans in good faith. When this is done, the staff will gradually become willing to assume a part in policy-making.

Group consensus should be sought in reaching solutions to school problems. Experience in group operation indicates that groups cooperate better if decisions are made by consensus rather than by simple majority. When decisions are made by 51 percent of the staff voting in favor and 49 percent of the staff voting against, the probability is great that there will be little real enthusiasm in the total staff for the program being inaugurated. If, however, decisions are held off, and no final commitments made until at least 80 to 90 percent of the staff are firmly convinced that the proposed steps should be taken, it is likely that unanimous support will develop.

Where authority is shared, the responsibility-assuming situation is a portion of the planning session in which all who are to have a part are included. The work to be done is analyzed, the specific tasks are listed, and agreement is sought on who should assume the various responsibilities. If decisions concerning responsibilities are made on the basis of an analysis of the work to be done, the allocation of responsibilities becomes a part of the solution of the problem.

The group leader will want to encourage small groups undertaking a task to establish criteria to guide them in the organization of a program and the assignment of tasks. Members should have the opportunity to volunteer or to suggest responsibilities they would like to have. People work harder and with less difficulty on tasks they like. Which person has the special skills needed? Which person will be least overloaded by the new assignment? Staff members should be given an opportunity to talk among themselves and to decide on specific responsibilities.

Some members of the staff may not have begun to assume much leadership. It may be necessary for members of the group to say to them, "The other members of the group are carrying many responsibilities, and their load is very heavy at the present time. Will you accept this particular job?" Group pressure, which results from group planning, is exerted on the individual who is not carrying his share of the load. Group pressure is much stronger than the pressure a group leader can bring on a member of the group to carry out his responsibilities. The person who does not want to assume more work can say "No" to a leader more easily than he can to a group of his fellows.

If possible, it is desirable to get a program organized so that responsibility is to the group. This can be accomplished if the program is actually group-planned, and if the delegation of responsibility is made at the planning session. When responsibility is assumed in a group planning session, the leader loses the temptation to reach for authority, and the teacher loses fear of the leader. But the teacher has an even more compelling responsibility: the responsibility to his fellow workers.

It is much easier to go to a principal with the excuse that it was impossible to do the work than it is to go to a group of one's peers and say that it was impossible to accomplish what one has agreed to do. By having the individual accept responsibility to the group, personal reaction to the principal is decreased. The group member assuming the responsibility does not feel that he is being imposed upon by an individual who happens to dislike him. Neither does he feel resentment toward the principal for giving him a load he is unable to bear. He has responsibility to the group, and his reactions toward his work are transferred to the group rather than to the principal.

GETTING OTHERS TO ASSUME RESPONSIBILITY

As staff members assume responsibility, deadlines should be agreed upon for the completion of the work. Members of the group who are assigned responsibility, or who volunteer to accept responsibility, should do so in terms of a date set by the group's production schedule. If deadlines are agreed upon, they serve as the control factors in the situation. They become the impersonal taskmasters. When a teacher agrees to a deadline, he commits himself and establishes his schedule without pressure from superior authority. If the official leader uses his personality or his force to control a situation, antagonism and personal antipathy may easily develop.

If a group leader wants others to assume responsibility more than once, he must insure that the persons allocated the responsibility have the necessary authority for carrying out the task they have assumed. Frustration often results when authority does not go with responsibility, and the acceptance of future responsibility is avoided. No one can do his best when he does not know how soon he will come to the limit of his authority or when he does not have the necessary authority to take action. A teacher must be secure in the knowledge that the immediate decisions he makes in carrying out the responsibility will be accepted and upheld by the group and the supervisor.

The supervisor must not grab control again when he thinks a teacher or a staff is making mistakes. When he retracts the authority that he has shared, he is telling all the staff members that he didn't share authority at all; that the person responsible for carrying out the action was really acting without authority, because no authority was actually shared. Whenever authority is revoked, it is apparent to the teacher that he has not had responsibility and that he will not have to assume responsibility in the future. He knows that if he gets into a difficult spot, he will be saved. The principal has continued to assume full responsibility and has indicated no real confidence in the ability of the staff members. After a few experiences of this type the teacher will refuse to accept new responsibility.

The supervisor must keep the channels of communication open if teachers are to discharge the responsibilities they have accepted. People are willing to work together when they are fully informed. They lose the desire to work for the achievement of goals they may have helped establish if they are not kept acquainted with the progress that is being made. Channels must be kept open both ways. If the people who are carrying out the program have no means of pointing out their difficulties to those who are in charge, the difficulties may assume such importance in the minds of the teachers that progress will stop. If, however, those who are expending the energy necessary to make the program succeed have a way of getting the attention of the total group focused on the difficulties encountered, they feel that they are not working alone, and that their obstacles are the concern of the group. When a worker feels that his problems are being considered by the group, his sense of belonging to the group and his sense of responsibility to the group increase in spite of the difficulties.

In a group situation, the supervisor should constantly encourage a group to recognize members who have made exceptional contributions to the completion of a program. As official leaders give praise, or encourage the group to give praise, for work well done, they are providing an additional stimulus for the assumption of further responsibility.

A principal invites trouble if he gives the impression that he is out to make a record for himself. If the members of the group receive this impression, it will be recognized that the participation in policy formation that the principal is suggesting is simply a device for manipulating the group. The techniques of a principal are judged in terms of the motives that the group attributes to him. If the principal takes all the credit when the program receives praise, the teachers will let him carry the full responsibility for his program. He has made it clear to the community and to the teachers that the program is his, and the teachers let him have both the program and the responsibility for it.

Some teachers feel that principals use them as stepping-stones to better positions. They say a principal comes to their building, institutes a new program, and is promoted to higher rank on the basis of the results of their efforts. They develop a feeling of resentment and are determined that they will not be exploited further by a man who stands to gain through their efforts.

When teachers see inequality in the workload, they develop resentment that keeps them from assuming new responsibilities. This inequality may be among teachers, as when some are asked to assume many extra duties or to carry a heavy pupil load while others have less responsibility, or it may exist between the teacher's load and the principal's load. When teachers see a principal taking life easy, they have a good reason for refusing to increase their own burden.

Another reason why many people do not assume more responsibility is that they are already overburdened. It is common practice in some schools to exploit the willing worker. If principals want people to assume responsibility, they must not overload the members of the staff who are quick to accept extra work. If people see that those who are willing to work hard are not protected from acquiring too much of a load, they become very reticent about assuming responsibility. One of the functions of a principal is to see that no member of the staff is overloaded. If the principal protects staff members from assuming too many responsibilities, the hesitancy to volunteer disappears. Teachers know that the principal wishes to protect, not overload, them.

A great number of insignificant chores may lead teachers to feel that they are being overworked. When they are asked to perform clerical duties that could be performed better elsewhere, they find a reason for not accepting more responsibility for the formation of policy, for participation in the community, or for doing the other things that lead to more effective teaching. If the school does not have a policy of substituting new responsibilities for old ones when the load becomes too heavy, it is only natural for teachers to fight against assuming new responsibilities. No one can be expected to assume more than his share of responsibility. If a teaching staff is already overburdened by a heavy pupil-teacher load, or by a large number of community activities, new responsibilities will not be accepted willingly.

In working with people and getting them to assume responsibility, the principal should always assume that they are going to say "Yes". He can make this assumption only when he has thought the proposition over and has no doubts in his mind that it is fair. If he doesn't think it is fair, he certainly questions whether the other person is going to say "Yes," and he is reduced to the status of seeking ways of overcoming the other person's objections; he relies on arguments in which he himself cannot have much faith. Asking an individual to assume a new responsibility for the group should not become a situation in which the principal sells his staff member on assuming a new assignment. It should be, instead, a conference to plan the work ahead and to discuss how the responsibility will be divided. It is looking at the facts together and seeking agreement on the next steps to be taken. On this basis, a conference may actually result in reduced or reassigned responsibilities!

It is evident that getting people to assume responsibility involves first of all working on the morale of the staff. It means: helping the staff have a part in deciding upon the work to be done; giving the staff an opportunity to plan and think through problems together; letting the staff assign the responsibilities to its members; making possible constant communication among all members of the working team; and building within the staff a habit of looking at the job distribution and making reassignments when any inequalities exist.

11 Staff Development in the Local School

Staff development in the local school is a continuous and comprehensive process which utilizes human learning in service, selecting additional staff members with appropriate competence, reassignment of staff members, and replacement of staff members. The purpose of Chapter 11 is to discuss these processes as they function in the local school.

Human Growth in the Local School

Professional growth is promoted through the kind of organization that encourages members to exert leadership by stating their problems, by devising ways of seeking solutions, by participating in decision-making, and by accepting responsibility for the outcome.

As a principal attempts to promote staff growth, his pattern of work corresponds to the principles that underlie all good learning situations. He recognizes that: (1) learning is occurring all the time; (2) the learning that an individual does in a situation is determined by his purposes, his needs, and his past experiences; (3) when force is applied, the learning that occurs may be the opposite of what is desired; (4) the learning of the teacher will be nearer what the supervisor expects when both the teacher and the supervisor feel secure and when both have had a part in establishing purposes; (5) all individuals in the situation, including coordinators, consultants and the teachers, are learning simultaneously. Teacher growth is promoted when teachers exchange ideas and when they are encouraged to test the hypotheses they establish.

Programs of curriculum improvement constitute in-service training. Too frequently, it has been assumed that in-service education and curriculum development are separate functions. As teachers work on identifying inadequacies in the present program, on preparing changes in policy or curriculum content, or on devising operational procedures, they are growing in insight and in teaching skill. They themselves improve as they work to improve the program.

Underlying any program of improvement is a belief in people. If staff development is to be successful, the supervisor must believe that the faculty can grow. Lack of such faith makes the staff development program a meaningless ritual.

Staff-development training is not something that is provided by the official leader for other members of the staff. He must participate, too. Many principals have made the mistake of assuming that it is their job to provide staff-development training for others. Such an assumption makes clear to the staff that the principal considers himself better than they. If, on the other hand, the principal shares the staff-development opportunities with the staff, he will grow with them in ability and in a sense of working together. He will be accepted as one of the group, rather than as an outsider who is trying to do something to the group.

Staff-development training must not be haphazard. The first task of the official leader is to learn what type is needed. Some clues come from evaluation. As a staff evaluates itself and the school program, the areas of weakness indicate the experiences that should be made available. A second source of guidance is the direction the school program is taking. If the faculty has agreed to institute certain changes in the curriculum, and if a practical approach is being made to the transition, an investigation must be undertaken to see if the faculty members possess the skills necessary to follow through. If they do not, the function of staff-development training is obvious. Curriculum programs have often failed because this step was not taken.

Changes in the nature of the community are clues to the human development that is needed. If teachers are not prepared to deal with the educational problems that arise from desegregation, the greater numbers of socially disadvantaged, and the increased demand for technically skilled people, and if these are the changes occurring in the school's community, then the education needed should be apparent to those planning the staff development program. Opportunities to build new skills are necessary in any situation where a new program is being evolved or where the nature of the community is undergoing rapid change.

Staff education is more profitable when it is centered on improving the school program. It is purposeful learning. Areas that have proved fruitful in many situations are:

Examination of the recent developments in theories of learning and child growth, and adapting the program to meet them.

Preparation of more adequate materials of instruction.
Reorganization of courses, marking schemes, promotion policies, and reporting systems.
Study of individual children, and the planning of experiences for them.

Staff development should not be confined to experiences that provoke only academic growth. Many times, a faculty will be further advanced in its academic learning than in other abilities that make the success of the school program possible. Growth in ability to work with others, improved skill in democratic processes, the development of social skill, and the rounding out of the individual as a social being may all be areas in which teachers need more help than they do with methods of teaching or with content.

A faculty may have emotional problems that create such a strain among members of the group that no cooperation can occur. In such a situation, a staff development program must provide as its first step experiences that will enable people to relieve themselves of the emotional tensions that hinder constructive work. For this purpose, the program may include recreation, dramatics, and arts and crafts as well as more formalized education.

Staff development needs to contribute to a growing together of the faculty. Any faculty needs to feel that it is a unit, that it is a team working for a common purpose. Some phase of the staff development program should be held at a place where the members of the group are away from distracting influences and have a chance to really learn to know each other in many different ways. Retreats or workshops held at camps or resorts enable the staff to play together, work together, and think together. Through such experiences, friendships and feelings of oneness emerge and make possible really cooperative solutions of the problems facing a school staff.

Development programs may take many forms. It is not always getting together for common experiences. Reading, attending conferences, or other types of individual experiences can be growth experiences. Some principals find that the best contribution they can make to teacher growth is to take the place of a teacher who is attending conferences or visiting some other school. Others have found that their most helpful contribution consists of making readily accessible to teachers professional material that contains suggestions and ideas. A strong professional library is a basic element of a good program.

Activities may take the form of study committees, workshops, clinics, participation in the evaluation of the school program, forums in which teachers, parents, and pupils exchange ideas, or study of learning problems based on direct classroom experience and on interschool studies of curriculum development and programs.

One of the most important kinds of experience is participation in an experimental program. An examination of the history of staffs in schools that have participated in experimental programs leads to the conclusion that such participation produces people who are stronger and more capable. People grow as they have a chance to try something new and come to look upon their jobs as a chance to explore better ways of teaching. To put it briefly, people grow as they try new things. When supervisors can make a teacher's day-by-day experiences an experimental attack on a problem, real professional development is being provided.

If teachers want to observe other teachers at work and are willing to be observed themselves, intervisitation and analysis of teacher-learning situations constitute a type of experience that promotes teacher growth. Frequently, principals find themselves faced by seemingly insurmountable problems in stimulating and conducting programs of intervisitation. Teachers don't want to observe. Teachers can't find time to observe. Teachers are unwilling to be observed. The classrooms observed are poor teaching-learning situations.

The following paragraphs describe how one South Carolina county system attempted to solve these problems as it conducted an observation program in which every elementary teacher participated:

As soon as the day of observation had been placed on the school calendar, the supervisors began working with other school staff personnel to study possible plans of conducting an organized observation program. Following their discussions, they adopted some general procedures for operating:

1. Observations were to be arranged for small groups of teachers, rather than for individuals.

2. If possible, teachers were to visit within their own administrative areas in order to encourage in each individual respect for power within his own group. In other words, teachers were to be encouraged to feel that each had a worthwhile contribution to make in the development of the school program, and therefore, that it would not be necessary to go outside the area to find good teaching situations.

3. As far as possible, the interests and special skill needs of teachers were to be considered in arranging for the day.

4. Because the major purpose in conducting the program was to provide situations and experiences in which teachers might continue to grow professionally and find better ways of meeting needs of individual children, as preparation for the day of observation, the supervisor would plan with and assist, wherever possible, the teacher who was to be observed.

5. Schedules were to be arranged to meet the needs of observers and the teacher who was to be observed.

6. A conference for readiness was to be held on the day of observation just prior to the classroom visitations.

7. A conference for evaluation and sharing of ideas was to be held in the afternoon of the day of observation.

The supervisor worked closely with the teacher who was to be observed. Help in planning the day's schedule was given; the teacher's general and specific plans of procedure for the various teaching situations were discussed; and any other help that the teacher requested or which the supervisor could suggest was provided.

Occasionally in setting up plans for the day of observation a teacher said to her supervisor, "If you will help me, I should like to attempt some work in an area where I am not good at all. With this day as an incentive, perhaps I can improve the quality of my own teaching." As a result, the teacher and the supervisor planned together some experiences with the requested topic. After a number of days with the two working in this manner, the teacher provided a period on the schedule for observers that was most valuable and satisfying to the visitors and also to the teacher herself.

The teacher who is to be observed desires help from the supervisor before she teaches. She does not want to feel that she has failed to carry forward the program on which agreement has been made. Teachers, like children, have needs that should be met. Each teacher who is engaged in one of these observation-teaching experiences has the need for a feeling of security — of warm acceptance by the supervisor; she has the need for a feeling of successful achievement and more self-respect; she has the need for a feeling of recognition for a valuable contribution from her fellow teachers who are her guests for the day; and she has the need for a feeling of belonging in the group.

While teacher and supervisor always planned very carefully each period for a day of observation, in no instance was the work rehearsed with children. The observation day was as natural as the teacher could make it. The teachers were concerned about doing as good a teaching job as possible, and therefore, some may not have been as relaxed as they would have been if the visitors had not been present. But every effort was made to provide the students with a normal day of work.

Between the middle of October and the last of March, every elementary teacher in the county experienced a day of observation. One hundred and thirteen teachers taught for the groups, and eight schools were visited in the tour pattern, with members of the group observing in classrooms from first through seventh grades.

A department in a large city high school made a less elaborate approach to intervisitation:

It was decided to make Mondays a film day for all social studies students. All classes of social studies meeting during the same period on that day would assemble in a large visual aids room. Because there were six periods during the day, six different instructors on any Monday would assume responsibility for the discussions accompanying the films. Because many teachers would be present each period, every member of the department would get a chance to see, over a period of time, every other member of the department handle a teaching situation. Because there was no pressure of any kind to imitate anyone or to follow any set procedure, individual teachers experimented in various ways, from traditional question and answer lessons to panels of students and committee work. The result was a stimulating experience for all members of the department to share experiences, observe each other informally, confront similar problems, and gain from each other's efforts.

Although the possibility of all classes being ready for a film at the same time might be questioned, the approach described above made it easy for teachers to begin to share ways of improving teaching-learning situations.

A small city system made a somewhat different approach to staff development:

A decision had been made to organize the elementary school faculties into teams consisting of a team leader, teachers, and teacher aids. The junior high school and high school faculty had been organized into departmental teams consisting of a team leader, teachers and teacher aids. The new arrangements had created some questions and even anxiety about the role of the team leader, the principal, teacher, teacher aid, and the ways these roles fit together.

A planning committee was formed and the problems and concerns were identified and discussed. They included such things as the need for role descriptions, communication development, improving group and leadership skills. Arrangements were made with a university to work cooperatively on these problems.

Role descriptions were first developed by team leaders and principals. Then, they were taken to teams for discussion and revision. When consensus was achieved the team leaders began to implement their new roles on an experimental basis and with feedback from team members. The continuing education meetings were used for principals and team leaders to share successes and failures and to continue to work for improvement.

The above program is an example of the way school improvement, continuing education, and college credit can be woven together to improve the quality of education for students.

It should be noted that the schools that have been most successful in their staff development programs have made the training a part of the teacher's normal workload. It has not been something added to the already full schedule of a hard-working teacher. It does not come at the end of a school day when the teacher's thoughts are focused upon aspects of life other than school work. Some schools have used preschool conferences for which teachers are paid; other schools have provided substitute teachers while excursions are provided for members of the staff. Still other schools have dismissed children for a portion of the school day and have held their staff development sessions at times that ordinarily would be devoted to regular teaching. Official leaders must let the public know that staff development costs money. It is an up-grading process to produce more effective teachers. It involves the expenditure of money to get better education.

Faculty Meetings Can Contribute
to Staff Growth

Faculty meetings can be a major aspect of the in-service program. The supervisory literature praises faculty meetings as a way of improving the quality of a staff and the school program. They are described as opportunities for cooperative thinking, for staff planning, for the presentation of stimulating talks by resource people, for getting to know the total school, and for interchange of ideas — all of which result in growth for the staff member.

When teachers are asked about faculty meetings, the story is altogether different. Most teachers rate faculty meetings very low as places for securing ideas about better teaching. Most teachers feel that they do not have any part in setting up faculty meetings, and that the meetings belong to an administration that is imposing on their time.

The meeting described below illustrates the frustration that many teachers and administrators feel in faculty meetings:

> We were summoned to a special teachers' meeting, to be held in the cafeteria, at 4:00 P.M. The district has few people but is large in area. The two out-of-town grade-school principals came from a distance of twenty miles. There were 27 teachers, one high-school principal, three grade-school principals, and the superintendent present.
>
> We all sat at a long narrow table facing each other, with the superintendent standing at one end. The superintendent called the meeting to order and presented to the group what he wanted done.
>
> "*I* want each of you to write a detailed course of study in language arts, explaining as closely as possible the exact procedure that you use in teaching language arts: reading, spelling, English, and so on. *I* want this so *I* will have something and *I* can show anyone that might want to see what *we* actually do in the field of language arts."
>
> The results speak for themselves. Three more meetings were scheduled. All were postponed. The superintendent was "saved" by the end of the school year. *Nothing* was accomplished!

As a result of teacher resistance, the usual practice is for the administration to announce a policy of one faculty meeting a month, with a definite amount of time set for the meeting, or to promise teachers at the beginning of the year that faculty meetings will be held to a minimum. Teachers have come to expect nothing from faculty meetings, and they wait impatiently for each meeting to end.

Principals must examine faculty meetings carefully. They must ascertain why a device that gives such high promise has yielded such poor results. Some schools have found that faculty meetings live up to all expectations. An examination of the faculty meetings in these schools gives some clues to ways they can be used effectively.

The faculty meeting must be centered on something that the teachers consider important. As long as the principal alone decides what the program of the faculty meetings will be, the topics chosen will be considered important by the administrators, but may be considered insignificant by the teachers. In the worst cases, such faculty meetings will consist entirely of a talk by the official leader that includes the announcements he considers important. If faculty meetings are to be vital to teachers, teachers must have a major part in selecting the problems to be studied.

In the beginning, the problems selected for study by the faculty may seem unworthy and unimportant to the principal. Indeed, they may be trivial problems, because teachers will start working on the minor things that bother them. If, however, teachers find that faculty meetings are effective in solving these irritating features of their work, they will be ready to move into the examination of more important issues. Analysis of apparently simple problems frequently leads the group back to a more basic problem.

A staff meeting should have an agenda, a definite plan. Too often, the plan of operation is only a list of ideas that the principal has in mind. It needs to be more than that. It should be a listing of items to be considered, and it should be made available to the staff prior to the time of the meeting. In this way, each member of the staff has an opportunity to be prepared to discuss and make decisions on any of the agenda items.

The agenda for a faculty meeting should be developed by the total staff, with each member, on an equal basis, offering any problem that he considers important. Acceptance of this principle means that the official leader does not have the right to put the items he considers important at the top of the list and, if there is time, allow discussion of other items. It means that the principal wants his items to receive the same treatment given to items turned in by other members of the staff. Unless the faculty has this assurance, the meetings still belong to the administration and are the principal's responsibility.

One way to insure that the staff knows that no special preference is given the principal is to use a faculty-meeting planning committee. Such a committee has the planning of the agenda as a major responsibility. Staff members who have items that they want included on the agenda turn them over to the chairman of the planning committee, not to the principal. In this way, the staff may be more sure that the agenda is established by the staff.

The total faculty should be free to change the order of items on the agenda at the beginning of a meeting. Something may have happened that makes it important to consider first an item that is far down on the agenda. Or the planning committee may have exercised poor judgment, in the opinion of the faculty, in their establishment of the agenda. In either case, the faculty should know that it has the right to change the order and should be provided with an opportunity at the beginning of each meeting to make necessary revisions.

One of the dangers of revising the agenda in the meeting is that too much faculty time will be taken up in arguing. If long arguments occur for two or three meetings, it would be well to suggest that the planning committee study the situation and come in with a recommendation for a more efficient way of satisfying the wishes of the faculty.

The planning committee should be chosen by the staff. This practice will eliminate the suspicion that the principal is merely pretending that the meetings belong to the staff. Having members of the planning committee chosen by the staff establishes the direct line of responsibility to the total staff more clearly and gives the staff greater freedom to go to the committee with recommended changes.

Membership on the planning committee should be changed frequently. In this way, the faculty keeps a constant control over the planning committee and over faculty meetings. More persons become involved in planning procedures and assume responsibility for the success of the program.

The planning committee, in addition to determining the agenda, may have responsibility for the other items needed to make a faculty meeting a success, such as the establishment of a meeting time, selection of the meeting place, arrangement of the furniture, provision for refreshments, and the securing of special consultants.

Much has been written about the appropriate time for holding faculty meetings. Some writers have advocated holding them before the school day starts. In some schools, the teachers' schedule for the day calls for being at the school half an hour before the children arrive. Faculty meetings are held daily at this time. In this way all faculty members can be kept informed of the developments that will occur during the day and have time to study school issues on a continuing basis. Other authorities urge that faculty meetings be held at the end of the day. Their argument is that a meeting held then does not tire the teacher before he begins teaching, will not be stopped in the middle of an important deliberation, and can be more relaxed. Those who believe that the end of the day is a poor time point out that teachers are tired and cannot give their full attention to the issue at hand, and that commuters will keep watching the clock.

Some schools have adopted the practice of holding faculty meetings on Saturdays. The arguments for Saturday meetings are that everyone is refreshed, and that time limitations do not interfere with the agenda. Opposed to this point of view is the opinion that weekends should be completely free from school work and used for relaxation and recreation.

During the past few years an increasing number of schools have devised ways to hold faculty meetings on regular school time, thus eliminating all feeling that faculty meetings are something beyond the regular job. Some confusion has arisen as to what constitutes a school day. Where administrations have not declared a policy, some teachers and teacher organizations have drawn the conclusion that the school day consists of the time classes are in session, and that the teacher is carrying a full job when he meets classes from nine in the morning to three in the afternoon. Other schools have stated officially that a school day includes time from 8:30 in the morning to one hour after classes end. These schools have faced less difficulty when they have attempted to bring staff meetings into the regular school day. In some schools with this policy an attempt has been made to secure a two-hour period for faculty meetings by shortening classes so that the regularly scheduled classes end an hour early and teachers' meetings can be held from 2:00 to 4:00 in the afternoon. Other schools have dismissed classes for half a day each month to carry on faculty meetings.

Another technique used to secure teacher planning time is to work out the schedule so that portions of the faculty with common school problems have nonteaching periods at the same time and can meet as small groups. But this practice does not eliminate the necessity for meetings of the total staff in which faculty unity and common purposes can be achieved.

There has also been much argument concerning the length of time for faculty meetings. Although many possible arrangements have been worked out, one thing is evident. All meetings cannot be of the short, half-hour variety. If all are short, they tend to become routine and used for administrative announcements. There must be some opportunity for long periods of uninterrupted thinking. One possibility is the short meeting for day-to-day decisions and longer meetings, once a month or oftener, for long-term planning and policy formation.

An important part of the planning for faculty development should be the arrangement for social activities that will help teachers get to know each other better and that will develop a feeling of unity that differences of opinion will not disrupt. Such activities build solid human relations on which the program can grow.

The social phase of the faculty meeting can be very simple. In some schools, it consists of serving coffee or tea at the beginning of the meeting, a particularly helpful practice if faculty meetings are held at the end of the day. It serves as a break between the mental exertion of classes and the thinking period of the meeting. It relieves tension and gives opportunity for an exchange of information, stories, and banter.

Faculty meetings should be held in the library or in some other room that is pleasant and has a flexible furniture arrangement. Too often meetings have been held in rooms with screwed-down desks that are too small for the teachers and that force them all to face in one direction. Both features tend to handicap the meeting. Thinking is more likely to occur in situations where people are comfortable and can relax. If principals want participation and interchange of ideas, people must be able to see each other.

In creating the environment for the faculty meeting, the furniture should be arranged so that all members of the staff can see each other face-to-face. Some schools have seated the faculty in a square formation. This has one disadvantage. Studies of the flow of discussion indicate that the persons in the two end positions on the side on which the discussion leader is sitting cannot participate freely. If the square is used, people who have facility in group discussion should be encouraged to take these "blind" spots so that timid members of the staff will not be further handicapped by these difficult positions. Other staffs have used the circle arrangement for discussion. If the staff is large, a double circle proves feasible, even if it isn't as efficient as a single circle. Some faculties have used the semicircle organization, with the chairman and a secretary of the faculty seated at a table faced by the semicircle. One definite recommendation is that no member of the staff, the discussion leader or any other member of the faculty, should be isolated by his seating position. The physical arrangement of the furniture should suggest unity without setting apart any member of the group.

If the small discussion group techniques are to be used to get wider participation, room arrangements must permit the staff to divide easily to consider issues that arise. Some schools have attempted to work out this difficulty by having several rooms available, so that small faculty groups can go to them for discussion. One of the difficulties of this plan is that time is wasted in moving from room to room, and the spirit of the meeting may be broken when the total group separates. Other schools hold their faculty meetings in a large room, such as the cafeteria, where small groups can isolate themselves and hold discussions without interfering with the conversation of other small groups.

Use of Classroom Observations

Observation can be used to improve instruction if it is a cooperative undertaking by teachers, coordinators and consultants. It is a technique for securing a basis for analysis of the specifics with which the teacher desires help. Observation is in disrepute with many teachers because of the ways in which it has been used. In fact, its misuse has done more to discredit supervision than has any other activity.

A teacher who began teaching less than ten years ago in a western state describes his principal's supervision as follows:

> Instead of coming into my room and observing my teaching, he would hide in a small storeroom next to my room and listen in on my classes. After I found out about this I felt ill at ease in anything I tried. It always seemed to me as though he were in the room.

Although he never entered the classroom, this principal made the beginning teacher insecure through what both the teacher and the principal called supervision.

Hasty visits to a classroom when neither the class nor the teacher were present have led to unwise actions that have harmed supervisor-teacher relationships:

> The students in the class were working on some creative projects in social studies and were so enthusiastic that they were only able to organize their work materials before bus time. These materials were to be used again first thing in the morning, so they were left out. No paints or any materials that would damage the room were left open. The principal saw the room and left the following note on the blackboard: "This room is a mess. It is to be cleaned up by nine o'clock, and the people responsible are to be sent to the office."

The teacher who wrote this description of supervision commented further that actions such as these convinced the faculty that the principal was concerned only with appearances, not with what teachers were doing to provide good teaching-learning situations.

Another teacher remembers his first experience with supervision as a visit from the superintendent of schools:

> My first teaching job was in an elementary school in a prosperous farming community in which the supervision was done by the superintendent. He felt that he knew good teaching when he saw it, and he was determined to see it done his way.
> Most of the teachers were very much afraid of him and his visits. I must admit that I wasn't exactly at ease when I saw him enter my room one Monday morning – the wrong time because Friday had been pay day, and I had been out of town the entire weekend. He stayed the entire day. After school he told me that he wished to see me in his office at the high school. He kept me waiting for almost an hour, and you can imagine how I was feeling by the time I was summoned into the "lion's den." The only thing he had to say was, "I couldn't find anything wrong."

By believing that the purpose of observation is to judge instruction and to tell teachers how to improve, a principal may destroy teachers' hopes. A beginning teacher describes her first experience with a general supervisor:

> One day she came into my room at nine o'clock. I had been glad she was coming and had written down some questions that I wanted her help in solving. When the reading lessons were over, and the children had gone to recess, I walked over to her, ready to discuss my problems. The very first thing she said to me was, "The group in the front of the room is not reading at a hard enough level." (I was proud of the fact that I had them reading out of a bound book finally.) Before I could recover, she said,

"The group by the door has seatwork using phonetic analysis, which I think is useless." (I had got the idea from a reading workshop.) "You should give your presentation as stated in the manual step by step." (I'd still be on the same page.) After all these negative statements before she had even offered to help me, I immediately said to myself, "I'd be darned if I will ask her for help."

This "evaluation" of my teaching lasted only about five minutes. She had ruined my whole day and many days that followed. Although this observation occurred early in the year, she never came into my room again.

Classroom observations should not be used until rapport has been established between the principal and the teacher, and until the teacher knows the supervisor and feels secure with him. After a basis of friendly understanding has been established, the supervisor should let the teacher know that help is available whenever the teacher wants it, and that the supervisor is on call to assist with difficulties that arise in the classroom.

One Washington teacher praised her principal for making the following statement about observation during the pre-planning session:

I want to feel free to come and go from room to room, not with the idea of criticizing, but to establish a feeling of understanding, to know you and your pupils better, and to be more able to talk with parents if a situation arises concerning certain teaching procedures. You are to feel free to come to me if at any time I can be of help to you.

The above statement is an excellent way for a supervisor to introduce his approach to direct participation in the teaching behavior system. But, saying these things does not make them true and certainly, does not guarantee that teachers will be more open, trusting, and accepting of supervisors. Rather, it is essential that these ideas be communicated behaviorally. This requires a collaborative approach, made up of mutual trust and respect, mutual help, and mutual openness. The supervisor needs to demonstrate openness and a willingness to be helped. This is a behavioral manifestation of trust and respect.

One problem with visitation programs has been the heavy focus on evaluation. The supervisor observed and communicated the "good" and "bad" things that were going on. This approach can be interpreted by teachers that the supervisor is superior; that the teacher is inferior; that the teacher needs help; that the teacher can't help himself; that the teacher must subordinate his initiative, creativeness, and need for freedom to the expectations of the supervisors. It is recommended that an approach with emphasis on helping the teacher get the kind of feedback she needs for self-evaluation might prove more effective. For example, after a certain level of rapport has been established, the supervisor and teacher arrange a conference to discuss the teacher's teaching plans for the day. The focus for the supervisor is trying to understand and not evaluate. If plans for a classroom visitation grow out of the conference, then the teacher and supervisor would decide on how the supervisor could be helpful. What kind of data are needed, and how will we go about collecting it? Questions about the analysis of the data, their implications for change, and the participation of the supervisor in the process of working toward improvement would be resolved through cooperative planning.

Two other types of visitation establish a satisfactory framework for cooperative analysis. The principal should convey his interest in projects that are being carried on in the classroom and should encourage the teacher to invite him to come and see new developments and experimental activities. Another basis for visiting the class is the planning of some joint activity that the supervisor and teacher carry on together with the teacher's class. If this approach is used, the supervisor must have time to plan with the teacher and to be in the classroom frequently while the project is under way.

When a supervisor has been invited to observe for these reasons, he appears as a visitor or a helper. In either role, he should plan to be in the classroom when the class starts and to stay in the background as much as possible. If his help is needed, it will be called for by students or by the teacher in charge. If the principal is merely observing, he should not interrupt class procedure or take over the class. A learning situation belongs to the class group and to the teacher. A principal is a visitor, and as such he should adapt himself to the class situation. When he interrupts, he interferes with the group operation and may put the teacher in a less secure position with the students. This is true when supervisors break in to say, "Perhaps a better way to explain that, Miss Brown . . ." or "Your information is not quite accurate. You should have stated that . . ."

The observer should sit where he can observe those things that he and the teacher have identified that need to be described and provided as feedback for the teacher.

Time should be made available to the teacher for discussion of the descriptions. Such discussions should be held as soon as possible after the classroom visit and should be held in a situation where the teacher feels at home and secure. They may take place in the classroom where the class session has been held or over coffee in the cafeteria. The important point is that the discussion be informal and that the teacher be made to feel he can assume a mature, equal part.

The focus of the conference after the observation is to share the descriptions of what happened in the teaching situation with the teacher. It is important for teacher and observer to attempt to reach agreement on "what happened" before any analysis is attempted.

The analysis involves examining the relationship between "what happened" and what was intended. Emphasis should be on the teacher's analysis.

It is a mistake for the resource person to make value judgments concerning what has gone on. His function is to assist the teacher in analyzing the situation and in formulating procedures for improving the work for the class. He should not ask leading questions designed to convince the teacher of his own point of view. The supervisor should give his opinion when it is called for and offer suggestions when the teacher asks for them, but it is not his function to tell the teacher what should be done. He is a resource person and not a director. He is there to help the teacher grow in self-direction and professional maturity, not to increase the dependence of the teacher on someone else's judgment.

In Chapter 8 collegial supervision was defined as a process for involving teachers in the supervision of each other. Such a process has important implications for staff development at the local school. Teachers have a broad base of competence that can be shared. Since they are colleagues, the threat factor is less significant. They also work in close proximity to each other and are therefore available when needed. Programs in schools and among schools develop and change on a "broken front." Therefore, teachers develop new skills and new understandings on a "broken front" and it is logical that teacher-teacher sharing of the new learning through interschool and/or interclassroom visitations could be an important part of the staff development program.

Classroom observation is not a supervisory tool to be used alone. It is one of a number of ways in which coordinators and consultants work with the teacher. Observation and the discussion that follows it are merely means by which the teacher obtains ideas of ways to implement the educational philosophy he has accepted.

THE PLACE OF EVALUATION IN STAFF DEVELOPMENT

Evaluation of teaching must be a part of an entire school program of evaluation. It must not be a treatment that is applied to teaching alone. Teachers cannot be expected to participate wholeheartedly in the evaluation of teaching unless it follows or goes concurrently with the school's goals, administrative procedures, and supervisory techniques. It cannot be something forced on them. It is a part of a total process of improvement.

The center of focus in an evaluation program must be improvement of the learning situation for pupils. The principal question must be, "How can we improve our procedures to bring about more desirable pupil growth?" A basic tenet of the evaluation approach is that all persons involved in the situation being evaluated should have a part in establishing the criteria by which the situation will be evaluated.

Everyone's participation in the evaluation process insures validity as far as purposes are concerned. Unless group activities and procedures are subjected to constant evaluation, the chances of individual improvement are greatly decreased. The principal must devote a large portion of his effort to helping the group improve its processes.

One of his first evaluation responsibilities is to help the group during planning sessions to devise a way of judging its progress. This cannot wait until late. He may call the group's attention to such questions as:

Have we decided upon long term and immediate goals?
Have we established a plan of action?
Has the responsibility of each staff member been defined?
Have we set deadlines for ourselves?
Have we agreed upon a method of coordinating our efforts?

These questions are designed to force a group to establish a plan definite enough to permit an estimate of subsequent progress. Answers to these questions may need to be revised later in terms of the group experience in carrying out the plan. As the work progresses, the supervisor will need to raise additional questions:

Are we meeting our deadlines?
Is each member fulfilling his accepted responsibilities?
Is there a need for revision of responsibilities?
Do we need to revise our time schedule?
Should our goals be revised?

Evaluation includes the work of the individual as well as the group. Each person should explicate his professional goals and ways of achieving them and discuss them with his coordinator. Then, as work proceeds toward the goals, evidence should be gathered and used as a basis for self-evaluation, peer evaluation, and coordinator evaluation. This makes it possible for each person to maintain professional and personal integrity because he is using a process to improve his ability in doing the things he values.

As facilities and organizational structures become more open and as teachers cooperate more and more in planning, actualizing, and evaluating teaching, evaluation of team and individual effectiveness will become more implicit in the total process. Teacher effort and results or lack of effort and lack of results will have greater visibility. Certainly, the process will contribute to the professional and personal development of the staff.

Selection of New Personnel

The addition of a staff member is an opportunity to strengthen the group. It is a chance to survey the skills and abilities of the group and to secure types of leadership that are lacking and needed. It is an occasion for the faculty to evaluate itself and ask for the assistance it wants.

Viewed in this manner, selection of new personnel is a concern of the school district and of the staff of a school. Local schools should select new personnel from candidates who have successfully passed the screening tests of the central personnel office. This process is time-consuming, but working groups cannot be built by the haphazard choice of new members by someone unfamiliar with the purposes and needs of the local school staff.

Let's be candid about the way many teachers are selected. In some small systems, when a position is open, teachers apply and are selected according to the whims of members of the board of education or of the superintendent of schools. In many cases local politics are considered before staff needs or candidate qualification. In many larger systems, the candidate must pass a paper-and-pencil test at a certain percentile level and must meet the personality requirements of a personnel interviewer. Of course, candidates in both systems must meet the basic requirement of certification for the state, unless an emergency exists. Sometimes, even the roughest kind of matching of qualifications and job requirements is overlooked. Such procedures do not hold the greatest promise for building effective work groups. Persons selected by such methods may not possess the competencies or ways of working with people needed in a particular situation.

The selection and employment of a new staff member should not be the job of the personnel office and the principal alone. Because teaching is an occupation in which staff members must work in close cooperation with other teachers, it is important that the members of a school staff have a part in determining what additions should be made to the group.

One of the best ways of getting faculty participation in the selection of new teachers is to have the faculty set up minimum standards that they feel the new staff member should meet. These standards should be permanent recommendations upon which the personnel office or the principal can act in an emergency. If, for example, a member of the staff resigns during August, and most of the faculty is away on vacation, the principal has the minimum standards to guide him in making a quick choice among candidates.

One criterion that most faculties will establish is that the new teacher must believe in a cooperative approach to problems and must have a willingness to consider all viewpoints in arriving at final solutions. If a new staff member does not have this point of view, he will be an unhappy, unsatisfactory member of a staff that works cooperatively.

If the principal can anticipate vacancies, it is desirable to have the staff members set up in detail a description of the type of staff member needed. For example, if a vacancy is to occur in the social studies department, the staff should meet to consider their respective knowledges and abilities and to decide upon the strengths that are needed to supplement their present abilities. If the department has a number of people with a strong background in economics, others who specialized in history and government, but few members with major training in sociology, then the staff may want to select a member with strength in this phase of social studies.

The members of the present staff should be asked for recommendations of people they feel are best qualified for the opening. Some persons question this procedure. They say that it develops cliques, increases the chances of favoritism and inbreeding, and is likely to produce narrow provincialism, because the staff will recommend people who think and act as they do. But if a staff has set up standards to guide themselves and the principal, objectivity will be introduced into the situation and there is little chance that the decision will be made on the basis of favoritism alone. Perhaps too little confidence has been placed in the professional attitude of teachers and too much confidence in the infallibility of administrators and supervisors. On the basis of numbers alone, an atmosphere that produces favoritism is less likely in a situation in which many faculty members participate.

After the standards of selection and, where possible, specific job qualifications have been established, the process of selection is ready to begin. The principal has the recommendations of present staff members. He should also secure recommendations from teacher education institutions and other sources of personnel. Too frequently, choices of new staff members are made from an inadequate list of candidates.

When a sufficient number of recommendations have been received and credentials have been secured, as many of the group as possible should participate in the initial screening. This screening can be done at a meeting of the faculty or personnel committee, or it can be done by having members of the staff look at the credentials individually and make a rank-order list of their choices. It has been the experience of the writer that the group examination of credentials results in better selection, because staff members have an opportunity to check their thinking against the thinking of others. Furthermore, it results in staff growth, because this process again calls attention to the selection of people in terms of the standards and the needs of the group rather than in terms of personal preference.

After the candidates have been reduced to a feasible number, arrangements for the interviews should be made. The principal should be aided by other staff members in conducting the interviews. If the staff is small, all members should have a part. If it is large, the principal will want to have representatives of the group work with him in the selection.

An interview is a two-way process. The candidate is making decisions about the principal, the staff, and the school, and they are reaching a conclusion about him. The candidate should be put at ease. If there is a real possibility that the candidate may be asked to consider the position — and there is, or he would not have survived the first screening — the atmosphere of the interview is the best example he has of the human relations of the group. Moreover, if the candidate is kept under tension, he will not show his full ability.

A part of the interview should be in the school. The candidate will want to see the situations in which he will teach, the arrangements that are made for teacher comfort and convenience, the facilities at his disposal, the community, living conditions, the provision made for personnel services in the school, and the working relationship among the staff. The candidate must be sure that the school offers a situation in which he would like to work, before the staff starts to make a decision as to whether or not he will fit into the situation. This process, though time-consuming, is not wasted effort. After all, the candidate being interviewed has already gone through the first rough screening successfully. If all these factors are not satisfactory to the candidate, his being chosen to fill the position may result in such dissatisfaction for him that it will hinder the harmonious relationship of the entire staff.

The staff will be concerned with certain reactions of the candidate. They will want to know the way he likes to work and the way he likes to teach. They will want to know the breadth of his interests and his creativeness in working out solutions to problems. One technique that some staffs have found effective for securing this type of evaluation is to talk over the problems of the school with the candidate and get his ideas on the way he feels answers should be reached and the solutions he thinks would be satisfactory.

If possible, a social situation should be brought into the interview. It may consist of a relaxation period for a cup of coffee in the school cafeteria or restaurant, or a meal for the group involved in the interview. In either case, the staff will have an opportunity to see how the candidate will fit into the social pattern of the group.

The interview should end with some type of definite understanding. The candidate may be told about the procedure the school is following in selecting the new staff members. If four or five candidates are being given a final interview, this fact should be made known to the candidate, and he should be told the approximate date on which the final selection will be made. If a final decision can be made at the time of the interview, an agreement should be reached before the interviews are over.

If a candidate is not selected, he should be notified of the final choice and the reasons for the final selection.

Whatever the outcome of an interview, the candidate should look back upon it as a pleasant, worthwhile, and stimulating experience. Conducting the interview in a manner that gives all candidates this reaction is merely good public relations.

Where possible, a part of the interview should be observation of the teacher in action with his own classes and in his own faculty. Seeing the way a person works in his own group is a more valid insight into his behavior than any interview can be.

Every essential detail of the position must be presented. Never oversell a job! If difficulties are ahead, present them. If the candidate has the strength to meet them, he will not be frightened by the prospect. If he is unable to work well under the conditions that exist, it will be better for all concerned to find that out before he is hired. The principal's honesty about the job is really a selling point for the position. Too frequently, a person considering a new position is shown only the desirable side of the work. One technique that proves helpful in eliminating this approach is to make it possible for the candidate to talk alone with members of the nonsupervisory staff and to make it clear to him that he should ask any questions he wishes about the workings of the school and the type of supervision.

In employing a staff member, no promises should be made that cannot be fulfilled. Failure to live up to promises will destroy the morale and effectiveness of the new teacher, and his dissatisfaction will spread to other members of the staff. If necessary, it is better to take a weaker person for the position than to secure a person who will be unable to take the position on its true merits.

When a candidate has been chosen, great care should be exercised to see that the final agreement reached is one on which there is complete understanding. No point should be left hazy that may result later in dissatisfaction or misunderstanding. Wherever possible, the final agreement should be put in writing by the principal, and a copy should be sent to the candidate. It is also desirable to have the candidate confirm the agreement in writing.

Induction of the New Teacher

One of the first responsibilities of a principal to a new teacher is to make him feel that he is wanted. Too often new employees get the feeling that no one cares whether they are on the job or not. Making a new teacher welcome involves such specific things as talking with him before the school year starts, greeting him the first morning, escorting him to the first faculty meeting, and introducing him to the members of the staff. The principal, or the department head in large schools, should take personal responsibility for introducing the new teacher to all the members of the teaching group. It increases the confidence of a new staff member to have a supervisor take the time to acquaint him with others, and it assures him that the supervisor has his welfare at heart. The introductions give the principal an opportunity to explain to the new teacher the type of help he will be able to obtain from each staff member.

The first gestures of friendship must be followed by a conference in which the new teacher really gets the impression of a sincere, warm welcome by the principal. Much of the difficulty of the first few days or weeks can be made insignificant by a friendly greeting. Above all, a new employee needs to feel that he is wanted on the staff he is entering.

Secondly, a new employee must have complete knowledge of the conditions of employment. During his employment interview, he will have raised certain questions about the school and the benefits of working in it, but many items, though they do not play an important part in his deciding whether or not to accept the position, are important for his successful operation as a teacher. He will need to know the length of the school day, when he is expected to arrive, how long he should remain after school, where the teachers eat, what special services are available in the system, and how to go about securing the benefits of employee group insurance, health and accident insurance, hospitalization, sick leave, credit unions, tenure, and pension rights.

Two of the most important bits of information a new employee needs to know are when to expect his pay check and how he will receive it. In one position the writer held, he was not told when or how he would be paid. The first month went by, and no check was received. Three or four days after the end of the month, his financial condition was becoming critical, so he began to make inquiries. But no one seemed to be able to answer him. Finally, he was referred to the bursar of the institution and found that his check was being held up until he signed certain papers and produced a birth certificate, which was needed to secure participation in the retirement fund. When he asked why he had not been told about these requirements before, the bursar's secretary replied, "Oh, we knew you would come around when you became sufficiently interested in getting your check." Such an introduction to the operation of the institution left a bad impression that lasted for many months. All this unpleasantness could have been avoided by informing the new employee of the steps necessary to secure his salary checks. Many institutions that provide employee benefits antagonize employees by treating them in such a way that the employees become disgusted with the institution, instead of being pleased to be part of an organization that takes an interest in them.

One of the most complicated types of information a new teacher needs is instruction in record keeping. Systems vary from school to school, and many difficulties and worries can be avoided if the school's record system and the teacher's responsibility are explained in the beginning.

A third step in the introduction of the new teacher is to give him a feeling of confidence in himself. The first few days on any new job are trying days that test the self-confidence of the teacher. Even though the teacher has been successful in a previous job, he always has a question in his mind about being able to achieve the same success in a new job. New people, new types of students, and new working conditions require new patterns of relationships and operations. The principal can help the new teacher by reaffirming the confidence felt in the employee when he was hired. This can be done by casually mentioning some of the previous successes the new teacher has had and by showing a genuine pleasure in having such skill added to the new staff.

Insecurity for the beginning teacher can be created by remarks that belittle the theory of teaching that has been acquired in a teacher education institution. At the first faculty meeting in the fall, a high-school principal in a southern state told his new teachers, with a knowing chuckle, "Put out of your minds all the theories that you learned in college, they just don't work in practice."

Certainly, the principal should avoid adding to the difficulty of getting started by pointing out mistakes that the teacher is making. Giving support and information is more important than pointing out mistakes to the newcomer.

> A teacher who had been absent from the teaching field for some time was finding it difficult to get started again. Knowing this teacher to be a person who loved and understood children, the principal refrained from making any suggestions. Later, this teacher commented to a group of fellow teachers, "One day when I first came back here, the principal came in to my room and saw me making a mistake of which I was not aware. She said nothing about it, although I am sure she observed it. A little later I became aware of it myself and corrected it. I could not help thinking that it takes a pretty big person to let you find your own mistakes without telling you about it."

One of the best ways of giving a new teacher this self-confidence is to carefully define his duties. By detailing the nature and amount of the work to be done, he is given confidence that his efforts will be successful. Much insecurity comes from not knowing exactly what is expected and when it is expected. When tasks are indefinite, the feelings of insecurity mount, because the new teacher has no standard of comparison by which he can measure his progress.

A fourth responsibility of the principal to a new employee is to give him a feeling of pride in the new institution. To do this involves giving an understanding of the background of the school, its past achievements, the goals for which it is striving, and the way in which it works. If the school organization does not make a person proud to be a part of it, the principal has not done the job that he should. He should indicate to the new employee the ways the staff is attempting to improve the school.

Pride can also be built by telling the new teacher something of the background and accomplishments of the various members of the staff. People like to feel that they are a part of a team that has other members as able as themselves. Teachers are no exception. The spirit and traditions of the school are part of a heritage into which a new teacher steps, and the supervisor can use them to build a sense of the power and function of the institution that will give the new employee pride in his association with the school.

The background provided by the principal will not supply enough information. He will not be able to make himself sufficiently accessible to answer all the detailed questions the employee has. To supply this deficiency the principal should ask one of the older members of the staff to assume responsibility for the guidance of the new teacher. Many schools have "buddy" systems. As new teachers enter the staff, one of the older members volunteers to sponsor him and to help him learn the purposes, philosophy, and method of operation of the school.

Some schools have a plan in which a teacher of approximately the same age as the new staff member assists with the introduction. The assumption underlying this practice is that new teachers will find it easier to ask someone near their own age the questions that trouble them. Also, the procedure increases the opportunity for the new teacher to make friends on the staff.

The community also can contribute to making the new teacher feel at home. In some communities all new additions to the staff are invited to dinner by families supporting the schools. The plan insures that during the first month in the community, each new teacher is a visitor in at least one home.

The principal must be as concerned about helping the new teacher make a successful adjustment to the community as to the school. Lack of success in learning to live in the community will prevent the teacher from making a maximum contribution in the classroom. Some school systems have worked out agreements with retail stores by which teachers obtain discounts. Giving the list of cooperating merchants to new teachers early is extremely important if the teacher is going to furnish a home or an apartment.

Many schools have asked community groups to assist by compiling a list of living quarters. The shift has been away from an approved list prepared by boards of education or the school administration to a nonofficial list that the teacher can reject or accept.

Teachers and parents are brought closer together through this cooperation. The principal who encourages such practices gives parents a greater feeling of participation in the school program and gives new teachers a sense that the community appreciates them. Getting started on the job means getting a sense of belonging in the community as well as learning the procedures of the school.

A number of schools have pre-school planning conferences for new teachers. Some last only an hour or two, while others continue throughout the week prior to the opening of school. As much help as the principal feels necessary is provided to get the new teacher settled and ready for a successful start.

Systems with pre-school planning conferences for all the staff members have a real advantage in helping new staff members get acquainted with their colleagues and the program. The new employee feels he is a part of the working team before he meets his classes.

But the principal cannot leave the induction solely to the buddy system or to tips from other teachers. He must determine from time to time whether the new teacher is adjusting satisfactorily. If things are not working out, the principal should sit down with the teacher and give him a chance to find solutions to his problems. If the teacher is successful, the visits of the supervisor are indications to the teacher of interest in his success.

A program that fulfills all these responsibilities is conducted in Oklahoma:

The city-wide program for the induction of teachers to the public schools provides for overall help such as: securing housing, tours of the city, trips through the administration building, breakfast and luncheon by organizations such as A.C.E.I. and the Chamber of Commerce to meet other school and business personnel, meetings with the personnel office about insurance programs, sick leave, and the teachers' credit union.

In addition, individual schools in the system conduct orientation programs for their new teachers.

During the pre-school week, the entire faculty meets as usual, to discuss implementation of the school philosophy. In these discussions each new teacher is assigned the customary "buddy teacher." In addition, a helping teacher, freed from other school duties, is assigned to the entire group of new teachers. It is the responsibility of this helping teacher to assist in any way that help is needed. A regularly scheduled meeting is set for each Friday morning before school. In these meetings, discussions center around such topics as:

1. School policies.
2. School forms and records.
3. Interpreting the cumulative records.
4. Studying the reading scores of the incoming ninth graders.
5. School philosophy.
6. Teaching techniques.
7. Case studies.
8. Pupil-teacher planning.
9. Reporting to parents.
10. Teaching that provides for individual differences.
11. Evaluation.

In these discussions, many supervisors and assistant superintendents from the city administration are used as resource people.

In addition to the regularly scheduled group meetings, the helping teacher attempts to do some of the following:

1. Be available at all times to answer questions, listen to problems, encourage, etc.
2. Substitute in classes, or find substitutes, so that new teachers can observe classrooms in other buildings in the city.
3. Do demonstration teaching in his teaching field.
4. Transfer problem pupils to more experienced teachers.
5. Help give objective tests.
6. Make suggestions for handling problem pupils.
7. Make suggestions for procedures after observing in classrooms.
8. Help teachers decide why problem children develop in class.
9. Suggest professional literature for general and specific problems.

An explanation to new teachers of the way a program has developed enables them to understand the things that have already been attempted, the types of difficulties that have been encountered, and the compromises that have been made. New teachers need to see how much progress has been made and the rate of speed involved. Such a background gives them an understanding of the types of skills that will be expected from them in working for change.

The orientation of the new teacher should also help him to get an understanding of the obstacles to progress in the school and community. Unless these obstacles are made clear, the new teacher may not have sufficient sympathy for the slow progress the staff has made, and he will not be able to help plan strategy for reducing or getting around the obstacles.

As soon as new teachers become members of the staff, they should be involved in faculty action to overcome obstacles. If they are exerting their energy in removing roadblocks, they will be less prone to criticize the lack of progress. Through meeting some of the hard knocks that come to those on the action front, they will gain a feeling of belonging and a greater appreciation of the contribution that present staff members are making. If possible, they should be working on committees composed of both older and younger teachers. The experience of the older teachers will help them avoid mistakes that their new ideas and enthusiasm will lead them to make.

Evaluation of Teachers

After a teacher is employed it is necessary to evaluate his contribution to the achievement of organizational goals. In many cases the evaluation has been a rating used by the administration to determine salary raises, tenure, and promotions. But rating, even though necessary, is not enough. It has major shortcomings.

When a principal rates teachers on the basis of one to three observations, and usually there is not time for more, the validity of the rating is open to serious question. Can it be assumed that the principal knows more about the teaching process? Suppose the principal has been in the profession for five years, but the teacher has taught for fifteen years and also has a year more of professional preparation than the principal.

Can it be assumed that the lessons observed by the rater are an accurate sample of the teaching that the class is receiving? The evidence points in the other direction. In the first place, if the teacher and pupils are not accustomed to visitors, they are under strain, and their actions are unnatural. Second, the principal may come into the class during an atypical situation. A poor teacher doing a good piece of work will receive a high rating. A visit to the room of an excellent teacher may come at a time when a disruption has occurred, and his rating will be poor. Third, the lesson observed may have been a carefully planned and rehearsed performance. The validity of ratings based on observations cannot be assumed, unless the visitations cover a more representative sampling of classroom time than is customary at present.

Some rating is based on classroom observation in which only portions of a lesson are seen. Some principals stop in the classroom for five- or ten-minute periods and decide upon the level of teaching on the basis of these small samples. They lift the sample out of its context and assume that they understand what is happening in the total learning situation. Such a naive approach to observation further decreases the possibility of a reliable rating.

Rating keeps the principal from helping the teacher with his weaknesses. Since salary increases and advancement are determined by what the principal sees in the teacher's classroom, the teacher puts on the very best show possible. Teachers do not dare say to the principal, "This is the type of help I need. What suggestions do you have?" To admit weakness decreases the possibility of a good rating.

Most serious of all, rating prevents cooperative working relationships between the supervisor and the supervised. The person supervised must always be on guard not to do anything that will indicate lack of strength or that will antagonize the supervisor. Under such conditions, the principal can never be sure about his relationships with teachers. He must always work under the suspicion that people are going along with him because they want his favor as a means of securing advancement.

Rating is unsatisfactory as an evaluation procedure. Although it produces a judgment that can be used by the administration, it prevents the teacher from asking for needed help and the supervisor from seeing a normal teaching situation; it eliminates any possibility for cooperative relations between the teacher and the status leader. Rating should be recognized as an administrative device used to establish a base for salary increases, promotion, or dismissal, and as a deterrent to improving instruction.

Some principals attempt to judge the work of teachers by the scores their pupils make on achievement tests. If a class does well on achievement tests, the teacher is assumed to be doing good teaching. If the class does not equal national or school norms, it is assumed that something is wrong.

Examination of this plan for judging teacher effectiveness reveals that it has many weaknesses. If, by chance, a teacher has an intelligent class, the pupils will learn in spite of anything the teacher does, and the results on the achievement tests will make it appear that the teacher has done excellent work. If the class is far below average ability, or has had poor teachers in previous years, superior teaching may not result in the attainment of school-wide or national norms. There is also the probability that teachers will teach toward specific tests and thus invalidate the results.

The primary purpose of the evaluation of staff members is to improve the quality of education for students. This can only be achieved through change in the behavior of organizational members. Each staff member occupies a position in the organization which exists to contribute to the achievement of organizational goals. It is assumed that each staff member is a professional person who is interested in the achievement of organizational goals and his own professional development. Therefore, it is suggested that each staff member should explicate the personal and organizationals goals he hopes to achieve each year, the processes he plans to utilize, and the effort he plans to make. These desires should be discussed in detail with his coordinator and they should reach agreement. During the course of the year evidence should be assembled to verify the actualization of the processes and the achieved outcomes by both the teacher and the coordinator in order to check for congruency between objectives agreed on and performance objectives reached.

It is essential that a systematic approach that is clearly understood by both evaluator and evaluatee be utilized. This will improve the probability that results will be valid and will be used to improve the performance of the teacher.

The evaluator and the evaluatee must collect many types of evidence concerning the work of the teacher if a valid judgment is to be made. Observations in the classroom, test results, pupil opinion, samples of pupils' creative effort, and teacher leadership in the faculty and the community all provide data to consider. The weaknesses of each type of evidence must be recognized and assigned a proper role in the total evaluation. Even though a judgment is an administrative necessity, the understanding of its fallibility will help to use it more intelligently and increase willingness to reexamine it. Under no circumstances should the judgment-making be confused with improvement of instruction.

REASSIGNMENT WHERE DESIRABLE

All staff members have their strong and their weak points. All will fail in some situations and most can be successful if placed in the right position. Administration has the responsibility for helping people find the situation in which they can be successful. Thousands of teachers are misfits in their work only because they have been assigned to the wrong job.

Advanced industries have recognized that untold productive hours are wasted because of misplaced people, and money is spent freely to match a person's skills to the job in which he can be most productive. In education, where a misplaced teacher squanders not only his own time but the efforts and energies of all his students, few systematic efforts have been attempted to make the most effective use of available skills. Proper placement means happier teachers, less frustration, less energy expended to achieve successful results, and greater accomplishments through the most effective use of available skills. Schools must face the facts squarely and begin to take systematic steps to put people into the jobs for which they are fitted.

What can the principal do? He can take a firm stand against permanent appointment to specific assignments, institute a careful analysis of job requirements, make a skills survey, and match people to the job for which they are best suited.

Assignment of a teacher to a new position should be temporary, for a probationary period. Any assignment for any teacher should be subject to change. If skills and abilities are to be used most effectively, the school administration must not allow a person to remain in an unsatisfactory position because of poor placement. In too many systems, teachers are frozen in jobs for which they are not fitted. In these systems, teachers feel that their rights are violated if they are moved to a different assignment; they see an unrequested transfer as punishment. No consideration is given to the rights of children who may be receiving poor education because of a mistake in placement.

It should be understood that positions are held on a basis of mutual satisfaction. Change may be made at any time, if the teacher's contribution is being hindered by the situation in which he is placed. Teachers should be as free to point out factors that limit their effectiveness as the administration is.

Does it take the same qualifications to teach seventh-grade mathematics as it does to teach twelfth-grade mathematics? Can the same teacher be equally successful with the youngsters in a poor neighborhood as with those in a wealthy community? Are teachers equally effective with slow and fast youngsters? Undoubtedly, the answer to all these questions is "No." A specific teaching situation must be analyzed to determine the qualities a teacher needs to fit it.

Suppose a supervisor has to find an English teacher for a junior high school in the Italian district of a large city. Certain requirements are immediately obvious. The teacher must not feel contempt for anyone whose ancestors did not come from northwestern Europe. Youthful energy and emotion must not be considered an evil to be driven out of the pupils. The teacher must have a thorough understanding of democracy and ways to make it work, as well as an earnest desire to help people meet everyday problems. All teachers will not have these qualities. Yet, if supervision is to make the program truly effective, it must make this kind of analysis in the assignment of teachers. A system cannot excuse itself on the plea of bigness.

Some leading industries have found it helpful to take an inventory of worker skills. Potential skills are classified, as well as the skills that the workers are using at the time of the inventory. When a new position opens, reference is made to the listed skills of each worker, and the one with the skills that fit the job description is promoted. The knowledge that the organization has a listing of his abilities, and that these will be considered when a better position opens up, has a good effect on a worker's morale.

Even if the supervisor doesn't make a formal survey, he should be on the alert for people with special skills, such as the teacher who is a good discussion leader or a skilled laboratory technician. As opportunities develop, a teacher's program should be changed in terms of his skills and his wishes.

The principal of a large New York City junior high school not only watches for special aptitudes and interests of the faculty members, but encourages teachers to express interests and to show their abilities. He studies the records of teachers, including the courses they have taken, and their past achievements. He listens to them in the course of their teaching and at individual and group conferences. One of his most effective approaches is encouraging people to talk freely in informal conversations, so that they can reveal their own thoughts and feelings without self-consciousness. He does this by showing interest in their ideas and respect for their opinions, whether he agrees with them or not. People in his school do not feel the metaphorical dash of cold water on their thoughts that has often led teachers to resolve never to express themselves again lest they be exposed to what is, in effect, veiled insult. He is willing to postpone work in which he is engaged so that he may talk to people who cannot see him at other times.

As a result, teachers voluntarily assume duties, such as special patrols, program-making, and running of bazaars and exhibitions, that have previously been to a great extent the responsibilities of supervisors. Another result is the uncovering of hitherto unsuspected abilities of many teachers.

In an important sense, the readjustment of teachers' programs in terms of skills is a program of curriculum reorganization. The teacher is, in large part, the curriculum. As teaching is improved, the curriculum becomes more satisfactory. As teachers' programs are adjusted to enable teachers to make better use of their talents, their teaching is improved, and the curriculum is enriched.

Some teachers have physical limitations that should be considered in placement and reassignment. Formulation of teaching schedules and assignment of rooms involve considerations other than knowledge of subject matter and number of students. Giving the teacher who is always cold a laboratory on the sunny side of the building, and the teacher with a bad heart a first-floor classroom is not coddling. It is efficient use of available manpower.

People can't be moved about like chessmen. Their human qualities, their strengths, and their frailties must be considered and accommodated. An adjustment to meet a handicap pays dividends in morale and improved teaching power, but it should be made in consultation with the persons involved. *Supervision is in part the removal of irritating features to free the creative potential of the teaching staff.*

Emphasis has been placed on putting the teacher where his talents are best utilized, and of matching the teacher to the job. What part does the teacher have in the decision? He must have a major part. Otherwise, the emotional upset caused by the shift will hinder the utilization of skills just as much as improper placement itself. The teacher should concur with the decision and should have a right and a way to appeal after the placement or shift has been made.

Will all teachers want the same positions? Not at all. Everyone likes the things he can do well. If a teacher is convinced that a placement or shift has been made because of special skills that enable him to do the job better than anyone else, he will want to do it. What people object to is being shifted as a punishment or to make way for someone with political influence. Everyone wants to feel needed and to have a sense of doing a job that no one else can do as well.

When a teacher fails, the administration has failed. Either the original selection and induction were poor, the placement was faulty, or the in-service training was inadequate.

12 Organization and Operation of the Faculty

A faculty cannot exist without organization. It may be an informal working arrangement or it may be a carefully charted plan in which the functions of each participant are enumerated. The plan of organization may be dictated by the principal or it may be developed by the group. But some structuring of the group, some organization of channels of communication and coordination of effort is necessary. This chapter deals with the questions of how coordination can be achieved, how the organization should be developed, what control is necessary, and how relationships should be established and maintained with other groups.

The Development of the Faculty Organization

If a supervisor starts with the basic premise that he wants to use all the intelligence of all the faculty members, he will apply it to the establishment of faculty structure as well as to the solution of problems. He will make provision for the faculty to participate in the establishment of its own organization. Let's look at two situations where that practice was followed.

In a large faculty of 200, a committee was appointed by the principal to draw up a plan of faculty organization. This committee consulted with other members of the faculty and formulated a proposed organization that was submitted to the entire faculty for revision. After the revisions had been made, the plan was voted on by the total faculty and became the official organizational structure. Under the plan, the final authority and decision in areas in which the school is autonomous rest with the total faculty. All committees, in the final analysis, report to the faculty, and no major change can be made in the program without the approval of the faculty.

Any member of the faculty can bring an issue before the total faculty at any meeting, but it is customary for policy changes to be presented to the faculty through regular committee channels. This right of faculty members to short-cut committee procedures is maintained to provide for emergency measures and to insure any faculty member the opportunity to make minority proposals in spite of opposition within the committees.

An elected group, the faculty council, serves as a screening body to keep faculty meetings from becoming overburdened with business items. In addition to the faculty council, the plan of organization calls for the establishment of committees to be responsible for development in various phases of the program. Every member of the faculty is asked to choose one of the committees on which he would like to serve. As far as possible, each faculty member is given his first preference. Under the plan, each committee meets and elects its chairman and decides upon the subcommittees that will be necessary to carry on its work.

Each subcommittee works on the problems in the areas assigned to it. From the subcommittees come recommendations for policy upon which the major committee is asked to act. If the committee accepts the recommendation of its subcommittee, the proposal is sent to the faculty council. All the general committees feed their proposals to the faculty council for acceptance or rejection. If a proposal is accepted by the faculty council, it is submitted to the faculty at the next faculty meeting. If a proposal is rejected by the faculty council, it is returned to the committee in which it originated. The plan for organization, however, provides that any faculty member can bring any proposal to the floor of the faculty meeting, if he so desires.

The business portions of the faculty meeting consist of a review by the faculty of the faculty council's actions. To facilitate this process, the minutes of the faculty council are submitted in writing to the faculty a week prior to the faculty meeting. If there is no disagreement with the actions of the council, the actions become faculty policy. If any specific action of the council is questioned, and if a motion to reject or revise the action is presented, the question is decided by the faculty as a whole at the faculty meeting.

An important part of the plan is a committee on committees that constantly reviews the success of the organizational structure and makes recommendations to the faculty for changes that the committee feels will make the organization more effective. No changes can be made by the committee on committees itself. It can only recommend; the faculty approves or rejects any proposals.

This plan is a cumbersome one designed to serve a large faculty, but several important principles are involved.

First, the structure of faculty organization is established by the faculty. No special committee responsible only to the administration has formed the plan. The procedure leaves no feeling that any group or individual is establishing a plan by which he can control faculty thinking and action.

Second, the plan calls for a structure built around the solution of current problems. It is functional. The major committees are working in areas in which many specific problems arise and in which rethinking of existing policy is needed.

Third, the organization is flexible. It can be changed as desired. When the focus of problems shifts, one committee can be abolished, and a new one can be formed. The procedures for constant study are defined in the description of the organization.

Fourth, faculty members are given an opportunity to work on the phases of the program in which they have the greatest interest. Under this procedure, it is possible for faculty members to relate their committee work on policy with their teaching problems and special research. Their participation and policy formation are not something apart from their customary thinking and activity.

Fifth, the plan makes use of an executive group to relieve the faculty of the responsibility for debating all the policy issues that arise. At the same time, it makes possible a review of the faculty council's actions, insuring that no faculty member will be denied the right to question and promote revision of any policies that are important to him.

Sixth, all members of the faculty have representation. This representation is indirect in the faculty council, whose members were elected by the total faculty, and direct through participation in the committee the faculty member selects.

Seventh, all matters of policy are referred to the faculty. No single, small group can gain control of faculty policy. No action becomes faculty policy without total faculty approval.

The faculty of a small two-school system put into practice the same principles. The administrator and two teachers of the system attended a workshop. At the workshop, they decided to work for more democratic practices in their faculty operation. Upon their return, the superintendent appointed a committee to get the faculty program under way. This committee, consisting of the superintendent, the principal of the high school, the principal of the elementary school, a teacher from the elementary school, and one from the high school, called the faculty together and explained its desire for more democratic determination of policy. The faculty was asked to state what they thought should be done. Three faculty meetings were devoted to the discussion of the problems of the school and of the ways the faculty might organize to solve them.

At the fourth meeting the committee appointed by the superintendent resigned, recommending to the faculty that it elect committee members who would more nearly represent the faculty and administration. A supplementary recommendation of the superintendent's committee was that the new committee, to be called a steering committee, be made up of the superintendent, the two principals, three teachers from the elementary school, three teachers from the high school, two members of the community, and a member of the board of education. This recommendation was accepted by the faculty by secret ballot, and an election was held to determine the membership of the steering committee.

The steering committee conducted a survey of the faculty to determine the problems around which they felt the faculty should be organized for study. On the basis of this survey, seven choices were offered to the faculty and each faculty member selected a committee on which he desired to work.

As the year progressed, committees explored their problems until they were ready to make recommendations. Faculty meetings were then called for a consideration of the reports of each committee. These reports consisted of recommendations for changes in the program of the school. Those that were accepted became school policy. If the recommendations were rejected, the committee was asked to study the situation further and to make revised recommendations or to drop the matter.

One aspect of the plan was a shifting of personnel in the steering committee. Each member, with the exception of the three representatives of the administration, was elected for a six-month term. In this way the faculty had a close control over the membership of the steering committee.

The primary function of the steering committee was to serve as a clearing house for the work of the general committees and to plan the faculty meetings. Members of the steering committee also advised the administration on ways in which the policies adopted by the faculty could be implemented.

It is important to point out that in both the plans described, the administration is a constant factor in all committees. In the large faculty, the official leader serves as chairman of the faculty council and faculty business meetings, and members of his staff are designated as ex-officio members on each of the major committees. In the small school, the three members of the administration are continuing members of the steering committee and have the responsibility for executing the policy arrived at through faculty deliberation.

A very simple type of faculty organization is that adopted by an elementary school in Colorado:

> At school this year, the teachers appointed a committee of three teachers to act with the principal in determining instructional problems. One committee member was chosen to represent the kindergarten, first-, and second-grade teachers; one to represent the third- and fourth-grade teachers; and one to represent fifth- and sixth-grade teachers. It is the job of this committee to interview other teachers and to decide problems that need to be considered for the improvement of instruction. One committee member presides at each faculty meeting.

Pitfalls To Be Avoided in a Faculty Organization

Any faculty considering a plan of organization should be aware of certain dangers inherent in the committee system. First, committee work is time-consuming, and provision must be made for meeting time as a part of the regular schedule; otherwise the work may be considered as extra and unimportant by some faculty members. Second, certain faculty members may become over-loaded with committee work. Faculties have a tendency to turn to certain members for leadership on any problem that arises. Unless some regulation is established that will keep any one faculty member from serving on too many committees, certain members may become so overloaded that their teaching will suffer. Third, the official leadership must learn to work through existing committees. It is easy to feel that none of the existing committees covers the particular problem facing the staff and to appoint a new committee to discharge the new function. Such a practice leads to many committee memberships for faculty members and to confusion about the way new committees fit into the existing committee structure. Fourth, the functions of the committees should be carefully defined. Unless they are, overlapping of committee activities occurs, and the sense of order is lost.

In setting up a new organizational structure, the functions of each group or individual must be stated. Such a practice does not stifle creativeness. It frees it. When energy does not have to be spent in wondering about function, full attention can be given to performing the role creatively. In planning, lack of restrictions are desirable. In execution, a planned framework gives guideposts and security that enable the person or work group to give full attention to the job.

Fifth, a way must be formulated to insure implementation of the policies established by the faculty. If the administration is not directly responsible to the faculty for such implementation, and if the policies are not put into practice, faculty members acquire a feeling of frustration and develop the opinion that committee work is a waste of time.

If the committee-work dangers are avoided, and if the faculty can see that the time spent in policy formulation really results in program change, faculty members assume real responsibility for the program and mature through their broader understanding of the overall program.

Any plan that is developed will be satisfactory if the faculty keeps in mind the desirability of widespread participation, the need for a functional organization that makes possible small groups working on problems that are their concern, continuity of problem solving and program development through standing committees with a responsibility for a portion of the program, and flexibility that permits necessary revision and necessary coordination under the authority of the total group. The productivity of a group depends upon the integration of a number of diversified abilities, interests, and needs into a unified endeavor.

Decision-Making in the Faculty

As the faculty moves into more use of group decisions and group responsibility, some insecurity may develop. Any change brings some tension. Supervisors can do certain things to help the group feel more secure during the transition.

In reaching a decision, much time must be spent on the what, the how, the when, and the who. The procedure to be followed will be definite, even though the results may be in doubt. Those staff members who gain responsibility from knowing what their specific jobs are will have security.

Do something. If too much time is spent discussing before any action is taken, the group will conclude that discussion is useless, a waste of time. As soon as possible, one of the hypotheses agreed upon by the group should be selected and put into action on an experimental basis. All members of the staff should be encouraged to watch the results and participate in an evaluation of its worth. By the process of taking action, the group will develop more faith in group work.

The leader must help the members of the group become aware of the process of interaction. Group efficiency must become a joint responsibility. Unless a group has control over its own actions and a responsibility for making them efficient, it has not really become a group; it is still directed and operated by the official leaders. Check lists of good group procedures against which the members of the group can check their own participation and group operation help group members to accept responsibility for the group operation. Asking some member of the group to keep a flow chart of the discussion, which can be presented to the group for their consideration at the end of the meeting, is another way of encouraging the group to examine itself.

Some teachers fear change. It adds to their insecurity. The techniques they already know may not work under the new conditions, and they are not sure they can acquire new ones that are as effective. In a changing situation, the only way a staff can achieve security is through the development of a method for the control of change.

As the group grows more mature, the principal will want to place greater personal emphasis on coordination and less on setting the stage. Other leadership will emerge in the group, and it must be used if the group is to develop. Other members of the group who show skill may be brought into service as chairmen of discussion meetings. A planning committee may be organized to take the lead in initiating ideas and establishing agenda for meetings. Subcommittees may be formed under the leadership of various staff members to assume responsibility for portions of the program.

Although as a result of group procedure, the entire staff will have an overall view of the program and the way the pieces fit together, someone must be alert for places where segmentation is developing, must call the staff's attention to the hazard, and must suggest ways of overcoming it. Someone must collect information about, and coordinate, the group's activities. That person is the principal. Someone must watch for places where leadership is beginning to falter and must be ready to serve as a resource person in group work procedures. That person, too, is the principal.

To make coordination of the program easier, the principal will avoid sole jurisdiction by any individual or group over any phase of the program. *All sub-groups, departments, and committees should be responsible to the total faculty.* All members of the staff should have a sense of responsibility for the total program if the faculty is to remain a group.

The decision-making process is the most important phase of successful democratic leadership, because sharing decisions is the only control a democratic leader has. If he cannot get group members to participate in decision-making, if he cannot help them to gain satisfaction from the process and believe in the soundness of the decisions, he must resort to authoritarian procedures.

When a problem has been identified, the next step is to define it and to explore its ramifications. This step involves analyzing the conditions of the school, making explicit the maladjustments of the situation, and advancing tentative solutions.

The official leader should recognize that the first attempts to reach joint decisions in a group are tests of the leader. As a result of past experience, various members of the group have different feelings about his sincerity in introducing the process. The leader should expect doubts and should welcome tests of his integrity.

A basis for decision should be sought. Are there any common values that the group seeks to promote? In school faculties it is usually easy to secure verbal agreement that all staff members want to improve the welfare of children. Of course, the decision-making process may reveal that other values are more important to some staff members, but verbal agreement serves as a working basis at the start.

The issues should be clearly defined. Time should be spent in examining the problem before study is undertaken. Individuals may be asked to cite specific examples. Opportunity must be provided for each member of the group to state the issue as he sees it.

More than one possible solution should be examined. Ask the committee to propose several solutions and provide time for the group to discuss the pros and cons of each. Other members of the group should be free to make other proposals. Expression of all opinions should be sought. Opinions cannot be repressed. If they are not stated in the meeting, they will be expressed elsewhere. The leader should watch for unspoken disagreements and should encourage the members to express them.

Examination of the problem should be started early. Most issues can be resolved if there is sufficient time. Rushed decisions do not permit everyone concerned to study issues and solutions and to talk through differences. One of the leader's functions is to help the group develop machinery for determining problems far enough ahead so that there is time for study and discussion.

The principal will want to encourage the group to seek consensus. If he allows decisions to be made on a simple majority basis, the group will not arrive at agreement on the problems they should investigate or on the ways of solving them. One way the leader can promote consensus is by taking straw votes with the definite understanding that any member of the group is voting in terms of the way he sees the solution of the problem at the moment and is not in any way committing himself to a final decision on the issue. Straw votes serve two purposes: they reveal how nearly the group has arrived at consensus, and they isolate differences that are still unresolved. When the leader finds that disagreements exist, he can call for those who have voted against the proposal to state their reasons and then give the persons who have voted for it an opportunity to explain theirs. In this way, a straw vote is a means of setting the stage for further analysis of the issue. Sometimes consensus on the total solution will be impossible. In such a case, it is better to proceed with the portions of the proposal on which agreement has been reached.

The areas of disagreement should not be forgotten, however. They are not liabilities. They constitute the problems on which further study is needed. By examining the unresolved differences, the faculty has an opportunity to gain new insight through mutual endeavor. If, however, the minority is forced to accept a program that it disapproves, wholehearted support of the program's implementation will be lacking.

Any innovation on which there is not consensus should be undertaken as an experiment. It is a trial run from which evidence is collected to be used as the basis for a more intelligent decision. Whether or not the leader recognizes this condition, it does exist. The proponents and opponents will be looking for data to support their positions. If the group officially recognizes the experimental nature of the situation, an evaluation can be undertaken to collect more comprehensive data to be used in subsequent decisions.

In the majority of cases, the principal will want to focus his attention on the process of reaching a decision rather than on getting any one solution accepted. If he is firmly convinced that one solution is essential, he should surrender the chair and work for it openly. Such action is additional proof to the staff of the principal's honesty.

Throughout his work with the faculty, the principal should continually put emphasis on *what* is right rather than on *who* is right. As the group is encouraged to center upon what is right, personalities and vested interests fade into the background.

In studying possible solutions, the principal will suggest possibilities that he sees too. Until the faculty has learned to trust him, he must emphasize that these are only possibilities, and not necessarily the course of action that should be accepted by the group.

NO VETO WHEN AUTHORITY IS SHARED

It is impossible to share authority and use the veto. It is a contradiction of terms. The use of shared authority means that the official leader is willing to share the power of decision making with the group. The use of a veto verifies that he did not share the authority in the first place. Many principals have felt that they could not eliminate the veto from their work with the group, but it really becomes an impossible instrument in a group that is operating cooperatively. A principal who starts with the idea that he is going to secure faculty advice and apply a veto will find that he cannot use it. If he has been unable to justify his point of view in faculty discussions, he will not be able to make his veto stick. As one principal stated it,

> I have a vote, and an important one, but only one. I suggest. I recommend. I try to persuade. I vigorously defend. But if my faculty doesn't understand, doesn't believe in, doesn't agree with my ideas, regardless of merit, then my ideas haven't much chance of being carried out effectively — and so I wait. I continue to work vigorously for those things that I believe, those things that seem to me to be best for the young people with whom I work.

This statement illustrates why a principal must state to his group that he will not use the veto. If he works as this man does, really thinking with his faculty, a veto is as ineffective as it is unnecessary. Holding it as an official club destroys most of the possibilities for sincere group work. If a group attacks a problem enthusiastically and arrives at an answer that is vetoed, it knows that the group study was a fake, a way of manipulating people. The result is the same if the principal holds the group together until it accepts his hypothesis.

A New Jersey junior high school faculty was assigned a new principal. The former principal had used good group process and teachers were accustomed to real participation in policy-making and planning. The new principal gave verbal allegiance to the procedure, but disagreement with him was a personal matter; he refused to let the group make a decision with which he disagreed even though the straw vote was as much as twenty to one against him. One of the faculty members finally said:

"It is no longer any use to participate in faculty planning sessions. We see they are used to manipulate us. The only thing to do is go back into our classrooms and teach and let the school program go hang. Yesterday

after the faculty council meeting the principal stopped me in the
auditorium and asked 'You are going along with my ideas, aren't you?' "

This statement from a strong, idealistic teacher is added evidence that the
principal must believe in group work and group thinking if group decision-
making is to succeed. If principals don't want, or understand, group thinking and
action, teachers will have to stage a revolution to get it, and most teachers find it
easier to submit or to change positions than to declare war on the principal.

The Control Necessary

The efforts of any organization must be coordinated if the organization is
to achieve its goals. A group cannot expect to be successful unless it plans its
goals carefully and devises ways of achieving them. It must also establish
effective control over the activities of its members. Anarchy has no program.
Laissez-faire does not lead to group accomplishment. Disciplinary control of
group members by each other is a necessity.

A group is more than the total of the individuals who compose it.
Individuals may be self-disciplined and able to control their own behavior, but as
a group they may still display anarchy. The purposes by which individuals
control their own decisions may be at such wide variance that no group control
exists, and coordination and progress are impossible. Self-discipline by individuals is not enough. To be successful, groups must have ways to bring
individual action into line with the goals of the group.

As a principal faces the responsibility of coordinating group activities, he is
confronted with the task of securing and maintaining discipline. If the group is
to exist, it must have discipline. It may be discipline that the group establishes to
carry out its purposes, or it may be discipline forced on the group by the official
leader. It may be developed by the group itself and administered by the leader.

Authoritarian discipline is control of the action of others by an individual
with greater power. The person with power over others decides what he wants
done, how he wants it done, and when he wants it done, and then forces others
to carry out his purposes and plans. As he becomes sure of the willingness and
ability of others to execute what he wants done, he gives them greater freedom
to plan and act within the framework of his purposes. A disciplined member of
the authoritarian group is one who has accepted the leader's wishes and guides
his actions by them. The leader's control is imposed. He regulates the action of
others through the power of fear or respect.

Group self-discipline comes from within. As the members of the group
accept common purposes, they develop a basis for coordination. As these
purposes become sufficiently strong to guide the group actions, group
self-discipline is achieved. The leader does not impose the control. He helps the

group form it. The official leader administers the controls the group imposes on itself.

Let's examine these concepts in terms of the operation of a school faculty. Members join the faculty of their own free will on a contract basis. They have accepted the official leadership of the principal, department head, or supervisors. They have agreed to provide their services to the school for a certain number of hours per day for a definite number of days per year. The school is to be operated within the regulations laid down by the state department of education, the local board of education, and accrediting agencies, and within the budget provided by the local board. Within this framework, any course of action may be taken by the official leader. He may tell teachers what to teach and how to teach, and he may present the purposes of the school and the rules by which they must abide. If he has enough power over the staff, he can enforce his decrees and have authoritarian discipline. If he does not have enough power, there will be no discipline. On the other hand, the official leader may seek to develop self-discipline within the framework of the faculty group by bringing teachers into the decisions regarding purposes, implementation, and execution.

The efficiency of the authoritarian approach is denied by available research on the ways to release group potential. The principal must seek ways of helping a group establish self-discipline.

Some official leaders have found it hard to make the transition. They have moved from authoritarianism to anarchy. Everyone is left to make his own decisions; the group disintegrates, and no progress is made in developing a school program. Such a condition is worse than authoritarian discipline.

Group self-discipline exists when a group has common purposes sufficiently strong to control the actions of individual members. A basketball team aspiring to win a tournament may develop such strong purpose that its members will abide by training rules and will help each other abide by them. Faculty members agreeing on the desire for a salary increase may be willing to levy a tax on themselves to underwrite a publicity campaign. In each case, personal plans and actions are subordinated to the group purpose that the individual has helped to establish.

As was described earlier, a part of the process of leadership is to help the staff evolve its purposes and plans. It is also the first step toward group self-discipline. A principal must meet with his staff to think out together common purposes that all accept. When the group becomes committed to certain purposes, each member of the staff is able to measure his actions by a yardstick he has helped to develop. A disciplined teacher, then, is a teacher with a clear understanding of the goals of the school and a compelling drive to reach them by working with, in, and for the group.

A second part of the achievement of common purposes is the development of group feeling. The members of the group must like and respect each other. They must trust each other and believe that each will assume his full share of responsibility. Otherwise, they will not be willing to undertake a common enterprise.

A third basis for group self-discipline is the clear definition of function and responsibility. Otherwise, there can be no wholehearted acceptance of purposes. Group members must see what the purposes involve in terms of time and energy before they are willing to accept responsibility. Without voluntary acceptance of responsibility, there is no basis for group self-discipline.

Fourth, the members of the group must know that changes in group purposes and procedures can be initiated. Without this assurance, individuals are afraid to submit to group discipline. They fear that group control may be unfair. They may be allocated more than their share of work. As long as it is possible to initiate change, there is no reason to resist group authority. If any person has a case, he can convince others of the need for change.

Fifth, the group must agree on the rules necessary for attaining its purposes. If rules are related to purposes, they will be logical and acceptable and they will coordinate activities. If they are established for the group without reference to the implementation of the common purposes that comprise the basic element of unity for the group, the group has no reason to accept them. They come from outside the group and can be enforced only by pressure from outside.

Sixth, the rules for the group must not involve unrelated activities. Teachers resent rules that affect personal living apart from the school program. Rules that emerge in group self-discipline are related to the coordination of the school program.

To make group discipline work, the principal himself must be disciplined by the group purposes. If he takes advantage of his position the staff can see that he is not really accepting its purposes. If, however, he accepts the purposes sufficiently to come to work before the other members of the staff and work longer than other members of the staff, many of the petty problems that exist in some schools will disappear during the time the staff participates in policy formation. A high correlation exists between clock-watchers on the staff and a clock-watching principal.

Group purposes will not be accepted equally by all members of the staff; some will deviate and will not carry their responsibilities. Some teachers may not even live up to their contract agreement. What then?

THE DISCIPLINING PROCESS

A clear distinction must be made between discipline and disciplining. Where discipline exists, no disciplining is necessary. Where an individual is not controlled by the group self-discipline, disciplinary action must be taken. It is polite in some circles to pretend that disciplining is never necessary. Such would be the case if a principal were perfect in his work with groups, but no one is. The principal, even though he is striving for group self-discipline, will find it necessary to take disciplinary action on behalf of the group. Group morale cannot be allowed to suffer because an individual refuses to be controlled by the self-imposed discipline of the group. Under the authoritarian type of administration a breach of discipline occurs when a teacher violates one of the rules set up by a principal. Under group self-discipline, undisciplined action on the part of a member of the group is activity that hinders the accomplishment of the purposes set up by all. If a teacher frequently fails to meet deadlines, the discipline problem is not that he is breaking a ruling of the principal, but that he is hindering the accomplishment of the purposes of the staff; and the discussion between principal and teacher must be on that basis.

How should disciplining be done? This topic is unpleasant, but certain procedures for treating persons who have broken the discipline of the group have been developed that give better results in helping the individual return to a voluntary acceptance of his responsibilities to the group.

The principal should, first of all, try to get all the pertinent facts. It is well to begin the discussion of the problem with a question designed to get the teacher's side of the story. As the teacher talks, all the facts should be brought out into the open to see whether or not there is complete agreement on them. Until agreement on facts has been established, the decision as to whether disciplinary action is necessary is on an unsound basis.

After facts have been ascertained and the breach of discipline is clear, an attempt should be made to discover the reason for the unsatisfactory behavior. Was it due to disagreement with group purposes? Was it the result of conflict with individuals in the group? Was it caused by distractions from the job? Was it promoted by lack of recognition for his contributions to the group? Was it·due to resentment of some act by the principal?

In dealing with the teacher, the principal must study his own behavior to eliminate anything that may be causing a breakdown of discipline in the group. He must attempt to be as objective concerning his own actions as he is concerning the teacher's actions. At no time during the discussion should there be an unnecessary display of authority. If the teacher agrees that he has violated the purposes or rules, the principal will seek to work out a mutually satisfactory solution, which may mean bringing in other members of the staff to think the problem through.

If the teacher refuses to accept the solution, it may be necessary to suspend, transfer, or fire him. These measures are a last resort; they are not to be taken to maintain the authority of the official leader but, instead, to enable the group to continue to be a self-disciplining group. Final decisions should be made in terms of the course of action that will do most to promote the purposes of the school. If there is agreement on facts, but disagreement on whether an action has been undisciplined, other members of the group should be brought in to help make the final decision. The situation should never be allowed to become an issue between the teacher and the principal.

At no time during the analysis of the situation and the attempt to reach a solution should the principal allow his emotions to come to the surface. He should maintain a calm, objective attitude and constantly seek facts and solutions, rather than attempt to overpower through emotional pressure. Always the paramount question should be: What is best for the pupils? What is best for the group? What is best for the teacher? It must be kept in mind, too, that every personal contact with a member of the group must be thought of in terms of its possible group implications.

The meetings involved in working out the problem should end pleasantly. The principal should seek to help the teacher regain his self-confidence and his place in the group. In this situation, a principal's responsibilities are twofold: to help the group maintain self-discipline and to help individuals to grow. Mistakes and lack of discipline should be looked upon as an opportunity to help the individual get new insight rather than as an occasion to punish.

These suggestions should not be interpreted to mean that the principal does not exert authority. He is empowered to act, and he does act to keep the staff members working together and making their full contribution to the success of the school program. He uses that power to implement the best thinking of all, including the one who violates group discipline. Action includes seeking solutions as well as punishing.

GUIDELINES
FOR A NEW SUPERVISOR

The "special" problems of the beginning supervisor are identified and discussed in this section.
An attempt is made to apply the "sense" of the
book to those special problems.

13   The Beginning Supervisor

The first few months of a new supervisor's work have a great effect on his success in the school system where he works. Whether he is a general supervisor, a subject matter resource person, a research or media specialist, a principal, or a helping teacher, he will create an impression with his beginning efforts that facilitates or hinders his work as a supervisor. Therefore, it is desirable that he think about the way he will attempt to work, formulate the theory that will guide his actions, and establish some criteria by which he will judge his progress.

The First Steps

A supervisor can reach his position by two routes. Either he can be promoted from the ranks or he can be brought into the situation from an outside position. Both routes have their difficulties.

If a man is promoted from the ranks, the staff knows his strengths and weaknesses before he starts exercising official leadership. He is a member of the group. He must not allow that relationship to change. His chief problem will be his own behavior. He will have to choose his words much more carefully. He will have to guard against actions that will be mistaken for assumptions of superiority. He will find that exercising leadership from the supervisor's spot requires different procedures from exercising leadership without official status in the group.

When a supervisor is brought in from the outside, first impressions can do much to win acceptance or to build up enormous hurdles that must be overcome.

Out of the first meeting with the staff should develop a feeling that a new official leader is friendly, has a sense of direction, and is willing to learn. Actions that tend to create feelings of antagonism, suspicion, distrust, or the impression that the official leader knows all the answers should be avoided.

Nor should the supervisor give the staff the impression that he is out to make a name for himself. The following excerpt from the letter of a beginning supervisor shows his awareness of this pitfall:

> The work here becomes increasingly exciting. Slowly and gradually, teachers are beginning to extend their confidence and enlarge their hopes. What's especially pleasing is that they are not pinning their hopes on me, but on themselves. In spite of this, however, I'm centering most of my activities in the system.
>
> The state executive committee proposed me to represent them on the national council. I asked them to reconsider the nomination. I have the feeling that as much as I'd like the growth that might come from this work, it might seriously impair my work here. I've had to overcome a certain amount of wariness in the teachers. They are afraid of the possibility of my using them and their work in the system as a stepping-stone of some sort. Nothing personal — just the result of sad experience. While I think few, if any, feel that way now, I don't want to give any reason for believing there is a possible element of opportunism in my work.

One way to get the staff members to work with the supervisor is to let them know that their help is desired. One of the first duties of the supervisor is to make clear that the program is not his, but rather that of the staff, that any progress that will be made will be progress of the staff and not the supervisor. He is there to help staff members develop the program, and he can help only if staff members indicate to him ways in which he can make a contribution. He needs also to indicate that he will make mistakes because he is new, but that these mistakes will be fewer if he has the guidance of the staff.

Many young supervisors experience difficulty because they fail to win the support of older, more experienced members of the staff who look upon the younger person as inexperienced and immature. Unless the supervisor goes out of his way to let them know that he intends to make use of their experience and knowledge, the chances are great that they will not give their full support to the program. One of the surest ways to secure their assistance is to let them know that he will be coming to them for information and help, that they have great responsibility for giving clear interpretations of the values of the present program, and that the staff needs these ideas as much as it does the thinking of new staff members.

In his opening remarks to the staff, the supervisor should get across the idea that the success of any program depends upon the extent to which staff members are able to work together and help each other.

One of the sources of help for a new supervisor is his predecessor. Even though the person who was in the position before is being relieved of his responsibility and feels bitterness toward those responsible, he will have much helpful information for the new supervisor. The newcomer will want to secure the former leader's analysis of the situation. Although this information may be biased, it should be weighed and evaluated to see what guidance may be obtained from it. Particularly helpful would be the outgoing supervisor's estimate of the strengths and weaknesses of various staff members, his description of the plan of operation of the program that is under way, and his statements concerning the pitfalls and problems involved.

The new supervisor should remember that he is on trial. It is not his function to go into a new position and judge his predecessor, the staff, or the program. He will want to avoid behaving like the supervisor that this Washington teacher described:

> Our supervisor was new to the district and unknown to nearly all the teachers, except by name. He walked into a room unannounced, sat for three hours and watched the proceedings of the class, and walked out without a word to the teacher he had observed.

The new supervisor must put the staff at ease. It is just as important for a supervisor to take this step as it is for him to devote the first part of an interview to making the other person feel at ease. Although the need for putting the other person at ease in an interview is widely recognized, the need for spending the first phase of work together in getting acquainted and making persons feel secure in their relationships with each other is not as well understood.

To put the staff at ease, one of the first things an official leader will want to do is to meet as many of the staff as possible on a social basis. This will give the staff members a chance to learn that the new supervisor is accessible and easy to know. It will give the official leader a chance to observe the personal qualities that will hinder or promote the socialization of the staff. Staff members will be glad to know that the official leader likes people and wants their friendship. They will try to discover whether they can respect him as a person as well as a professional leader. Professional leadership is not enough. Staff members need the type of relaxed, tension-free social relationships that enable them to accept, understand, and work with one another. The staff watches to see whether the official leader contributes to this type of emotional environment.

Another aspect of putting the staff at ease is to start with the assumption that all members of the staff are strong. A supervisor will want to start by looking for good qualities that he can commend. As he gives recognition to the positive side of the existing program, he will build the confidence of staff members in their relationship with him. An analysis of weak points at the beginning of working together will alienate some members of the staff who would otherwise be willing to give the new official leader a chance. Starting out with an accent on the positive serves the same purpose as discussing common interests in the beginning of an interview.

If the official leader stresses his role as a coordinator, rather than as a dictator of policy, he will help put people at ease. They will feel certain that no one is going to come into the situation and institute change more rapidly than they can accept it. Emphasis on the coordinator role makes it clear that the supervisor conceives of his job as a service function rather than as a directing function.

The official leader should assure the staff that he will continue the present method of operating. Drastic changes will not be made immediately. Unless the staff requests it, he should not make changes just to assert his authority or to let the staff know that a new man is on the job. The staff knows the situation, and any action taken by a newcomer without the knowledge supplied by the staff would be rash.

The procedure outlined in this section eliminates any upset or confusion when a new official leader is introduced. It provides for a smooth transition from the previous leadership to the new. By proceeding in this way, the official leader has an opportunity to learn, and to know the job and the staff.

Initiation of Change

Any change should be made on the basis of evaluation. The supervisor will want to approach the program from an evaluation point of view. He will want to collect the facts, pass judgment with the staff on these facts, and make plans for revision in terms of the judgments made. Through this approach, he will show that he is not making changes just to be different. He will emphasize his respect for evidence. He will demonstrate his respect for the members of the staff by accepting the effort and work that they have put into the existing program. He must remember that the program he finds represents the best thinking and effort that the staff he has inherited has been able to achieve. Any negative judgment on his part without evidence that the staff has examined with him is a destructive criticism of the staff members as persons. It builds antagonism.

By following the evaluation approach, the new supervisor is making clear to the staff that the program is its program and its responsibility. This approach keeps the staff from feeling that programs belong to official leaders and that they change completely as official leaders are changed.

A new supervisor should listen more than he talks. Any person going into a new situation will make mistakes based on lack of information about the job. The more experienced members of the staff will know many details of the method of operation that the supervisor cannot hope to know. Foolish statements based on this lack of information will put the new supervisor in the unfavorable position of having to correct or revise any mistake that he has made.

> An industrial engineer was placed in charge of the sales department of a large concern. One of the members of the department who had hoped to be appointed supervisor came to the engineer and asked how he should conduct the mailing campaign that was then in progress. The new supervisor wisely recommended that the older employee go ahead with the program the way it had been planned until the new supervisor had become thoroughly acquainted with the department and its operation.
>
> Another supervisor in the same organization proceeded on an entirely different basis. When he met his staff for the first time, he stated publicly that he did not like the way the program was being conducted and from now on everything would be done differently. He put his declaration into effect immediately. Although his staff went along with his program, they did not thoroughly accept it, and as soon as the man moved to a new job they began working for the return of the practices that had been used in the department before he came. This man never thoroughly sold his staff on his program and his procedure, because he had discarded without a fair evaluation a system to which they had contributed and to which they felt loyalty.

A supervisor's first job is to become acquainted with the program in which he is to work. If he does most of the talking, his chance of becoming acquainted with it is decreased.

If the supervisor conceives of his job as one of helping his staff, he will want to start with the problems that the members of the staff have. This approach will be a way of demonstrating that he is sincere in his desire to help and in his acceptance of the value of the program that the staff has developed, even though these problems may be unimportant from the supervisor's point of view.

A new supervisor cannot tell his staff which problems are important in the school. He can only create a situation in which the staff will bring its important problems into the open, and in which the supervisor may be of assistance in solving them.

One technique for bringing the problems of a school to the surface was followed by a new superintendent. He wrote to all the teachers in the system and asked them to list the problems on which they felt the staff should be working. Using the statements of the teachers, he compiled a list of the twenty-five problems mentioned most frequently. He requested the staff to select those problems from the list thus created to serve as the basis for an in-service training program that was to be instituted in the school system that year.

In talking with the staff to learn about the program and the personnel involved, the new supervisor must be careful not to build up a caste system in the faculty. All persons should have equal access to the door of a new supervisor. If it becomes apparent that the supervisor is depending upon certain members of the staff for information and guidance, the teachers not included in this inner circle will begin to form resistance groups to the program being evolved by the unofficial cabinet. This condition is particularly likely to arise if the stated functions of the persons to whom the new official leader turns for advice do not include leadership in portions of the program about which decisions are made.

One way to avoid the development of feeling that the advice of only a portion of the staff is sought is to make many decisions in an open conference. Thereby, the staff will have the opportunity to see how the supervisor brings out all the evidence, encourages everyone to listen to all data and opinions, considers with the staff all the possible solutions suggested, and seeks consensus before a decision is reached. Even though such conferences are time-consuming, they will ultimately pay dividends and will be effective in building morale and saving time. The staff will acquire confidence in the way the official leader works and will develop a trust in the fairness of decisions that are made when they are not present.

Another important task of a new supervisor is to convince teachers that he knows that it is his job to release the talents of those with whom he works. He must let teachers know that he wants suggestions on steps he can take to remove hindrances to creative teaching.

The official leader helps set the pattern of work in the organization. If the new supervisor wants members of the staff to be on the job on time and to work at a high level of efficiency, he must set that pattern himself from the moment he begins his new job. If he is prompt, hard-working, and thorough, if he sets an example of coming to work early and not leaving before the day is over, the staff will more likely assume the same responsibility. A new executive director was appointed in an organization in which tardiness and leaving the job early were a consistent pattern. The new official leader made it a habit to get to work half an hour earlier than anyone else and to stay half an hour after the last person left. Without a word being spoken, the staff began to work a full day. The example was more forceful than anything the supervisor could have said.

As he enters a new job, the supervisor must avoid any change in his personality. New responsibility must not be allowed to interfere with his friendliness and relaxed manner. It is so easy to become overwhelmed by new duties and responsibilities, so that new formality, hurriedness, and hardness may begin to appear in the supervisor's actions.

One exception to being natural is being more careful about chance remarks. Comments of supervisors have much wider implication than remarks made by other members of the staff. Much humor in ordinary situations is at the expense of others. Belittling remarks are accompanied by a smile and are usually accepted in the same spirit in which they are given. When such remarks are made by a supervisor, they have a far different implication. As a person steps into a supervisory role, he has a much greater effect on the future of his coworkers.

Remarks made by a supervisor may be misunderstood. Remarks that are made in jest may be taken seriously. Statements that are understood perfectly by everyone present in a given situation may cause much misunderstanding when they are told to persons who were not present. Care must be exercised to avoid the type of statement that will be misunderstood if it is repeated out of the context in which it was spoken. A remark made in good faith may be twisted by repeated tellings until it becomes a barbed threat by the time it reaches the person concerned. Persons in positions of responsibility must be constantly on their guard to be sure they say what they mean and do not depend upon inflection of the voice or upon gestures to convey the impressions they wish.

Loyalty to Ideas

The new official leader must win acceptance and respect. He cannot demand loyalty to himself, even if he wants it. A former college professor went into a job as the head of a department in a national organization. On the first day, he called the staff together and opened the meeting with the remark, "I expect all of you to be loyal to me." One of the members of the staff spoke up immediately, "I do not know whether or not I can be loyal to you." The college professor, taken aback by the response, asked why; the staff member replied that he would develop loyalty if he found the supervisor deserved it.

An industrial relations director, in discussing the problem of winning support of a staff, put it in another way. "Loyalty is a two-way proposition, and a supervisor must be the one to demonstrate it first. Workers are loyal when the supervisor earns their loyalty by being loyal to them."

Lillian Smith, in *The Journey,* writes:

As totalitarianism increases – in a school or a country or a church – the use of the word loyalty increases. A strange and frightening word. The mob's word. The gang's word. A word people shout in unison – while honor and responsibility and integrity are words only an individual can speak and act out.

How does one measure the quality of a man's relationship with a large entity such as a church or school or government? It is an interesting fact, and one many of us have observed all our lives, that people demand loyalty of us only when they are doing something to us (or somebody else) of which we don't approve and cannot wholeheartedly participate in, and that weakens our love and admiration. Let's admit it: loyalty is a verbal switch-blade used by little, and big, bosses to force us quickly to accept a questionable situation that our intelligence and conscience should reject.

In the cooperative approach, loyalty to an individual official leader is not the quality desired. Teachers must develop loyalty to the values that they accept, and loyalty to the program that emerges through the implementation of these values. Official leaders should not be concerned over whether people develop a personal loyalty to them. Staff members should be unfettered by personal loyalties that keep them from taking issue with official leaders when the leaders violate the values that the group is seeking. Official leaders should seek, instead of loyalty, acceptance as worthwhile contributors to the development of a good program and respect for their abilities and skills that make the school more effective. Acceptance and respect are built through the way the leader works. It is a longtime proposition.

The New Supervisor's Theory of Change

Any supervisor who operates intelligently must have a theory of change that guides his behavior. A theory is especially important for a new supervisor. He knows his new role makes him more responsible for change in a desirable direction. Although he may approach the process of inducing change in a haphazard manner, he will not be as effective as if he worked in terms of a well thought out theory of change that gives him perspective in his decisions and his actions.

Although most people recognize that the fundamental function of a supervisor is to induce change, little attention has been given to the theory of change that should guide his behavior. How does change take place? What are the things that a change agent can do to bring about change? The theory of change that seems most productive to the writer has five assumptions.

First, change occurs in programs and institutions as people change. What people believe, how they think, and the skill that they develop all determine what happens as they live and operate. A change in policy statement, or in an organization table, will mean nothing unless the people who operate in terms of it believe that the change has occurred and that it makes a difference. People are what they believe. Their beliefs govern their behavior.

Second, people change as they change their perception of themselves, their role, or the situation. People do what they do because of the way they see themselves in the situation. As their picture of themselves in the situation changes, they operate differently. And the situation changes because they have changed. If a person feels that he is more adequate, he begins to behave differently. If he sees that his role has not been what he thought, he tends to live up to his new expectation of himself in the situation. If he gains greater understanding of the realities of the situation, or becomes less sure of his reality, his behavior changes. Therefore, if a person hopes to bring about change, he places his effort on helping people change their perception of themselves, their role, or of the situation.

Third, people change as they interact with each other on matters that concern them. People don't change because someone else wishes they would, or because someone tells them they must. People change themselves as they become involved in matters that are important to them. They are affected by the comments or the actions of a person in the situation that is important; the way others behave toward them affects their perception of themselves, or their role. The additional facts that others bring to them about the situation change their perception of the situation. If a change agent hopes to bring about change in people, he seeks to create the kind of situation where they will interact with others.

Fourth, desirable change occurs when people examine intelligently the issues that divide them. Individuals do not see the situation, themselves, or their role in the same way as other people see it. Each person approaches a given situation uniquely and interprets it uniquely. Out of this uniqueness of perception comes the difference that leads to conflict. Whether people grow as a result of difference, or whether they regress and withdraw depends upon the way the situation develops. If people can be helped to objectively examine and thoroughly explore the data and the alternate courses of action, desirable change will occur. If on the other hand, people make emotional, hasty attempts to resolve their differences, or they are not brought into contact with a wide variety of data and courses of action, the change that occurs will probably not be desirable, because it will be unintelligent.

Fifth, the place of the change agent is to develop an organization, a structure, and a procedure by which the next steps for any given group can be considered intelligently. This is the major function of the official leader who hopes to bring about intelligent change. He can't produce lasting change by coercion, or bribery, or threat. People will live with the force that he is able to apply only until they are able to extricate themselves from the situation. But if a change agent wants the change to be lasting, he will bring it about by creating the kind of situation where people can interact in an intelligent manner on problems that concern them. Attention will be given to the kind of structure, which enables such interaction, and to guiding the procedure, which frees intelligence to collect data concerning a variety of alternatives and to make choices in terms of consequences.

The supervisor, in applying these assumptions in his attempt to create change in the public school program will recognize that there are internal and external forces that work for change in a public institution. Pressure groups in the world, national and community bases seek to bring about change in school programs. The government at the local, the state and the national level attempts to influence the direction of education. Boards of education attempt to establish policy and to give direction. Administrators pressure for change. Teachers are attempting to make their purposes and needs felt. Students are a real force working for change. There is no question that change will occur. The question is really whether or not the change will be an intelligent one in a desired direction. Haphazard change will not produce the most desirable change. Decisions in such situations will be made by power rather than by intelligence. Where power is the determining factor, the change may be in the direction of advantage for a few at the expense of the many.

An institutional structure must be created that makes possible free and open consideration of the alternatives and choice based on evidence and the prevailing values. This means that all who will be involved should have the opportunity for suggesting items for consideration, should be free to supply data, should have the opportunity to advance alternatives, and to question and to discuss, and to ask that the values be made clear and the course of action taken be an implementation of the prevailing values.

Of course it is recognized that if the values are wrong, the direction of change will be wrong. Those who hold different values will see the direction of change as regression rather than progress. If, however, those who will be affected have an opportunity to participate in the decision-making and if ideas and values are brought into the open and stand in the open market place, tested by all concerned, the choices of values made will be the most intelligent that people in the situation can make.

One of the real problems is deciding which people shall be involved in which decision. It is important that the areas of decision and the degrees of freedom of choice to be allocated to each decision-making element of the organization be defined. The safest criterion that the writer knows is that those who will be affected by a decision should be involved. In a school situation, this is obviously an impossible criterion to apply in all cases. The school system must fall back on representative participation in decision-making. This means that the official leader must be concerned with the structure that determines the method of choice and the kind of communication channels that exist between those represented and their representative. If the structure established is such that the communication is not good and not two-way, the participation in the decision-making by all will fail.

Implicit in what is being said is that the structure that is created must be of the type in which people can be deeply involved in the decision-making through their representatives. If the supervisory staff hopes to bring about lasting change in the program, the primary concern must be with the degree of involvement. If people change only to the extent that they are involved, the change agent must put his primary focus in examining the structure on the degree to which people have an opportunity to participate and feel a responsibility for the decision taken. This theory of change serves the new supervisor as a frame of reference against which to evaluate all of his decisions and actions.

Assumptions That Cause Difficulty for Supervisors

A new supervisor should know that persons in positions of official leadership have found themselves in difficulty in the past because they have operated on the basis of false assumptions about the nature of human beings, human groups, communication, and learning. Some of these trouble-causing assumptions will now be examined.

1. Appointment to a status position gives one leadership.   A principal in a midwestern city was appointed to the position of assistant superintendent in charge of instruction. In one of his first meetings with a large group of teachers, he began to tell them what he wanted them to do. Several teachers raised objections. The man lost his temper and told the group in angry words that he was the assistant superintendent, and they would do what he said.

This man assumed that teachers should and would follow him because of his appointment. He did not realize that leadership is earned and does not come automatically with the title. Two years later, the assistant superintendent was replaced.

2. Communication follows the organization chart.   An organization chart is a picture of someone's wishes. It may be drawn to coincide with the flow of communication, but it does not always reflect the true organization or the true flow of communication. Unless supervisors recognize that decisions are made in informal situations, and unless they discover the real channels of communication, chances are they will be ineffective.

3. Loyalty is to persons rather than ideas.   Many official leaders become unhappy and begin to distrust the members of the staff because they make this assumption. They become insecure, because they cannot understand why persons who are their friends, persons they have helped, persons who have stood shoulder to shoulder with them in previous battles, do not support them in the present situation. They feel that their colleagues are being treacherous and guilty of disloyalty, when actually the colleagues are being moral and living up to their values. A concept of loyalty that requires that a person must agree with the official leader and support him on all issues weakens the leader's self-confidence and leads to disruption of the group.

4. Staff members should adjust to the official leader.   When a supervisor assumes that he can be moody, nagging, and inconsiderate, and that others must still work with him, the rocks of failure are immediately ahead. He may retain his position, but he will lose his leadership. Leadership is bestowed by a group upon an individual who is sensitive to the feelings of its members.

5. Feelings are not important.   It is easy to say that staff members should be adult and not become disturbed over an action. But saying what should be does not make it true. The way a staff member feels about an action of the supervisor is more important than the action itself. If a teacher interprets an action as a reprimand or a recrimination, his future behavior is governed by his interpretation, not by the leader's intention. Unless a supervisor attempts constantly to place himself in the other person's position and to see how actions look from there, his leadership is in jeopardy.

6. Administration is decision-making.   A principal from an eastern state objected vigorously to the idea of sharing decisions. He said, "My job is making decisions. If you take that function away, I have no function." His point of view is one that is held by many.

The concept of "power over" has been a part of human culture for many years. It is only as supervisors begin to discover that sharing decisions is a more effective way to release the power of a group that they see a different function for the leader. Conceiving of the leader's role as that of decision-maker is only possible in situations where teachers are willing to surrender their professional judgment. Cornell's study (1954) indicates that the better teachers are unwilling to do this.

7. *The status quo can be maintained.* When a person tries to keep the program as it is, he is attempting the impossible. People change day by day, and the program continues to be dynamic. When leaders fail to recognize this fact and do not plan for growth, they are left with the choice of either repressing change or withdrawing from active leadership.

8. *People can be told what their problems are.* A high-school principal wanted his staff to work on the student-activity problem. The teachers felt they would profit more by studying techniques of pupil-teacher planning. For four days of a preschool planning conference, the struggle continued. At last the principal capitulated.

Even if he had won, the work would not have been productive. People must believe there is a real problem before they are willing to give their full energy to a project. When supervisors attempt to tell people what the problems are on which they should work, they encounter resistance.

9. *People grow by being told.* When teachers were asked where they secured the new ideas they put into practice, they placed the suggestions of supervisors twenty-seventh on the list. This discouraging condition is not the result of lack of ideas among supervisors. It is a reflection of how we learn. Teachers learn when they are ready. When they want help on a problem, and when they discover a solution by reading or by talking with someone of their choosing, they learn.

10. *People can be forced to be democratic.* Unless a staff wants to participate in policy formation, going through the process is fruitless. Democracy cannot be achieved in a staff by autocratic means. Frequently a staff rebels and accuses the official leader of asking it to do his work and to assume his responsibility. Securing staff participation is a gradual process in which the official leader continues to offer to share the decisions he has the authority to make.

11. *Actions between an official leader and a staff member are individual.* A Texas principal spent many hours attempting to help a beginning teacher become a successful one. Because the teacher was an attractive girl and the principal was a man, other teachers began to talk. Although this supervisor was making a professional effort to help an individual teacher, it affected the work of the entire school adversely.

The assumptions listed above conflict with the implications of existing research. They constitute stumbling blocks to supervisors who continue to accept them.

Working Conditions Promoted

The direction supervision will take in the future depends upon the type of working situation that is desired. Actions are attempts to realize ideals and visions. Thus, any attempt to state the future of supervision must involve an effort to define the staff relationships that are deemed desirable.

Assistance in the development of more effective learning situations for students is the primary function of the supervisor. But a direct attack does not produce the results desired. Unless a teacher feels right about himself, about his job, about his fellow staff members, and about his supervisor, he is not ready to consider his teaching processes.

What are the qualities of a school situation in which a supervisor can hope to improve instruction?

1. Each member values himself and others.   When an individual dislikes himself or feels inadequate, he attempts to hurt himself or to find solace in proving himself superior to others. Either type of action decreases the power of a group. The productivity of a staff is increased when its members take steps that enhance the individual's sense of worth by recognizing contributions and supporting his efforts.

2. A deep concern for the welfare and feeling of each individual exists.   A superintendent in a western school system faced a problem that was serious enough to cost him his job. As he sat in his office trying to decide what to do, he put his head in his hands for five full minutes. An observer might have guessed that he was worried about losing his position. When he raised his head, his questions were: "What will this do to John? How will Sally feel about this action?" His constant concern was how the individuals involved would feel. The success of his solution was to be measured in terms of people's emotions as well as other factors.

Such concern for the feeling and welfare of each individual has its effect on the group. In such a situation, teachers feel more secure and are more concerned with the feelings of their students and the improvement of the school program.

3. Each member of the staff feels that he belongs to the group.   When an individual does not feel that the other members of the group accept him or want to be associated with him, the chances are great that he will not be able to make much of a contribution to the school. He will be so involved in discovering ways to become accepted that he will not be able to concentrate on staff projects or on improving the quality of his work. Or he may reverse the procedure. He may be so full of resentment at being excluded that he will engage in harmful and aggressive activity toward the group members. The supervisor will want to do the things that help each person feel "free to come and safe to go." He will strive to help each staff member to feel that he may enter any informal group without a sense of intruding and that he may leave without fear that he will be talked about in a derogatory manner.

4. People trust each other.   When there is no trust, individuals must be on the defensive and more concerned about protecting themselves and their status than with seeking more effective ways of doing the work or of becoming more productive. Trust is the foundation stone of communication. Unless we trust the other person, we resist his ideas and refuse to share our deep convictions. Unless trust is established, persons in the situation will deal with superficial topics or attempt to outmaneuver others.

Trust cannot be achieved by the official leader's stating that he wants to be trusted. Trust is something that is earned, and each action of the individual affects it. It is a two-way street. If we hope to see it prevail in the staff with which we work, we must be the first to demonstrate it.

The way in which the official leader works with group members demonstrates his faith or his lack of faith; it determines whether group members will trust him or trust each other. One of the best tests we can apply to our own actions is to ask these questions: Does the step that we are about to take make future working together possible? Will the action increase the possibility of honest communication? If an action fails to meet these tests, it probably is not a good supervisory procedure.

5. The administration shares decisions within its authority.   The simple process of sharing decisions is the most powerful tool a leader has. It is the key to the securing of leadership, the assumption of responsibility, the acceptance of assignments, and the development of high morale.

Any decision within the authority of the official leader may be shared, but care should be exercised to distinguish between those decisions that the official leader can make and those that are made by a higher authority, such as the board of education. Failure to make the boundaries of authority clear may cause frustration and may lead the group to reject further participation in decision-making.

If there are certain decisions within the authority of the official leader that he wishes to retain for himself, he should make these clear to the staff with which he works. Such action will be more acceptable than pretending to share all decisions and then vetoing decisions in areas in which the leader feels the staff to be incompetent.

6. All who will be vitally affected by a policy participate in its formation.   When the official leader makes it possible for staff members to participate in making decisions, he increases their assumption of responsibility, which in turn promotes better performance of the tasks at hand. When people share in a decision, they are concerned about its outcome.

7. Each person can maintain his integrity.   Permissiveness is the foundation of self-respect. Unless each person is free to express his disagreement, the situation is one in which he cannot behave morally; he cannot work in terms of the values he holds. A person who must forfeit his integrity to hold his job cannot value himself or those who force him to debase himself. Growth and increased contributions come only when individuals value both themselves and their colleagues.

8. Increased self-direction by each staff member is sought. Although it seems contradictory, a group grows in strength as its members become increasingly self-directing. As staff members define together what they hope to accomplish and plan the procedures by which these goals will be achieved, each individual becomes better able to make valid decisions. As he has access to more information and as he becomes more familiar with the thinking of the group, an individual develops the security that enables him to make judgments without turning to someone else. Confusion and indecision are eliminated.

9. Individuals gain a sense of direction by participating in establishing group goals. An individual may obtain a sense of direction either by being told, or by participating in forming, the goals. When he is told, he may misunderstand or resist the goals that are set for him. If he participates, he understands the goals, because he has helped establish them, and he expends more effort to obtain them because he is sure of their worth.

10. Information is available to all. A staff cannot be expected to make wise decisions if it does not have access to relevant information. Inaccessibility of information, caused by the administration's refusal to share it or by clogged channels of communication, may cause the group to make a poor decision. And a poor decision results in loss of faith in its own ability or in its leadership.

Because of the official leader's position, bulletins and other documents come to him. He attends meetings in which information is shared by the administration. It is difficult for him to know which information to share. He does not want to bore staff members with unnecessary and unimportant details. He wants to keep them as free and unburdened with unnecessary information as he can. But screening is dangerous. Sometimes the information he considers unimportant will be very important to certain members of the staff. The safest procedure is to make available to all the information the official leader possesses.

11. Ideas are considered the property of the group. When ideas are identified with people, decisions are too often made on the basis of the proponent's status rather than on the inherent value of the ideas. If ideas are considered a resource of the group, teachers share them freely. But if proposals and practices are constantly related to the individual who originates them, selfishness begins to operate. For example, at one major teacher-training institution, the staff members are very careful to keep the new materials they develop away from other staff members. Materials are hidden in filing cabinets and desk drawers. Each person wants to be sure that he keeps control of his innovation until it is recognized by the total staff as his contribution. In another teacher-training institution, great emphasis is placed on joint planning, and staff members frequently share the materials they develop. Very infrequently is any material labeled with the name of an individual staff member. In the first situation, suspicion and jealousy prevail. In the second, conflict and distrust are the exception.

12. Loyalty is to ideas and values, not to persons. This condition is closely related to the one above. If disagreement with the official leader is considered disloyalty, the only type of creativity that can exist within the staff is improvement within the areas in which the official leader has interest.

13. Teachers speak out, and the administration capitalizes on their ideas. In some situations, the person with ideas that differ from those of the official leader is considered a trouble-maker. He finds himself unwanted in the school. He is ignored in faculty meetings, and if he persists, attempts are made to belittle him and his ideas. The easy path for him is to keep quiet and to accept the policies of the administration.

If the supervisor wants to release the full potential of the staff, this procedure cannot be accepted. Insight comes as differences are examined. If all members of the faculty believe the same thing, progress is unlikely, because of the complacency that the uniformity of ideas develops. If morale and a sense of group unity have been developed to the point where the staff feels that it belongs together, disagreement is not dangerous; it will not destroy the group; it is a source of creativeness.

14. Decision by consensus is sought. A decision leads to action when the group members are convinced of its value. If only a majority is in favor of the proposed course of action, the full power of the group will not be back of it. Decision by majority is only second-best. When time and the skill of the group permit, achieving consensus insures the group's total commitment to the enterprise.

15. Teachers and administrators have the opportunity to tell each other frankly what they expect of each other and the help they would like to receive from each other. At a principal's conference in a midwestern city, each principal brought one member of his teaching staff. Small groups of teachers and principals were formed, with no teacher in the same group with his principal. For the major portion of the week, the members of each small group considered what they expected and the help they wanted. New understandings, more common perception of roles, and more satisfying ways of working resulted.

16. The staff accepts responsibility for decisions made and is willing to live with the consequences. Participation in decision-making has little meaning if it is divorced from the responsibility of living up to the decision. If it is not expected that all will be bound by the decision, behavior will be irresponsible. Every staff member should expect that the official leader will hold himself and every member of the group accountable for fulfilling the obligation imposed by the decision reached.

In light of present knowledge, the sixteen conditions listed above make possible the greatest productivity of a staff and should be the basic goals of a supervisor.

When a teacher has assurance of his own worth and the importance of his job, a sense of belonging to the group, and a trust in the official leadership, he is ready to attempt to improve instruction. The official leader can assist in improving the teaching-learning situation in many ways such as:

seeking agreement on purposes.

making provision for sharing of ideas.

stimulating and assisting the staff to prepare self-evaluation check lists.

keeping all teachers well supplied with up-to-date materials.

asking as frequently for proof of why a new method should not be tried as for reasons why it should.

encouraging teachers to develop distinctive classrooms that reflect the work and activities of their classes.

recognizing persons who are trying new procedures.

establishing a petty-cash fund for the purchase of expendable materials.

providing in-service training experience in self-expression in a variety of media.

helping teachers develop techniques for evaluating a variety of types of pupil growth.

organizing staff meetings around the study of teacher problems and the improvement of the school program.

using workshops as a procedure for program change.

assisting with the experimentation that grows out of a workshop.

encouraging pupil-teacher planning.

encouraging teachers to meet and plan the curriculum with parents.

encouraging self-evaluation of teachers and their classes.

using faculty meetings to discuss evaluation techniques that individual teachers have found helpful.

stimulating intervisitation as a method of providing more data on which to base judgments.

Self-Evaluation Procedures for Supervisors

Self-evaluation is going on all the time. A man takes a furtive glance at the toes of his shoes as he goes by the bootblack. A woman takes out her compact to see whether her lipstick is still as it should be. Persons judge themselves against unstated standards.

People do not, however, take stock as frequently of the way they do their jobs. They are more inclined to let others judge them. They feel that they can tell how well they are doing if they get a satisfactory number of promotions and raises and if the people working with them are happy and fond of them. Many of them will even refuse to evaluate their work when they are not pleasing their superiors or co-workers. They escape by blaming the other person for their inadequacies.

Few people do the type of work they are capable of doing. They work at less than full efficiency because they have not analyzed their position and evaluated their work in terms of the requirements.

The supervisor's need for evaluation is both personal and professional. To preserve his own self-respect, he seeks ways of increasing his strengths and decreasing his weaknesses. To grow professionally and to be sure that he is doing an adequate job, he needs to establish goals or criteria and measure his actions by them.

What are the ways he can judge his work? At least two phases should be examined constantly: How well does he manage his activities? What are the results he achieves? Let's first examine the way he works. The following questions have significance:

1. Do I set up a schedule of activities for each week? for each day? Supervisory work will control a man unless he makes some attempt to organize it. No one can do a hundred tasks at once, and the supervisor has that many ahead of him constantly. The tasks seem overwhelming, unless he lists one by one the things he is going to do and eliminates the others from his mind until the immediate task is finished. Setting up a schedule of work is a way of freeing himself from the burden of a work load, because it enables him to carry only a portion of it at one time.

2. Am I flexible in my schedule without becoming disturbed? Schedules are made to be broken. They constitute the best organizational hypothesis at the start of the day. They give stability and form to the day. But they are not sacred. As the day progresses, the supervisor gets more information; new situations arise that render unwise the schedule he had planned. The need for his changing the schedule should not disturb him. A change is a decision that he makes because he thinks it is best or because people have operated in a way that he did not expect.

3. Do I get upset when my plans don't go as I hoped? When a person plans cooperatively, the plans developed are rarely the ones he brought to the situation. He expects them to be revised as more people participate in studying and executing them. He expects that plans will be changed in the light of other people's thinking and in the light of his inaccuracy in predicting the outcomes of action. If he gets disturbed by the failure of his plans to develop exactly as he had devised them, he probably is more concerned with controlling people than he wants to admit.

4. Do I check off the things I've accomplished? Everyone needs a sense of achievement. Records that show the completion of tasks a person has established for himself give this satisfaction. Failure to record the things done continues the burden. Each task finished remains a part of the mental load he must carry unless he has a way of recording its accomplishment and forgetting it.

5. Do I get my feelings hurt? Helen Jennings (1950) found that the main qualities of those whom others select as leaders are the ability to keep their personal feelings under control and sensitivity to the feelings of others. When a person is suspicious of others and their actions, when he spends a large portion of his time trying to guess the hidden motives that underlie the actions of others, when he views actions of others as threats to him, he is displaying his insecurity. To exert leadership, a man must be the type of person in whom others can place confidence. If he is insecure, afraid, or suspicious, he decreases the strength of the group of which he is a part, rather than supplying assistance, support, and hope.

6. Am I able to take criticism?   This criterion is related to the preceding one. A weak, insecure person is threatened by criticism from others. Instead of using criticism as information that helps him grow, he tries to avoid it and fights against those who offer it.

Some persons are able to take criticism from their superiors, but not from individuals they consider to have less rank or importance. Two factors may account for this condition. The first is their expectations. Their stereotype of a superior may be a person who tells them what to do, how to do it, and how well it has been done. When criticism comes from a superior, it is the expected thing and not a threat. The person with less status, on the other hand, may be stereotyped as an individual who takes orders and is in no position to criticize. Second, he may have feelings of superiority toward persons of less status. He may believe that he holds his present position because of superior intelligence and ability. Either of these feelings deprives him of access to the intelligence of a large percentage of those with whom he works and of the opportunity to provide real leadership for them.

7. Am I able to put myself in the other person's position?   In supervision, a person works through the efforts of others. He succeeds as they succeed and fails as they fail. To be effective necessitates that he experience empathy with others. He needs to be able to see the way in which difficulties, purposes, surprises, actions, and assets look to others. As he approximates their feelings about the events of the day, he is able to plan and work with them. If he isn't able to put himself in the other person's shoes, his actions may be a constant threat to others without his knowing it.

8. Am I making a sincere effort to learn more about the staff?   Much of a supervisor's success in placing himself in the other person's position depends upon knowing a lot about the other person. If he doesn't want to know about his colleague, he probably won't have much empathy for him. It is difficult for a supervisor to understand a teacher's reaction to the lack of a salary increase, if the supervisor does not know that the teacher has five children and a mother and father whom he helps to support. If he isn't taking the steps that will help him learn how he can help the people around him, the probability that he will be a successful supervisor is decreased.

9. Do I consult those who will be affected by an action before I take it?   Action that is taken without consultation is frequently misunderstood. If a supervisor wants to be sure that those who will be affected by a step that he takes will accept it, he needs to provide an opportunity for them to have it explained and for them to react to the proposal. By telling the supervisor how they feel about it, the teachers suggest revisions that he should make in the proposed procedure. Furthermore, individuals who will be affected will have a greater sense of commitment to the change, because they have had a chance to express their opinions about it and to propose revisions that would make it more acceptable to them. Even though the supervisor is not able to adapt the action to the interests of all, he knows the risk he runs and is in a better position to make a decision on whether the gamble is a good one.

10. Do I live up to commitments? If a supervisor wants people to have faith in him, it is necessary for those people to be able to rely on his word. When a decision has been reached in a group of which he is a part, staff members have a right to expect that the commitment will be honored. If staff time is spent reaching a decision, and then the supervisor does not put into action the agreements reached, he breeds disillusionment and dissatisfaction.

Now let's turn to the ways of evaluating what we accomplish.

The measure of a supervisor's success lies in the worthwhile change he is able to effect. Unless severe social upheaval is placing undue strain on the school, the supervisor's contribution should be evaluated in terms of the increased curriculum improvement activities in the school. These are important questions in judging the effectiveness of a supervisor.

1. How many more teachers are experimenting?   Teachers grow as they try new procedures and measure the results. If a supervisor is effective, teachers are trying more new things than they were a year ago. If a supervisor is not effective, more teachers will have discontinued their search for better ways of teaching and will be following lesson plans and procedures that they developed last year or several years before. As a supervisor looks around him in the schools in which he works, he should find more faculty groups attempting to develop better procedures of evaluation, seeking to improve the living in the community, and searching for better ways of meeting the emotional needs of youngsters. He should see more faculties seriously attempting to measure the results of their innovations, rather than carrying out hunches without any attempt to collect evidence concerning the results. If his work has been effective, then more and more teachers will be basing their decisions on the scientific approach. A greater number of teachers will be spending time seeking evidence and basing conclusions on it.

2. Has there been an increase in the calls for help in thinking through problems?   Not an increase in calls for answers, because if people are coming more and more for answers, they are increasing their dependence and not developing their leadership. Calls that are of a type that indicate that people value our thinking as they look at a problem, want our help as they analyze the various facets of a problem, and value our ideas as they plan possible courses of action and make selections are the evidences we want to look for.

3. Has there been a change in the nature of the problems presented?   For example, are people bringing fewer problems that deal with how to do something and fewer questions that deal with interpretation of policy? Are they moving toward types of problems that call for thinking together about the application of values and principles held? If people are asking the supervisor more and more questions about how he interprets policy, then he isn't getting anywhere in this matter of spreading leadership and encouraging the emergence of other leadership; if they are asking specifically how to do something, this is not the kind of growth the supervisor should try to achieve for professional people. Supervision should develop people who are able to supply their own creative ways of applying the principles and values to which they are committed.

4. Is there an increased demand in the staff for professional materials?   Are more people asking for professional materials on certain topics? Is there more pressure within the staff for an adequate professional library? Are people sharing their magazines and books? Although reading professional books is not an end in itself, the number of teachers who are interested enough to sample what is being published in their field is an index to the extent of professional alertness in the staff. Are more new professional books available? Has the circulation increased? Are more teachers telling other teachers about books and recommending them? Is a greater proportion of the staff searching for suggestions on ways to improve their work?

5. Is there more sharing of materials among members of the staff?   When someone gets a book or some teaching material that he's really sold on, does he share it with the other people? Is there less hiding in cupboards and closets of materials that are especially valuable? Is there more experimentation by the faculty? Do more teachers say, "I'm dissatisfied with this phase of my work. What's the best hunch I have? How can I try it out? What kind of help can I get? How do I collect evidence as to whether the new procedure is any better than the present one?"

6. Is the faculty identifying the problems it has to face farther ahead, so that it isn't confronted with so many emergencies?   Does it say, "Here's a problem that is coming up. We'd better get on it."

7. Is there a greater use of evidence in deciding issues?   Is the faculty moving away from saying, "How do we feel about it?" to "What is the evidence?" or, "On the evidence, what is the best course of action to take?"

8. Is there within the faculty a greater acceptance of difference?   Are there fewer derogatory remarks by teachers about other teachers? Are there more questions about how we can get into a more effective working relationship with people with whom we disagree? Or how to focus the question when a conflict arises, "How can we work together?" not, "How can we isolate this person who is on the other side of the fence?"

9. How many more parents are involved in the school?   Teachers alone cannot improve the school. Adults of the community are needed to help plan the program and to serve as resource persons for classes and activity groups. In schools without an adequate staff, they may assist with the service functions of the school. If a supervisor has been effective in increasing the vision of the staff concerning the potential contribution of community members to education and to his community relations, more parents will be involved in school activities.

10. How many more rooms are more attractive?   If pupils and teachers are to spend six hours a day in a room, it should be attractive — a place in which a person likes to be. It is becoming widely recognized that barren, empty, harsh classrooms do not stimulate the kind of learning the teacher desires. How many more rooms have color, pictures, drapes, displays, and other devices that teachers and pupils have used to give rooms personality and to make them reflect and support the quality of teaching that is sought?

11. How many more teachers are active in professional organizations?   Although activity in a professional organization does not guarantee classroom competency, participation in local, state, and national organizations is another indication of the professional spirit of the staff. A supervisor's behavior and attitudes should motivate teachers to exert leadership in improving education through professional organizations.

12. How many more teachers are seeking in-service experience?   Some school systems require that staff members take alertness courses every few years, as a minimum insurance of curriculum improvement. Teachers should be looking for opportunities to improve. Has the system made available the types of workshops and resource people that the teachers consider helpful? Have staff members requested the supervisor to provide a seminar or workshop on some problem facing them? When a volunteer workshop or meeting is announced, does a greater percentage of the staff attend? Are more teachers attending summer school even though they are not required to do so for certification or salary-increase purposes?

13. How many more teachers are planning with other teachers?   Teachers grow through interaction. As much teacher growth occurs through teachers planning with other teachers as through organized in-service programs. When teachers recognize the value of sharing experiences and materials, the faculty moves toward a common point of view with regard to learning and curriculum. If a supervisor's work is effective, more teachers will find value in this joint planning.

14. How many more pupils are being included in planning and evaluating?   The learning situation improves as the people involved in it have an opportunity to make their purposes clear and to make judgments about the success of their activities. A supervisor improves the learning situation as he assists teachers to gain the security and the techniques that make it possible for them to utilize the intelligence of pupils in making judgments about what is to happen and what has already happened. One of the barometers by which to judge a supervisor's productivity is the extent to which increased pupil-teacher planning is occurring.

15. Is a larger percentage of the staff assuming responsibility for the improvement of the program? Through individual efforts, a supervisor is able to effect some changes in the curriculum, but his own shouldering of responsibility is not enough. It is only as he works in such a way that more and more people begin to desire change and to assume responsibility for making it that a supervisory program has any impact on a school system.

16. Are staff meetings becoming more faculty-directed? If staff meetings remain the exclusive property of the administrators, changes of lasting significance are unlikely. Is the administrator invites staff members to assume responsibility, and no teacher leadership emerges, then nothing happens except an increase in the dissatisfaction of the staff. When a supervisor's work procedures are effective, the faculty gives more and more attention to the planning of meetings and to the use of meetings to make decisions concerning school policy. If only 25 percent of the staff is interested in making decisions concerning policy, it is difficult to make a judgment about the quality of the supervision. If next year, only the same 25 percent is interested in making decisions, it is apparent that the supervisory procedures being followed are not the kind that increase the staff's self-direction. If a supervisor is doing his job effectively, staff members become increasingly able to conduct their own meetings and to decide on policy. The staff becomes concerned with knowing limitations and possibilities and in making judgments concerning the next best steps in the situation.

17. How many more teachers are using a wider range of materials? A good learning situation is one that makes it possible for pupils to find materials and media through which they can learn better. In order to provide for differences in reading ability, the books available must cover reading levels of a number of grades. To make it possible for many youngsters to express themselves easily, the classroom should contain art materials and other media through which they may express how they feel about the experiences they have been having. To provide information, references, film strips, tapes, and pictures should be available. If supervision has been effective, the teaching staff has sought to increase its acquaintance with, and skill in using, a variety of media. More teachers are making available to youngsters different ways of learning and sharing.

18. How are students scoring on achievement tests? The end result of all efforts is to increase the learning of children. Under ordinary circumstances, pupil achievement should be higher each year as the result of a supervisor's efforts. However, it is important to consider the external factors that bear on the school situation before judgments based on the achievement of youngsters are made. The nature of the community may have changed, and the intellectual environment of the homes may have become lower or higher. Decreased funds for schools may have deprived youngsters of instructional materials and lowered the teacher morale so that less learning for pupils results. However, if the situation has remained approximately the same, and if a supervisor's efforts have been successful, the achievement level of pupils will have been raised.

In spite of all the questions above, self-evaluation by the official leader is not enough. The leader must obtain the judgments of others in determining the revisions he will make in his procedures.

The supervisor's work should be evaluated as a part of the judgments concerning the total group effort. He is working within the group. His function is to contribute to the group's accomplishment of its goals. Acceptance of this principle keeps the faculty from stating that the official leader is strong or weak. Rather, faculty members say, "We have achieved these goals, but failed to reach those. Our supervisor has been very helpful on certain points and would strengthen us if he would put more emphasis on these other activities during the next few months."

If goals have been established, the only way to judge the success of the group *and the supervisor* is by the amount of progress made toward the goals. The goals of the school are the criteria against which the work of the official leader must ultimately be judged. If no progress has been made, the supervisor is failing, even though he has built morale and has increased job satisfaction. Maintaining the status quo in a school program is failure unless it is being maintained in the face of constantly increasing difficulties.

In order to determine progress, it is necessary to know where the group starts. Some base line must be established. The program of the school must be accurately recorded so that the group will be able to determine exactly the amount of change that has taken place. Either the beginning of the school year may be used or the time at which the evaluative criteria are applied to the school program. The starting point chosen doesn't matter if it is recent enough to permit detection of change that is occurring under the impact of present activity. But some complete picture of existing conditions at the base-line date is essential.

As a group evaluates its work and that of its supervisor, it is necessary to determine the amount of change that has been produced in the direction of the group goals since the base line was established. How does the school program now differ from the school program at the previous date?

When the types and amount of change have been determined, the group is ready to make judgments. If no change has occurred, the judgment is obvious. If some change has been effected, the group must decide whether that progress is satisfactory in light of existing conditions. At this point the judgment becomes subjective.

Everyone involved in the situation — supervisors, teachers, parents, pupils, community groups — should be a part of the judgment process. The amount of change can be determined by individuals — a teacher, the principal, or an outside group — but the judgments about the amount of progress must be made by all concerned. Whether or not the supervisor desires this condition, it will occur.

The skillful supervisor devises situations for obtaining these judgments and uses them in improving the school program. The unskillful official leader will pretend that he can ignore them and find that he has missed an opportunity to build group spirit and a solid backing for the program. He will wonder why opposition is developing in those whose judgments were not obtained and used.

The judgments that name areas of less than satisfactory progress will indicate the points where analysis and revision are needed, either in the work of the supervisor or of others in the group. The specific criteria by which a program and the official leader should be judged fall into four categories:

1. More responsible participation of students, teachers, and community members in the improvement of the program.
2. Enrichment of the school program through an increase in opportunities and activities for all.
3. Improvement of learning situations for students.
4. Greater contribution of the school to the improvement of community living.

Evaluation of a supervisor must be an evaluation of program development, with specific attention devoted to the procedures by which more group potential for progress can be released.

The supervisor who has formulated a theory to guide his action and criteria to evaluate his success will grow in skill and competency. He will use the results of his evaluation to test his theory and identify the areas in which he needs to search for new knowledge and insight and more possible courses of action from which to choose.

EPILOGUE

In this last section the authors attempt to logically
derive an alternative future for instructional supervision. An action proposal for moving toward
that future is presented and discussed.

14   The Future of
Supervision

The sixties and early seventies have seen an increase in man's growing concern about the future. Concern for the future quality of air, water, land, and more importantly the quality of human interaction have all been expressed in numerous publications. A common thread running through much of the literature is the assumption that man is not just a victim of the future, not just a reactor to a large variety of social and physical forces, but that man can identify and define alternative futures, plan for the future, and make a significant difference in the kind of future that develops. If it is assumed that the future is a part of an inevitable cycle and is therefore, already determined then man would attempt to understand the cycle, define the future of supervision, and make preparations to adjust to it. But, it is our assumption that the future of supervision is indeterminate. Rather, it is a function of a multiplicity of factors that are also indeterminate and interdependent. Therefore, it is possible for man to identify and study these factors, influence their distinctive character, and control to some extent their emergence and, therefore, the nature of the evolvement of instructional supervision. It is proposed here that the future nature of teachers, teaching and learning, and the educational organization will be significant factors in the evolvement of educational supervision. An attempt will be made to describe assumed futures for these factors and to discuss the implications for instructional supervision. Further, a proposal for moving toward the future in supervision is presented and discussed.

The purpose of Chapter 14 is not to "sell" or convince the reader of anything. It is hoped that the discussion will stimulate thinking and action and therefore, contribute to our efforts as educators to establish a future of greater effectiveness for instructional supervision.

Assumptions About the Future Nature of Teachers

There is every reason to believe that teachers of the future will continue to have the basic physiological, sociological, and psychological needs that were defined by Maslow (1954). They will continue to have a need for food, clothing, shelter, love, belonging, esteem and "self-realization." The difference will be in the relative currency of these needs and the means and possibilities for their satisfaction.

Teachers will continue to become more specialized and more competent as a result of the following factors:

1. Growing organizational complexity
2. Broadening and deepening needs of students
3. Improvement of professional preparation and continuing professional growth
4. Improvement of recruitment and selection practices
5. Growing knowledge base from which the conditions of learning are derived including both content and methodology

The growing diversity of professional members of the educational organization will be intensified by growing differences in life styles, increasing mobility, deepening specialization, and more significant staff differentiation. The need to communicate will be greater and so will the difficulty of communicating. The greater specialization and differentiation of the staff indicates a need for more cooperation, mutual trust, and understanding. But the temporary nature of people and positions, differences in backgrounds, and purposes all work against a climate of trust, mutual support, and cooperation.

The future will bring a growing recognition of the organization member's right of personal freedom and obligation of accountability. Teachers will be expected to utilize their expertise in the pursuit of organizational goals. But, they will also have a part in decisions on the goals and developing the structure in which the goals are achieved.

Assumptions About the Future of Teaching and Learning

There will be a growing recognition of the students' rights of individual freedom, self-realization and personal responsibility. (Briner and Sroufe, 1971, pp. 82-83). Learning conditions will be geared to the individual needs of students. Special consideration will be given to psychological needs of students. Examples would include positive support for trying new things, psychological support and technical help in failure, self discipline, and free exploration of ideas. Each individual right for self-realization will be cherished. More specifically the schools will be characterized by:

1. More emphasis will be placed on student involvement in the identification of educational needs and programs for achieving those needs.
2. Programs will be planned for each student
3. Students will pursue their goals both in independent study and in cooperation with other students and professional helpers.
4. A comprehensive "feedback system" will be available to both students and teachers so that both can be continuously aware of the extent of goal achievement.

The school will be seen as an agent of social change and improvement. Transmitting the cultural heritage will continue as an important school mission, but it will be only one among many. Other missions will include providing the arena for the discussion of the kind of society we want and how we can achieve it and the socialization of societal members. (Knezevich, 1971)

The nature of engagement opportunities will change drastically. There will be broad changes in the things to be learned and the ways to help students learn them. "Open schools" will provide more freedom of movement, and availability of many kinds of human and materials resources. Highly specialized differentiated and available resources will be available to work with students on a continuing basis. There will be independent study, group study, school in the community and home, computer-assisted instruction, video tape-assisted instruction and television.

The curriculum will be more open. There will be fewer constraints; but more importantly, new retrieval and storage systems will enhance the availability and usability of new knowledge for achieving multiple objectives and program conditions.

There will be a new concept of the "place" for schooling to occur. Rather than being highly centralized and place bound, schooling will occur in the home, the community, and special school buildings. The coordination of home learning centers, neighborhood centers, and specialized learning centers will be facilitated by the use of computers and other electronic devices.

The possible use of laser-assisted instruction, three-dimensional TV and films, direct electronic communication through implanted electrodes, and the use of drugs to stimulate learning excite the imagination. (Knezevich, 1971, pp. 50-57)

Assumptions About the Future
Nature of Educational Organizations

It is predicted that educational organizations will become more open. (Toffler, 1970, pp. 124-51). Individuals including both teachers and students will move in and out of organizations more freely and frequently. A large urban school system in the southeast reported 100 percent student turnover in one school during one school year. Teachers will move and be moved from school to school and system to system according to changing organizational and individual needs.

Within the organization there will be more temporary systems. One school system reported the formation of well over one hundred projects to facilitate student learning. Most of these were temporary, lasting one to four years. Professional members of the organization were brought into and out of these special projects. They had to adapt, learn appropriate new skills, take on new responsibilities, and "let go." In future educational organizations individuals will be expected to move from role to role through temporary systems to meet temporary needs.

The rapidity of organizational change coming about as a result of both internal and external forces will cause organizations to move toward relatively greater concern with rapidity of response, creative response and adaptability, and relatively less concern with stability, control, compliance, and predictability of response. The organization of the future will have to be more concerned with providing a psychological support system that will help members change rapidly, adapt to new situations, give up old situations, learn to quickly develop new relationships with effective communcation and problem solving, and deal with loneliness, failure, success, and impersonality. It will also be necessary to sensitize educational workers to new ideas and help them develop new skills to implement them.

Implications for
Instructional Supervision

Some educators have predicted that supervision will be eliminated from the educational organization. Perhaps they are right, if they are referring to a position labeled general supervisor. But if supervision is viewed as seeking improvement of curriculum and instruction, it will continue to grow in importance and in the number of personnel involved.

In many small school systems from the 1920s through the early 1950s, a person labeled "general supervisor" attempted to perform the entire supervisory function – instructional improvement, curriculum development, in-service education, media, remedial, and special service. Now, the number of people with the label "general supervisor" who have responsibility for all of these functions will probably decrease. School systems are being enlarged to make possible the provision of more services to the classroom teacher. It is being recognized that more specialized assistance is needed.

It is true that there will be a need for more supervisors. But more importantly the growing specialization of teaching and the rapidly developing knowledge base from which the content and process of teaching are derived will require more highly specialized and accessible expert assistance to help teachers be sensitive to changes, develop new skills, and implement appropriate innovations.

Rapid changes in both the content and process of teaching will generate greater psychological stress on teachers. The growing diversity of students, teachers, and supervisors indicates the growing difficulty of meeting certain basic requirements of a quality learning environment and points toward certain necessary functions of instructional supervision:

1. Provision for psychological support.
2. Helping people to communicate.
3. Helping people to help and be helped by each other.
4. Helping people to accept each other.
5. Coordination of the contributions of highly specialized people toward the needs of human beings in the learning environment.
6. Utilization of the total staff in the system of instructional supervisory behavior.

The supervisory and teaching staff will be more specialized and diverse than it has been in the past. The specialists in subject matter, learning disabilities, mental health, media, and research will not have a common background or depth of teaching experience. In fact, some may never have been teachers. They will be added to the task force because they have a competency that can be used. They will not all know the curriculum design or even quality teaching if they see it. Yet, each will be able to make his contribution as a part of the overall effort coordinated by the head of the supervisory staff. Greater independence of learners, teachers, and supervisors, and greater diversity and specialization of human learning resources require effective coordination in order to provide internally consistent learning environments.

Since the background, training, and professional goals of all of the supervisory staff will not be similar, the coordinating skill of the head of the staff will be extremely important. All that this book contains about group development and leadership will be critical for this person. He will need to develop common goals, mutual trust, cohesiveness, and a way of sharing decisions that gives the task force a plan and a strategy.

Even though all supervisors will not need to have the same knowledge or the same skills, all will need to have understanding and competency in leadership, communication, and the ability to release human potential. More diversity in the supervisory staff is coming, and it is desirable, but it must be accompanied by a common theory of change and common principles of working with people.

There will be a broadened base of participation in instructional supervision. The growing competence and specialization of teachers and administrators contributes to their capability to help each other. It is also true that students develop certain skills and understandings in the education process, and it is predicted that they will be utilized in the instructional supervisory behavior system of the future. It is also anticipated that a broad range of resources outside particular school systems will be provided and utilized. These outside agencies will emanate from state and federal government, local and national industrial agencies, private citizens and others. The proper coordination and utilization of these resources will become a major task for instructional supervision.

The "opening up" of the learning-teaching environment enhances the possibility for teachers, administrators, supervisors, and students to share engagement opportunities, describe each other's work, help each other analyze the learning environment; and, in general, participate in "self-supervision" and the supervision of each other. A systematic approach for facilitating this process follows:

Collaborative Supervision:
An Action Proposal*

During the period of "scientific management" teachers were thought of as passive instruments of management which could be manipulated to participate in that behavior which was conceived by management as being the most likely to facilitate the achievement of organizational goals. The goals of the organization were predetermined by management as was the best methodology for achieving them. It was the function of instructional supervisory behavior to maintain quality control by telling, showing, enforcing, monitoring, rating, and rewarding. Naturally, the model was built on the assumption of the "super-vision" of the superordinate and the "lack of vision," creativeness, and problem solving ability of the subordinate. In a sense the role of the supervisor was to examine, diagnose, prescribe, and monitor the behavior of the teacher in such a way as to insure the achievement of the goals of the organization. The classical model was an important factor in the evolvement of supervisory behavior in the educational organization.

The latter part of the first quarter of the twentieth century saw a challenge to the classical model of supervision that developed out of the human relations movement. Emphasis shifted from the needs of the organization and the worker as instrument to the needs of the worker as a thinking and feeling organism. Supervision in the educational organization was profoundly affected. In some

*The idea for collaborative supervision was developed from many sources most of which are unidentifiable. But, special credit is due Peter Husen, Amy Pace, Arthur Earp, Robert Simerly, Dewey Stollar, and Larry Hughes, all of The University of Tennessee. These colleagues discussed the idea, criticized the manuscript, and made suggestions.

quarters supervisors were resource people without authority, on call, waiting for requests for services. In some cases the "happiness index" became the important criterion of supervisory effectiveness. It is true that organizational members have needs and that these needs are important factors in their behavior. But, it is also true that organizations have goals; and they need organizational members that behave in ways that will contribute to the achievement of these goals.

This proposal challenges both the "traditional" model for supervision and the human relations model. The proposed model calls not only for the cooperation of professional workers in efforts to improve the instructional program, but also recognizes the reality and essentiality of differentiated roles of educational workers and the necessity for their collaboration in educational endeavors. An essential ingredient in the proposed model is the assumption of a broad base of competence and expertise among educational workers. The "need" is for the identification, analysis, and delivery of the reservoir of specialized competence to the appropriate problem solving situations. It is recognized that individuals such as supervisors, coordinators, consultants, and principals who are formally assigned to the supervisory behavior system have specialized competence that should be utilized. But it is also assumed that they can't be competent in all things or available in all situations. Therefore, it is proposed that the competence of organizational and nonorganizational members be utilized on an ad hoc basis. What is required is an organizational structure that facilitates this kind of flexibility.

THE CHALLENGE TO THE "CLASSICAL" MODEL

The challenge to the classical model and the proposal for a different model is necessarily based on a number of propositions that need to be explicated at the outset:

Teachers in educational organizations are capable of providing leadership in curriculum development and policy formulation activities. Educational organizations are characterized by the fact that the basic worker, the teacher, normally has a very high level of preparation and specialization. As the educational enterprise has become more and more complex, the teacher has become better prepared, more specialized, and more competent. Growing specialization not only means that workers must achieve a greater expertise in certain areas, but it also precludes the possibility that certain workers, "supervisors," can be expert in all things. It, therefore, follows that it is logical for educational organizations to utilize the broad base of special skills and knowledges represented by teachers in the continuous effort to improve the learning environment for students. It is critical to get the person with the appropriate competence in the appropriate position with the necessary authority and time to "supervise" the achievement of a particular task. This requires a broad base of instructional supervisory behavior, rather than a narrow base.

Teachers in educational organizations are capable of giving help to and receiving help from each other. Teachers engage in similar kinds of activities with similar students. Sometimes they share students. Therefore, the special conceptual, human, and technical skills that a teacher has developed through the years could have relevance for other teachers. But it is not only help of a technical nature that can be shared; teachers also need psychological support. Teachers who are attempting innovations need the encouragement and support of fellow teachers. They need to know that someone cares — someone accepts the importance of their activities; and fellow teachers can be in the right place at the right time to provide this kind of "supervision."

Teachers and superordinates can give and need to give help to and receive help from each other. Superordinates such as supervisors, coordinators, and principals are in a special position to provide support for the teaching behavior system. They can be highly specialized both in training and activities since they are not required to participate in the teaching behavior system. Thus, they can come with an expertise that is not generally available. They also have the time, and freedom to facilitate the process of teachers helping teachers. It is significant that teachers expect supervisors to participate in these kinds of activities, and this contributes to the potential effectiveness of the supervisor in facilitating teacher-teacher supervision.

Since teachers are involved in the direct process of actualizing engagement opportunities for students, they are in an excellent position to try out "new" content and methods and are therefore an excellent source of feedback on the effectiveness of ideas developed by "supervisors." Working directly with teachers in the teaching behavior system is also a way that "supervisors" can maintain close and direct contact with students.

It is also true that the process of teachers helping supervisors and supervisors helping teachers can be a psychologically rewarding experience. Either giving or receiving help can be a source of recognition. It is a way of saying, "I care about what you are doing and want to be a part of it." The opportunity to share successes in teaching with other adults can contribute to the feelings of satisfaction. Recognition and satisfactions from the work itself have been identified as important sources of teacher satisfaction in various research studies.

Effective supervisory behavior is not just a function of formal position but rather is a function of many factors such as competence in area of group concern and level of esteem by fellow group members. Since organizational members have a broad base of expertise, esteem, and creativity and since individuals have different strengths and weaknesses in different areas, it will be necessary for organizations to broaden the base of supervisory behavior throughout the organization on an ad hoc basis. This will make it possible to get the appropriate supervisory behavior where and when it is needed; and, thus, the organization will be able to utilize the special competence and esteem of a much larger number of organizational members.

Students have the competence to be effective participants in instructional supervision. Students have the opportunity to participate in a wide range of innovative activities. For example, a school system may start a nongraded program, open facility, open curriculum, or individualized program and self-directed learning. During the course of the student's participation in these activities he has an opportunity to develop a "feel" for the innovation as well as certain "special" skills. If the school wanted to spread the innovation to other student groups in the same school or different schools, it is proposed that students with these special understandings and skills be assigned to the innovative groups on a temporary basis as teacher helpers. Thus, they would be participating in the supervisory support system on an ad hoc basis.

There is a need for authority in the educational organization, but it need not be static nor just "role" determined. When a task requires the coordination of human and material resources, there is a need for organizationally bestowed authority. Such authority can increase the probability of people working together and the availability of appropriate human and material resources. It is crucial that just enough authority for the particular task be provided on the basis of an individual's expertise for this particular task. The difference between supervisor and supervisee is one of function in a particular task situation rather than a general assumption of superiority and inferiority. In fact, in the next task situation the roles might be reversed.

The supervisory behavior system should be a product of a scientific system for the allocation of human effort to improve the quality of learning for children. When supervisory behavior is thought of as organizational behavior that is provided to interact with teaching behavior in such a way as to improve the quality of learning for students, it is apparent that it can be a function of any person in the organization. A teacher who has been assigned to demonstrate a particular technique to fellow teachers is participating in instructional supervisory behavior. A supervisor who is observing for the purpose of describing a particular teaching procedure so as to make this "feedback" available to the teacher is participating in instructional supervision. The need is to allocate these functions on the basis of expertise, esteem by fellow teachers, needs of the situation, availability and other factors rather than to allocate such functions on the basis of role title.

It is impossible for the person occupying the official role, "supervisor" to have the availability, esteem of fellow professionals, and expertise in all situations. The educational organization is highly complex; it requires organizational behavior of a sophisticated and specialized nature. It is also true that each learning environment is itself made up of unique individuals (both teachers and learners) in constant interaction. Effectiveness in the environment requires a depth of specialization unique to the environment. Therefore, supervisors could not possibly be expected to have the expertise to diagnose and prescribe for each learning environment.

New developments in the educational organization have contributed to the possibility of providing a broad base of instructional supervisory behavior. "New" developments such as open space, team teaching, differentiated staffing, media utilization, independent study, and large group instruction contribute to the possibility of teacher-teacher visibility, interaction, cooperation and therefore availability for, and competence in, participating in collaborative supervision.

The prescriptive model is not appropriate for supervision in the educational organization. Teachers in educational organizations are assumed to be professionally competent practitioners who can be held responsible and accountable for the outcomes of their teaching behavior. Therefore, it would be inappropriate for the "superior" to examine, diagnose, and prescribe a certain learning environment because the "superior" would then have to be held accountable for the outcomes.

The supervisory behavior system should utilize resources from the teacher behavior system, supervisory behavior system, and the internal administrative behavior system. Human competence which is needed to support the teaching behavior system will be broadly dispersed throughout the organization. What is needed is an organizational structure that is open and flexible enough to recognize, release and utilize human resources when and where they are needed. The fact that a person is a principal of a school does not mean that he either has or does not have a certain expertise that is needed in the instructional supervisory behavior system. What is needed is a way of knowing if he has it and a way of allocating that human resource where it can be helpful. The same could be said for a superintendent, teacher, or supervisor.

COLLABORATIVE SUPERVISION

The foregoing set of propositions provides the framework for a proposed system of collaborative supervision. The concept, "collaboration" was chosen over either possibilities such as collegial, cooperative, and others for several reasons. First, the proposition that organizational members are specialized, competent, and interdependent workers leads to the need for a system of cooperation in curriculum and instruction decision making and problem solving. The lack of availability of a large enough group of people titled supervisors with a broad enough spectrum of expertise and the availability of teachers indicated a need to get the people with the expertise and esteem where they could collaborate with individuals needing psychological or technical support. But it was also assumed that the organizational members achieve different levels of prestige and organizational authority. Therefore, it was assumed that organizational members would not always be collaborating from equal positions of power. Rather, it was assumed two or more people nearly always collaborate from positions of unequal influence.* Therefore, collaboration, defined also as cooperating with a perceived adversary or person with greater power seemed to describe the situation as it often exists. But, the need for cooperative help, sharing of ideas, coordination, and caring also exists; and so does the need for collaborative supervision.

It is proposed that a system of collaborative supervision will improve the probability of certain kinds of learning outcomes for students. It is hoped that the conceptual scheme in Figure 9 will clarify the major components of a model for collaborative supervision.

The "student behavior system" is a target. The teaching behavior interacts with the student behavior system and is defined as having five dimensions:

*This idea was generated during a discussion with Dr. Peter Husen of the University of Tennessee.

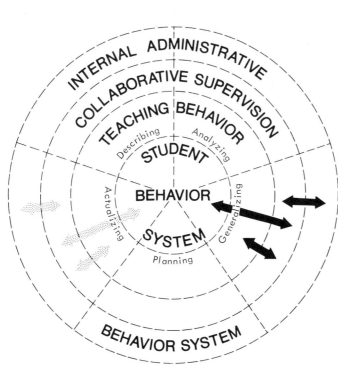

FIGURE 9
Collaborative Supervision

1. Planning
2. Actualizing
3. Describing
4. Analyzing
5. Generalizing

The five dimensions of teaching were defined and discussed in Chapter 8. They are used as points of entry for the system of collaborative supervision. Teachers must plan engagement opportunities for students. Other teachers, supervisors, students or principals may have special competence to contribute to this process. A teacher may want to try a new idea. There may be a fellow teacher who is already utilizing the idea. The "fellow teacher" could be released on an ad hoc basis to work with the teacher who is developing plans for the implementation of the new idea, or the teacher could be assigned to the teacher who is already utilizing the idea to get a feel of its implementation before trying it in his own teaching situation. Obviously, the person with the special competence could be a principal from another school, a consultant, or a supervisor. The idea is to make the resource available when it is needed.

When teachers teach, it is helpful to get descriptive data on what happens. Competent colleagues can provide this kind of help. A teacher may be concerned about the amount, quality or direction of interaction among a group of students with whom she is working. Fellow teachers or administrators who have the necessary expertise and rapport with the teacher could come in and provide descriptive data on the pattern of interaction. Flow charts, observation checklists, or video tapes are examples of techniques that could be used. The idea is to provide valid feedback for the teacher and leave the evaluation of the data to the teacher.

When teachers actualize new approaches, there may be human resources that could be used on a temporary basis. School A may be actualizing a "new" open facility, structure and curriculum. School B has been using a similar approach for several years. Certain teachers from School B could be assigned to School A on an ad hoc basis to "collaborate" in the implementation of the "new" program. Similarly the principal of School B could work in School A on a temporary basis as an instructional consultant. Students from School B have had several years to become familiar with the new approach and to develop skills of independent study, using tapes and vertical files and working in small groups. Certain students could be assigned to School A on a temporary basis to help get things going. These students would be participating in the system of collaborative supervision.

Teachers could use fellow teachers, administrators, and students to discuss the meaning and implication of the descriptive data. The opportunity to get this kind of help from an outside source could make a critical difference.

Curriculum designing, experimenting with "new" approaches, and developing the new approaches are examples of activities that could draw on the specialized competence of human resources throughout the organization. A principal of an elementary school could be released from his assignment to conduct a system-wide experiment. A group of teachers could be released to form a temporary system to facilitate development of an open curriculum in another school. During this period they would be participating in the system of collaborative supervision.

The system of collaborative supervision draws on human resources from the teaching behavior system, the internal administration system, and the student behavior system according to expertise, esteem, availability and needs of the teaching behavior system. It is also apparent that certain human resources are needed whose primary focus of effort is in the instructional supervisory behavior system. It is considered to be a primary function of the supervisory behavior system continuously to study the needs of the teaching behavior system and the human resources available from teachers, supervisors, internal administrators, and students and to develop strategies for the utilization of these resources.

Strategies to Actualize
Collaborative Supervision

THE "RIFLE APPROACH"

Supervisors often elaborate on the great difficulty of working with each teacher in each school in the system. They explain that there are just too many schools with too many teachers and not enough supervisors to go around. They also speak of the difficulty of being available at the right place at the right time with the necessary rapport and competence to be truly effective in their efforts to work in terms of the needs of teachers. With so many teachers to see it is difficult to establish a true basis of mutual trust and respect. When these same teachers are confronted with the idea of a system of "collaborative supervision" in which teachers are encouraged to participate in self-supervision and the supervision of each other, they like it but raise some serious questions. Do teachers have the necessary skills and understandings to supervise each other? Have they had the necessary training in group process, human relations skills, micro-teaching, observation and description skills such as the interaction analysis, videotaping and analysis, and evaluation: They also wonder if teachers "really" want to help each other and if they have the time. These are appropriate questions and certainly the answers are not all "in." But the "rifle approach" is suggested as one possible way to get started.

The rifle approach requires the identification of a school and some teachers in that school who have an authentic interest and readiness for "trying" collaborative supervision. Then a great effort would be made from the "central administration" to concentrate needed material and human resources in that school in order to get the program started on a limited and experimental basis. Supervisors could be assigned temporarily to work with the teachers in this school. Consultants could be employed to help teachers develop the necessary skills. The teachers could be released from part of their teaching responsibilities to develop needed skills and to help each other. The rifle approach provides a "multiplier effect." As the small group of teachers who are directly involved become more interested and secure, the idea will spread to other teachers in the school. Further, as the program becomes successful in one school, it will spread to other schools. The concentrated support system could be withdrawn and used in other situations since the teachers involved would have developed the necessary skills, interest, and understandings to maintain and extend the program.

THE CADRE OF "FLOATING TEACHERS"

The idea is to provide a group of "supervisor-teacher" professionals at the central office who are competent and willing to participate in either the teaching behavior or supervisory behavior system. Members of this cadre could be assigned teaching and/or supervisory responsibility. For example, if a "regular" teacher had the special expertise to help a fellow teacher, the floating teacher could be assigned to replace the regular teacher. It would also be possible, where appropriate, for the floating teacher to collaborate directly with teachers in a supervisory role or to work with teachers to help them develop needed supervisory skills. The cadre makes it possible to loosen up the availability of teachers and thus spread the potential for teacher participation in the collaborative supervision system.

TEAM TEACHING

Team teaching is an organizational structure to facilitate the process through which teachers can cooperate in planning, teaching, and evaluating what has been done. This team approach provides for teacher-teacher visibility, interaction, and sharing and thereby provides the potential for collaborative supervision. Teachers can share each other's plans, make suggestions, observe and describe the learning environment, provide feedback, and participate in cooperative evaluation. The potential is there for collaboration; all that is needed is desire, effort and competence.

OPEN SPACE

Numerous school systems are beginning to use open space as a way of promoting cooperative teaching and learning, availability of specialized resources, differentiated staffing, independent study, and use of multi-media. The open space frees teachers to see each other work, to collaborate, to evaluate each other, and to describe each other. It also makes it possible to introduce "external" personnel with specialized expertise in "supervision" without so much threat since the situation is already open. The cooperative approach to teaching makes it more difficult to fix individual responsibility and thus provides more teacher openness to continuous study of the learning environment and student learning outcomes. These processes are collaborative supervision and can be nurtured and extended. But, it does not happen automatically with the development of open space. Professionals working in the open space need an opportunity to develop the skills and understandings of collaborative supervision and an internal system of administrative behavior that rewards and participates in that kind of action.

MICRO-TEACHING

Micro-teaching can be defined as a process of "boiling down" a teaching situation in terms of time, methodology, or content. It provides an opportunity for teachers and supervisors to "try out" teaching ideas without the risk of an actual situation but with the opportunity for immediate feedback from fellow teachers and supervisors. It provides opportunities for teachers to learn the skills of collaborative supervision through actual participation in the planning, teaching, describing, and analyzing phases of teaching as collaborative supervisors.

No attempt has been made to exhaust the possible strategies. Others could be mentioned and those already mentioned could be further elaborated. Rather, the idea of collaborative supervision was developed together with the rationale for the idea. Action strategies were presented to demonstrate the application of the idea.

A Final Word

Our discussion of supervision has defined more questions than it has answered. The future of supervision rests on success in asking and answering relevant questions. Anyone working in the field of supervision or entering it should recognize how scanty and tentative the evidence is and should be committed to an endless search for data that will enable him to test the hypotheses on which his supervisory actions are based. There is no one pattern of instructional supervision to which an individual may conform with security. Supervisory effectiveness is a function of a multiplicity of factors. Supervisors are different; they have unique needs, skills and expectations of others. The people with whom supervisors interact are also unique and have different needs, expectations for help, and variable strengths and weaknesses. The "key" is to somehow identify and release variable human resources in the continuous effort for educational improvement.

Bibliography

Abbott, M. 1965. Unpublished Paper, Auburn University.

Ainsworth, L. H. 1958. "Rigidity, insecurity and stress," *Journal of Abnormal and Social Psychology*, 56:67-74.

Alexander, W. M. 1969. *The high school of the future: a memorial to Kimball Wiles*. Columbus, Ohio: Charles E. Merrill.

_____ and R. J. Havighurst. 1962. "Bases for curriculum decision," *National Elementary Principal*, 42:8-12.

Allen, D. W. 1971. "In-service teacher training: a modest proposal," in *Improving in-service education*, ed., L. J. Rubin. Boston: Allyn and Bacon.

Allingham, R. B., et al. 1961. "How Supervise Instruction in the Large Urban Secondary School?" *National Association of Secondary School Principals Bulletin*, 45:7-11.

American Association of School Administrators. 1971. *Profiles of the administrative team*. Washington, D.C.: American Association of School Administrators.

Amidon, E. J., and E. Hunter. 1966. *Improving teaching: analyzing verbal interaction in the classroom*. New York: Holt, Rinehart, and Winston.

Anderson, J. G. 1968. *Bureaucracy in education*. Baltimore, Maryland: Johns Hopkins.

Anderson, L. R., and F. E. Fiedler. 1964. "The effect of participatory and supervisory leadership on group creativity," *Journal of Applied Psychology*, 48:227-36.

Anderson, R. C., et al. 1969. *Current research on instruction*. Englewood Cliffs, N.J.: Prentice-Hall.

Anderson, R. H. 1966. *Teaching in a world of change.* New York: Harcourt Brace and World.

Argyris, C. 1961. "Organizational leadership," in *Leadership and interpersonal behavior,* eds. L. Petrullo and B. M. Bass. New York: Holt, Rinehart and Winston.

Arnstine, D. 1971. "Freedom and bureaucracy in the schools," in *Freedom, bureaucracy and schooling,* ed. V. F. Haubrick. Curriculum Development.

Aronson, E., and **B. W. Godlen.** 1962. "The effect of relevant and irrelevant aspects of communicator credibility on opinion change," *Journal of Personality,* 30:135-46.

Association for Supervision and Curriculum Development. 1962. *Perceiving behaving becoming.* Washington, D.C.: The Association.

Ayer, F. C., and **A. S. Barr.** 1928. *The organization of supervision.* New York: D. Appleton and Co.

Back, K. W. 1951. "Influence through social communications," *Journal of Abnormal and Social Psychology,* 46:9-23.

Bahrick, H. P. 1954. "Incidental learning under two incentive conditions," *Journal of Experimental Psychology,* 47:170-72.

Bales, R. F., et al. 1951. "Channels of communication in small groups," *American Sociological Review,* 16:461-68.

Barnard, C. I. 1938. *The Functions of the Executive.* Cambridge, Mass.: Harvard University Press.

Barnett, H. 1962. *Innovation: the basic of cultural change.* New York: McGraw-Hill.

Baskin, S. 1962. "Experiment in independent study (1956-1960)," *Journal of Experimental Education,* 31:183.

Bass, B. M. 1960. *Leadership, psychology and organizational behavior.* New York: Harper and Row.

Bavelas, A. 1942. "Morale and the training of leaders," in *Civilian morale,* ed. G. Watson. Boston: Houghton Mifflin.

―――. 1950. "Communication patterns in task-oriented groups," *Journal of the Acoustical Society of America,* 22:725-30.

―――, and **P. Barrett.** 1951. "An Experimental Approach to Organizational Communication," *Personnel,* 27:366-71.

Beal, G. M., E. M. Rogers, and **J. M. Bohlen.** 1957. "Validity of the concept of stages in the adoption process," Rural Sociology, 22:166-68.

Bellack, A. A., et al. 1968. "The language of the classroom," in *Teaching: vantage points for study,* ed. R. T. Hyman. New York: Lippincott.

Bennett, J. and **R. McKnight.** 1956. "Misunderstandings in communications between Japanese students and Americans," *Social Problems,* 3:243-56.

Bennis, W. G., K. D. Benne, and R. Chin. 1961. *The planning of change.* New York: Holt, Rinehart, and Winston.

Bennis, W. G. and E. H. Schein, eds. 1966. *Leadership and motivation: Essays of Douglas McGregor.* Cambridge, Massachusetts: M.I.T. Press.

Bergin, A. E. 1962. "The effect of dissonant persuasive communications upon changes in a self-referring attitude," *Journal of Personality,* 30:423-38.

Berkowitz, L. 1951. "Some effects of leadership sharing in small decision-making conference groups," Unpublished Doctor's Dissertation, University of Michigan.

Berman, L. M., ed. 1963. *The nature of teaching.* Milwaukee, Wisc.: University of Wisconsin.

_____. 1968. *New priorities in the curriculum.* Columbus, Ohio: Charles E. Merrill.

Blau, P. M. 1956. *Bureaucracy in modern society.* New York: Random House.

_____, and R. W. Scott. 1962. *Formal organizations: A comparative approach.* San Francisco: Chandler.

Blumberg, A., and E. Amidon. 1965. "Teacher perceptions of supervisor-teacher interaction," *Administrator's Notebook,* XIV.

Boag, T. J. 1952. "The white man in the Arctic, a preliminary study of problems of adjustments," *American Journal of Psychiatry,* 109:444-49.

Bobbitt, J. F. 1912. "The elimination of waste in education," *The Elementary School Teacher,* 12:260.

_____. 1913. "Some general principles of management applied to the problems of city school systems," in *Twelfth Yearbook of the National Society for the Study of Education,* Part I. Chicago: University of Chicago Press.

_____. 1920. "The objectives of secondary education," *The School Review,* 28:738.

Bovard, E. W., Jr. 1951. "Group structure and perception," *Journal of Abnormal and Social Psychology,* 46:398-405.

Briner, C., and G. Sroufe. 1971. "Organization for education in 1985," in *Educational futurism 1985,* eds. W. G. Hack et al., Berkeley, Cal.: McCutchan Publishing.

Brown, C. G., and T. S. Cohn. 1958. *The study of leadership.* Danville, Illinois: Interstate Printers and Publishers.

Brown, R. W., and E. H. Lenneberg. 1954. "Studies in linguistic relativity," *Journal of Abnormal and Social Psychology,* 49:454-62.

Bruner, J. S. 1961. "The act of discovery," *Harvard Educational Review,* 31:21-32.

_____. 1966. *Toward a theory of instruction.* Cambridge, Massachusetts: The Belknap Press of Harvard University Press.

Burnham, R. M. 1962. "A neglected resource in the education of teachers," *The Journal of Teacher Education,* 13:85-87.

Burnham, R., and **M. King.** 1961. *Supervision in action.* Washington, D.C.: Association for Supervision and Curriculum Development.

Burton, W. H., and **L. J. Brueckner.** 1966. *Supervision, a social process.* New York: Appleton-Century Crofts.

Callahan, R. E. 1962. *Education and the cult of efficiency.* Chicago: University of Chicago Press.

Campbell, R. F., and **J. M. Lipham, eds.** 1960. *Administrative theory as a guide to action.* Chicago: University of Chicago Press.

Carp, F. M., et al. 1963. "Human relations knowledge and social distance set in supervisors," *Journal of Applied Psychology,* 47:178-80.

Carter, L. F. 1951. "Appointed leaders less authoritarian than 'natural' ones, study indicates," *Research Reviews.*

Cartwright, D., and **A. Zander, eds.** 1960. *Group dynamics: research and theory.* Evanston, Illinois: Row, Peterson.

Castetter, W. B. 1971. *The personnel function in educational administration.* New York: Macmillan.

Caswell, H. L., and **D. Campbell.** 1935. *Curriculum development.* New York: American Book.

Cattell, R. B. 1951. "New concepts for measuring leadership in terms of group syntality," *Human Relations,* 4:161-84.

Chowdhrey, K., and **T. Newcomb.** 1952. "The relative abilities of leaders and non-leaders to estimate opinions of their own groups," *Journal of Abnormal and Social Psychology,* 47:51-71.

Clark, R. S. 1968. *A study of the relation of instructional supervision behavior to teacher satisfaction and to teacher-pupil relationships, Ed.D. Dissertation, Auburn University.*

Coch, L., and **J. R. French.** 1948. "Overcoming resistance to change," *Human Relations,* 1:512-32.

Cogan, M. L. 1973. *Clinical supervision.* Boston: Houghton Mifflin.

Cohen, A. R. 1958. "Upward communication in experimentally created hierarchies," *Human Relations,* 11:41-52.

————, **et al.** 1962. "The effects of changes in communication networks on the behaviors of problem-solving groups." *Sociometry,* 25:177.

Combs, A. W., and **D. Snygg.** 1959. *Individual behavior.* New York: Harper and Row.

Commoss, H. H. 1962. "Some characteristics related to social isolation of second grade children," *Journal of Educational Psychology,* 53:38-42.

Cooperative Development of Public School Administration, *Instructional staff administrators.* Albany, New York, 1957, in Daniel Griffiths, et al. 1962. "Organizing schools for effective education." Danville, Illinois: The Interstate Printers and Publishers.

Cornell, F. 1954. "When should teachers share in making administrative decisions?" *The Nation's Schools,* 53:43-45.

Cowley, W. H. 1928. "Three distinctions in the study of leaders," *Journal of Abnormal and Social Psychology,* 23:144-57.

———. 1931. "The traits of fact-to-face leaders," *Journal of Abnormal and Social Psychology,* 26:304-13.

Cubberley, E. 1916. *Public school administration.* Boston: Houghton Mifflin.

Culbertson, J. 1959. "Recognizing roadblocks in communication channels," *Administrator's Notebook,* 7:1-4.

Cunningham, L. L. 1959. "The process of educational policy development," *The Administrator's Notebook,* 11:1-4.

———. 1963. "Effecting change through leadership," *Educational Leadership,* 21:75-79.

Davis, K. E., and C. C. Florquist. 1965. "Perceived threat and dependence as determinants of the tactical usage of opinion conformity," *Journal of Experimental Psychology,* 1:219-36.

Davis, K., and W. G. Scott, eds. 1964. *Readings in human relations.* New York: McGraw-Hill.

Davits, J. R., and D. J. Mason. 1960. "Manifest Anxiety and Social Perception," *Journal of Consulting Psychology,* 24:554.

Doll, R. C. 1962. "In-service training in communication," *Overview,* 3:57.

———. 1972. *Leadership to improve schools.* Worthington, Ohio: Charles A. Jones.

Dowis, J. L., and O. Diethelam. 1958. "Anxiety, stress and thinking: an experimental investigation," *Journal of Psychology,* 45:227-238.

Dykes, A. 1963. "Influencing the power elite," *The Education Digest,* 29:28.

Eagle, M. 1959. "The effects of subliminal stimuli of aggressive content on conscious cognition," *Journal of Personality,* 27:578.

Easterbrook, J. A. 1955. "The effect of emotion on cue utilization and the organization of behavior," *Journal of Abnormal and Social Psychology,* 51:458-63.

Elkin, F., G. Halpern, and A. Cooper. 1962. "Leadership in a student mob," *Canadian Journal of Psychology,* 16:199-201.

Emmer, E. T., and G. B. Millett. 1970. *Improving teaching through experimentation.* Englewood Cliffs, N.J.: Prentice-Hall.

Epperson, D. C. 1962. "Stimulating teacher collaboration in the improvement of educational practice," *National Association of Secondary School Principals Bulletin,* 46:45-49.

Feldhusen, J. F., and **H. J. Klausmeier.** 1962. "Anxiety, intelligence and achievement in children of low, average and high intelligence," *Child Development,* 33:403-10.

Festinger, L., and **H. A. Hutte.** 1954. "An experimental investigation of the effect of unstable interpersonal relations in a group," *The Journal of Abnormal and Social Psychology,* 49:513-22.

Festinger, L., and **J. Thibaut.** 1951. "Interpersonal communication in small groups," *Journal of Abnormal and Social Psychology,* 46:92-99.

Festinger, L., J. Torrey, and **B. Willerman.** 1954. "Self-evaluation as a function of attraction to the group," *Human Relations,* 7:161-74.

Fiedler, F. E., and **W. A. T. Meauwese.** 1963. "Leader's contribution to task performance in cohesive and uncohesive groups," *Journal of Abnormal Psychology,* 67:83-87.

Fine, B. J. 1957. "Conclusion-drawing, communicator credibility, and anxiety as factors in opinion change," *Journal of Abnormal and Social Psychology,* 54:369-74.

Flanders, N. A. 1951. "Personal-social anxiety as a factor in experimental learning situations," *Journal of Educational Research,* 45:100-110.

———. 1962. "Using interaction analysis in the in-service training of teachers," *Journal of Experimental Education,* 30:313.

———. 1963. "Teacher behavior and in-service programs," *Educational Leadership,* 21:25-29.

Fleming, J. N. 1963. "An analysis and a comparison of the decision-making processes in two school faculties," Unpublished Doctor's Dissertation, University of Florida.

Frazier, A. 1963. "The new teacher – and a new kind of supervision?" *Educational Leadership,* 21: 97-100.

———. 1972. *Open schools for children.* Washington, D.C.: Association for Supervision and Curriculum Development.

Gagne, R. M., and **L. T. Brown.** 1961. "Some factors in the programming of conceptual learning," *Journal of Experimental Psychology,* 62:313-21.

Gaier, E. L. 1952. "The relationship between selected personality variables and the thinking of students in discussion classes," *School Review,* 60:404-11.

Gellerman, S. 1968. *Management for motivation.* New York: American Management Association.

Getzels, J. W. 1960. "Theory and practice in educational administration: an old question revisited," in *Administrative Theory* as a Guide to Action, ed.

R. F. Campbell and J. M. Lipham. Chicago, Illinois: University of Chicago Press.

————, and **E. G. Guba**. 1954. "Role, role conflict and effectiveness," *American Sociological Review*, 19:164-75.

————. 1957. "Social behavior and the administrative process," *The School Review*, 45:423-42.

Gilchrist, J. C., M. E. Shaw, and **L. C. Walker**. 1954. "Some effects of unequal distribution of information in wheel group structure," *Journal of Abnormal and Social Psychology*, 49:554-56.

Glass, D. C. 1964. "Changes in liking as a means of reducing cognitive discrepancies between self-esteem and aggression," *Journal of Personality Psychology*, 32:531-49.

Goetzinger, C., and **M. Valentine**. 1964. "Problems in executive interpersonal communication," *Personnel Administration*, 27:24-29.

Goldhammer, R. 1969. *Clinical supervision*. New York: Holt, Rinehart and Winston.

Goodlad, J. 1969. In an address delivered in Connecticut in 1969.

————, **M. Francis Klein**, and **Associates**. 1970. *Behind the classroom door*. Worthington, Ohio: Charles A. Jones.

Gouldner, A. W. 1954. *Patterns of industrial bureaucracy*. Glencoe, Illinois: Free Press.

Greer, E. S. 1961. "Human relations in supervision," *Education*, 82:203-6.

Griffiths, D. E., et al. 1962. *Organizing schools for effective education*. Danville, Illinois: The Interstate Printers and Publishers.

Grobman, H. G. 1958. "The public school principal's operational behavior, theory and practice and related school and community interactions based on data from the investigations of the University of Florida CPEA leadership project," Unpublished Doctor's Dissertation, Gainesville, Florida: University of Florida.

Gross, N., and **R. E. Herriott**. 1965. *Staff leadership in public schools: a sociological inquiry*. New York: John Wiley.

Guba, E. G. 1968. "Diffusion of innovations," *Educational Leadership*, 25:292-95.

Guelcher, W., T. Jackson, and **F. Necheles**. 1970. *Microteaching and teacher training, a refined version*. Chicago, Ill.: University of Chicago.

Guetzkow, H., and **W. R. Dill**. 1957. "Factors in the organizational development of task-oriented groups," *Sociometry*, 20:175-204.

————, and **H. A. Simon**. 1955. "The impact of certain communication nets upon organization and performance in task-oriented groups," *Management Science*, 1:233-50.

Gustad, J. W. 1962. "Communication failures in higher education," *Journal of Communication,* 12:11.

Gynther, R. A. 1957. "The effects of anxiety and of situational stress on communicative efficiency," *Journal of Abnormal and Social Psychology,* 54:274-76.

Hackman, R. C., and R. G. Moon. 1950. "Are leaders and followers identified by similar criteria?" *American Psychologist,* 5:312.

Hahn, C. P. 1961. "Collection of data for utilization in curriculum planning of the U.S. Air Force Academy," in *Leadership and interpersonal behavior,* eds., L. Petrullo and B. M. Bass. New York: Holt, Rinehart and Winston.

Hale, W. T. 1961. "UICSM's decade of experimentation," *The mathematics teacher,* 54:613-18.

Hall, E. J., J. S. Mouton, and R. R. Blake. 1963. "Group problem-solving effectiveness under conditions of pooling versus interaction," *Journal of Social Psychology,* 1:147-57.

Hall, E. T. 1959. *The silent language.* Garden City, New York: Doubleday.

Hallworth, H. J. 1961. "Anxiety in secondary modern and grammar school children," *The British Journal of Educational Psychology,* 31:281.

Halpin, A. W. 1966. *Theory and research in administration.* New York: Macmillan.

———, and D. B. Croft. 1963. *The organizational climate of schools.* Chicago, Illinois: University of Chicago Press.

Hare, A. P. 1952. "A study of interaction and consensus in different sized groups," *American Sociological Review,* 17:261-67.

Harris, B. 1963. *Supervisory behavior in education.* Englewood Cliffs, N.J.: Prentice-Hall.

Harris, B. M. 1962. "Instructional improvement — how adequate is your staff?" *The American School Board Journal,* 145:11-13.

Harrison, R., and B. Lubin. 1965. "Personal style group composition and learning," *Journal of Applied Behavioral Science,* 1:286-301.

Hartley, H. J. 1968. *Educational planning-programming-budgeting.* Englewood Cliffs, N.J.: Prentice-Hall.

Hebb, D. O. 1958. "The motivating effects of exteroceptive stimulation," *American Psychologist,* 13:109-13.

Heinicke, C., and R. F. Bales. 1953. "Developmental trends in the structure of small groups," *Sociometry,* 16:7-38.

Hemphill, J. K. 1949. *Situational factors in leadership.* Columbus, Ohio: Ohio State University.

———, D. Griffiths, and N. Frederickson. 1962. *Administrative performance and personality.* New York: Bureau of Publications, Teachers College, Columbia University.

Herzberg, F., B. Mausner, and B. Snyderman. 1959. *The motivation to work.* New York: Wiley.

Hicks, J. A., and J. B. Stone. 1962. "The identification of traits related to managerial success," *Journal of Applied Psychology,* 46:428-32

Hoffman, L. R., E. Harburg, and N. R. F. Maier. 1962. "Differences and disagreement as factors in creative group problem solving," *Journal of Abnormal and Social Psychology,* 64:206-14.

Homans, G. C. 1950. *The human group.* New York: Harcourt, Brace, Jovanovich.

Horowitz, M. W., J. Lyons, and H. V. Perlmutter. 1950. "Induction of forces in discussion groups," *American Psychologist,* 5:301.

Horton, D., and R. R. Wohl. 1956. "Mass communications and para-social interaction, observations on intimacy at a distance," *Psychiatry,* 19:215-30.

Hovland, C. I., and W. Weiss. 1951. "The influence of source credibility on communication effectiveness," *Public Opinion Quarterly,* 15:235-650.

James, H. E. O. 1955. "Personal contact in school and change in inter-group attitudes," *International School Science Bulletin,* 7:66-71.

Jenkins, D. H., and R. Lippitt. 1951. *Interpersonal perceptions of teachers, students, and parents.* Washington: Division of Adult Education Service, National Education Association.

Jennings, H. H. 1950. *Leadership and isolation.* New York: Longmans, Green.

Johnson, E. S. 1961. "Human dimensions of supervision," *Educational Leadership,* 18:222-27.

Johnson, R. I., M. Schalkamp, and L. A. Garrison. 1956. *Communication: handling ideas effectively.* New York: McGraw-Hill.

Kallegian, V., P. Brown, and I. R. Weschler. 1953. "The impact of interpersonal relations on ratings of performance," *Public Personnel Review,* 14:166-70.

Katz, E. 1961. "The social itinerary of technological change: two studies on the diffusion of innovation," *Human Organization,* 20:70-82.

Kay, E., and H. H. Meyer. 1965. "Effects of threat in a performance appraisal interview," *Journal of Applied Psychology,* 49:311-17.

Kelley, H. H. 1951. "Communication in experimentally created hierarchies," *Human Relations,* 4:39-56.

———, and E. H. Volkart. 1952. "The resistance to change of group anchored attitudes," *American Sociological Review,* 18:453-65.

Kelly, E. C., and M. I. Rasey. 1952. *Education and the nature of man.* New York: Harper and Brothers.

Kersh, B. Y. 1958. "The adequacy of 'meaning' as an explanation for the superiority of learning by independent discovery," *Journal of Educational Psychology,* 49:282-92.

———. 1962. "The motivating effect of learning by directed discovery," *Journal of Educational Psychology,* 53:65-71.

———, and **M. C. Wittrock.** 1962. "Learning by discovery: an interpretation of recent research," *Journal of Teacher Education,* 13:461-68.

Kiesler, C. A. 1963. "Attraction to the group and conformity to group norms," *Journal of Personality,* 31:559-69.

Kimbrough, R. B. 1965. "Community power structure and curriculum change," *Strategy for Curriculum Change.* Washington, D.C.: NEA-ASCD.

———. 1964. *Political power and educational decision-making.* Chicago: Rand McNally.

———, **and M. Y. Nunnery.** 1971. *Politics, Power, Polls, and School Elections.* Berkeley, California: McCutchan.

Kipnis, D., and **W. P. Lane.** 1962. "Self-confidence and leadership," *Journal of Applied Psychology,* 46:291-95.

Kirsch, P. E. 1960. "Classroom visitation," *National Association of Secondary School Principals Bulletin,* 44:34-39.

Kitane, H. H. L. 1962. "Adjustment of Problem and Nonproblem Children to Specific Situations: A Study in Role Theory," *Child Development,* 33:229-33.

Kittell, J. E. 1957. "An experiential study of the effect of external direction during learning on transfer and retention of principles," *Journal of Educational Psychology,* 48:391-405.

Kliebard, H. M. 1971. "Bureaucracy and curriculum theory," in *Freedom, bureaucracy, and schooling,* ed. V. F. Haubrick. Washington, D.C.: Association for Supervision and Curriculum Development.

Knezevich, S. J. 1971. "Perspectives on the educational program in 1985," in *Educational futurism 1985,* eds. W. G. Hack, et al. Berkeley, Cal.: McCutchan Publishing.

Koopman, R. G., A. Miel, and **P. J. Misner.** 1943. *Democracy in school administration.* New York: Appleton-Century-Crofts.

Langworthy, R. L. 1964. "Process," in *A dictionary of the social sciences,* eds. J. Gould and W. L. Kolb. New York: Free Press.

Larson, O. N., and **R. J. Mill.** 1958. "Social structure and interpersonal communication," *American Journal of Sociology,* 63:497-505.

Lawler, M. 1961. "New frontiers for supervision," *Educational Leadership,* 19:82.

Leavitt, H. 1951. "Some effects of certain communication patterns on group performance," *Journal of Abnormal and Social Psychology,* 46:38-50.

———, **and R. A. Meuller.** 1951. "Some effects of feedback on communication," *Human Relations,* 4:401-10.

Lee, I. J. 1952. *How to talk with people.* New York: Harper and Row.

Leeper, R. R., ed. 1965. *Role of supervisor and curriculum director in a climate* *of change.* Washington, D.C.: Association for Supervision and Curriculum Development.

Lewin, K. 1939. "Experiments in social space," *Harvard Educational Review,* 9:21-32.

_____. 1943. "Forces behind food habits and methods of change," *The problem of changing food habits.* Bulletin of the National Research Council, No. 108.

_____. 1944. "The dynamics of group action," *Educational Leadership,* 1:195-200.

Lewis, A. J. and A. Miel. 1972. *Supervision for improved instruction.* Belmont, California: Wadsworth Publishing.

Likert, R. 1961. "An emerging theory of organization, leadership, and management," in *Leadership and interpersonal behavior,* eds. L. Petrullo and B. M. Bass. New York: Holt, Rinehart and Winston.

Lionberger, H. F. 1961. *Adoption of new ideas and practices.* Cedar Falls, Iowa: Iowa State Press.

_____. 1965. "Diffusion of innovations in agricultural research and in schools, *Strategy for curriculum change.* Washington, D.C.: NEA-ASCD.

_____, and R. R. Campbell. 1963. *The potential of interpersonal networks for message transfer from outside information sources: a study of two Missouri communities.* Columbia, Missouri: Agricultural Experiment Station, Research Bulletin 842.

Lionberger, H. F. and C. M. Milton. 1957. *Social structure and diffusion of farm information.* Columbia, Missouri: Agricultural Experiment Station, Research Bulletin 631.

Lippitt, G. L. 1955. "What do we know about leadership?" *National Education Association Journal,* 44:556-57.

_____, ed. 1961. *Leadership in action.* Washington: National Training Laboratories, National Education Association.

Lippitt, R. 1965. "Roles and processes in curriculum development and change," *Strategy for curriculum change.* Washington, D.C.: NEA-ASCD.

Lippitt, R., N. Polansky, and S. Rosen. 1952. "The dynamics of power: a field study of social influence in groups of children," *Human Relations,* 5:37-64.

_____, J. Watson, and B. Westley. 1958. *The dynamics of planned change.* New York: Harcourt, Brace and World.

Lippitt, R. and R. K. White. 1947. "An experimental study of leadership and group life," in *Readings in Social Psychology,* eds. T. Newcomb and E. Hartley. New York: Holt, Rinehart and Winston.

Lonsdale, B. J. 1963. "The Guese of Supervision," *Educational Leadership,* 21:69-74.

Lovell, J. T. 1967. "A perspective for viewing instructional supervisory behavior," in *Supervision: perspectives and propositions,* ed. W. H. Lucio. Washington, D.C.: Association for Supervision and Curriculum Development.

Lucio, W. H. 1962. "Instructional Improvement: Considerations for supervision," *Educational Leadership,* 20:211-17.

————, ed. 1967. *Supervision: perspectives and propositions.* Washington, D.C.: Association for Supervision and Curriculum Development.

Lucio, W. H. and J. D. McNeil. 1969. *Supervision: a synthesis of thought and action.* New York: McGraw-Hill.

Lyda, W. L. 1960. "A suggested conceptual system for decision-making in curriculum development," *Educational Record,* 41:74-83.

Lysgaard, S. 1955. "Adjustment in a foreign society: Norwegian Fulbright grantees visiting the U.S.," *International Social Science Bulletin,* 7:45-51.

Mackenzie, G. N. 1964. "Curricular change: participants, power, and process," in *Innovation in Education,* ed., M. B. Miles. New York: Teachers College Press.

MacKinnon, W. J., and R. Centers. 1957-58. "Social psychological factors in public orientation toward an outgroup," *American Journal of Sociology,* 63:415.

Macy, J. Jr., L. S. Christie, and R. D. Luce. 1953. "Coding noise in a task-oriented group," *Journal of Abnormal and Social Psychology,* 48:401.9.

Mandler, G., and S. B. Sarason. 1952. "A study of anxiety and learning," *Journal of Abnormal and Social Psychology,* 47:166-73.

March, J. G., and H. A. Simon. 1961. *Organizations.* New York: John Wiley.

Markey, O. B., and G. Herbkersman. 1961. "An experiment in student responsibility," *The School Review,* 69:169-80.

Marks, A., J. P. Guilford, and P. R. Merrifield. 1959. "A study of militancy leadership in relation to selected intellectual factors," Los Angeles, California: Psychological Laboratory of the University of Southern California, Report No. 21. In *Leadership and Interpersonal Behavior,* eds. L. Petrullo and B. M. Bass. New York: Holt, Rinehart and Winston. 1961.

Maslow, A. 1954. *Motivation and personality.* New York: Harper and Row.

Mayo, E. 1933. *The human problems of an industrial civilization.* New York: Macmillan.

Maxon, R. C., and W. E. Sistrunk. 1973. *A systems approach to educational administration.* Dubuque, Iowa: William C. Brown.

McCarthy, I. J. 1962. "Professional library in the school: a tool for supervisors," *Elementary School Journal,* 63:166-67.

McCleary, L. E. 1968. "Communications in large secondary schools," *NASSP Bulletin,* 52:48-61.

McClintock, C. G. 1963. "Group support and the behavior of leaders and nonleaders," *Journal of Abnormal and Social Psychology,* 67:105-13.

_____. 1965. "Group support, satisfaction and the behavior profiles of group members," *British Journal of Social and Clinical Psychology,* 4:169-74.

McGrath, J. E. 1962. "The influence of positive interpersonal relations on adjustment and effectiveness in rifle teams," *Journal of Abnormal and Social Psychology,* 65:365-75.

_____, and I. Altman. 1966. *Small group research.* New York: Holt, Rinehart and Winston.

McKeachie, W. J., D. Pollie, and J. Speisman. 1955. "Relieving anxiety in classroom examinations," *Journal of Abnormal and Social Psychology,* 50:93-98.

Merei, F. 1949. "Group leadership and institutionalization," *Human Relations,* 2:23-29.

Merton, R. K. 1940. "Bureaucratic structure and personality," *Social Forces,* 18:560-68.

Miel, A. 1946. *Changing curriculum.* New York: Appleton-Century-Crofts.

_____. 1962. "In service education re-examined," *The National Elementary Principal,* 41:6-11.

Miles, M. 1959. *Learning to work in groups.* New York: Bureau of Publications, Teachers College, Columbia University.

_____. 1965. "Education and innovation: the organization as context," in *Change perspectives in educational administration,* eds., M. G. Abbott and J. T. Lovell. Auburn, Alabama: Auburn University.

_____. 1971. *Innovation in education.* New York: Bureau of Publications, Teachers College, Columbia University.

Miller, V. 1965. *The public administration of American school systems.* New York: Macmillan.

Millinger, G. D. 1956. "Interpersonal trust as a factor in communication," *Journal of Abnormal and Social Psychology,* 52:304-9.

Moeller, G. H., and W. W. Charters. 1966. "Relation of bureaucratization to sense of power among teachers," *Administrative Science Quarterly,* 10:444-65.

Montague, E. K. 1953. "The role of anxiety in serial rote learning," *Journal of Experimental Psychology,* 45:91-96.

Moos, R. H., and J. C. Speisman. 1962. "Group compatibility and productivity," *Journal of Abnormal and Social Psychology,* 65:190-96.

Myers, A. 1962. "Team competition, success, and the adjustment of group members," *Journal of Abnormal and Social Psychology,* 65:325-32.

Myers, R. 1954. "The development and implications of a conception of leadership for leadership education," Unpublished Doctor's Dissertation, Gainesville, Florida: University of Florida.

National Training Laboratory in Group Development. 1953. *Explorations in human relations training.* Washington, D.C.: NEA.

Nelson, H., et al. 1956. "Attitudes as adjustment to stimulus, background and residual factors," *Journal of Abnormal and Social Psychology,* 52:314-22.

Netzer, L. A., et al. 1970. *Interdisciplinary foundations of supervision.* Boston: Allyn and Bacon.

Ober, R. L., E. L. Bentley, and **E. Miller.** 1971. *Systematic observation of teaching.* Englewood Cliffs, N.J.: Prentice-Hall.

Olson, A. R. 1960. "Organizing a faculty for curriculum improvement," *National Association of Secondary Schools Bulletin,* 44:94-97.

Owens, R. G. 1970. *Organizational behavior in schools.* Englewood Cliffs, N.J.: Prentice-Hall.

Palermo, D. S., A. Castaneda, and **B. R. McCandless.** 1956. "The relationship of anxiety in children to performance in a complex learning task," *Child Development,* 27:333-37.

Pascoe, D. 1963. "Three concepts of democratic district leadership," *Educational Leadership,* 21:89-92.

Petrullo, L., and **B. M. Bass.** 1961. *Leadership and interpersonal behavior,* New York: Holt, Rinehart and Winston.

Phillips, B. N. 1955. "An experimental study of the effects of cooperation and competition, intelligence and cohesiveness on the task efficiency and process behavior of small groups," Indiana University: *Thesis Abstract Series #6.*

Polansky, N., R. Lippitt, and **F. Redl.** 1950. "An investigation of behavioral contagion in groups," *Human Relations,* 3:319-48.

Pratt, W. E., and **D. G. McGarey.** 1958. *A guide to curriculum improvement in elementary and secondary schools.* Cincinnati, Ohio: Public School Publishing.

Preston, M. G., and **R. K. Heintz.** 1949. "Effects of participatory vs. supervisory leadership on group judgment," *Journal of Abnormal and Social Psychology,* 44:345-55.

Pryer, M. W., A. W. Flint, and **B. M. Bass.** 1962. "Group effectiveness and consistency of leadership," *Sociometry,* 25:391-97.

Read, W. H. 1962. "Upward communication in industrial hierarchies," *Human Relations,* 15:3-16.

Reader, N., and **H. B. English.** 1947. "Personality factors in adolescent female friendships," *Journal of Consulting Psychology,* 11:212-20.

Reeves, J. M., and **L. Goldman,** 1957. "Social class perceptions and school maladjustment," *Personnel and Guidance Journal,* 35:414-19.

Reger, R. 1962. "An attempt to integrate a group isolate," *Journal of Educational Sociology*, 36:154.

Revans, R. N. 1971. *Standards for morals: cause and effect.* Oxford, London, 1964, cited in Sugiovanni, T. J. and R. J. Starratt, *Emerging patterns of supervision: human perspectives.* New York: McGraw-Hill.

Rogers, C. R. 1961. *On becoming a person.* Boston: Houghton Mifflin.

_____. 1969. *Freedom to learn.* Columbus, Ohio: Charles E. Merrill.

_____. 1971. "Can schools grow persons?" *Educational Leadership*, 29:215-17.

Rogers, E. M. 1962. *Diffusion of innovations.* New York: Free Press.

Roethlisberger, F. J., and W. J. Dickson. 1947. *Management and the worker.* Cambridge, Massachusetts: Harvard University Press.

Rubin, L. J., ed. 1971. *Improving in-service education: proposals and procedures for change.* Boston: Allyn and Bacon.

Runkel, P. J. 1956. "Cognitive similarity in facilitating communication," *Sociometry*, 19:178-91.

Sand, O., et al. 1960. "Components of the curriculum: curriculum decisions in secondary education," *Review of Educational Research*, 30:233-37.

Savage, R. 1967. "A study of teacher satisfaction and attitudes," Unpublished Doctor's Dissertation, Auburn, Alabama: Auburn University.

Schein, E. H., and W. G. Bennis. 1965. *Personal and organizational change through group methods: the laboratory approach.* New York: John Wiley.

Schrag, C. C., and O. N. Larsen. 1954. *Sociology.* New York: Harper and Brothers.

Selznick, R. 1949. *T.V.A. and the grass roots.* Berkeley: University of California Press.

Sergiovanni, T. J. 1967. "Factors which affect satisfaction and dissatisfaction of teachers," *Journal of Educational Administration*, 5:66-82.

_____, and R. J. Starratt. 1971. *Emerging patterns of supervision: human perspectives.* New York: McGraw-Hill.

Shaw, M. E. 1954. "Some effects of unequal distribution of information upon group performance in various communication nets," *Journal of Abnormal and Social Psychology*, 49:547-53.

_____. 1955. "A comparison of two types of leadership in various communication nets," *Journal of Abnormal and Social Psychology*, 50:127-34.

_____. 1963. "Some effects of varying amounts of information exclusively possessed by a group member upon his behavior in the group," *Journal of General Psychology*, 68:71.

_____, G. H. Rothschild, and J. F. Strickland. 1957. "Decision processes in communication nets," *Journal of Abnormal and Social Psychology*, 54:323-30.

Spears, H. 1957. *Curriculum planning through in-service programs,* Englewood Cliffs, N.J.: Prentice-Hall.

Steiner, I. D., and E. D. Rogers. 1963. "Alternative responses to dissonance," *Journal of Abnormal and Social Psychology,* 66:128-36.

Sterling, T. D., and B. G. Rosenthal. 1950. "The relationship of changing leadership and followership in a group to the changing phases of group activity," *American Psychologist,* 5:311.

Stith, M., and R. Connor. 1962. "Dependency and helpfulness in young children," *Child Development,* 33:15-20.

Stogdill, R. M. 1948. 'Personal factors associated with leadership, a survey of the literature," *Journal of Psychology,* 25:35-71.

———. 1950. "Leadership, membership and organization," *Psychological Bulletin,* 47:1-14.

———. 1957. *Leader behavior: Its description and measurement.* Columbus, Ohio: Bureau of Business Research, College of Commerce and Administration, Ohio State University.

Strickland, L. H., E. E. Jones, and W. P. Smith. 1960. "Effects of group support on the evaluation of an antagonist," *Journal of Abnormal and Social Psychology,* 61:73-81.

Suchman, J. R. 1961. "Inquiry training: building skills for autonomous discovery," *Merill-Palmer Quarterly of Behavior and Development,* 7:147-69.

Sugg, W. B. 1955. "A study of the relationship between program development and the working patterns of school principals," Unpublished Doctor's Dissertation, Gainesville, Florida: University of Florida.

Swearingen, M. E. 1960. "Identifying needs for in-service growth," *Educational Leadership,* 17:332-35.

Tabachnick, B. R. 1962. "Some correlates of prejudice toward negroes in elementary age children," *The Journal of Genetic Psychology,* 100:193-204.

Tannenbaum, R., I. Weschler, and F. Massarils. 1959. *Leadership and organization.* New York: McGraw-Hill.

———. 1961. *Leadership and organization: a behavioral science approach.* New York: McGraw-Hill.

Thibaut, J. 1950. "An experimental study of the cohesiveness of underprivileged groups," *Human Relations,* 3:25-78.

Toffler, A. 1970. *Future shock.* New York: Bantam.

Tyler, R. W. 1950. *Basic principles of curriculum and instruction.* Chicago, Illinois: The University of Chicago Press.

Waterhouse, I. K., and I. L. Child. 1953. "Frustration and the quality of performance: III. An experimental study," *Journal of Personality,* 21:298-311.

Watson, D., and B. Bromberg. 1965. "Power communication and positive satisfaction in task-oriented groups," *Journal of Personality and Social Psychology,* 2:859-964.

Weigan, J., ed. 1971. *Developing teacher competencies.* Englewood Cliffs, N.J.: Prentice-Hall.

White, R., and R. Lippitt. 1960. "Leader behavior and member reaction in three social climates," in *Group dynamics,* ed., D. Cartwright and A. Zander. Evanston, Illinois: Row Peterson.

Whitman, R. M., and D. Stock. 1958. "The group focal conflict," *Psychiatry,* 21:269-76.

Whyte, W. F. 1943. *Street corner society.* Chicago: The University of Chicago Press.

Wick, J. W., and D. L. Beggs. 1971. *Evaluation for decision making in the schools.* New York: Houghton Mifflin.

Wiles, K. 1950. *Supervision for better schools.* Englewood Cliffs, N.J.: Prentice-Hall.

Wilkening, E. A. 1956. "Roles of communicating agents in technological change in agriculture," *Social Focus,* 34:361-67.

Wilkins, E. J., and R. Decharms. 1962. "Authoritarianism and response to power cues," *Journal of Personality,* 30:439-43.

Wilson, L. C. 1971. *The open access curriculum.* Boston: Allyn and Bacon.

———, et al. 1969. *Sociology of supervision.* Boston: Allyn and Bacon.

Zander, A., and A. R. Cohen. 1955. "Attributed social power and group acceptance: A classroom experimental demonstration," *Journal of Abnormal and Social Psychology,* 51:490-92.

Index